THE IMPACT OF PRIVATIZATION IN THE AMERICAS

Edited by
Melissa H. Birch and Jerry Haar

North·South Center Press
UNIVERSITY OF MIAMI

The publisher of this book is the North-South Center Press at the University of Miami.

The mission of The Dante B. Fascell North-South Center is to promote better relations and serve as a catalyst for change among the United States, Canada, and the nations of Latin America and the Caribbean by advancing knowledge and understanding of the major political, social, economic, and cultural issues affecting the nations and peoples of the Western Hemisphere.

© 2000 North-South Center Press at the University of Miami.

 Published by the North-South Center Press at the University of Miami and distributed by Lynne Rienner Publishers, Inc., 1800 30th Street, Suite 314, Boulder, CO 80301-1026. All rights reserved under International and Pan-American Conventions. No portion of the contents may be reproduced or transmitted in any form, or by any means, including photocopying, recording, or any information storage retrieval system, without prior permission in writing from the North-South Center Press.

All copyright inquiries should be addressed to the publisher: North-South Center Press, 1500 Monza Avenue, Coral Gables, Florida 33146-3027, U.S.A., phone 305-284-8912, fax 305-284-5089, or e-mail mmapes@miami.edu.

To order or to return books, contact Lynne Rienner Publishers, Inc., 1800 30th Street, Suite 314, Boulder, CO 80301-1026, 303-444-6684, fax 303-444-0824.

Cataloging-in-Publication Data on file in the Library of Congress

The impact of privatization in the Americas
/edited by Melissa H. Birch and Jerry Haar
   p. cm.
Includes bibliographical references and index.
ISBN 1-57454-054-8 (alk. paper: paperback)

Printed in the United States of America

⊚ The paper used in this publication meets the requirements of the American National Standards for Information Sciences —Permanence of Paper for Printed Library Materials, ANSI Z39.48.1984.

04 03 02 01 00   6 5 4 3 2 1

DEDICATION

In memory of Carlos Raúl Ramírez Díaz de Espada, assassinated in the honest practice of his profession, on January 29, 1997.

Melissa H. Birch

In loving memory of Samuel Winik, humanitarian, philanthropist, and proud promoter of his nephew's accomplishments.

Jerry Haar

Table of Contents

Preface
   Melissa H. Birch and Jerry Haar i

Chapter 1
Privatization in the Americas: The Challenge of Adjustment 1
   Melissa H. Birch and Jerry Haar

Chapter 2
Early, Massive, Broad, and Successful Privatizations:
   The Case of Chile 13
   Rolf J. Lüders

Chapter 3
The Evolution, Rationale, and Impact of Mexico's
   Privatization Program: A Critical Assessment 51
   Miguel D. Ramírez

Chapter 4
The Argentine Privatization Process and Its Aftermath:
   Some Preliminary Conclusions 77
   Sebastián Galiani and Diego Petrecolla

Chapter 5
The Impact of Privatization in Peru 99
   Pedro-Pablo Kuczynski

Chapter 6
The Experience of Privatization in the Caribbean 115
   Richard L. Bernal and Winsome J. Leslie

Chapter 7
The Tortuous Road to Privatization in Venezuela 141
   Gerver Torres

Chapter 8
Privatization in Brazil: Toward an Evaluation 177
   Juarez de Souza

Chapter 9
Privatization in Colombia: Competition and Labor Adjustment in the
    Electric Power and Telecommunications Industries 203
    Mauricio Cárdenas

Chapter 10
Conclusion: Comparative Analysis of the Privatization Experience ... 217
    Melissa H. Birch and Jerry Haar

Contributors 237

Index 239

Preface and Acknowledgments

Privatization, for many nations in the Americas, has been the centerpiece of neoliberal reform economic policies adopted a decade and a half ago. Nearly all of these countries have pursued market-based solutions as they have sought to reform and restructure their economies and stimulate sustainable growth. Recognizably, the shape, pace, and level of commitment to the privatization process have varied widely, and external as well as internal forces and factors have affected each nation's efforts to privatize state-owned enterprises.

The results of privatization have been mixed, with differing levels of success within individual countries, industries, and sectors. Although it is still too early to offer a definitive assessment of privatization's contribution to economic renewal in the Americas, one can nevertheless offer an interim assessment of the progress being made. The authors of this volume have done precisely that by examining the impact of privatization in the areas of macroeconomics, quality and quantity of goods and services, labor and productivity, and trade liberalization.

We gratefully acknowledge the support of The Dante B. Fascell North-South Center at the University of Miami and its Director, Ambler H. Moss; Deputy Director Robin L. Rosenberg; and Jeffrey Stark, Director of Research and Studies, for their financial and academic support of the project.

The second author thanks The David Rockefeller Center for Latin American Studies, Harvard University, and its director, John H. Coatsworth, for their help as well. Research assistance from Barbara Cross and Garrett Halton has greatly improved the readability and consistency of the manuscript.

Invaluable assistance was also provided by Kathleen A. Hamman, Editorial Director of the North-South Center Press; José F. Grave de Peralta, Senior Editor, who performed the lion's share of the editing; Michelle Pérez, Editorial Assistant; Patricia Rosas, Free-lance Copy Editor; Susan K. Holler, Graphic Artist and Indexer; and Mary M. Mapes, Publications Director.

Melissa H. Birch
Jerry Haar

CHAPTER 1

Privatization in the Americas: The Challenge of Adjustment

MELISSA H. BIRCH AND JERRY HAAR

For Latin America and the Caribbean, the "lost decade" of the 1980s has given way to an era of economic reform, structural change, and, in some cases, renewed growth. The adoption of neoliberal economic policies, which first began in Chile in the early 1970s and then swept through the Latin American continent in the wake of the debt crisis, has resulted generally in lower rates of inflation, slower rates of debt accumulation, improvements in rates of economic growth and investment compared to those experienced in the 1980s, significant trade expansion, and, most notably, a diminished role of the state in terms of asset ownership. Privatization has been, for more than a decade, the centerpiece of neoliberal reform, reflecting the preeminence given by policymakers to private sector actors and the role of market forces in achieving sustainable growth.

By the late 1980s, many Latin American policymakers had come to suspect that the development model that had produced significant growth in the 1950s, 1960s, and early 1970s was exhausted and that a new strategy for economic development was needed. In some countries, such as Chile and Argentina, a sudden and significant shift in prevailing ideology and an ambitious privatization program were visible ways to attract international attention. In some countries, however, privatization programs were driven less by an ideological commitment and more by pragmatism. In Bolivia, for example, the word privatization was politically unacceptable, and that country's program to increase private ownership of historically state-owned firms was known as the "capitalization" program. In Colombia, where macroeconomic instability in the 1980s was not as severe as in other parts of Latin America, there has been no comprehensive privatization program. Instead, the state has divested itself of certain enterprises in response to particular concerns about the quantity, quality, or price of the services provided by those entities.

In the cases of Mexico and Brazil, the stubborn burden of internal and external public debt and the macroeconomic instability it generated made privatization an attractive way to raise revenues, retire debt, and decrease budget deficits.[1] The World Bank cited the huge budget deficits associated with subsidies to public enterprise in many developing countries as one of the major obstacles to their economic growth (World Bank 1995). The way in which a privatization program was structured and the use of the resulting funds are of special interest, then, in the context of stunning growth rates in some Latin American countries in the 1990s. If funds from the sale of public enterprises are added to current income, the need for structural adjustment of the public accounts is postponed, but fundamental problems remain uncorrected. Although extensive earmarking of funds is generally frowned upon in public finance, the one-time swap of physical assets for financial assets may be a case that justifies the creation of a special fund. The experience in Latin America in this regard is quite varied and will be discussed below.

Although public enterprise investment was easily postponed in the early stages of the debt crisis, the absence of investment over time eroded the quantity and quality of goods and services provided. Technological change, particularly in such industries as telecommunications, exacerbated the problems of public enterprises, magnifying their deficiencies and reducing public support for their existence. In some cases, newer technologies seemed to suggest that the concept of natural monopoly was quickly becoming a thing of the past, negating one of the principal reasons for the creation of public enterprises in some countries.[2] In the absence of government funds, the combination of a need for additional investment and the availability of new technologies was a compelling reason to seek a new source of funds and to look to private investors for their provision.

Thus, by the beginning of the 1990s, foreign and domestic political forces and fiscal and technological concerns all converged and pointed toward a redefinition of the scope of private and public sectors in Latin America. Instead of fostering the creation of public enterprises, the International Monetary Fund (IMF) and the World Bank now imposed conditions for structural adjustment loans that required a reduction in the role of the state in the economy. World Bank support specifically for privatization was extremely important to the form and speed of privatization in Argentina, for example (World Bank 1993). Contested markets and international competition were to replace the government as owner and, to a great extent, regulator in many sectors of the economy. Latin American governments, short of funds and long on obligations, had to rethink their priorities in a changing context. Privatization, in all its forms, became the centerpiece of economic reform in Latin America.[3]

PRIVATIZATION IN THEORY AND PRACTICE

Much of the faith in the salutary effect of privatization derives from a belief that private ownership of assets and the removal of government from business decisionmaking results in efficiency gains. Because a government is more likely to pursue multiple objectives in its management of a firm (such as employment creation and provision of services to areas that are not commercially profitable), it will create a series of disincentives that reduce the efficiency and, therefore, the profitability, of the firm. In its generally critical review of public enterprise performance in developing countries, the World Bank pointed out, "Bureaucrats typically perform poorly in business not because they are incompetent (they aren't), but because they face contradictory goals and perverse incentives that can distract and discourage even very able and dedicated public servants" (World Bank 1995, 3).

Privatization is believed to simplify the operational objectives of the firm and, by exposing it to the forces of market competition, reduce costs, increase output, and improve overall performance. Yet, many state-owned enterprises in Latin America operate in markets characterized by a lack of competition, as is the case with natural monopolies or industries that occur where required economies of scale are such that a country is unlikely to support more than one efficient plant. In a comprehensive review of the contribution of ownership to firm efficiency, John Vickers and George Yarrow (1988) concluded that private ownership was superior to public ownership only in industries where healthy competition existed. In markets without competitive forces, they argued that the introduction of competition (via the elimination of statutory monopolies, for example) or regulatory measures that mimicked competitive forces probably provided greater efficiency gains than could be expected from the transfer of ownership to the private sector. Substitution of a private monopoly for a public one could produce only limited gains in efficiency, due principally to a reduction of employment and the restriction of services to financially rewarding markets.

Thus, it is clear that although privatization has become nearly synonymous with economic reform, economic theory cannot guarantee that the economic efficiency of the firm or the performance of the economy as a whole will necessarily improve under private ownership. Given the ambiguity, it seems useful to examine the initial experience of Latin American privatization programs and their contribution to the success of the market-based reforms undertaken in the 1980s and early 1990s. The chapters in this book examine the impact of privatization in four key areas: 1) macroeconomic stability and fiscal balance; 2) the quality and quantity of supply in privatized industries; 3) levels of employment, wages, and productivity; and 4) promotion of free trade. Of course, the results of privatization vary across countries and can only be evaluated against the scope and structure of the program and the specific objectives of each country. With this in mind, the rest of this chapter will highlight the differences in the nature and scope of privatization programs in the Latin American countries considered in this book, while the initial impact of privatization on the four variables noted above will be reviewed in the country chapters and summarized in the volume's final chapter.

PRIVATIZATION PROGRAMS IN LATIN AMERICA

Although the timing, extent, techniques, and motivations of privatization programs have varied considerably across Latin America, there are few countries in the region where privatization has not become an important feature of the economic reform package. Privatization has been expected to produce revenues for the state, attract foreign investment and new technology, improve and extend basic services, and lower costs and increase efficiency in key sectors of the economy. While the sale of state-owned firms has often resulted in performance improvements, in other cases the outcomes have been unexpected. Political, social, macroeconomic, and managerial factors all affect privatization — a process far more complex than the mere sale of a public entity to a private concern. In examining the varied experiences across the sample of countries considered here, it becomes clear that the way in which these four factors interact determines a unique outcome for privatization in each country.

The explanation for the widespread divestiture of public enterprises by Latin American governments in the 1980s, especially in the absence of other regulatory and liberalization measures, must include objectives other than economic efficiency. In its study of privatization, the United Nations Economic Commission for Latin America and the Caribbean (ECLAC) identified a series of both structural and cyclical reasons for the prevalence of privatization in Latin America in the 1980s (see Table 1). Even though one may disagree with ECLAC's calibration of the importance of possible motivations, the list of reasons — and the varying importance given to them in different Latin American countries — suggests that one should expect a potentially wide array of outcomes from privatization. Thus, a unique privatization experience can be found in each nation, even when the same industries are compared across different countries.

Table 1.
Reasons for Privatization in Latin America

	Argentina	Brazil (a)	Chile (b)	Mexico	Venezuela
Structural					
Ideological	*	*	***	***	**
Internal Efficiency/ Modernization	***	**	*	**	***
Change in Market Structures	***	***	***	***	***
Circumstantial					
Political Credibility	***	***	*	*	***
Fiscal Urgency	***	*	**	**	**
Restricted Investment	***	*	**	**	**
Catalytic Effects	***	**	**	***	***
External Pressure	***	**	*	*	*

Key: Three stars indicate motivation was of primary importance, two stars indicate it was of secondary importance, and one star indicates it was of tertiary importance. (a) Refers to the government of Collor de Mello and (b) refers to the second round of privatization.

Argentina

In Argentina, privatization had been part of the agenda of both military and civilian governments since the mid-1970s. Although the military government in power between 1976 and 1983 sold a large number of small state-owned enterprises (SOEs), their significance to the economy and the public sector was very small. Raúl Alfonsín, Argentina's first democratically elected president after the military dictatorship, included privatization in his reform program, but political opposition and pressing issues of macroeconomic stabilization precluded much progress. Thus, it was under the unlikely circumstances of the Peronist administration of President Carlos Saúl Menem that the greatest strides toward privatization were made.

Sebastián Galiani and Diego Petrecolla (Chapter 4, this volume) identify four phases of the Argentine privatization program undertaken by the Menem government with different objectives taking priority in each period. In the first phase, which included the privatization of ENTel and Aerolíneas Argentinas (the national telephone company and international airlines, respectively), maximization of the sale price of the firm seemed to be the primary objective. Monopoly power was allowed to persist, high profits were assured, and regulatory issues were left vague. In the second stage, including the privatization of the national oil company, sales of the remaining shares of ENTel, and the granting of concessions for operation of toll roads, attention shifted to reducing inflation and bolstering the Convertibility Plan.[4] Thus, in the privatization arena, pricing and indexation issues dominated the debate. By the time the third phase began, some financial constraints had been eased, and attention focused more on questions of market structure and allocative efficiency following the privatization of the state-owned gas and electricity companies. In the fourth phase, the onset of recession in the Argentine economy and the faltering confidence of international markets resulted in a return to the dominance of financial objectives, which, in turn, led the government to sell the remaining shares it held in some previously privatized firms.

Argentina rivals Chile in terms of the breadth of industries subject to privatization. From public utilities and telecommunications to steel and even the national oil industry, nearly all the SOEs created in the post-war period have been sold. In most cases, majority ownership and operating control passed into foreign hands, while some portion of the privatized firm was sold on the local stock exchange. Some 10 percent of the shares usually were reserved for the firms' workers. Outstanding foreign debt, purchased by buyers in the secondary market, was the most common form of payment. It is estimated that, by mid-1993, proceeds from the sale of SOEs amounted to US$18.8 billion, of which less than half (47 percent) was paid in cash (Galiani and Petrecolla, Chapter 4).

Brazil

Serious attention to privatization in Brazil also began in the late 1970s, with the creation of the Special Secretariat for the Control of State Enterprises in 1979. The secretariat did not undertake the sale or closure of public enterprises but did centralize reporting and increase government control over SOEs. The creation of the Special Commission for De-Statization in 1981 marked the beginning of the government's formal intent to divest itself of some of its enterprises and, as in Argentina and Mexico, the first to be privatized in Brazil were small firms of relatively little significance in terms of the size and scope of public sector economic activity.

The government of José Sarney, Brazil's first civilian president in 20 years, showed little serious interest in privatization, perhaps because no strong domestic constituency existed for the program. Firms sold during his administration were generally those that had fallen into state hands as a result of their financial problems while under private control. Thus, privatization in this period was seen as a return of these entities to their former owners. The large SOEs that had played such an important part in Brazil's post-war development strategy were not seriously considered for privatization at that time.

Sarney's successor, Fernando Collor de Mello, campaigned on a neoliberal platform of eliminating government corruption and creating a smaller and more modern state sector. Upon taking office in early 1990, President Collor announced the ambitious National Privatization Program (Programa Nacional de Desestatização — PND), which promised to sell one government-owned firm per month. Although this goal was never attained, the implementation of the PND marked the beginning of a process that privatized the steel, petrochemical, and fertilizer industries. The PND, managed by the National Bank for Economic and Social Development (Banco Nacional do Desenvolvimento Econômico e Social — BNDES), stressed transparency and checks and balances, requiring two independent professional valuations of the target firm, and it established auctions and public offerings of shares as the predominant form of sale. Most of the firms sold through the first half of 1998 have been purchased by other Brazilian entities, often pension funds of other public enterprises.

The Brazilian privatization program initially was distinctive in terms of 1) the absence of foreign participation, which was limited by statute to 40 percent of voting equity; 2) the extensive use of relatively worthless domestic public debt instruments;[5] and 3) the focus on manufacturing industries rather than on public utilities and other non-tradables. It is estimated that almost three quarters of the total paid for privatized firms was in the form of domestic public debt certificates swapped at par, what Brazilians have termed "rotten money" because of the deep discount at which it trades in the secondary market.

In the wake of Collor's impeachment in late 1992, the Brazilian privatization program was significantly revised. The new president, Itamar Franco, changed the structure of the privatization program, by 1) limiting the participation of pension funds, 2) requiring an increased use of cash instead of domestic debt instruments, and 3) easing restrictions on foreign participation. Despite these mid-course corrections, the program seemed to lose momentum, and few new privatizations were completed. Instead, policy attention turned to the implementation of the Real Plan, and its seeming success virtually guaranteed its designer, Fernando Henrique Cardoso, a successful bid for the presidency.

Despite some initial uncertainty among investors regarding Cardoso's plans for privatization, he took steps to signal his intent to continue selling public enterprises. The Companhia Vale do Rio Doce (CVRD), the very profitable state-owned mining company, was added to the list of firms slated for privatization, and, in July 1995, the state-owned electric company in the state of Espírito Santo was sold to private investors. The Cardoso administration sought constitutional reforms to "flexibilize" the petroleum industry, introduced legislation to increase private participation in electricity generation, and established a commission to study the reorganization of telecommunications — an industry of particular interest to foreign investors.

Caribbean

State-owned enterprises have tended to play a key role in the development of the Caribbean economies. In response to a colonial heritage, many governments have used state ownership to assert sovereignty and economic independence and to implement a nationalist economic policy. This began to change in the 1980s, however, when governments in the Caribbean, as elsewhere in Latin America, were forced to undertake significant economic reforms as part of the conditionality associated with multilateral assistance and bilateral aid. Although support for state ownership was already waning in some Caribbean countries due to poor service, financial losses, and overstaffing, privatization programs often were met with some public skepticism, which focused on the potential for corruption, the lack of transparency in some privatization procedures, and the unrealistic pricing of state assets slated to be sold.

Although the extensiveness both of government ownership and subsequent privatization has varied among Caribbean countries, privatization has tended to include hotels, banks, public utilities, sugar, and chemical and cement plants, while bauxite and, in some cases, sanitation and *transportation services* have been explicitly excluded. The methods of privatization have varied somewhat depending on the country and the organization sold; yet, the Caribbean programs are noteworthy in their reliance on cash sales and exclusion of the use of debt instruments. Privatization in the Caribbean region has made extensive use of leases, concessions, contracting-out, and joint ventures to supplement a more limited number of divestitures. Care was taken in most of the Caribbean programs to include worker participation in the sale, often through the use of employee stock ownership plans.

Chile

Chile was the pioneer in privatization not only in Latin America but also in the international arena. Its program began in 1973 when a military coup ended decades of democratic civilian rule. Between 1974 and 1992, Chile privatized more than 500 state-owned firms in a process that can be divided into two periods separated by a short reversal. Gen. Augusto Pinochet's military government demonstrated a strong ideological commitment to a market economy. A cadre of economists trained at the University of Chicago designed and implemented the extensive privatization program, which has had wide-ranging effects — from production of goods and economic services to areas such as pension funds, education, and health.[6]

The first round of privatizations, undertaken between 1974 and 1982, involved the return of recently nationalized assets to their former owners, the liquidation of some small state firms, and the sale of banks and a few traditionally state-owned companies. Done in haste, improperly financed, and poorly supervised, this phase of privatization was relatively short-lived and unsuccessful because many of the highly leveraged privatized firms fell into bankruptcy during the severe recession of the early 1980s. Ownership of some 50 firms reverted to the state when a recessionary economy combined with a lack of internal liquidity to create a financial crisis in 1982. While the firms were privately held, ownership was highly concentrated among the country's leading *grupos* (holding companies), and questions about the proper valuation of the firms and the lack of transparency of those transactions still linger.

The second round of privatization in Chile (1984-1990) consisted of re-privatizing the firms that had fallen back into the hands of the state and extending the scope of privatization to include a number of traditionally state-owned firms, including public utilities, airlines, and steel. This second round, characterized by greater transparency and a commitment to increase share diffusion and decrease leverage, has attracted significant international attention. Various methods were used to sell firms, and shares were sold to workers, managers, foreigners, pension funds, and other companies. Foreigners could utilize a debt-equity scheme known as Chapter 19 to finance their purchases, but debt financing of sales was very limited. Shares in large firms were also sold on foreign stock exchanges.

Chile's privatization program is unique in many ways. It is the only Latin American privatization program undertaken in an environment where political discussion and dissent were severely limited. Privatization in Chile was also part of a broad set of policy changes that substantially increased competition in the economy, in both output and capital markets. The extent of privatization in Chile exceeds that undertaken in other Latin American economies, especially as it affects education, health, and other social services. Additionally, Chile's privatization marks a complete turnaround from a tradition of state entrepreneurship to a staunch commitment to a free market economy.

Colombia

Colombia's privatization experience has been unique in that there was little to privatize from the beginning. The state's share of gross national product (GNP) has never exceeded 25 percent, and the private sector has enjoyed wide participation in all industries.

The government's privatization efforts began with the transportation sector, which had impeded significant growth in exports and imports due to its inefficiency. Subsequently, the government directed its attention to the telecommunications and power sectors, the former a particularly significant net cash generator for the government. In both sectors, the government has chosen concessions, subcontracting, and joint ventures as the preferred modes of privatization while simultaneously pursuing measures to boost the efficiency and performance of state-owned enterprises. The Colombian government then privatized much of the highway infrastructure and social security.

Although privatization results to date demonstrate improvements across the board in service quality, higher consumer prices have had negative effects on Colombians. Nevertheless, the Colombian Congress has displayed growing support of privatization, and greater competition — among private providers as well as between state and private providers — is expected to usher in decreases in costs and prices.

Mexico

Privatization was an important part of Mexico's stabilization and reform program and, as in Chile, it was a long process that evolved in several distinct stages, spanning three presidential terms (each term lasts six years and is called a *sexenio*). The Mexican privatization program, initially referred to as disincorporation, began in 1983 with the closure of hundreds of unprofitable, small, public-sector firms and was followed, in the mid-1980s, by the divestiture of more significant enterprises. The privatization program has involved the sale or closure of nearly 1,000 state-owned firms, valued at about $18 billion. Although Mexico has privatized telecommunications, airlines, steel, and granted concessions for toll roads, its program is distinctive in the Latin American context for the inclusion of the banking sector and the exclusion of electricity and oil. In fact, the 18 banks sold in 1993 accounted for more than half of all privatization revenue ($12.6 billion).

Although foreign participation in the banking sector faces statutory limitations, foreign investors played a major role in Mexican privatization, which also appeared to have attracted significant sums of returning Mexican flight capital. Recent legislation would permit 100 percent foreign ownership of the Mexican railroads. Shares of privatized firms have been sold in both foreign and domestic stock markets, though voting rights are often reserved to Mexican buyers. The sale of TELMEX stock in the United States attracted significant interest; its success may have initiated the wave of Latin American Depositary Receipts that followed.

Peru

A government with little previous political or administrative experience launched Peru's privatization program at a time of considerable political and economic turmoil. Despite such an inauspicious setting, the program successfully completed 71 divestitures, ranging from gas stations, hotels, and fishmeal plants to mines, cement, public utilities, and refineries. The program started slowly in 1992, some two years after Alberto Fujimori took office, as part of a larger program of economic stabilization and reform. Early privatization included the sale of an iron mine, the national airlines, a coastal shipping operation, and the granting of a concession to operate oil fields off the north coast of the country. Perhaps the best reported privatization was the sale in 1994 of the operating control of Peru's telephone company to Telefónica de España for some $2 billion. Although the pace of privatization slowed somewhat in Fujimori's second term, the government's determination to privatize was not in question. Rather, the complexity of the remaining SOEs seemed to require a more measured pace.

By mid-1996, privatization in Peru had generated some $3.8 billion for the state treasury and an additional $2.7 billion in commitments for additional investment. Most enterprises were sold for cash to the highest bidder, usually a private foreign investor. Private domestic investors participated in many of the smaller privatizations, but little attempt was made to include small investors in anything like the "popular capitalism" schemes of Chile and Great Britain. Stock market sales of shares were not widely used, principally because of the small size of the local stock market. The increase in private foreign investment in Peru in recent years, however, has led to increased activity and liquidity in that market.

Venezuela

Venezuela undertook privatization as part of a broader set of economic reforms that included economic stabilization, structural adjustment, and compensatory social policies aimed at reducing the effects of adjustment on the poor. Privatization, as part of a process of structural adjustment that also included the elimination of some statutory monopolies, began in 1990 with the sale of a bank and reached its peak in late 1991 with the sale of the national telephone company. In the intervening period, state assets, including banks, hotels, an airline, sugar refineries, and a shipyard, were sold. Between 1990 and 1995, a total of 26 firms were sold for $2.4 billion, with the sale of the telephone company accounting for 78.5 percent of that revenue. Since then, political unrest and economic crisis have nearly halted privatization. Although steel and aluminum remain slated for privatization, there has been little activity in those sectors under current conditions. Interestingly, the petroleum sector, nationalized in 1976, has been making frequent use of concessions and contracting out increasingly. The petroleum industry was officially opened to private sector participation in 1996, when exploration contracts were sold at auction.

The objectives of the Venezuelan privatization program included increased competition, greater efficiency, higher levels of output, development of capital markets, the democratization of wealth, and the improvement of fiscal balances. The primary focus of privatization in Venezuela, however, was on a redefinition of the role of the state in the economy. Thus, the privatization program was designed to remove the state from the ownership of economic assets. The program was also designed to sell firms without restructuring, for cash rather than debt instruments, in a process of public bidding for a controlling share with extensive private sector participation in the process of valuation and sale. In each sale, between 10 percent to 20 percent of equity was reserved for sale to workers at a preferential rate. In several cases, the state reserved for itself a portion of the shares of companies being privatized, in hopes of later selling them to develop local capital markets.

CONCLUSION

The wave of neoliberal economic reforms that began in Chile and Great Britain in the 1980s has resulted in a significant transfer of assets and, perhaps less obviously, a transfer of responsibilities from the public sector to the private sector. The world has put a great deal of faith into what market forces and private sector managers can create in Latin America. Perhaps inspired by the faith and confidence of the world community in its regenerative powers or attracted by the bargain-basement prices of some large SOEs, private capital began to flow back to Latin America in the late 1980s. However, the collapse of the peso in Mexico at the end of 1994 and the financial repercussions of this event on the rest of Latin America indicate how fragile the process of economic and political reform can be. And while it is too early to evaluate the full contribution of privatization to economic renewal in Latin America, it is time to examine the progress being made. That is the focus of the remaining chapters of this book. The full impact of current privatization in Latin America and the Caribbean will only be known sometime in the next century.

Notes

1. For the fragile democracies taking hold in Latin America, a revenue-enhancing tax reform might have accomplished the same task but was politically impossible and unfashionable in the international arena, which had become dominated by the neoliberal policy agenda.

2. For a thorough review of the Latin American experience with privatization of the telecommunications and transport sectors, see Ramamurti 1996.

3. The term "privatization" can refer to many different policies whose common purpose is to reduce the influence of the state in the economy and to strengthen the role of market forces. In its broadest interpretation, market liberalization, deregulation, divestiture (sometimes called denationalization), and contracting out are all included under the privatization rubric. In this book, the term focuses more narrowly on divestiture, that is, the sale of publicly owned assets.

4. The Convertibility Plan, introduced in March 1991 as part of a stabilization program, pegged the Argentine peso to the U.S. dollar at a 1:1 ratio and eliminated all exchange and capital controls. It also established that the money supply could be expanded only if the quantity of money was fully backed by international reserves.

5. Acceptable currencies for Brazilian privatization included *cruzeiros* (local currency), *cruzados novos* (originally those held in blocked accounts), agricultural development debt, privatization certificates, and other government public debt instruments, all of which would be accepted at nominal face value. Foreign debt could be used but with a 25-percent discount.

6. CODELCO, the large state-owned copper mining company, however, remains in state hands.

CHAPTER 2

Early, Massive, Broad, and Successful Privatizations: The Case of Chile

ROLF J. LÜDERS

C hile began to privatize even before the United Kingdom, making a number of significant mistakes in the process. The Chilean privatizations were massive, in the sense that a large number of state-owned enterprises (SOEs) were privatized in a relatively short period of time, using a variety of original privatization modes. The privatization process was broad, as it not only affected firms offering commercial products but also certain government-provided social services, such as education, health, pensions, and housing. The privatizations were successful because they contributed to a more efficient economy, generated more employment, and broadened stock ownership and because the process was widely accepted by most Chileans. This chapter describes the relatively novel privatizations undertaken in Chile. It discusses the mistakes made and the impact of program, while highlighting the conditions that contributed to its ultimate success.

PRIVATIZATION AND ECONOMIC REFORM

P rivatization in Chile, as in many other places, was one of many instruments applied by the economic authorities to improve efficiency in the use of the country's resources. Thus, the impact of privatization cannot be judged without considering the measures that accompanied the process. In addition, the political will involved in carrying out the privatization program must also be taken into account. Before describing the modes used to privatize and analyzing the impact of privatization for the country, this chapter will examine the context of Chilean privatization.

Economic Background

Chilean privatizations were a reaction against the socioeconomic development process leading up to September 1973. After the depression of the early 1930s, Chile adopted a state-led, inward-looking economic development model. Producers were protected from international competition through customs duties and other trade barriers. The government intervened heavily in the economy by fixing prices, wages, and interest rates. Moreover, through the Corporation for Production Development (Corporación de Fomento de la Producción — CORFO), the official development bank, the government created a number of large SOEs to produce private goods and services. The intention was to provide the basic industrial infrastructure — steel, electricity, petroleum — that the private sector supposedly could not produce due to lack of capital, technological knowledge, and entrepreneurial capacity.[1]

After a brief initial period of successful growth and in spite of the government's deepening intervention in the economy, Chile's relative economic growth rates stayed below those of some of its Latin American neighbors and, after the 1950s, well below those of the Asian Tigers. During the 1950s, the government increasingly felt popular pressure to accelerate growth. Three alternative models were proposed by the leadership of the country's three large political groups then beginning to divide the country more or less evenly: the Marxists, the Christian Democrats, and the Independent-Conservatives. The Marxists sought to apply a centralized model, along the lines of the Cuban or Central European economies. The Christian Democrats believed that it was necessary to carry out deep structural reforms, including land reform, while maintaining a mixed market economy. The third group, the Independent-Conservatives, favored stronger direct and indirect investment incentives for the private sector and, in general, heavier reliance on the latter to produce goods and services (see Lüders 1988).

Between the late 1950s and the early 1970s, all three political groups had a chance to apply their policy proposals at least partially. Between 1958 and 1964, the Independent-Conservatives were in power. Thereafter, the Christian Democrats were elected with the support of the Independents and stayed in power until 1970.[2] In both cases, after two very successful initial years, growth and inflation rates deteriorated but were kept under control. Between 1964 and 1970, important structural reforms were implemented with respect to land, taxes, and monetary activities, generating a significant redistribution of wealth and hurting only a relatively small number of people, most of them supporters of the Independents. This made a Christian Democratic-Independent coalition for the following election very difficult, if not impossible. In the three-way 1970 presidential election, Marxist representative Salvador Allende won the election with 34 percent of the vote and immediately began to apply his economic program that led to a centralized economy.[3]

Allende established fixed prices for almost all goods and services, interest rates, and wages. With the support of the representatives of all political parties, the new government nationalized the large foreign-owned copper companies without compensation.[4] The controlling shares of over 200 other private firms also were purchased, including all but one of the commercial banks, and these companies became SOEs.[5] Additionally, the government took control of 240 other medium- and large-sized private firms, invoking a decree that had been passed by a de facto government during the depression of the 1930s and never been repealed. This law allowed governments to expropriate those firms producing "essential" goods or services when labor conflicts threatened to halt production.[6] Moreover, the Marxists accelerated the land reform process, nationalizing about 50 percent of the country's irrigated lands.

Among other negative effects on the economy, the Allende government's measures generated an increasing central government deficit, which reached 24.7 percent of gross domestic product (GDP) for 1973, resulting in the loss of all international reserves and in an annual inflation rate exceeding 1,000 percent for September 1973. The effects of the government's land reform process and poor macroeconomic management largely explain the severe food shortage of 1972 and 1973. Moreover, by implementing its program of expropriations despite having only minority support in Congress, the government violated the law, as Congress and the Comptroller's Office publicly and officially pointed out. The fear of the loss of personal freedom resulting from these expropriations[7] and the lack of food motivated over 1 million women to protest in the streets of Santiago by banging their empty pots and pans, demanding that the Allende government step down. Eventually, after an impressive truck drivers' strike that paralyzed all transportation in the country, the military took over the government to make fundamental reforms in Chile's economic, social, and political institutions.

The legacy of socioeconomic development between 1940 and 1973 is very important for understanding the privatization process in Chile. During that period, the role of the government expanded rapidly (see Cortés and Wagner 1980), as did the SOE sector. By the early 1970s, many Chileans were beginning to associate the operations of the government and the SOEs with bad service and inefficiency.

The Military and the Chicago Boys

Chileans were in search of a model that would produce growth within a democratic framework. In 1973, they clearly and popularly rejected the totalitarian regime's attempts to implement a centralized economy, although this meant that Chileans had to accept an authoritarian government that claimed it would reestablish a viable democracy. The military recognized that, given Chile's relatively low income levels and its uneven income distribution,[8] this could be accomplished only within the framework of a rapidly growing economy. Otherwise, the redistributive pressures were going to be too strong and destructive, as had been proved at other times between 1940 and 1973. The military also felt that the economy needed to be radically restructured to be able to achieve rapid growth, although it did not offer a particular model. The military had been very isolated from civil society ever since it was thrown out of government following a brief period in power during the late 1920s and early 1930s. The military had concentrated strictly on defense matters since then. Augusto Pinochet, the strongest member of the military junta, said that he favored a "social market economy," without specifying exactly what he meant by that. He did know that in designing and implementing the new economic institutions, he did not want to go back to past practices, nor did he want or initially need to invite input from pressure groups, labor, business leaders, or political parties, all of whom he deeply distrusted.

The military, therefore, invited a group of young economists, most of them from the Pontifical Catholic University of Chile (Pontificia Universidad Católica de Chile — PUC), to lead the economic reform process. During the 1950s, the U.S. Agency for International Development (USAID) had initiated a collaborative project between that university and the University of Chicago to improve Chile's capacity for economic analysis. An economic research center was created in Santiago, and dozens of Chilean students received Ph.D.-level training at the University of Chicago. Upon returning to Chile, many of these graduates did research on a full-time basis at the Catholic University. The relatively homogenous, upper-middle class background of these professors, their common professional training, and the strong empirical (factual) nature of the research explain the development during the 1960s of a shared diagnosis about the ills of the Chilean economy and the institutional and policy reforms necessary to accelerate growth. In general terms, the "Chicago Boys," as they came to be known, advocated a competitive market economy, open to international trade and finance — a radical departure from the highly protected and regulated economy then in place. This view was, of course, transmitted to hundreds of elite students, who eventually played a very important role during the structural reform process when, in key positions in the public and private sectors, they understood, supported, and contributed to the implementation of the process.

At the time, the open market economy advocated by the Chicago Boys had very little support in Chile or elsewhere for that matter (Valdés 1995). The idea of a market economy ran counter to the notion, espoused by academics and practitioners, that poor economies could develop only with very heavy government intervention. Labor leaders opposed the model because it implied a drastic reduction of labor's bargaining power and favored the institutionalization of a competitive labor market. Business leaders opposed it because it would end existing protectionism and expose domestic firms to foreign competition. Although some of the PUC economists had helped develop the platform of Jorge Alessandri, a right-wing presidential candidate running against Salvador Allende, a more traditional, protectionist view defended by a group of leading businessmen prevailed.

By 1972, the dramatic economic and political failures of the Allende regime suggested that his government might be replaced before the end of the constitutionally established term. This led a multipartisan group of economists to prepare the basic guidelines of a new economic program, to be offered to the next president to govern the country after Allende (CEP 1994). This economic program differed from those applied in the previous two decades, fulfilling one of the conditions sought by the military, namely, that it indeed was a social market economy. After a year of indecision, the new government adopted the program. The Chicago Boys, without ties to political parties or interest groups, were put in charge of its implementation. They were led by Sergio de Castro, former dean of the Faculty of Economics and Social Sciences of the Pontifical Catholic University of Chile.

In summary, several decades of increasing protectionism and state intervention in the economy culminated in a severe sociopolitical and economic crisis in 1973, when the Allende government tried to force a centralized economy on the country. This set the stage for a very strong, popularly supported reaction, led politically by the military and technically by the Chicago Boys.

Basic Outline of the Economic Model

The Chilean model can indeed be called a social market economy in the sense that it is a free market economy in which the government plays a role in correcting external and human-capital endowment disparities among citizens (Wisecarver 1992). It differs from the German model in that, during the Pinochet regime, divergences between private and social costs and benefits (externalities) were judged "technically" by the economic team, instead of being "revealed" through the political process.

This "market-based" model aims to let markets work with the least government intervention advisable. The model is based on 1) creating the right climate for private enterprise development, 2) having a sound macroeconomic foundation, 3) integrating into the global economy, and 4) investing more in people. The state is not to intervene in those areas where markets work or can be made to work well, and, above everything else, it is to foster competition wherever possible, destroying any monopolies. The government should not manage productive activities, since this can best be done by the private sector.[9] Therefore, one of the basic policies followed by the military regime was the privatization of SOEs as well as of social goods and services formerly provided by the state (education, health, housing, and pensions).

The government, rather than create market-distorting interventions as it had in the past, would concentrate its efforts on achieving 1) higher rates of investment in education, health, and other human-capital areas, in order to equalize initial conditions for all citizens, while correcting for externalities in this area; 2) alleviation of poverty of children and the elderly; 3) improvements in the country's social, physical, administrative, and legal infrastructure; and 4) a sound macroeconomic environment.

This market-based model today is generally accepted as the paradigm for developing countries (World Bank 1995). Contrary to what was then believed, its goal is an efficient and powerful government that can carry out the activities listed above, through its comparative advantage over the private sector. The private sector, in turn, is to produce *all* goods and services in the economy at the lowest possible cost. This objective requires privatization within a competitive framework. It was believed at the time that most existing monopolies were legal monopolies, created by the state to satisfy rent-seeking pressure groups. The view was that technological progress had sharply diminished the number of natural monopolies. It was further asserted that most of the state-owned public utilities could be unbundled into a number of firms, most of them competitive. A need was recognized, however, for regulation of the few remaining natural monopolies, and antimonopoly institutions had to exist. This alone was not enough (Akin and Spiller 1994). Without the right business climate, privatization would not produce the expected results because, in an unfavorable economy, the privatized firms would be likely to invest less than the optimum, leading to the potential for a reversal of the whole process. As had occurred with nationalizations in the past, this would happen if goods and services provided by the privatized firms did not satisfy existing demands or were of low quality or both.

The economic team of the military regime believed that the private sector would develop as desired only if the expected rates of return to investment were still attractive at high investment rates relative to GDP *and* if, at the same time, the sector had access to the necessary financial and human resources. In Chile before 1973,

expected rates of return were relatively low. This was mainly because of expropriation episodes, which sometimes occurred directly — as in the cases of the large
foreign copper company, some of the public utilities, and land reform — but
generally took place indirectly — through the government maximum price-fixing
mechanism and other incomes policies. At the same time, governments repressed
financial markets by fixing low deposit interest rates and, in general, by crowding
out the private sector.

> To generate the desired private sector development, these latter conditions had to
> change drastically. Property rights needed to be strengthened through constitu-
> tional and legal means, in such a way that direct or indirect expropriations would
> become highly unlikely (Corbo, Lüders, and Spiller 1996). Prices had to be freed
> credibly and the economy had to be opened up as much as possible to international
> trade and finance. In this way, a floor was to be put on expected local rates of return
> to investment, equal to international rates plus a reasonably low risk premium for
> Chile. On the supply-of-financial-resources side, Chilean governments had to
> generate budget surpluses to eliminate the crowding-out effect, and a number of
> measures had to be taken to strengthen the domestic capital market, the most
> important of which would probably be the privatization of the pension system (to
> be discussed below), and the opening of the capital account. When the process
> started, human resources in Chile were relatively developed, but people had to
> receive the necessary incentives to continue to invest heavily in human capital
> (Hachette and Lüders 1993).

Thus, the economic team believed that a successful privatization process
could take place only in a price-stable economy within a competitive environment
in which institutional stability were paramount, expropriation threats were absent,
and financial and human resources would become available as required by the
development process. Today, it is also accepted that the country had a need for
"social capital," initially available through the network of Catholic University
graduates (Montero 1996).

Privatizations and the Economic Cycle

The evolution of the privatization process — its impact, successes, and
failures — is closely related to some of the more outstanding features of the
country's economic development. Different privatization phases clearly are tied to
phases of the Chilean economy starting in late 1973. The privatizations were
designed to accomplish short-term, specific objectives related to the particular
phase of the economic cycle. Additionally, there were two long-run objectives:
from a political perspective, to reduce the power of the state and, from an economic
perspective, to increase the efficiency of the enterprises and the economy.

The first round of privatizations coincided with a period that began with a
major recession (1975) and ended with an even deeper one (1982-1983). It was a
"revolutionary" period during which the military regime made almost all substantive institutional adjustments, including those to increase competition drastically in
all markets, to reestablish macroeconomic balances, and to implement painful
stabilization efforts. Most Chileans were willing to make the necessary sacrifices
to reestablish the economic health of the country. During this period, those
enterprises nationalized during the Allende government were privatized; land

expropriated as part of the land reform process was allocated to peasants and, therefore, privatized; and social services were reformed to allow private sector production of formerly government-provided (financed) services. The specific short-term objective of the privatizations was to collect resources to finance the government deficit. Since the Chilean private sector had virtually no liquid assets and foreigners would not become interested in investing in Chile until the late 1970s, the government granted credit to purchasers of SOEs, which eventually had disastrous consequences.

The deepest recession since the 1930s, caused by external factors but aggravated by macroeconomic management errors, ended this hectic period. In 1982 and 1983, about 50 of the most important privatized firms reverted to state control as a consequence of the impact on their holding companies of the significant reduction in economic activity linked to the recession and to the massive disruption in the financial sector, which had been aggravated by the debt-led privatizations of 1975 to 1978.[10] Immediately following the recession, especially during 1984, some of the structural reforms described below were reversed; in particular, customs duties were raised significantly.

Beginning in late 1984, there was a period of recovery, adjustments, consolidation of the main institutional developments of the 1970s, policy changes to increase savings rates and exports, and rapid economic growth. The successful operation of the firms privatized during the 1970s allowed the government to engage in additional privatizations, while firms that had been expropriated during the downturn were reprivatized and a second round of privatization involving the large, core SOEs, many of them public utilities, took place. The government did not have any pressing budget financing problems, and, therefore, the privatizations now had different short-run objectives, including the reduction of the foreign debt (to be achieved through debt-for-equity swaps), the provision of investment possibilities for the new private pension funds (through sales of SOE shares to them), and the creation of a notion of private ownership (Larroulet 1994).

In 1990, a democratically elected president, supported by a broad center-to-left coalition,[11] took office, and rather than modify the basic features of the economic model, his administration deepened some of its characteristics. For example, customs duties were lowered even further, from 15 percent to 11 percent. A second democratically elected government, supported by the same coalition, also retained the economic model. For example, it further liberalized international capital flows and negotiated free trade agreements with North American Free Trade Agreement (NAFTA), Southern Cone Common Market — Mercado Común del Sur (MERCOSUR), and the European Union, among others. These new center-to-left-leaning democratic governments embraced the economic and social institutions of the right-wing military government, mainly because the system was proving to be effective in generating economic growth and reducing poverty, and also because the old protectionist, state-led model had been discredited worldwide.

Since 1990, however, the privatization process has come to a virtual halt (see Table 1). Before 1990, the military government had taken the privatization process as far as it was willing to carry it. In that year, the remaining SOEs were relatively few, although some were very large. One of these was the huge and inefficient

Table 1.
Chilean State-Owned and State-Managed Enterprises in Selected
Years, 1970-1995 (number of enterprises)

	1970	1973	1983	1989	1995
Enterprises related to CORFO	46	571	24	24	20
Subsidiaries	46	228	23	24	20 [a,b,c]
State-managed enterprises	0	325	0	0	0
Banks	0	18	1	0	0
Other state-owned enterprises	20	22	21	18	14 [d]
Other financial institutions	2	2	2	2	2
CODELCO	0	1	1	1	1
Total of state-owned and managed enterprises	**68**	**596**	**48**	**45**	**37**

Notes: a) ZOFRI, S.A. 48% privatized   b) Edelnor, S.A. 30% privatized
          c) Colbún, S.A. 7.6% privatized   d) Minsal, S.A. 18% privatized
Sources: Hachette and Lüders (1993) and data provided by CORFO for the 1990-1995 privatizations.

National Copper Corporation (Corporación Nacional de Cobre — CODELCO), valued at least at US$10 billion (Lüders 1992). This company was nationalized in 1971 by unanimous vote in Congress to establish a law by which 10 percent of its sales are automatically turned over to the military. However, the new democratic governments have not wanted to privatize CODELCO outright. Another SOE was National Petroleum Company (Empresa Nacional de Petróleo — ENAP), the worthless petroleum company (Hachette, Kaufmann, and Lüders 1989). A third is the well-managed Santiago Subway (Metro de Santiago — METRO), whose main asset, the right-of-way below the surface, is very difficult to appraise. Another SOE is Colbún-Machicura, a large electricity-generating firm, which was to be used as a yardstick to regulate the private generators but which is now being partially privatized. There were also a number of smaller SOEs, among them several water and sewerage companies, most of which have been or will be privatized.[12]

Although the privatization of existing SOEs is proceeding very slowly, new needs have emerged as the export-led economy grows rapidly and at a steady pace. The new democratic governments must make very large road, railroad, and port infrastructure investments to support the growth of exports, while at the same time expanding investments in human capital. These administrations have been inviting the private sector to carry out the infrastructure investments through concessions. The government also is planning to invest most of its limited budget to build roads and other infrastructure in relatively isolated regions of the country, where these investments have low private, but high social, rates of return. Meanwhile, the private sector will develop the commercially viable infrastructure, including urban streets, to be financed on the basis of tolls, as has been done, for example, in Singapore. In another tactic, CODELCO has been inviting private sector firms to develop joint ventures to exploit certain of its mineral rights, and, more often than not, it grants company control to its private partners.

Structural Reforms and Privatization

As part of the privatization process and with varying degrees of success, Chilean governments since 1973 have carried out key policy or institutional changes (Hachette and Lüders 1993; Wisecarver 1992). Although practically all the institutional changes took place during the 1970s and the early 1980s, significant improvements have taken place thereafter. In particular, the core SOEs were privatized between 1985 and 1989. A significant shift in economic policy occurred after the recession of the early 1980s, with the goal of increasing savings and exports. The following are among the changes that have provided a framework for Chilean privatization:

Stabilization policies were implemented to achieve a low and stable inflation rate. Predictable price levels were considered necessary for rapid private sector development. Measures taken initially to bring down the extremely high inflation rates included restrictive fiscal and monetary policies, the use of the exchange rate to control inflationary expectations, and mandatory wage adjustments. The Central Bank became independent in 1989. It is responsible only for price stability, since a provision in the 1980 Constitution prohibits it from lending to the public sector. The Central Bank allowed SOEs to raise their prices significantly, while subjecting them to self-financing and marginal-cost pricing. This policy is still in effect. SOEs had accounted for one-third of the overall public sector deficit in 1973. The government was able to achieve a public sector budget surplus in 1979, which, except for the period of the recession, has continued ever since.

Public sector reforms were made to shape the new economic development model. The objective was to transfer productive activities to the private sector, concentrate government efforts to finance human capital development for the poor, and correct for significant market imperfections, including the provision of public goods. The government transferred more than 550 state-controlled firms to the private sector. In addition, educational and health services, the administration of the pension system, and the construction of houses also have been partially or totally transferred to the private sector. All commercial subsidies, except one for new forest plantations, have been eliminated.

Tax reforms were implemented to raise revenues to finance government expenditures in the least distorting way possible. Chile's expenditures were relatively high due to the level of social expenditures. Measures taken in the 1980s included comprehensive tax reforms that introduced a value-added tax affecting *all* activities (an even 18-percent rate as of 1994) in place of a progressive sales tax,[13] eliminated all exemptions, increased real estate assessments, and exempted undistributed profits from income taxation. Although the last measure has recently been partly and temporarily reversed, tax administration was significantly improved.

Price policies were implemented to allow prices to become the market signal and to restrict governments from using price controls to expropriate the private sector indirectly. All price controls were eliminated, and the 1980 Constitution, which explicitly prohibits discriminatory government interventions, virtually assures that they will not be used again.[14]

Trade policies were implemented to insert the Chilean economy into the global economy and to use resources more efficiently. Tariffs were reduced from a range of 0 to 750 percent to a single flat rate of 11 percent on *all* items. Nontariff barriers were eliminated. Exports diversified significantly and increased from $1.4093 billion in 1973 to $12.3477 billion during 1995 (based on 1986 U.S. dollars). The liberal import policy became the most effective way to introduce competition into all tradable activities, including those involving privatized enterprises.

Domestic financial policies were implemented to create efficient and deep financial and capital markets to allocate domestic and foreign savings efficiently. The availability of financial resources at market-determined interest rates was considered another necessary condition for private sector development and successful privatization. Measures included the complete liberalization of interest rates; the elimination of qualitative and quantitative credit controls; the establishment of new domestic banks, other financial intermediaries, and foreign banks; the privatization of the existing banks (in 1973, all but one were in government hands); and the permission to issue indexed securities and deposits in the capital market. Initially, no priority was given to establishing prudential or market-based regulation mechanisms, since the leaders of the economic team expected depositors to exercise the necessary control over the solvency of the financial institutions. This oversight contributed to the severity of the crisis during the early 1980s, so that by 1981, a mixture of prudential and market-based regulatory measures was being implemented. The substitution in 1980 and 1981 of the pay-as-you-go pension system by a new mandatory, privately managed system was another major institutional change. This individual-account, defined contribution system was related only indirectly to the private financial markets, but it has had a significant impact on their development, on the allocation of private savings and investment, and on the success of SOE privatizations.

Measures were designed to improve foreign capital flows and to promote the insertion of the Chilean economy into the global economy. The new policies made it possible for Chileans to invest their resources at home or abroad, wherever their risk-adjusted return was higher. Measures included the elimination of medium- and long-term quantitative limits on capital inflows and the approval, in July 1974, of a new foreign investment code, Decree 600, which gave parity to foreign investors with respect to domestic investors.

Labor market reforms were undertaken to break the existing semi-monopoly power of unions and to improve the functioning of the labor market. These reforms allowed employment to increase when unemployment was high and wages to rise when labor market conditions were tight. They also removed government from the wage-setting process, while allowing it to set the minimum wage. Measures included a sharp reduction in workers' severance payment rights, free union membership, multiple unions at each firm, collective bargaining at the firm level, and the right of firms to replace workers on strike, among others. Some of these reforms have now been reversed.

Modernization in social services was pursued to increase efficiency in government-financed education, health, housing, and pensions. Public sector expenditures in these areas exceeded 14 percent of GDP, one of the highest levels among developing countries; therefore, making the best use of these resources was a government priority. The basic principle was to subsidize demand instead of supply, contrary to what had been done in the past, and to focus these subsidies on the poor instead of on the middle class. Subsidies in response to demand provided beneficiaries with a choice and introduced competition from private sector producers. Measures included the financing of education on the basis of a fee per student-day of school attendance, to be paid to municipal or privately subsidized schools, both of which now compete; the creation of specialized private health insurance companies that can provide social security-financed health services in competition with the official health organizations; focused lump-sum housing subsidies to be used by the beneficiaries to purchase houses in the housing market; and the introduction of a private pension system.

A competition policy to regulate natural monopolies and discourage collusion by private sector firms was undertaken. Measures have included the unbundling of the large public utility monopolies; regulatory laws and institutions for the electricity, telecommunications, and water and sewerage sectors; and the creation of a relatively sophisticated antimonopoly mechanism. These institutional measures and economic policies provided a framework within which to carry out the Chilean privatizations. Wherever possible, competition was introduced into the economy, and where not possible, regulation was applied. Moreover, once the economy was integrated into the global market, conditions allowed privatized firms to prosper by providing institutional stability and financial and human resources at free market rates.

Overall Economic Results

Since the mid-1980s, Chile's GDP has grown at a relatively steady and high annual average rate of 6.3 percent (the highest since the 8.4-percent annual rates experienced from 1932 to 1941). The inflation rate was 8.2 percent in 1995, down from 608.7 percent in 1973 and below the average for any year since 1960. Exports, which were $1.4093 billion in 1973, grew to $12.3477 billion by 1995. Total employment has grown since 1973 at an average annual rate of 2.43 percent, and the 1995 unemployment rate was 4.70 percent.[15] Real wages are 39.33 percent higher than in 1985 and 19.01 percent higher than during their peak in 1981. Data on the evolution of income distribution is contradictory, while indicators suggest that poverty is rapidly being reduced. The so-called macroeconomic fundamentals have been under control since the recession of the early 1980s, and the economy seems to be continuing its fast expansion. Moreover, opinion leaders widely agree that the basic principles underlying the current model should not be modified.

These good results cannot be attributed to any one feature of the model; that is, they cannot be identified with privatization alone. However, it can be said that without the privatizations, given the large size of the SOE sector in Chile in 1973, the highly successful market-based model implemented in Chile would never have been possible.

THE PRIVATIZATION MODES

In Chile, SOEs, land, and certain government-provided social services were privatized. Concessions also were granted to private sector firms to exploit roads, ports, and other infrastructure projects, which the public sector had previously built and operated. Some of the privatization modes used in Chile are novel and are an alternative to the voucher scheme used in Central European and former Soviet Union countries.

State-Owned Enterprises (SOEs)

SOEs were privatized in three rounds (1974-1978, 1984-1988, 1990 and beyond). In the first two rounds, SOEs were divested in two phases each.

First Round, First Phase: 1974 (Return of Expropriated Firms). During the first phase of privatization, 325 expropriated enterprises, with a net book value of about $2.33 billion,[16] were returned to their owners on the condition that they would formally agree not to litigate against the government for any losses of working capital or deterioration of machinery and other assets. In special cases, additional conditions were imposed to ensure the maintenance of employment levels, competitiveness among related industries, and levels of new investments. Compliance with this second set of conditions was, however, not enforced.

First Round, Second Phase: 1975-1978 (Debt-Led Privatizations). The second phase of the first round of privatizations in Chile consisted mainly of the transfer (for the equivalent of about $1.2 billion) of 207 financial institutions, industries, wholesale distribution companies, and other corporations that had been acquired by the public sector, primarily during the Allende government. This phase generated revenues of $2.45 billion.[17] Only a handful of CORFO subsidiaries were retained for "strategic reasons," along with the core SOEs, those enterprises established by special law. Most of these latter corporations either were considered natural monopolies or controlled a high percentage of the business in their fields.

The SOEs sold between 1975 and 1978 were divested via liquidation, auction, or direct sale. If the value of an enterprise as a going concern was less than the value of its separate assets, the company was closed down, and the individual assets were either auctioned off or sold directly.

Decree 1068 regulated the auctions. Bidders were offered controlling shares in the SOEs and allowed to pay in installments in order to raise divestiture prices. This was a major flaw in the process, since it produced a moral hazard, as the bidders offered such "high" prices that they were forced to go further in debt or engage in risky operations to meet the installment payments. During the recession of the early 1980s, the holding companies that had bid for the SOEs went bankrupt, inflicting huge losses on commercial banks. In expectation of large privatization revenues, the government had not reduced its expenditure levels, which may partly explain the extremely high interest rates between 1975 and 1979 (see Table 2). In the end, the government was induced to bail out the banks, which means that the government was maintaining a high level of social expenditures, financed at a cost that surely exceeded its rate of return. The lesson is that debt-led divestitures, with low down payments and no additional guarantees, should never be made to controlling parties.

The use of direct sales was a third mode of privatization, usually applied to smaller enterprises where organizing an auction was too costly in relation to the expected sale price.

Second Round, First Phase: 1984-1985 ("Second-Tier" Privatizations).[18] During this phase, about 30 "productive" companies of lesser prominence than big industrial firms were divested, generally by auction, generating about $785 million.[19] The controlling shares were offered as a package, but no credit was granted, and bidders were obliged to prove their solvency. With foreign investors showing new interest, some of the larger reprivatized companies invited foreign partners to join them. The government welcomed these foreign investments because they made multimillion dollar export projects planned by certain firms possible (Larroulet 1994). These investments were made more attractive by allowing debt-equity swaps that allowed investors to pay with Chile's foreign debt instruments at about 60 percent of face value.

Second Round, Second Phase: 1985-1989 (Core SOEs). The last phase of privatizations under the military government affected the large, traditional SOEs, as well as large financial institutions. Total revenues exceeded $1.45 billion.[20] These privatizations were politically more sensitive and, as a rule, the government divested each one incrementally in order to gain gradual support for its policy. The government also took care to achieve as wide a distribution of the shares as was reasonable. SOEs were first transformed into corporations whose shares could be traded on the stock exchange and whose accounts and operations would be subject to audits. The government would then announce, for example, the privatization of 30 percent of the equity, using one or at most two of the divestiture modes described below. As soon as that percentage had been successfully divested, the government would announce the privatization of another 19 percent, perhaps making use of a different privatization mode. The announcement of the privatization of an additional 2 percent would then complete the transfer of control to the private sector. Privatization of the remaining stock, up to 100 percent, usually by offering small to medium-sized share packages on the Santiago Stock Exchange, followed immediately.

Regulation of natural monopolies also was put in place: in 1982, for electric power and local and long-distance communications (the latter was revised in 1987)

Table 2. Economic Indicators for Chile, 1971-1976

	1971	1972	1973	1974	1975	1976
Real Sector						
GDP (millions $ 1986)	2,835,922	2,801,517	2,645,612	2,671,393	2,326,511	2,408,358
GDP Growth Rate (%)	9.0	-1.2	-5.6	1.0	-12.9	3.5
Gross Investment/GDP (%)	14.7	12.4	8.0	21.5	13.6	13.2
National Saving/GDP (%)	12.4	8.3	5.2	20.7	7.9	14.5
Unemployment Rate (%)	3.8	3.1	4.8	9.2	14.5	12.9
Prices						
Inflation Rate (%)[a]	28.2	255.4	608.7	369.2	343.3	198.0
Real Wages Index (1977=100)[b]	164.8	136.6	77.5	91.5	87.3	91.5
Short-term Real Interest Rate (lending rate, %)	n.a.	n.a.	-76.1	-36.9	16.0	64.3
Real Exchange Rate (1977=100)	71.1	71.2	90.2	87.9	149.7	114.0
Real Exchange Rate (1986=100)[c]	n.a.	n.a.	n.a.	n.a.	n.a.	n.a.
Terms of Trade (1977=100)	205.6	201.8	220.3	183.5	104.0	111.1
Monetary and Financial Sector						
Total Change in Monetary Base (% GDP)[d]	8.27	-3.82	-2.83	-3.06	-1.56	1.61
M2/GDP (%)[d]	17.0	11.7	8.1	5.8	6.2	7.7
Consolidated Banking Credit to the Private Sector/Total Credit (%)	28.5	22.2	18.6	15.2	15.9	15.6
Public Sector						
Public Sector Expenditures (% GDP)	31.1	31.2	44.9	32.4	27.4	25.8
Fiscal Deficit of the Central Government (% GDP)	10.7	13.0	24.7	10.5	2.6	2.3
Foreign Sector						
Export in Constant Prices of 1986 (millions)	311,597	264,519	271,900	396,840	406,620	505,418
Export Growth in Constant Prices (%)	0.8	-15.1	2.8	46.0	2.5	24.3
Current Account Surplus/export (%)	-17.8	-48.1	-19.7	-12.9	-27.1	5.4
Annual Change in External Debt (US$ millions)	73.0	406.0	446.0	726.0	80.0	-134.0
Annual Change in Foreign Reserves (US$ millions)	-231.0	-87.0	92.0	-73.0	-223.0	237.0
External Debt Service/Exports (%, medium and long term)	36.8	15.6	11.9	15.1	31.2	39.0

n.a. = not available a) December to December; b) Up to 1989, original figures from Jadresic (1989) were combined with the changes of the real wage index published by the Central Bank of Chile (1989), and, thereafter, up to 1995, various figures were obtained from the Central Bank's *Boletines Mensuales;* c) Central Bank of Chile figures; d) 1986 pesos, December balances.

Table 2a. Economic Indicators for Chile, 1977-1983

	1977	1978	1979	1980	1981	1982	1983
Real Sector							
GDP (millions $ 1986)	2,645,796	2,863,639	3,093,913	3,330,684	3,527,938	3,044,338	2,969,004
GDP Growth Rate (%)	9.9	8.2	8.0	7.7	5.9	-13.7	-2.5
Gross Investment/GDP (%)	14.8	18.3	18.4	21.7	23.9	11.3	9.8
National Saving/GDP (%)	10.7	12.6	12.4	13.9	8.2	2.1	4.4
Unemployment Rate (%)	11.8	14.2	13.6	10.4	11.3	19.6	14.6
Prices							
Inflation Rate (%)[a]	84.2	37.2	38.9	31.2	9.5	20.7	23
Real Wages Index (1977=100)[b]	100.0	105.6	115.5	125.4	135.2	135.2	121.1
Short-term Real Interest Rate (lending rate, %)	56.8	42.2	16.6	11.9	38.7	35.1	15
Real Exchange Rate (1977=100)	100.0	106.9	97.2	88.4	79.1	83.7	100.1
Real Exchange Rate (1986=100)[c]	n.a.	68.1	70.2	60.8	52.9	59.0	70.8
Terms of Trade (1977=100)	100.0	98.9	111.1	111.2	100.4	94.1	95
Monetary and Financial Sector							
Total Change in Monetary Base (% GDP)[d]	1.19	1.15	0.21	0.55	-1.30	-2.92	-0.
M2/GDP (%)[d]	9.5	13.2	14.6	18.8	23.7	24.2	19
Consolidated Banking Credit to the Private Sector/Total Credit (%)	37.7	50.6	54.7	68.1	81.1	83.0	80.8
Public Sector							
Public Sector Expenditures (% GDP)	24.9	23.8	22.8	23.1	24.9	28.5	28
Fiscal Deficit of the Central Government (% GDP)	1.8	0.8	-1.7	-3.1	-1.7	2.3	3.8
Foreign Sector							
Export in Constant Prices of 1986 (millions)	565,873	632,486	722,506	826,982	752,544	786,337	786,853
Export Growth in Constant Prices (%)	12.0	11.8	14.2	14.5	-9.0	4.5	0.1
Current Account Surplus/export (%)	-21.8	-37.8	-26.1	-33.9	-88.4	-62.2	-29.2
Annual Change in External Debt (US$ millions)	481.0	1,463.0	1,820.0	2,600.0	4,458.0	1,611.0	278
Annual Change in Foreign Reserves (US$ millions)	165.0	785.0	11256.0	1244.0	67.0	-1165.0	-541
External Debt Service/Exports (%, medium and long term)	43.9	44.6	41.2	39.6	64.2	64.4	65.7

SOURCES: Central Bank of Chile (1989) *Indicadores Económicos y Sociales,* 1960-1988; *Boletines Mensuales,* various years; *Memoria Anual 1994 and 1995*; PIMA/PUC Database; De la Cuadra, Sergio and Dominique Hachette (1988); Jadresic, E. (1989); Lüders, Rolf (1986); Superintendency of Banks and Financial Institutions; Ramos, Joseph (1986).

Table 2b. Economic Indicators for Chile, 1984-1989

	1984	1985	1986	1987	1988	1989
Real Sector						
GDP (millions $ 1986)	3,144,616	3,242,387	3,419,209	3,644,681	3,911,154	4,297,337
GDP Growth Rate (%)	5.9	3.1	5.5	6.6	7.3	9.9
Gross Investment/GDP (%)	13.6	13.7	14.6	16.9	17.3	18.2
National Saving/GDP (%)	2.9	5.4	7.7	12.6	16.3	16.9
Unemployment Rate (%)	13.9	11.4	8.8	7.9	6.3	5.3
Prices						
Inflation Rate (%)[a]	23.0	26.4	17.4	21.5	12.7	21.4
Real Wages Index (1977=100)[b]	121.1	115.5	118.3	118.3	125.4	127.8
Short-term Real Interest Rate (lending rate, %)	11.5	11.0	7.5	9.2	7.4	11.8
Real Exchange Rate (1977=100)	104.8	128.8	141.8	146.9	157.3	151.7
Real Exchenge Rate (1986=100)[c]	74.0	90.9	100.0	104.3	111.2	108.6
Terms of Trade (1977=100)	89.3	83.0	83.0	91.2	104.5	102.8
Monetary and Financial Sector						
Total Change in Monetary Base (% GDP)[d]	-0.04	-0.03	0.46	-0.13	0.98	-0.35
M2/GDP (%)[d]	19.9	20.9	21.6	24.5	26.9	26.6
Consolidated Banking Credit to the Private Sector/ Total Credit (%)[e]	79.8	83.4	84.1	82.9	83.7	82.7-97.8
Public Sector						
Public Sector Expenditures (% GDP)	28.8	32.5	30.0	28.3	30.7-25.5	22.1
Fiscal Deficit of the Central Government (% GDP)[f]	4.0	6.3	2.8	0.1	1.7- -6.2	-6.3
Foreign Sector						
Export in Constant Prices of 1986 (millions)	804,106	903,429	994,634	1,061,675	1,184,359	1,375,171
Export Growth in Constant Prices (%)	2.2	12.4	10.1	6.7	11.6	16.1
Current Account Surplus/Export (%)	-56.4	-34.9	-27.1	-15.5	-2.5	-8.7
Annual Change in External Debt (US$ millions)	1,446.0	441.0	70.0	-180.0	-1,559.0	-1,386.0
Annual Change in Foreign Reserves (US$ millions)	17.0	-99.0	-228.0	45.0	-732.0	-437.0
External Debt Service/Exports (%, medium and long term)	60.9	65.4	57.1	36.5	23.8	26.5

n.a. = not available a) December to December; b) Up to 1989, original figures from Jadresic (1989) were combined with the changes of the real wage index published by the Central Bank of Chile (1989), and, thereafter, up to 1995, various figures were obtained from *Boletines Mensuales;* c) Central Bank of Chile figures; d) 1986 pesos, December balances; e) Superintendency of Banks and Financial Institutions; f) PIMA/PUC Database.

Table 2c. Economic Indicators for Chile, 1990-1995

	1990	1991	1992	1993	1994	1995
Real Sector						
GDP (millions $ 1986)	4,437,355	4,759,419	5,284,882	5,616,414	5,855,011	6,355,325
GDP Growth Rate (%)	3.3	7.3	11.0	6.3	4.2	8.5
Gross Investment/GDP (%)	26.2	24.8	28.2	29.8	28.9	31.7
National Saving/GDP (%)	24.3	24.1	24.8	24.2	25.4	27.6
Unemployment Rate (%)	5.7	5.3	4.4	4.5	5.9	4.7
Prices						
Inflation Rate (%)[a]	27.3	18.7	12.7	12.2	8.9	8.2
Real Wages Index (1977=100)[b]	130.1	136.5	142.7	147.4	154.6	160.9
Short-term Real Interest Rate (lending rate, %)	16.4	8.0	9.8	10.5	10.5	9.2
Real Exchange Rate (1977=100)*	-	-	-	-	-	-
Real Exchange Rate (1986=100)[c]	112.7	106.4	97.8	96.9	94.2	89.1
Terms of Trade (1977=100)	93.9	94.3	94.8	88.8	98.5	109.7
Monetary and Financial Sector						
Total Change in Monetary Base (% GDP)[d]	0.01	0.38	0.55	0.15	0.58	n.a.
M2/GDP (%)[d]	25.7	29.0	30.6	31.9	33.2	n.a.
Consolidated Banking Credit to the Private Sector/ Total Credit (%)[e]	98.4	98.8	99.2	98.8	99.0	99.3
Public Sector						
Public Sector Expenditures (% GDP)	20.7	21.9	22.0	22.2	22.8	n.a.
Fiscal Deficit of the Central Government (% GDP)[f]	-3.1	-2.2	-2.6	-1.8	-1.9	n.a.
Foreign Sector						
Export in Constant Prices of 1986 (millions)	1,508,335	1,669,676	1,895,505	1,974,801	2,137,562	2,382,234
Export Growth in Constant Prices (%)	9.7	10.7	13.5	4.2	8.2	11
Current Account Surplus/Export (%)	-6.4	1.2	-7.0	-22.8	-5.5	1.0
Annual Change in External Debt (US$ millions)	1,173.0	-1,061.0	1,878.0	944.0	2,292.0	347.0
Annual Change in Foreign Reserves (US$ millions)	-2,369.0	-1,238.0	-2,499.0	-577.0	-3,194.0	-1061
External Debt Service/Exports (%, medium and long term)	24.9	24.6	22.3	25.9	20.3	25.0

SOURCES: Central Bank of Chile (1989) *Indicadores Económicos y Sociales,* 1960-1988; *Boletines Mensuales,* various years; *Memoria Anual 1994 and 1995*; PIMA/PUC Database; De la Cuadra, Sergio and Dominique Hachette (1988); Jadresic, E. (1989); Lüders, Rolf (1986); Superintendency of Banks and Financial Institutions; Ramos, Joseph (1986).

and, in 1988, for water and sewerage services. This tested the regulatory framework for the electric and telecommunications sectors prior to privatization. In addition, it was decided to unbundle these companies before privatizing them. In the case of electricity, several generating and distribution companies were spun off from the National Electric Company (Empresa Nacional de Electricidad — ENDESA), the state-owned monopoly. ENDESA retained the transmission company and most of the generating plants and, more important, practically all the water rights necessary to put into operation new hydroelectric power plants. In the case of telecommunications, long-distance (ENTEL) and local telephone (Compañía de Teléfonos de Chile — CTC) companies remained separated. Some regional telephone companies were spun off from CTC, but the latter continued to cover the central part of the country, including Santiago, by far the country's largest market. According to the regulations, there is free entry into both the electricity and the telecommunications sectors, and fierce competition has developed in the long-distance telecommunications market, but some would argue that in the remaining markets (local telephone and electricity generation), competition could be much stronger if unbundling had been carried further (Bitrán and Sáez 1994).

Once the core SOEs and the sector in which the privatized firms would operate had been "prepared" for privatization, the government applied one or more of four privatization modes:

The *popular capitalism* mode was used to privatize the large, second-tier financial institutions (Banco de Chile and Banco de Santiago) and the largest private pension fund administrators (Provida and Santa María).[21] It was also applied to the privatization of shares in a few other core SOEs, such as ENDESA, the large electricity generating firm. Under popular capitalism, the SOEs to be privatized offered new shares to the general public. CORFO, the official development bank, offered an automatic, long-term loan without interest or at very low real interest rates to individuals purchasing shares. In addition, the government granted such a generous investment tax credit that most income tax payers expected to receive the shares free, given the foreseeable dividends. The number of shares each person could buy was limited. Both the favorable investment conditions and the quotas of up to about $5,000 per person were designed to spread ownership of these shares as widely as possible.

Under *labor capitalism*, shares were sold directly to the workers of a divested enterprise or, in a few cases, notably that of ENDESA, to public servants in general. With relatively few exceptions, workers would acquire between 5 percent and 10 percent of the stock of the divested corporations. To pay for the stock, workers received an advance on their severance pay and, to make the purchase attractive, the stock was offered at a low price, with a repurchase guarantee at the time of retirement. If the value of the stock dropped below the value of the severance payment, the workers would have the right to sell their shares back to the corporation at the time of their retirement for an amount equivalent to the severance payment. That is, workers received an offer to buy shares at below market price, without having to put up any money and without risking any loss. They could, however, gain substantially if the stock turned out to be a good investment. The main purpose of this generous offer was to gain worker support for privatization, but the system also contributed to distribution of stock ownership among the general population. In some cases, workers became so enthusiastic about these investments that they went into debt in order to expand their share holdings, even to the point of becoming, as a group, the largest or one of the largest shareholders.

Institutional capitalism involved selling SOE stock to institutional investors in general and to the privately run pension funds in particular. This method was used during the last phase of the second-round privatizations to divest about 25 percent of the stock of the privatized SOEs through auctions on the Santiago Stock Exchange. However, investment in shares of privatized SOEs initially made up less than 5 percent of the total investment portfolio of the pension funds. The two structural reforms, privatization and pension reform, thus reinforced each other through this divestiture mode, having a significant positive effect on the development of the capital market (to be discussed below).

Traditional capitalism included other forms of divestiture used during the second phase of the second round of privatizations. After the divestiture modes described above had been used to sell roughly 50 percent of the stock of the core SOEs, the remainder of the SOE stock was auctioned on the stock exchange in small to medium-sized packages. Significant exceptions to this privatization pattern were the divestiture of a controlling interest in CTC, the largest local telephone company, and CAP, Chile's largest steel mill, but for both companies, the last step still involved this auctioning of shares in small packages. In the case of CTC, a 51-percent share of the company was offered through an international bidding process, with the requirement that the purchaser invest more than $200 million in telephone-line expansion. The bid was won by Bond, an Australian investor, who later sold its interest to Telefónica, the Spanish telephone company. The privatization of CAP became possible when, taking advantage of a very favorable cash position, it repurchased its own shares and, in the process, increased significantly the participation of its private shareholders.

Third Round: Privatizations During the 1990s. Table 1 clearly shows that the pace of the privatizations slowed during the 1990s. Between 1989 and 1995, only four SOEs were privatized for a total of $27.2 million. The problem was not a lack of state-owned assets to be privatized, as many believed, but the lack of political will. In 1989, the state still controlled 45 firms. CODELCO, the large copper producing company, was valued at $18 billion. Among the remaining SOEs, several had a relatively high net worth (the government sold minority shares in six of them, amounting to $542.4 million).[22] The government also announced that, in certain companies, in particular COLBUN, S.A., it would continue to divest shares while retaining a controlling interest. Since 1989, two contradictory forces within the governing coalition have shaped privatization policy. The "reformed" Socialists and some neoliberal-minded members of the Christian Democratic Party favor privatization, whereas the rest of the Christian Democrats and the traditional Socialists oppose it. Within the political opposition, which generally favors privatization, some strongly advocate for it, while the more traditional groups, especially within Renovación Nacional, are more skeptical about the process. In particular, the latter are unlikely to support legislation in Congress to privatize CODELCO. This means that unless a considerable political realignment takes place, the privatization of the remaining SOEs will continue to proceed at a slow pace, if at all.

Divestiture of Land and Water in the Agricultural Sector

The privatization of most of the land expropriated by the Agrarian Reform Corporation (Corporación de la Reforma Agraria — CORA), the institution in charge of the Chilean land reform, affected about 50 percent of the irrigated land in Chile and implied a land transfer worth about $1.631 billion.[23] Twenty-eight percent of CORA's landholdings had been expropriated illegally, and they were returned immediately to the legitimate owners. Another 52 percent were divested to 52,603 laborers, who received relatively small plots, called *parcelas CORA*, at subsidized prices and favorable payment terms. The remaining land was either sold through public auction or turned over to the National Forest Corporation (Corporación Nacional Forestal — CONAF). Over 40 percent of the owners of small plots have since sold the land, half of it to the old landlords, realizing significant capital gains in the process. Most of the new landowners were professionals, who, by way of capital improvements, marketing, and management techniques, have contributed significantly to the transformation of the country's old-fashioned agricultural practices and to increases in productivity.

The military government was particularly interested in creating a smoothly functioning agricultural land market, as part of its drive toward an efficient market economy. The definition of strong property rights at the constitutional level and regulatory measures designed to eliminate most impediments to free trade in land helped. During the 1980s, with the same objective, the government also made water-use rights for irrigation purposes, which up to then had been tied by tradition to the land, freely tradable.

Privatization in the Social Sector[24]

During the late 1970s and early 1980s, the government initiated a number of structural changes, known as "modernizations," mainly in social services. As a general rule, policy definition, financing, and operational functions — all previously carried out by one government institution for each service — were separated. This separation allowed the government to subsidize demand for these services, rather than subsidize supply as it had in the past. The process also permitted "privatization" and the introduction of competition into the provision of certain social services. This meant that the provision of public education, public health, public housing, and pensions, previously carried out by the public sector, was transferred to the private sector, while being largely financed through targeted demand subsidies paid by the government.

Pension Funds. Decree Law 3500 of 1980 revolutionized the Chilean pension system. Until then, the system was based on mandatory contributions and government-operated institutions and was of the "pay-as-you-go," defined-benefit variety still used in most countries. Benefits were indexed to the monetary-corrected salary levels of the last five active years, while social security taxes were paid during the whole active life of the employee. As a result, powerful incentives existed to underreport salaries during all but the last five years, as well as to retire as early as possible. Fraud and the mounting political pressures to increase benefits without raising contributions eventually forced the government to subsidize the system heavily. At its peak, this subsidy reached 30 percent of the system outlay. In addition, the lack of incentives for efficient administration resulted in extremely poor service at relatively high operating costs.

The new pension system is also mandatory, but it is of the funded, individual account, privately managed, and defined-contribution variety. These characteristics replace the perverse incentives of the old system. People will ask for more benefits only if they are willing to contribute more; in general, they will not try to avoid making contributions since these no longer are a "tax." Management is more efficient because it is competitive. Solidarity is guaranteed by a minimum pension to which all Chileans have a right, regardless of the payments they have made into the system. Contributions are capitalized with returns obtained from the investment of the funds and are to be paid out at retirement to the beneficiaries, who, in essence, must then use those accumulated funds to buy an annuity or similar alternative.

Pension funds are privately administered by profit-seeking fund administrators (Administradoras de Fondos de Pensiones — AFPs) that are heavily regulated and closely supervised. These companies compete for the right to manage individual funds on the basis of commissions and quality of service (rates of return, amount of paper work, speed of service, information, and so on). All employees can freely choose among these AFPs and switch from one to the other if they believe the cost is lower or the service better elsewhere. The AFPs are regulated by law and by the Superintendency of AFPs. Investments are made in domestic and foreign financial instruments, whose risk is assessed by private risk-classification companies. By regulation, the average risk level of an AFP portfolio must be relatively low. Contributors could lose if the market as a whole drops; however, they are protected by the government against fraud or bad investments made by any one AFP.

Overall, the experience with the new pension system has been very positive. It has resolved the main problems of the "pay-as-you-go" system, and AFP clients are generally satisfied with the level of services they receive. As a proportion of salary at the time of retirement, pensions are higher than before. Of course, due to Chile's favorable economic conditions, rates of return on invested funds have been very high. It remains to be seen how the labor force will react during a prolonged business downturn, when the funds might experience heavy losses. Major criticisms of the system mention its relatively high administration costs and the low degree of "solidarity" and affiliation.[25] The new pension system has played an important role in the spectacular development of the domestic capital market, as well as in the privatization process, to which it contributed as an institutional purchaser of shares of the privatized SOEs.

Health Services. Since the 1920s, social security in Chile has included a health insurance component. The system's health facilities were by far the most important in the country. Private hospitals and other health services were few and generally served the well-to-do. The official system achieved wide coverage and had a relatively good reputation for competence, but it was inefficiently managed.

Reform during the military government consisted of both 1) the decentralization of the official system, which meant, in essence, the separation of finance from the operation of health facilities, while decentralizing operations to regional levels where they are financed on the basis of fixed fees for services rendered, and 2) the introduction of choice, one form of which was the privatization of some services for the benefit of middle-income families. Workers were allowed to contribute to private, specialized health insurance companies (Instituciones de Salud Previsional — ISAPREs) instead of to the official system. ISAPREs are private, highly regulated and supervised, competitive institutions. Many own their own health facilities and have become health management organizations. Today, about one-third of the work force is, as a matter of choice, affiliated with ISAPREs. Many of these workers choose health insurance plans that require contributions exceeding the mandatory social security tax. Lower-income workers generally cannot afford to belong to an ISAPRE because the mandatory contribution, 7 percent of a worker's salary, is not enough to finance the minimum health insurance premium. The official system is able to provide adequate minimum health coverage to everybody because it receives a significant subsidy from the government.

The results of these health reforms have been positive but far from ideal. Workers are, in general, satisfied with the service provided by the ISAPREs, although no adequate solution has been found yet for older and retired workers, whose insurance premium rates are so high that some have had to switch back to the government-subsidized system.[26] The latter provides excellent coverage, and the services provided are technically competent but badly organized. Often, people have to wait in long lines for hours to see a doctor, and some must wait months for an operation. The last two administrations have significantly increased the system's subsidy, but, not surprisingly, that increase has been "captured" almost entirely by the existing staff of doctors and nurses in the form of wage increases. Service seems to have improved very little.

Housing. Some aspects of public sector housing programs were also priva-tized during the 1970s. Before the reforms took place, a considerable proportion of housing for low- and lower-middle-income families (most of the families in the country) was financed and provided (at times, even constructed) by the state. Housing turned out to be expensive, and choices of location, style, internal space distribution, and so forth were nonexistent for the heavily subsidized "buyer." Reform consisted mainly in reducing the role of government in this process by providing and managing a housing subsidy, distributed on the basis of a point system. In this way, the supply of housing for low- and lower-middle-income families has become extremely competitive, and construction has become more efficient.

Education. Until the early 1980s in Chile, a centralized national educational system provided primary and secondary education free of charge for most people. The country also had a number of private schools and a few universities, most of them belonging to the state. Educational reform has consisted of adopting a system that, in practice, follows the basic principles of the voucher system; that is, the government subsidizes demand, and educational services are provided in a competi-tive fashion. In the Chilean case, subsidized primary and secondary education are provided by municipal schools, which are the "old" national schools, whose property and management have been handed over to the municipalities, and by "privately subsidized" schools that compete with the former. Parents can send their children to either type of school, and the schools, both municipal and privately subsidized, get paid a certain amount per student-day of attendance. To help parents choose a school, yearly testing at the fourth, eighth, and twelfth grades is administered, and the results, per school, are made public. Similar principles are applied to university-level education.

The results of the education reform have been very good. The quality of public education (that is, at municipal and privately subsidized schools) has improved dramatically with respect to that of private, unsubsidized schools. Even if a difference in quality still exists in favor of the latter, it seems small in relation to the cost per student in both systems (Büchi and Sancho 1996). Similarly, competition among different universities has increased.

Overall Accomplishments

Early in 1990, when the new civilian administration took over, the military government had accomplished its objective of transferring to the private sector the property and management of all but a handful of approximately 590 enterprises that it had controlled in late 1973. The government, it could be argued, had accomplished significantly more than initially intended, since no privatization of "traditional" public service or infrastructure SOEs had been planned. When these were divested during the last round of the privatization process, their equity exceeded that of all other privatized SOEs.

Perhaps even more important, the privatization process, including that of the traditional SOEs created by law, came to be generally accepted.[27] This acceptance can be attributed, in large part, to the competitiveness of the environment or the types of regulation that monitored the privatized enterprises and made them socially efficient and to the privatization modes utilized to spread stock ownership.

In regard to the latter, at the end of December 1988, workers directly controlled over 50 percent of the members of the board of directors in IANSA (the large sugar beet company) and over 40 percent in CAP (the steel mill), SOQUIMICH (the Chilean nitrate monopoly), and Laboratorio Chile (a pharmaceutical company). If directors appointed by the pension fund administration firms are included, all these enterprises are now controlled by workers and their representatives. Today, ENDESA (the electricity generating company) can also be included in the list and, in most remaining large ex-SOEs, worker-appointed directors make up significant proportions of the companies' boards.

In terms of the evolution of the number of enterprises under public sector control and the increase in value added by them, changes in the SOE sector during the military government were impressive. Although today the government owns and runs fewer companies than in 1970, the value added by existing SOEs is similar to that of the late 1960s, a period in which, for many citizens, the entrepreneurial activity of the state was already too great. However, this should not lead to a misinterpretation. CODELCO, a company the military regime never sought to privatize, for "strategic" reasons,[28] and whose large copper mines were foreign owned up to the late 1960s, makes a significant difference in this measurement. Without CODELCO, SOEs as of 1994 accounted for only about 5 percent of GDP (versus about 16 percent during the 1960s), a level well below that of most nations in the Western Hemisphere. That is, leaving aside "big copper," which during the 1960s was in many respects a foreign enclave and today remains as such under state ownership, privatization and deregulation have contributed significantly to the transformation of the Chilean economy.

Moreover, largely due to the "Chileanization" and subsequent nationalization of the large copper mines during the late 1960s and early 1970s, the first round of privatizations, which did not affect the traditional SOEs created or nationalized as a result of specific laws, still left the state's entrepreneurial activities generating almost one-quarter of GDP, a very high percentage for a market economy. In that sense, the last round of privatization was important for the achievement of the government's overall political objectives. During that stage, the entrepreneurial role of the state was drastically reduced, while individual freedom to choose increased, certainly in economic matters and perhaps also in political terms.

In terms of revenue, it is estimated that the public sector received over $2.5 billion up to the end of 1989 (see Table 2). On a yearly basis, revenues varied between 0.1 percent and 3.3 percent of GDP and 0.3 percent and 10.6 percent of fiscal revenues. Relative to GDP, these revenues were more significant than privatization revenues in Great Britain during the late 1970s and the 1980s. Given the fiscal discipline of the government, privatization permitted implementation of important expenditure projects that would have been avoided otherwise. As a result, during the first round, privatization expanded the level of social expenditures, while during the second round, it increased investment and reduced indebtedness (see Hachette and Lüders 1993, Chapter 5).

Another way to put these revenues in perspective is to compare them with the net worth of the remaining SOEs. CODELCO, whose net worth is by far the largest of any of the current SOEs, has an estimated market value of about $4 billion. That is, through the divestiture of about 550 enterprises, some of which were relatively large public service and infrastructure companies, the state divested at most about 40 percent of the net worth of the enterprises it controlled in 1973.

Again, this should not lead to misinterpretations. Privatization led the public sector to eliminate, for all practical purposes, its participation in all economic sectors except mining (copper and petroleum — the value added of the latter sector is rapidly shrinking because of the exhaustion of the natural resource), making ample room for the private sector to become the "engine of economic growth." Privatization is perhaps the clearest expression of the revolutionary change in economic policy that took place during the military regime, which set the country on a new course that has been reconfirmed by the current democratic government.

THE GAINS IN EFFICIENCY AND OTHER IMPACTS

E conomic theory suggests that private firms operating in a competitive environment will be more efficient than SOEs, especially state-run companies that are legal monopolies. The same theory also suggests that allocation of resources and overall economic efficiency will improve if SOEs are privatized while legal monopolies are abolished (see Vickers and Yarrow 1988). International experience seems to confirm this hypothesis.[29] However, what has been the Chilean experience?

The first Chilean massive privatizations took place over 20 years ago, enough time to allow measurement of some of the process's effects. Dominique Hachette and Rolf Lüders (1993), among others, have studied privatization's fiscal, employment, capital market, and investment effects. The next paragraphs contain a summary of the main conclusions of these studies, supported by data about the effects of the privatizations on the quality and diversity of products and services produced by the privatized SOEs.

Before examining these studies, however, it should be emphasized that the privatization process in Chile had two major effects, one on the economic system as a whole and another on expectations. Expectations probably cannot be measured or, at least, they have not as yet been measured.

First, in economies that privatize only a few SOEs, the contribution of privatization to overall growth can be measured by its contribution to raising efficiency. In Chile, however, the significance of the SOE sector made implementation of a market economy inconceivable without privatization. Given the success of the system in raising Chile's living standards, privatization should receive its due share of the credit.

Second, privatization, perhaps more than any other policy, acts as a powerful signal to investors that a country is following a market approach to economic development (see World Bank 1988). In Chile, the massive privatizations of the 1970s conveyed a clear signal to all investors, domestic and foreign, that the government really meant to implement a market economy. This signal must have positively influenced the investments in the country. The message was sent again, after the recession of 1982-1983, when a significant number of firms again fell into the government's fold, and a vigorous privatization program was announced and implemented. The success of this privatization probably was one reason why Chile was able to recover from the recession more quickly than other countries in the region.

The Fiscal Impact of Privatization

It can be proved that if the following conditions are in place, privatizations of commercial ventures *in and of themselves* will not have fiscal or private wealth effects:

1. A country has a relatively efficient capital market,

2. The private and public sectors use the same discount rate,

3. The efficiency of a given firm does not change with privatization, and

4. The privatization process is effective and transparent.

The final outcome, however, will be a function of the use made by the government of the privatization revenues. If they are consumed, fiscal wealth will diminish,[30] whereas if the government invests them (in foreign assets, for example), fiscal wealth will not change. However, if they are "invested," for example, in human capital (that is, education, health, or even public housing), fiscal wealth will still diminish, and private wealth will increase correspondingly. In all cases, privatization does change the fiscal cash flow, because the government receives a cash flow that without privatization would not have materialized.

Thus, it is also clear that if a privatized firm is expected to be more efficiently managed in the private sector than in the public sector and if all the conditions mentioned above remain the same, a privatization *in itself* will increase fiscal wealth and leave private wealth practically unchanged. This outcome is the result of competitive bidding of private investors for a firm that can generate a potentially higher rate of return. The final wealth effect will, of course, depend on the use made by the government of the privatization revenues.

What happened in Chile? The economic policy of the country since 1974 has been oriented toward improving the workings of the capital market and toward establishing competitive conditions all around. In the early 1980s, relatively sophisticated mechanisms were developed to regulate natural monopolies, including those in the hands of the state, with the objective of inducing the monopolies to behave as if they were operating in competitive markets. Early on during its administration, the military regime decided to treat SOEs as if they were private enterprises, requiring from them profit maximization but granting them management autonomy. As a result, Chilean SOEs improved their efficiency to the point that, during the 1980s, statistically, their behavior could not be distinguished from those in the private sector, although average rates of return were still slightly higher in the private sector (Hachette and Lüders 1993).

Therefore, in order to estimate the fiscal wealth effect of privatization in Chile, Hachette and Lüders (1993) assumed that cash flows would not change if an SOE were privatized. Then, they calculated what price should have been paid for the shares of a sample of 10 large SOEs, the "perfect-market price," and compared it to the price actually received by the government. To estimate the perfect-market price, a number of assumptions had to be made, and these were all intentionally overestimations.

Hachette and Lüders (1993) concluded that the last round of privatizations, those of the large traditional SOEs, generated only a small fiscal wealth loss, if any at all. These results are consistent with those of a study of a smaller sample by Ahmed Galal and Mary Shirley (1993).[31] In their study, Hachette and Lüders estimated that the price differential between the perfect-market price of shares and the actual revenues per share received by the government from the privatizations in the sample of firms amounted to 15.4 percent. However, that percentage includes 1) the effect of subsidies the government granted to "popular" and "labor" capitalists, 2) the effect of the bias introduced on purpose into the estimates, and 3) a likely underestimation of the discount rate for privatizations in 1986. Arguably, if corrected for these effects, any remaining difference must be very small and probably statistically insignificant.

Hachette and Lüders (1993) also present evidence that suggests that the first-round, second-phase privatizations generated an initial *perceived* fiscal wealth gain. As explained above, judged ex-post facto, divestiture share prices turned out to be "high" as a result of the credit-led divestitures. As a consequence of moral hazard, during the crisis of the early 1980s, many privatized firms failed, and management of them was returned to the government. Moreover, the government decided, as the best alternative, to cover most of the unpaid loans of these same firms to avoid the bankruptcy of commercial banks. That is, the government believed it was gaining fiscal wealth as a result of the privatizations of the 1970s, and it spent accordingly. Once it became evident that such a gain did not exist, the government, to minimize the social cost of the crisis, was forced to repay at least those loans and the accumulated interest that the purchasers of SOEs had obtained to pay for part of the privatization installments.

What did the government do with the privatization revenues? Hachette and Lüders (1993) concluded that during the 1970s, privatization revenues allowed the government to spend more on higher social (human capital) expenditures, while during the 1980s, these revenues permitted increased infrastructure investments, especially in telecommunications and public works. Total privatization revenue amounted to 13.1 percent of GDP, about 60 percent of it generated during the second round of privatizations — until 1991 the highest percentage of any country in the world (see Hachette and Lüders 1993; Kikeri, Nellis, and Shirley 1992).

The Employment Effects of Privatization

Labor always fears the employment effects of privatization. The Chilean case actually proves that privatization, as distinguished from measures in general to increase "X" efficiency, probably has a positive employment effect. Because Chile implemented a set of policies to introduce competition and regulation to induce natural monopolies to operate as if they were in a competitive market, while simultaneously treating all SOEs as if they were private, excess labor tended to be eliminated even before privatization.[32]

The implication is that lean SOEs, once privatized and freed of the usual public sector investment restrictions, should expand employment more or less in line with output.[33] Sample evidence indicates that between 1976 and 1979, when business was expanding, privatized firms increased employment by 21.2 percent, faster than in the rest of the private sector, whose rate was only 1.5 percent. This "catching-up" process was to be expected since public sector investment restrictions previously existed. Something similar but less dramatic happened during the second-round, last-phase privatizations. Larroulet (1994) reports that, if one compares employment levels of a sample of 10 core SOEs two years before and two years after privatization, employment increased in *all* of them by an average of 10 percent.

Thus, negative employment will always accompany a drive to induce firms with a higher than optimum labor-capital ratio to become more efficient, which is a necessary condition for achieving high economic growth rates. In Chile, however, excess employment was reduced significantly before privatization, a consequence of measures to increase competition and to treat SOEs as if they were private enterprises. Thus, privatization was not accompanied by the anticipated employment reductions, proving that privatization per se does not have negative employment effects. This implies that the opposition of labor to privatization is, in the last analysis, an opposition to any measure to increase SOE efficiency.

The Impact of Privatization on Capital Markets

Privatization had a profound impact on the development of the Chilean financial and capital markets. The first- and second-round privatizations influenced this development in different ways.

The first-round privatizations, the return of the expropriated firms to their legitimate owners, and the debt-led divestiture of controlling shares of the non-core SOEs nationalized by the Allende regime recreated the capital market structure of the 1960s. At that time, commercial banks, operating basically in the short end of the market, dominated finance in the country. Almost all Chilean firms, including those whose shares were traded on the stock exchanges, were in essence "closed"; that is, they were controlled by a few shareholders. Share turnover in the stock exchanges was very low by international standards and did not differ much from that of the 1960s. Of course, freely operating interest rates, significantly lower reserve requirements, the opening of the local market to international capital flows, and the absence of qualitative and quantitative credit controls made a big difference in the operations of the capital markets. In particular, these policy changes allowed commercial banks to grow rapidly and induced them to operate increasingly in the medium and long terms. The failure of most commercial banks, which induced the government to intervene and to gain control of many industrial, commercial, and mining firms indirectly, ended this phase of the privatization process and created conditions favorable to more dynamic and dispersed financial and capital markets.

The second-round privatization of the core SOEs, as well as the pension system reform of the early 1980s, generated a new and different capital market structure, while the whole market continued to grow very rapidly. Total financial liabilities, which had reached 54.4 percent of GDP in 1981, doubled to 108 percent in 1989.[34] During that period, liabilities of financial institutions increased by about 70 percent in absolute real terms, but the net worth of corporations increased by 127 percent. This reduced the share of the liabilities of the financial institutions in 1989 to 48 percent of total private sector liabilities, down from 56 percent in 1981, while the share of corporate net worth increased to 48 percent from 41 percent in 1981. Other liabilities made up the difference in both years (Hachette and Lüders 1993). The growth of both the financial and capital markets, as well as increased diversification, gave domestic entrepreneurs better access to financing.

The privatization methods used during the 1980s largely explain the capital market's relatively faster development compared to the financial market at that time. Both labor and popular capitalism rapidly increased the total number of shareholders in the economy. By 1989, privatization had generated 200,000 shareholders, about 32 percent of all shareholders in the country.[35] Moreover, the demand for shares made by institutional investors, especially those of the privately managed pension funds, increased elevenfold between 1985 and 1989 (Larroulet 1994). Although the pension funds were created only in the early 1980s, by 1989, they already held shares worth about five times those held by the insurance companies and more than 80 percent of the value of those held by all institutional investors (Larroulet 1994).

The spreading of shared ownership among workers and popular capitalists, the latter essentially income tax payers, and the increasing and significant participation of institutional investors in the capital market reduced the degree of ownership concentration of financial institutions and corporations in general and also activated the capital market. According to Cristián Larroulet (1994), the 10 largest shareholders of the two largest private commercial banks owned 66.2 percent of the shares of those banks before the state took them over during the 1982-1983 crisis; after privatization, they controlled only 5.5 percent of the net worth of the same banks. In the case of the remaining SOEs privatized by CORFO, the percentages of shares were 95.4 percent before and 62.8 percent after privatization. All along, private corporations whose shares are traded on the Chilean stock exchanges experienced during the same period no significant change in the degree of shared ownership, slightly over 73 percent.

Total trading of shares of capital stock increased rapidly at the Santiago Stock Exchange during the 1980s, heavily influenced by privatization. In 1984, when the country was recovering from the recent economic and financial crisis, capital stock shares of corporations divested during the first round of privatizations made up slightly over 6 percent of the total stock traded, about the same percentage as during the latter part of the 1970s. In 1989, after the second round of privatizations was practically complete and total stock trade had increased about 22 times, the share of the privatized stock had increased to almost 66 percent.

The Impact of Privatization on Investment

Privatization's impact on investment has several dimensions: Privatization during the 1970s induced the government to increase its investment in "human capital," especially education and health, and it allowed the government to increase infrastructure expenditures during the 1980s. Privatization also generated new investment opportunities in the private sector, especially in the privatized SOEs. Comparing the three years before and after privatization, the Chilean Telephone Company (CTC) invested enough to increase the number of telephones by 174 percent; ENERSIS, the Santiago electricity distribution holding, increased investment by 254 percent; CAP, the steel mill, by 564 percent; and SOQUIMICH, the Chilean nitrate producer, by 196 percent (Larroulet 1994). Compared with the cases of Argentina and Peru, for example, purchases of stock in the privatized Chilean SOEs by foreigners were moderate, and almost all of them took place during the second round. Most foreign investment took the form of debt-for-equity swaps, totaling about $500 million, half of it in second-tier privatizations.

However, Chilean privatization's main impact on savings and investment may have been indirect, as a signal that the government was serious about the implementation of a market economy. Especially during the 1980s, privatization was accompanied by a rapid increase in private sector savings and investment rates (Hachette and Lüders 1993). Foreign investment, both direct as well as swaps, followed the same trend (Larroulet 1994).

The increase in savings and capital inflows and the accompanying changes in the capital-movement legislation generated some of the necessary incentives for Chilean firms to invest abroad. The experience gained in Chile during the liberalization phase also helped, since neighboring countries began implementing similar policies only 15 or more years later. The privatized core SOEs, especially those in the electric utilities sector, given their size and advanced technology, became the leading Chilean firms investing abroad, especially in the Southern Cone countries. These investments, supported by all governments since the late 1980s, are generating a very different business sector structure[36] and a rapidly increasing integration between Chile and the rest of the world, especially its neighboring countries. Without privatization, this would scarcely have been possible, because the Chilean private sector was too small.

The Impact of Privatization on the Quality and Variety of Products and Services

On the basis of the information provided by some of the privatized core SOEs, it is possible to infer that privatization increased the variety of products offered. The effect on quality has not been measured, since companies that replied to Hachette and Lüders'(1993) questionnaire had not carried out surveys on the subject prior to their privatization. As of 1994, former SOEs were gathering information about the quality of their products and services, data which is meaningful in itself. Moreover, some of them have become significant exporters since privatizing, which suggests that their products are now of international quality. The following are summaries of the case studies made on the subject:

ENTEL Chile. The state monopoly in charge of international long-distance telecommunications, ENTEL Chile, was also one of the two national long-distance carriers. The company was privatized starting in 1986 and maintained its international long-distance monopoly position until 1994, when the multi-carrier system was introduced in Chile and eight competitors appeared. Since privatizing, ENTEL has created subsidiaries to offer long-distance service in other countries, including the United States and many Latin American nations, and to offer data transmission, mobile telephony, and, recently, local telephony.[37] Today, since it has to compete, ENTEL gathers information about completed calls, causes of failures to complete calls, complaints received, time taken by its employees to respond to those complaints, and other service issues.

ENTEL's international traffic increased from 33.6 million minutes in 1985 to 137 million minutes in 1993; the number of its employees increased by about 200 between 1985 and 1991, reaching almost 1,600; its profits increased by 257 percent between 1985 and 1983, and then fell drastically with the introduction of the multi-carrier system; the rate of return on assets, which had been below the 12.6 percent reached in 1985 while the firm was state owned, ranged between 20 percent and 34.9 percent between 1986 and 1993, falling to 8.8 percent during 1994[38]; the rate of return on monetary corrected net worth, in the 11.2 percent to 20 percent range before privatization, ranged between 31.8 percent and 45.6 percent between 1986 and1993; and new investment increased rapidly after privatization, averaging, until 1992, about five times pre-privatization levels, and, thereafter, increasing to over eight times pre-privatization levels.

Celulosa Arauco and Constitución, S.A. These SOEs were privatized during the 1970s and were merged into one firm, which was indirectly expropriated by the government in 1983 and later reprivatized as a second-tier firm. Although basically no new products were introduced, as the firms had always produced cellulose, paper, and wood, the privatization carried along with it major investments to "modernize" existing operations ($120 million); to build a new cellulose production plant ($600 million); and to remodel another plant ($426 million). In the wood-processing sector, production capacity increased from 120,000 to 600,000 cubic meters and cellulose production from 280,000 to 400,000 tons. Before privatization, exports went to 30 countries, with 80 percent going to Latin America. As of 1994, exports reached almost 100 countries, with only 20 percent destined for Latin America.

Laboratorio Chile, S.A. This pharmaceutical firm was created to allow the government to regulate the pharmaceutical market. Following privatization in 1986, its production facilities changed little,[39] but 1) the number of new products introduced each year increased significantly; 2) exports increased rapidly, which suggests improvements in the quality of the products; and 3) the firm invested in facilities in Argentina and Peru. After the price and trade liberalization of the 1970s, the pharmaceutical business became very competitive. Since SOEs were treated as if they were private enterprises and faced tight budget constraints, Laboratorio Chile had to adjust to the new conditions. It did so with success, by increasing its number of products and its scope of marketing. While the firm had introduced about 20 new products per year during the early 1980s, that figure increased to more than 40 after privatization. Exports, which reached a peak of only $0.2 million in 1985, increased rapidly after privatization, reaching $6.5 million in 1994. New investments, almost nonexistent during the early 1980s, increased rapidly after privatization to 7.5 percent of sales and 43 percent of profits between 1992 and 1994. Profits also increased after privatization, rising from less than 10 percent to more than 15 percent of sales.

IANSA, S.A. This firm was created during the 1950s by the government to develop Chile's sugar beet industry. After privatization, its holding company was the first large corporation to go bankrupt during the crisis of the early 1980s. It was reprivatized between 1988 and 1991, and, in 1992, after a long period of conflict among its main shareholders, one of the new Chilean conglomerates, Pathfinder, achieved definitive control of it. Before privatization, IANSA was in the business of selling sugar and some of its derivatives, including alcohol, and also agricultural inputs. After privatization, it expanded to include alfalfa, dog food, fish food, fruit concentrates, tomatoes marketed in different forms, and new high-quality sugars. To produce and market these products, it created two new subsidiaries: IANSAFRUT and BIOMASTER. In 1994, IANSA was in the process of investing over $290 million in 1) a new sugar refinery in Peru, with a production capacity of one-hundred thousand tons per year; 2) a tomato processing plant in Peru; 3) marketing facilities for agricultural inputs in Peru; 4) production facilities for corn syrup; and 5) retail marketing facilities in Chile for agricultural inputs through "Farmcenter" outlets of IANSAGRO, another subsidiary of IANSA.

IANSA was not particularly concerned about satisfying consumers while it monopolized the sugar beet industry in Chile. During the 1970s, before its privatization, IANSA still received privileged treatment, one of the few exceptions among the SOEs. After the reprivatization, it had to compete with imported sugar, alcohol, and most agricultural inputs and with other local producers of fruits and vegetables. Now, IANSA is constantly making market surveys to adapt its product characteristics and packaging to local demand.

IANSA's sugar sales in metric tons have increased by more than 50 percent since privatization, as has employment, and profits have multiplied tenfold in U.S. dollar terms. Investments have averaged almost $10 million per year since 1986, reaching $20 million in 1995, and they will average in excess of $40 million per year through 1999.

In summary, the limited information available suggests that privatization in Chile has been accompanied by an awakening about consumer satisfaction and, therefore, about product quality and diversity. This concern is closely related to all Chilean firms' strong competition and powerful incentives to increase exports, requiring products of international quality tailored to the needs of targeted markets. Companies' concern for consumer satisfaction has required considerable new investments. As a result, the privatized SOEs have been able to expand output at rates exceeding Chile's national GDP growth rate, and they have become more profitable to the Chilean economy. The firms that were studied also expanded employment, although at rates below those of output growth, and increased productivity as a result of privatization.

Notes

1. See Vittorio Corbo (1992) and Cecilia Montero (1996) for accounts of the economic policies followed between 1940 and 1970, as well as the rationale behind them.

2. Both traditionally and currently, Chilean presidential terms last six years.

3. According to the election law of that time, members of Congress had to vote for one of the two highest polling candidates. Traditionally, however, Congress always voted for the candidate with the biggest majority, and the Christian Democrats followed that practice, in spite of the stakes involved, but only after negotiating a set of "guarantees" with Salvador Allende. Today the law stipulates a second-round, direct popular runoff election between the two highest polling candidates.

4. It was argued that past profit repatriations were already high enough to compensate for the investment and a "fair" rate of return.

5. This occurred only after the government had reduced the value of the shares significantly by imposing low prices and high wages.

6. In most cases, these conflicts were illegal and had been organized to produce the government takeovers.

7. The government was in the process of acquiring a very large number of firms and, therefore, control over their hiring power.

8. For income distributions in different countries, see the World Bank (1994, 220-21). Although this data is recent, income distributions tend to change only over very long periods of time.

9. There are solid theoretical reasons, based on principal-agent theory, to expect private enterprises in a competitive environment to outperform SOEs (Vickers and Yarrow 1988).

10. Hachette and Lüders (1993, 46-51) describe in depth the phenomenon of moral hazard generated by the debt-led privatization.

11. This coalition is known as the Alliance for Democracy (Concertación por la Democracia — CODE) and is dominated by the Christian Democrats and two factions of the ex-Socialist parties.

12. Among these smaller SOEs, a commercial bank, Banco del Estado de Chile, is still in state hands. Toward the end of its regime, the military government attempted to privatize the bank, but labor opposition aborted the attempt. There is today no discussion about privatizing it, although there seems to be no reason from the standpoint of efficiency to have a state-owned commercial bank within the framework of Chile's developed and competitive financial system.

13. The value-added tax, a neutral tax from an allocative point of view, raised total tax revenue by 49.21 percent in 1994.

14. After December 1980, legislation was required for the implementation of any new price controls.

15. The National Statistical Institute has begun to produce new labor statistics suggesting that unemployment may be as great as two percentage points above the official rate.

16. Amounts obtained from Hachette and Lüders (1993) and readjusted.

17. Amounts obtained from Hachette and Lüders (1993) and readjusted.

18. Larroulet (1994) estimated that the "second-tier" firms generated 8.6 percent of GDP, about half of the total of the SOEs at the time of the recession. The enterprises belonging to this sector were of a very high caliber and included Banco de Chile; Banco Santiago and Banco Concepción (commercial banking); AFP Provida and AFP Santa María (pension fund administrators); COPEC; Forestal Arauco and INFORSA (forestry); Textil Viña (textiles); Industria de Radio y Televisión (electronics); CCU (soft drinks and beer); INDUS (cooking oil); Compañía Minera Pudahuel (mining); Chilean Airlines (Línea Aérea del Cobre — LADECO); CTI (white-line goods); and a part of Compañía Sudamericana de Vapores (shipping).

19. Amounts obtained from Francisco Javier Labbé and M. Yévenes (1988), readjusted by the increase in the U.S. Wholesale Price Index (WPI) between 1985 and 1995.

20. Amounts obtained from Hachette and Lüders (1993), readjusted by the increase in the U.S. Wholesale Price Index (WPI) between 1987 and 1995.

21. Some other second-tier banks were sold directly to "interest groups": one to a medium-sized group of miners, another to a group of businessmen from northern Chile, a third to citizens from the Israeli community, and so forth. In all cases, care was taken to ensure that, initially at least, control was directly or indirectly distributed among a relatively large number of people.

22. Zofri, S.A. (a free port, 48 percent divested for $23.9 million); Colbún (an electricity generating firm, 7.6 percent divested for $65 million); EDELNOR, S.A. (an electricity generation and distribution firm, 30 percent divested for $86.4 million); MINSAL, S.A. (minerals, 18 percent divested for $7.1 million); El Abra (a new joint venture of CODELCO, in which CODELCO supplied the mineral rights in return for $330 million and 49 percent of profits); and FEPASA, S.A. (a new joint venture of the Chilean Railroad Co., EFE, to transport cargo, whereby EFE sold the use of the railway rights for $30 million plus 49 percent of the profits).

23. US$800 million, amount readjusted.

24. This section is based on Tarsicio Castañeda (1992) and Larroulet (1991).

25. The administrative costs are high in comparison to a "pay-as-you-go" system but low in comparison to private pension funds elsewhere. The competitive nature of the Chilean system induces AFPs to expend large amounts on marketing, but measures have been implemented to allow for a reduction in those costs. The issue of solidarity is largely ideological in nature. Some argue that the minimum pension should not be financed by the government but by the high-income, more privileged contributors, who would thus express their solidarity with poorer workers. From a technical perspective, however, this would introduce a "tax" element into the system, and with it, an incentive to contribute less. The self-employed are not forced to contribute to the system and although they can do it on a voluntary basis, few have affiliated.

26. This, it is argued, reduces "solidarity." Highly paid workers, whose contributions to the official system are likely to be below costs while they are relatively young, switch to

the ISAPREs, where they can get high-quality service for their 7 percent. When they get older, and the 7 percent does not allow them to pay the minimum insurance premium of the private system, they switch back to the official system, which then will subsidize them. The only way to get the incentives right may be for the government to subsidize demand for health services in a targeted fashion and privatize the supply of these services completely, introducing as much competition as possible.

27. Privatization became so accepted that Carlos Ominami, Minister of Economics in the Aylwin administration, in a report to Congress denouncing the capital loss of CORFO as a result of privatizations and CORFO credit operations during the military government, emphasized that the government in no way intended to reverse the privatizations.

28. Similarly, a percentage of overseas copper sales traditionally have been transferred directly to the Armed Forces to finance arms purchases. Although the fraction of the sales transferred is established by law, neither this income nor the purchases financed with those resources are reflected in Chile's trade balance.

29. Rölf J. Lüders (1996) presents a brief review of recent surveys on this topic.

30. What happens in this case with private wealth is a matter of speculation. At one extreme, under the hypothesis of rational expectations, private wealth would increase, and consumption would fall, to offset the expected increase in taxation brought about by the loss of government revenue from the privatized assets. At the other extreme, economists assume that economic agents do not alter their consumption pattern as a consequence of government behavior. Most empirical studies have, up to now, rejected both hypotheses.

31. Mario Marcel (1989), using a methodology similar to that of Hachette and Lüders (1993), has concluded that fiscal wealth loss from privatizations was very high. As Hachette and Lüders explain at length, among other differences, Marcel used an arbitrary 10 percent rate of discount, which is much lower than the rate estimated on the basis of the Capital Asset Pricing Model.

32. Between 1974 and 1976, SOEs reduced employment by 9.7 percent; private firms, by 8.7 percent; and privatized firms, by only 4 percent (Hachette and Lüders 1993).

33. Corrected for normal productivity increases.

34. In 1961 and 1973, financial liabilities amounted to less than 6 percent of GDP (Hachette and Lüders 1993).

35. See Larroulet (1994), on the basis of data gathered by Cecilia Cifuentes. At the end of 1989, the country had 629,300 shareholders, a high number if one considers that Chile has fewer than six million families.

36. In the past, limited by the size of the country, business expansion had to take place by diversifying investment into different sectors of the economy. Today most of the large conglomerates are not very diversified sectorally, but they are internationally. Also, foreigners invest significant amounts in Chile, but Chilean firms also invest significant amounts abroad, although in countries different from those attracting foreign investors into Chile.

37. In Chile, free entry into the local telephone business exists. Three carriers offer services in some parts of Santiago, and ENTEL will be the fourth competitor in that market. Competition is made possible because the interconnection of different networks is regulated, as are the tariffs for such interconnections.

38. In Chile, the balance sheet information is monetary corrected.

39. Ten years after its privatization, Laboratorio Chile inaugurated its first new production plant.

References

Akin, K., and Pablo T. Spiller. 1994. "Consideraciones sobre aspectos regulatorios en la privatización." In *Economía política de las reformas estructurales*, eds. J. De Brun and Rolf Lüders. San Francisco and Santiago: International Center for Economic Growth (ICEG) and CERES.

Bitrán, E., and Raúl E. Sáez. 1994. "Privatization and Regulation in Chile." In *The Chilean Economy: Policy Lessons and Challenges*, eds. Barry P. Bosworth, Rudiger Dornbusch, and Raúl Laban. Washington, D.C.: The Brookings Institution.

Büchi, H., and A. Sancho. 1996. "Social Expenditures." Paper presented to the Tinker Forum on the Role of the State in Latin America, Cancún, Mexico, October.

Castañeda, Tarsicio. 1992. *Combating Poverty*. San Francisco: International Center for Economic Growth.

Central Bank of Chile. 1989. *Indicadores Económicos y Sociales, 1960-1988*. Santiago: Central Bank of Chile.

Central Bank of Chile. 1989. *Boletines Mensuales*. Various years. Santiago: Central Bank of Chile.

Central Bank of Chile. 1989. *Memoria Annual, 1994-1995*. Santiago: Central Bank of Chile.

Centro de Estudios Públicos (CEP). 1994. *El ladrillo. Bases de la política económica del gobierno militar chileno*. Santiago: CEP.

Corbo, Vittorio. 1992. *Development Strategies and Policies in Latin America: A Historical Perspective*. Occasional Paper Series (March). San Francisco: International Center for Economic Growth (ICEG).

Corbo, Vittorio, Rolf Lüders, and Pablo T. Spiller. 1996. "The Foundations of Successful Economic Reforms: The Case of Chile." Unpublished study. Santiago and Berkeley, Calif.: Pontifical Catholic University of Chile (PUC) and the University of California.

Cortés, Hernán, and Gert Wagner. 1980. "Un enfoque económico de la acción del Estado. Evidencia empírica chilena e internacional." Research Paper. Department of Economics, Pontifical Catholic University of Chile (PUC).

De la Cuadra, Sergio and Dominique Hachette. 1988. *The Timing and Sequencing of a Trade Liberalization Policy: The Case of Chile*. Santiago: Pontificia Universidad Católica de Chile (PUC), Instituto de Economía, Oficina de Publicaciones.

Galal, Ahmed, and Mary Shirley. 1993. *Does Privatization Deliver?: Highlights from a World Bank Conference,* eds. Ahmed Galal and Mary Shirley. Washington, D.C.: World Bank.

Hachette, Dominique and Rolf Lüders. 1993. *Privatization in Chile: An Economic Appraisal*. San Francisco: International Center for Economic Growth (ICEG).

Hachette, Dominique, J. Kaufmann, and Rolf Lüders. 1989. "Estimación del patrimonio y del flujo de caja de cuatro empresas públicas chilenas: Banco del Estado, CODELCO, CORFO y ENAP." Washington, D.C.: The World Bank. Mimeo.

Jadresic, Esteban. 1989. *Salarios Reales en Chile: 1960-1988*. Nota Técnica No. 134. Santiago: Corporación de Investigaciones Económicas para Latinoamérica (CIEPLAN).

Kikeri, Sunita, John Nellis, and Mary Shirley. 1992. *Privatization: The Lessons of Experience*. Washington, D.C.: The World Bank.

Labbé, Francisco Javier, and M. Yévenes. 1988. "Evolución del proceso de privatización chileno." *Punto de Referencia* (Santiago: Centro de Estudios Públicos) 33.

Larroulet, Cristián, ed. 1991. *Soluciones privadas a problemas públicos*. Santiago: Instituto Libertad y Desarrollo (ILD).

Larroulet, Cristián. 1994. "Efectos de un programa de privatizaciones: El caso de Chile (1985-1989)." *Estudios Públicos* (Santiago) 54 (Autumn).

Lüders, Rolf J. 1986. *Lessons from the Financial Liberalization of Chile: 1974-1982*. Santiago: Pontifical Catholic University of Chile (PUC).

Lüders, Rolf J. 1988. "Veinticinco años de ingeniería social: un breve ensayo sobre la historia económica del período 1960-1988." *Cuadernos de Economía* (Pontifical Catholic University of Chile) 25 (76, December): 331-380.

Lüders, Rolf J. 1992. "La imprescindible modernización de CODELCO: Un enfoque económico." Santiago:Pontifical Catholic University of Chile, November. Mimeo.

Lüders, Rolf J. 1996. "Enterprise Reform, Privatization, and Public Sector Reform." Paper presented to the Organisation of Economic Cooperation and Development, the Korean Development Institute, and the International Center for Economic Growth. Conference on Growth and Competition in the New Global Economy, Seoul, Korea. June 27-28.

Marcel, Mario. 1989. "Privatización y finanzas públicas: El caso de Chile 1985-1988." *Colección Estudios* Corporación de Investigaciones Económicas para Latinoamérica (CIEPLAN) 26 (June).

Montero, Cecilia. 1996. *El modelo empresarial chileno*. Santiago: CIEPLAN.

PIMA/PUC Database. Pontificia Universidad Católica de Chile (PUC): Programa Interamericano de Macroeconomía Aplicada (PIMA). http://www.sol.facea.puc.cl/pima.htm#atras

Ramos, Joseph R. 1986. *Neoconservative Economics in the Southern Cone of Latin America, 1973-1983*. Baltimore: The Johns Hopkins University Press.

Superintendency of Banks and Financial Institutions. *Información Financiera*. Various Years. Santiago.

Valdés, Juan Gabriel. 1995. *Pinochet's Economics: The Chicago School in Chile*. Cambridge, England, and New York: Cambridge University Press.

Valdés, Salvador. 1994. *Administrative Charges in Pensions in Chile, Malaysia, Zambia, and the United States*. Policy Research Working Paper (The World Bank) No. 1372 (October).

Vickers, John, and George Yarrow. 1988. *Privatization: An Economic Analysis*. Cambridge, Mass.: The MIT Press.

Wisecarver, Daniel L., ed. 1992. *El modelo económico chileno*. San Francisco: International Center for Economic Growth.

World Bank. 1988. *Techniques of Privatization of State-Owned Enterprises*. World Bank Technical Paper No. 88-90. Washington, D.C.: World Bank.

World Bank. 1994. *World Development Report: Infrastructure for Development*. New York: Oxford University Press.

World Bank. 1995. *Bureaucrats in Business: The Economics and Politics of Government Ownership*. New York: Oxford University Press.

CHAPTER THREE

The Evolution, Rationale, and Impact of Mexico's Privatization Program: A Critical Assessment

MIGUEL D. RAMÍREZ

The wholesale dismantling of Mexico's massive parastatal sector since the mid-1980s represents a complete reversal of the public sector's long-standing interventionist role in economic affairs. The reversal has been part of the Mexican state's implementation of sweeping neoliberal reforms, which have included liberalization of the export-import sector; deregulation of markets for goods, factors, and financial assets; and the opening of the economy to international trade and investment under the auspices of the General Agreement on Tariffs and Trade (GATT) and the North American Free Trade Agreement (NAFTA). Although the country's economic and financial debacle following the December 1994 devaluation represented a major setback to the neoliberal strategy, in the long run, the harsh, orthodox steps taken to "resolve" that crisis have helped solidify the reform program. This chapter contends that reform of the state apparatus and deregulation of the Mexican economy between 1983 and 1994 have limited the state's ability to promote long-term economic growth and broad-based development.

Privatization, the most radical element of neoliberal restructuring, took place in Mexico under crisis conditions over a span of three presidential administrations (called *sexenios*, since Mexican presidents serve six-year terms). The first sexenio was that of Miguel de la Madrid, who held office from late 1982, following the onset of the Mexican (and Latin American) foreign debt crisis, to late 1988. The second sexenio, that of Carlos Salinas de Gortari, lasted from late 1988 to late 1994. During the Salinas administration, the major privatizations took place, and the macroeconomic imbalances that led to the 1994 foreign exchange crisis developed. The third sexenio, that of Ernesto Zedillo Ponce de León, began in late 1994 and has been marked by the foreign exchange crisis, subsequent devaluation, recession, and a harsh, orthodox anti-inflation program.

Background and Overview

The full economic consequences of privatization must be placed in the context of the macroeconomic imbalances of the Salinas period and the subsequent exchange rate and economic stabilization crises. The Mexican economy experienced slow growth after 1990, and, in 1993 (mirroring most of the 1980s), it posted a decline in real gross domestic product (GDP) per capita (see Table 1). The slowing of the economy was caused by the government's successful policy of reducing the rate of inflation to one digit, implemented in order to maintain the country's exchange rate and ensure the passage of NAFTA. As a result, the peso's real value increased steadily, stimulating imports of consumer goods, intermediate parts, and capital inputs, while doing little to promote nontraditional exports.[1] The ballooning current account balance reached an unprecedented and unsustainable deficit of 8.1 percent of GDP (close to US$30 billion) by the end of 1994 (see Table 1).

Table 1.
Mexico: Selected Economic Indicators, 1989-1994

Indicator	1989	1990	1991	1992	1993	1994
	(Percent Change)					
Real GDP	2.9	4.0	3.6	2.6	0.3	3.0
Real GDP Per Capita	0.7	1.7	1.4	0.4	-1.9	0.8
Consumer Prices	19.7	30.0	18.8	11.9	8.0	7.0
Real Minimum Wage	-7.9	-7.0	-6.5	-7.2	-5.6	-5.0
Urban Unemployment	2.9	2.7	2.7	2.8	3.4	3.9
	(Percent of GDP)					
Fiscal Deficit	6.0	3.5	1.3	-1.0	-0.2	0.5
Domestic Investment	17.8	18.9	20.4	23.0	20.5	20.8
National Savings	16.2	15.5	14.1	13.8	14.0	13.5
Current Account Balance	-2.8	-3.2	-4.8	-6.8	-6.4	-8.1
Public External Debt	32.5	31.7	26.1	31.0	31.1	29.8
Real Effective Exchange Rate (1990=100)	103.2	100.0	91.1	83.8	78.0	80.0

Sources: ECLAC 1996; IDB, various reports, 1989-1994.

The drop in the national savings rate can be traced to the consumption induced by the overvalued exchange rate and the debt-led nature of the consumption and investment recovery of the early 1990s. The shortfalls in domestic savings and the growing current account deficit after 1990 were financed by a steep increase in the net inflow of largely short-term foreign portfolio investment. Contributing to this inflow were the relatively low real interest rates in the United States and the prospects that the passage of NAFTA would solidify the Mexican government's market-oriented reforms. For example, in 1993, Mexico received an estimated $17 billion in foreign investments, with 69 percent going into portfolio investments — not into direct investments in plant, machinery, and equipment. Mexico's reliance on short-term debt was great, relative to other highly indebted nations in the region (see Table 2).

Table 2.
External Debt of Five Latin American Countries, 1994

	Total Debt as Percentage of GDP	Short-Term Debt as Percentage of GDP
Argentina	31	3.6
Brazil	26	6.0
Chile	43	8.3
Mexico	47	18.0
Peru	54	5.6

Source: Federal Reserve Bank of Dallas, 1995, 7.

The bulk of these funds were attracted by overly generous terms offered to investors in the privatizations of banks and major state-owned enterprises and also by the issuance of short-term government debt, or *tesobonos*, through which the Mexican government absorbed the risk of devaluation by indexing the principal (in pesos) to the peso/dollar exchange rate. Political instability in 1994 forced the Mexican government to issue these "risk-free" obligations in order to attract short-term funds and prevent apprehensive investors from transferring their money out of the country. When, in late 1994, both the stability of the exchange rate and the availability of dollars came into question, the volatile stock of tesobono investments seeking conversion to dollars became a major contributor to the crisis.

In terms of prospects for economic growth, real domestic investment was weak during the Salinas sexenio. Even though from 1989 through 1993 gross domestic investment rose as a percentage of GDP, only some of the ground lost in the 1980s was recovered (Table 3). Both in absolute and relative terms, and despite rapid expansion of the privatization program, the highest level recorded for total domestic investment during the Salinas sexenio — that of 1992 — was still well below levels attained in the early 1980s.

More important, aggregate-investment data mask the underlying deterioration in public investment in economic and social infrastructure that took place during the Salinas administration. In 1985, public investment as a proportion of GDP stood at 6.5 percent, but, by the end of 1993, it had dropped to only 4 percent (see Table 3). A portion of this decline can be attributed to the neoliberal shrinking of the state and to the privatization process in particular. In that same period, private investment rose from 11.4 percent to 16.5 percent of GDP.

Compared to Chile — the only other country in the hemisphere where market-oriented policies have been pursued as avidly as in Mexico — the Mexican state performed poorly in terms of its share of overall investment, which declined from 34 percent in 1986 to 19.5 percent by the end of 1993 (Figure 1). In Chile, the ratio of public investment to overall investment rose from 25.8 percent in 1990 to 31 percent in 1993, while overall investment as a percentage of GDP rose from 18.8 percent to 22 percent (Miller and Sumlinski 1994), strikingly different from Mexico's performance.

Table 3.
Gross Domestic Investment in Mexico and Latin America
(billions of real pesos, 1980=100)

Year	Public Investment	Private Investment	Total Investment	Public/GDP	Private/GDP	Total/GDP
1980	476.4	630.4	1,106.8	10.7	14.0	24.7
1981	583.4	703.0	1,286.4	12.0	14.5	26.5
1982	473.5	596.9	1,070.4	9.8	12.3	22.1
1983	303.0	464.7	767.7	6.5	10.0	16.5
1984	315.4	501.6	817.0	6.6	10.5	17.1
1985	318.2	563.0	881.2	6.5	11.4	17.9
1986	272.9	504.3	777.2	5.7	10.5	16.2
1987	239.5	536.7	776.2	5.0	11.0	16.0
1988	229.3	591.8	821.1	4.7	12.0	16.7
1989	237.6	653.5	873.1	4.7	12.5	17.2
1990	268.0	720.6	988.6	5.0	13.6	18.6
1991	250.0	822.5	1,072.5	4.5	15.0	19.5
1992	241.4	993.5	1,234.8	4.3	17.7	22.0
1993	225.4	929.8	1,155.3	4.0	16.5	20.5

Country	Public and Private Investment as a Proportion of GDP		Growth Rates	
	1970-79	1980-89	1971-80	1981-91
Argentina	21.7	16.1	3.7	-12.1
Brazil	24.5	17.9	9.5	-2.4
Chile	17.9	16.3	2.8	0.6
Mexico	23.0	18.4	8.6	-3.6
Venezuela	26.5	18.9	4.6	-7.0
Latin America	23.0	17.3	7.3	-3.2

Sources: IDB 1991, 267, Table B-5; IDB 1992, 275, Table B-4; OECD 1992, 253, Table B; ECLAC 1993.

    Mexico's decline in public investment is worrisome in light of empirical evidence suggesting that public investment in economic and social infrastructure has a lagged positive effect on private capital formation and that indiscriminate cuts in government spending, which fall disproportionately on public investment, will sharply reduce the overall rate of capital formation and future economic growth (Cardoso 1993; Calderón 1988; Ramírez 1994). Therefore, contrary to neoliberal claims, cuts in public investment might undermine the efficiency gains promised by the proponents of privatization and economic liberalization.

Figure 1. Mexican State's Share in Overall Investment, 1950-1993

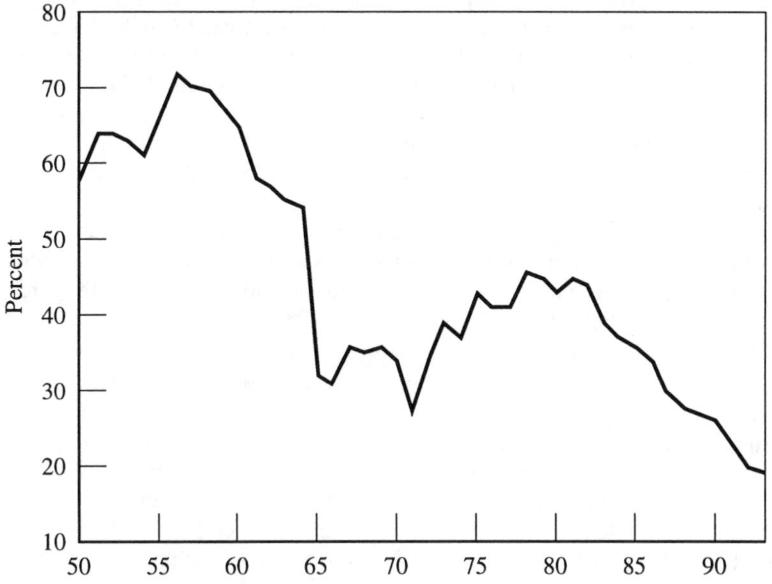

Source: Author.

PRIVATIZATION: EVOLUTION AND RATIONALE

The de la Madrid Sexenio: 1982-1988

Mexico's privatization program during the sexenio of Miguel de la Madrid can be subdivided into three major periods: December 1982 to January 1985; February 1985 to November 1987; and the most decisive phase, beginning in December 1987 (OECD 1992, 85-94; Romero 1991).

During the de la Madrid administration, Mexico's privatization program was labeled "disincorporation," in response to the administration's politically sensitive nature in regard to employment effects, the relative power of the state vis-à-vis the private sector, and the issue of national sovereignty over the country's vast natural resources (Ferrer 1991, 35-57; Romero 1991). The administration portrayed the withdrawal of the state from key subsectors of the economy, not as a sign of weakness or abandonment of the state's commitment to meeting pressing social welfare needs, but as a strategy designed to increase its relative effectiveness in meeting selected economic and social objectives. Government officials argued that disincorporation promised to render the state more capable of fulfilling its long-standing commitment to attaining social justice via specific social programs, such as the National Food Program (Programa Nacional de Alimentación — PRONAL) and the National Program for Integrated Rural Development (Programa Nacional de Desarrollo Rural Integrado — PRONADRI), precursors of the National Solidarity Program (Programa Nacional de Solidaridad — PRONASOL) and the Agricultural Promotion Program (Programa Nacional del Campo — PROCAMPO).

The central features of the privatization program were outlined in the administration's National Development Plan (Plan Nacional de Desarrollo) for 1983-1988 and were implemented via constitutional reforms of Articles 25, 26, and 28 in 1983 and the promulgation of the Law of Federal and Parastatal Entities in 1986, which provided differentiated treatment for various subsectors of the economy. Article 28 asserted that the state would retain control over strategic productive subsectors, such as oil, basic petrochemicals, electric power, the minting of money, nuclear energy, satellite communications, the railroads, and the postal service (Romero 1991). In so-called priority areas, such as the media, transportation, mining, and banking, only domestic private investors would be allowed majority holdings. In secondary or nonpriority subsectors, the state's participation would be eliminated, and, under certain conditions, firms would be open to 100-percent foreign ownership (BIC 1990, 41-54; Cornelius 1986).

The first phase of the privatization strategy was confined to the sale, merger, or elimination of mostly small, nonpriority enterprises in manufacturing, textiles, chemicals, and consumer durables (BIC 1990, 41-54). During this phase, the government authorized nearly 200 divestitures, of which 143 were outright liquidations, 41 were mergers or transfers, and only 11 were sales to the private sector (Romero 1991). By the end of the first phase, the number of public entities had dropped from 1,155 to somewhere between 941 and 993 (see Table 4).[2] The figures for the first three years, December 1982 through January 1985, reveal that the government proceeded cautiously in order to minimize the political repercussions of what was, at the time, a highly sensitive issue, as well as to gain valuable experience with the privatization process before tackling the larger enterprises. The sale, elimination, and transfer of nonpriority state enterprises during this phase reduced public production and employment very little (Ferrer 1991, 46; Machado and Peres 1986).

Table 4. Number of State-Owned Enterprises in Mexico, 1982-1993

Year	Companies Actually Sold	Companies Slated for Sale
1982	1,155	1,155
1983	1,082	1,074
1984	1,056	1,049
1985	993	941
1986	889	737
1987	851	617
1988	—	412
1989	—	379
1990	—	280
1991	—	239
1992	—	223
1993	—	205*

*As of December 1993.

Sources: Ferrer 1991, 45; *Mexico Business Monthly* 1994a, 5; IDB 1991, 123-25; OECD 1992, 89, Table 18.

The so-called disincorporation process, however, would intensify during the second phase, particularly after 1985, in part due to conjunctural factors that played an important role in forcing the hand of the de la Madrid administration. In the second half of 1985, as oil prices dropped sharply and earthquakes devastated Mexico City, a renewed crisis of confidence emerged in the private sector, which resulted in declining investment and accelerating capital flight (Murguía 1986, 6-9; Cornelius 1986, 20-21). Faced with the threat of hyperinflation, reduced access to external financing, and capital outflows, the government had little choice but to sell its larger and more profitable state-owned enterprises to garner needed resources.

The Mexican state began to divest itself of a number of enterprises in which its equity investments were between 25 percent and 50 percent — including many *fideicomisos* or public trust funds (see Table 5). Between February 1985 and November 1987, the state authorized 406 disincorporations, of which 205 were liquidations, 54 mergers or transfers, and 147 sales. Among the major enterprises affected were the country's oldest integrated steel mill (located in Monterrey and employing more than 10,000 workers); Mexicana Airlines (sold to a consortium headed by AeroMexico, Mexico's Grupo Xabre and the Chase Manhattan Bank); and a large hotel chain (Nacional Hotelera). The sale of public enterprises during the second phase generated approximately $1.03 billion in revenue, representing a modest fiscal impact on the government's net wealth (Sánchez 1993, 101-104).

Table 5.
Number and Type of State-Owned Enterprises in Mexico, 1982-1992

	1982	1983	1984	1985	1986	1987	1988	1989	1990	1991	1992
Firms with a Majority Share	744	700	703	629	528	437	252	229	147	119	106
Firms with a Minority Share	78	78	78	69	7	3	0	0	0	0	0
Public Trusts	231	199	173	147	108	83	71	62	51	43	40
Decentralized Organizations	102	97	95	96	94	94	89	88	82	77	77
Total	1155	1074	1049	941	737	617	412	379	280	239	223

Sources: OECD 1992, 89, Table 18; INEGI 1992a.

The third, and most decisive, phase of the disincorporation process began in 1987, near the end of the de la Madrid administration. Once again, it was precipitated by a grim economic outlook, as Mexico faced an inflation rate of 159.2 percent, a fiscal deficit of over 16 percent, and a fast-falling stock market, which led to the resurgence of capital flight in the last quarter of that year. The government responded to the economic turmoil by introducing a heterodox stabilization program, the Solidarity Pact (Pacto de Solidaridad Económica). The program's heterodox elements consisted of the systematic implementation of negotiated wage and price restraints and a deliberate deceleration of the nominal rate of peso devaluation in order to control inflationary expectations (and, from a political standpoint, the rate of decrease in real minimum wages). It also included fairly orthodox recommendations, in the form of further cuts in public investment, a policy of tight credit, and, notably, a renewed effort to dismantle what were once considered to be priority (and even strategic) subsectors of the state's productive apparatus, thereby rendering useless for operational purposes the former distinction between priority and nonpriority subsectors (for further details, see Banco de México 1989, 17-42).

During 1988, the last year of the de la Madrid administration, 205 new privatizations were undertaken, of which 185 involved companies in which the state had a majority participation. In contrast, from 1982 through 1987, 743 state-owned enterprises were sold, with the state having majority participation in 492 of those companies. The state also divested itself of all enterprises in which it had a minority participation, including 173 trust funds and decentralized entities.

The Salinas de Gortari Sexenio: 1988-1994

The favorable international climate for market-based reforms created by the collapse of the socialist states in Eastern Europe and the former Soviet Union and the lack of a viable economic and political alternative to the status quo enabled the Salinas administration to attain a national consensus regarding neoliberal reforms. Without delay, Salinas proceeded to consolidate the modernization project initiated by his predecessor via the privatization of priority subsectors of the economy, formerly considered strategic, such as basic petrochemicals, banking, steel, mining, telecommunications, and the railroads (Cárdenas 1990, 1-25; Lustig 1992, 103-107; OECD 1992; Romero 1991).

By December 1993, the number of parastatal enterprises had dropped to 210, the state having divested itself between 1989 and 1992 of more than 100 firms in which it had had a majority share. Notably, these sales had included prominent and profitable enterprises, such as the following:

1. The state-owned telephone company, TELMEX;
2. The country's largest steel producer, ALTOS HORNOS DE MÉXICO, S.A.;
3. The Cananea and Mexicobre copper mines;
4. The fertilizer company, FERTIMEX;
5. The warehouses and subsidiaries (including oilseed-processing facilities and sugar mills) of CONASUPO, the giant food distribution and market-ing firm;
6. Peripheral businesses associated with Petróleos Mexicanos (PEMEX);
7. Mexicana Airlines;
8. The petrochemical company (Tereftálatos de México — Temex); and,
9. The country's 18 nationalized banks.

With the streamlining of the parastatal sector almost complete by the end of the Salinas sexenio, the administration announced that, during 1994, another 12 enterprises would be sold, including Almacenes Nacionales de Depósito (government commodity warehouses); EXPORTADORES ASOCIADOS; Ocean Garden (aquatic farms); *El Nacional* newspaper; and three paper manufacturers (*Mexico Business Monthly* 1994a, 4).

Over the 1989-1992 period, the accumulated proceeds from privatizations amounted to 6.5 percent of GDP, with the sale of the nationalized banks accounting for more than one-half of that figure. (In absolute terms, the sale of the 18 banks netted the government $12.6 billion.) The lion's share of the privatization proceeds were placed in a special contingency fund used to retire government debt (both internal and external). Thus, the state's use of privatization proceeds benefited foreign creditors and investors, and a relatively small number of domestic financiers and bankers who held most of the internal and external debt — the very same individuals and firms that profited from the debt-expansion, debt-service cycle in the first place (Noguera and López 1987, 105-126; MacEwan 1990, 1-13).

In the wake of the country's recent economic, political, and social difficulties, an increasing, if still inadequate, share of these proceeds are also being used to finance the National Solidarity Program (Programa Nacional de Solidaridad — PRONASOL), which the Salinas administration created in 1988 to channel resources and social programs to the poorest, mostly rural, segments of Mexican society. Critics of the program, however, contended that the primary objective of PRONASOL was political, that is, to undermine the strength of opposition forces on the left and act as a "social tranquilizer" for the same groups that were being marginalized by the government's neoliberal policies (Dresser 1991, 12-14).[3]

Perhaps the most significant and controversial policy initiative launched during this phase of the privatization process was the 1992 restructuring of PEMEX, the state-owned oil company, into four decentralized divisions. Under the Constitutional Law on Mexican Petroleum and Subsidiary Bodies (Ley Orgánica de Petróleos Mexicanos y Organismos Subsidiarios), PEMEX continued as the parent company of four independent units: exploration and production; refining; gas and basic petrochemicals (reserved for state control); and nonbasic petrochemicals (open to private Mexican companies and foreign investors). The new structure established a separate division, PEMEX Internacional, to conduct international trade in crude and petroleum products. Although the president's office, during all three administrations, has gone out of its way to reassure the public that the oil company will remain in state hands, similar statements were made about the airlines, mining companies, telephone company, and banks before they were privatized, and many industry analysts believe the PEMEX restructuring is paving the way for a partial or complete privatization of the company.

To a significant degree, this process is already well under way in 1994. For example, PEMEX has sold its majority share in certain activities, such as the production of lubricants and petrochemicals, and it has opened the exploration and development of several oil fields to foreign companies, including Triton Engineering Corporation of Houston and Sonat Corporation.[4] In addition, beginning in 1990, the Salinas administration removed 15 products from its list of 34 basic petrochemicals reserved for state development, and, under the terms of NAFTA, it agreed to reduce the number of "exclusive" basic petrochemicals to only six, thus facilitating the eventual privatization of the subsidiary for secondary petrochemicals.[5] Needless to say, the 1994 economic debacle forced the Zedillo administration to intensify the privatization of the lucrative petrochemical subsector in order to raise immediate revenues with which to meet the public sector's pressing financial and social demands. Conservative groups, within and outside the country, pressured the administration to sell PEMEX's shares in its various enterprises (representing a potential market value of $150 billion), while preserving the government's sole ownership of subsoil hydrocarbon reserves, estimated by PEMEX to be worth $900 billion at 1995 world prices (see, for example, Pazos 1995, 123-127).

INITIAL IMPACTS OF THE PRIVATIZATION PROGRAM

Output

The impact of privatization on production and output can be analyzed at the level of the economy as a whole and by specific subsector. Mexican investigators, such as René Villarreal (1988) and María Amparo Casar and Wilson Peres (1988), initially regarded privatization primarily as a rationalization mechanism for establishing guidelines and incentives for the efficient utilization of dwindling public resources. They minimized the importance of its global impact by pointing to government studies that showed that as of 1989, the privatization process had only reduced the state enterprises' share of GDP by between 2.1 and 3.2 percent (IDB 1990, 150).

By subsector, however, the disincorporation process involved a total or partial withdrawal of the state from key industries, such as mining, steel, capital goods, motor vehicles, consumer durables, and airlines. For example, the state withdrew completely from the production of cars, trucks, buses, and diesel engines, as a result of the sale, merger, or elimination of Renault de México, Diesel Nacional, S.A. and its subsidiaries Dicuminsa (with Cummings Engine), Motores Perkins, Dina Autobuses, and Dina Camiones (trucks) (for further details, see Romero 1991; BIC 1990, 46). Even before the decisive third phase of the divestiture process, the state had withdrawn from 15 of the 28 productive subsectors in which it had been participating in 1982.

The impact in specific subsectors is corroborated by Jaime B. Romero (1991), who reports that, between 1982 and 1987, the divestiture process in mining reduced the state enterprises' share of total output by 30 percent, while in manufacturing, the reduction was close to 32 percent (see also BIC 1990, 46). Even Villarreal's own research shows that, between 1982 and 1986, the privatization process reduced the state's contribution to total national output by 27 percent (Cypher 1990, 148). These figures are incomplete because they do not take into account the impact of the latest wave of divestitures in major mining companies, secondary petrochemicals, steel, sugar mills, airlines, the telephone company, and, above all, banking (*Latin American Weekly Report* 1992, 9). The pace of privatization has increased to the point where it is no longer a question of simply rationalizing public expenditures but one of fundamentally transforming the structure of the state and its role in the economy.

Employment

The privatization process has eliminated tens of thousands of jobs in those industries that experienced major sales, liquidations, or mergers — including mining, steel, trucks and auto parts, airlines, fertilizers, sugar, and secondary petrochemicals. Privatizations affecting these industries resulted in the direct total loss of about 250,000 jobs, according to a study conducted between 1983 and 1989 by the Finance and Public Credit Secretariat (Secretaría de Hacienda y Crédito Público) (*Latin American Weekly Report* 1992). Unions affiliated with the Mexican Workers Union (Confederación de Trabajadores Mexicanos — CTM) reported losses of up to 200,000 jobs: steel (40,000); petroleum (20,000 to 135, 000);[6] mining (15,000 to 20,000); truck and auto parts (5,000); fertilizers (3,000); and sugar (2,000) (*Latin American Economy and Business* 1992d, 5; Latin American News-letters 1992, 5). The privatization of AeroMexico and Mexicana Airlines alone eliminated more than 13,000 jobs between 1988 and 1992. In the case of the country' s largest steel mill, Altos Hornos de México, in Monclova, privatization resulted in the layoff of some 10,000 workers and the reduction in working hours and benefits for many others (Latin American Newsletters 1992, 4-5). Moreover, according to Juan José Jiménez, director of the Monclova Chamber of Commerce, the "privatization of the steel plant has resulted in the closings of more than 200 local businesses, and large supermarkets and shopping centers are in danger of becoming white elephants because of the city's economic stagnation" (*Mexico Business Monthly* 1991b, 10). Moreover, between 300,000 and 400,000 public sector jobs have been eliminated since the implementation of the third phase of the privatization process (OECD 1992, 90; Pazos 1993, 21; Latin American Newsletters 1992, 4-5).

In addition to job losses, privatization has resulted in a deterioration of labor standards, including enforcement of existing contracts, the right to bargain collectively, and the right to strike. In many cases, the government has used bankruptcy proceedings to void labor contracts, or it has "sanitized" state-owned enterprises before launching formal privatization procedures.

The example of the Cananea Mining Company (Compañía Minera de Cananea — CMC) illustrates the impact of privatization on employment. In 1988, after failed attempts to sell the company to private mining interests, the state stepped in and declared the company bankrupt, "dismissed 2,800 miners, closed the mine, and moved in 3,400 troops to insure that workers would not destroy valuable equipment" (BIC 1990, 65). The Salinas administration underestimated the public outcry that would follow its actions. Given the symbolic importance of CMC during the Mexican Revolution, the government was forced to reopen the copper mine and promise that every effort would be made to preserve existing jobs and worker benefits. Once public outrage died down, the company's new owners were able to exert effective pressure on the government to allow them to cut the workforce by 23 percent and rehire the remaining workers under new contracts that "included fewer labor categories (from 400 to only six) and established continuous shifts and round-the-clock, seven-day-a-week operations" (BIC 1990, 65). MexCobre, an affiliate of Grupo Minero de México, as the company's major shareholder with 78.8 percent, also reneged on a promise made, following bankruptcy proceedings, to sell 25 percent of the company's shares to unionized workers; instead, it allotted the union less than 4 percent of the stock (for further details, see Sánchez and Corona 1993, 115-130).

In the case of the airline industry, the government declared AeroMexico bankrupt in April 1988 in order to punish the union for a major strike initiated in response to the government's decision to privatize the carrier. By that action, the existing labor contract was voided, and the company's new owners, Grupo Dictum, were given a free hand in firing 9,000 union members and replacing them with 3,000 new workers from outside the union (Hanson 1994, 204). Mexicana's privatization, although initiated earlier, was not completed until shortly after that of AeroMexico. Although the government did not subject Mexicana to bankruptcy proceedings, the implicit threat that it could resort to this legal mechanism to "sanitize" the privatization process enabled the new owners, Grupo Falcón, to pressure the union successfully to abrogate the existing collective bargaining agreement and accept a new labor contract that, inter alia, decreased the company's workforce from 14,000 to 11,000, reduced the number of justifications for absences, eliminated over 100 job categories, established 24-hour operations in all production areas, and eliminated the seniority-based promotion system (Hanson 1994, 204).

The actions of the government against organized labor reveal an important aspect of the neoliberal strategy. As Barry Carr observed some years ago:

> By putting workers on the defensive . . . the crisis (and now the "sanitization" policy) has allowed the most dynamic and aggressive sector of Mexican capitalism . . . to advance the modernization process in order to secure major productivity gains. The "devaluation of labor power" involves not only reductions in real wages, but also a managerial onslaught on worker rights, a reduction in the amount of leverage exercised by workers in the production process, and a freer hand for management revolutionizing production processes through microelectronic technology (Carr 1986, 4).

This aspect of neoliberal strategy has received little attention in the literature, even though it promises to change permanently, if it has not already done so, the balance of power in the labor markets of less-developed countries such as Mexico.

NAFTA will accentuate this trend because it makes it far easier for economically powerful and politically influential Mexican and U.S. capitalists to pool financial, managerial, legal, and technical resources, and, in so doing, bring them to bear against workers, both within Mexico and across the border. The increased leverage and power of employers relative to workers, which has been secured through the globalization and economic integration of the country, promises further to erode hard-won workers' rights in areas such as job classification, seniority clauses, shop-floor representation, nonwage benefits, and the right to strike. In other words, the current privatization and liberalization movement in Mexico and elsewhere has vastly increased the pool of relatively unskilled workers that employers can utilize to perform any given job (with highly standardized technology), thus increasing the employers' power inside the workplace, lowering unit labor costs, and improving the conditions for profitable investment.

Distribution of Income and Wealth

The unprecedented concentration of productive and financial resources and the resulting worsening of income distribution are other unfavorable outcomes of the privatization process. Although Mexico has long suffered from a highly inequitable distribution of income and wealth, the austerity policies and neoliberal reforms of the 1980s further polarized Mexican society (Table 6). Between 1984 and 1989, the income share of the top decile rose from 32.8 to 37.9 percent, while the cumulative income share of the "bottom" 90 percent of the Mexican population fell from 67.2 to 62.1 percent. The gap between the very rich and the very poor increased dramatically. In 1984, the richest 10 percent had incomes that were 19 times greater than those of the poorest 10 percent. By the end of the decade, the income of the richest 10 percent had soared to 24 times the income of the poorest 10 percent.

Table 6.
Mexico: Distribution of Household Income

Deciles	1984 %	1984 Cumulative %	1989 %	1989 Cumulative %	1989 Average Income[1]
I	1.7	1.7	1.6	1.6	548
II	3.1	4.8	2.8	4.4	972
III	4.2	9.1	3.7	8.1	1,294
IV	5.3	14.4	4.7	12.9	1,636
V	6.4	20.8	5.9	18.8	2,043
VI	7.9	28.6	7.3	26.1	2,522
VII	9.7	38.3	9.0	35.0	3,108
VIII	12.2	50.5	11.4	46.5	3,952
IX	16.7	67.2	15.6	62.1	5,408
X	32.8	100.0	37.9	100.0	13,126
Total	100.0	————	100.0	————	3,461[2]

1. Average household income (monetary and nonmonetary) per quarter (in 1989 thousands of pesos).

2. Equivalent to US$1,384.

Sources: INEGI 1992b; OECD 1992, 110, Table 27.

Perhaps not surprisingly, the functional distribution of income has also become highly unequal over the past decade. According to Mexican economist Ifigenia Martínez (1995, 157, Table 2), the share of national income received by capitalists increased from 48 percent in 1982 to 57.1 percent in 1994, while that going to labor fell from 41.7 percent in 1982 to 30.9 percent in 1994 (the residual share is absorbed by indirect taxes). Thus, both the functional and size distribution of income figures reveal, in no uncertain terms, that only the very rich and powerful have been able to escape the painful adjustment costs borne by the rest of the population and, in many instances, their incomes and wealth have even increased. This group has also benefited disproportionately from their ownership and acquisition of productive and financial assets and tight monetary policies, which have encouraged relatively high real interest rates in the domestic financial sector.

The trend toward greater concentration of assets is most evident in the reprivatization of the nation's 18 commercial banks. Despite the stated goal of the Finance and Public Credit Secretariat to distribute the country's financial power more equitably by prohibiting individual investors from owning more than 5 percent of a privatized bank's shares, ex-bankers and new private financiers — the latter having amassed large fortunes as a result of the stock market boom of the second half of the de la Madrid administration — have created new financial *grupos* that can obtain up to 100 percent of shares of the privatized banks. For example, Mexican financial specialist Carlos Elizondo observed that only 44 economic grupos bid for the 18 nationalized banks and that the bulk of the savings of these privatized banks are now concentrated in a small number of individuals and firms:

> Deposits of 18,649 people and firms with accounts of one billion pesos or more, 0.07 percent of total accounts, make up 53 percent of total deposits. Those with accounts of 250 million or more, 96,382 firms or people, represent 0.37 percent of total accounts and 66.1 percent of total deposits . . . . [T]he number of shareholders after privatization amounts to nearly 130,000 people. This implies that the most important savers may own part of the banks, thus privatization allows them to directly or indirectly manage their savings (Elizondo 1993, 11).[7]

Not surprisingly, some of the same families that owned and controlled the banking system before the 1982 nationalization have returned, along with powerful industrialists and new private financiers. The latter are mainly owners of brokerage houses who, according to Carlos Elizondo (1993, 15), "knew [how to profit from] the stock market much better than former bankers."[8]

To illustrate this turn of events, take the case of the National Bank of Mexico (Banco Nacional de México — BANAMEX), one of the three largest banks in Latin America and one of the oldest banks in Mexico, with assets totaling more than $15 billion, 31,797 employees, and 720 banks throughout the country. The institution was sold in 1991 for $4.6 billion to Grupo Regional, which includes the nation's largest brokerage house, Acciones y Valores de México (Accival). The group is headed by Alfredo Harp Helu, Roberto Hernández Ramírez, and José G. Aguilera Medrano. Hernández Ramírez and Harp Helu are partners in Accival, and Harp Helu is the former president of the Mexican stock exchange and a close friend of former President Carlos Salinas de Gortari (for further details, see *Mexico Business Monthly* 1991a, 6-7). The Commerce Bank (Banco de Comercio — BANCOMER) the country's second largest retail bank, with $25 billion in assets, was sold to individual investors led by Eugenio Garza Laguera, former owner of Banco SERFIN and chairman of grupos VAMSA and VISA. VAMSA is a leading financial firm based in Monterrey, Mexico, with investments in securities, brokerage firms, leasing, factoring, and warehousing.[9] Its principal subsidiary, Seguros de México, S.A., is Mexico's largest individual life insurer.

Even the relatively smaller banks have been sold to individuals and firms belonging to powerful financial and industrial grupos. For example, multiregional banks, such as Banco Atlántico (the seventh largest) and Banco Promex (the twelfth largest), were sold to Alonso de Garay Gutiérrez and Jorge Rojas Mota Velasco. The new owners are closely connected to Grupo Bursátil Mexicano, the country's second largest stock brokerage house. Banco Atlántico is the largest multiregional bank with assets of $3.5 billion and a network of 204 branches spread over 26 of Mexico's 30 states (*Mexico Business Monthly* 1991b; *Latin American Economy and Business*, 1992a, 16). In addition, Banco Mercantil del Norte, the country's largest regional bank, was sold to a group of investors led by Roberto González, Juan Antonio Gonzáles, and Federico Graf. These investors are closely affiliated with Grupo Industrial Maseca, Mexico's largest tortilla-flour producer (*Mexico Business Monthly* 1992b, 4-5).

The concentration of banking assets in a relatively small number of financial and banking institutions has given rise to legitimate concerns about the degree of competition present in the privatized banking system. Economic theory suggests that one measure of market power is whether the industry sustains above-normal profits. In Mexico, banks' profits, as measured by the real return on their assets, soared between 1992 and 1994 — even as their portfolio of nonperforming loans rose dramatically. More revealing, perhaps, is the relatively high price-to-book value the new owners paid for the banks, reflecting their belief that above-normal profits are likely to persist (McComb, Gruben, and Welch 1994, 220). Economic theory also suggests that as competition and efficiency in the banking industry are enhanced, the spread between lending and deposit rates should shrink. However, the spreads have widened significantly since the completion of the bank reprivatizations (Table 7). For example, they rose from an already high 11.33 point margin in 1992 to 14.63 in 1993. Although these figures do not constitute prima facie evidence that concentration has enhanced market power in the privatized banking system, they indicate that one has to look elsewhere for evidence that reprivatization has enhanced competition and efficiency in the industry.

Table 7.
Mexico: Real Interest Rates and Financial Margins, 1987-1994

Year	Deposit Rates (mean percentage cost)	Average Lending Rates	Margins
1987	-14.61	-4.71	9.90
1988	-25.12	-14.18	10.94
1989	20.31	33.40	13.09
1990	8.45	19.08	10.63
1991	-0.22	11.58	11.79
1992	2.71	14.05	11.33
1993	6.18	20.80	14.63
1994*	9.08	24.74	15.66

*As of July 1994.

Source: Calva 1995, 92, Table 15.

The Domestic Fiscal Deficit

One particularly "favorable" outcome of deregulation and privatization was the immediate provision of resources to reduce the fiscal deficit, a feature that government officials and the international banking and financial community publicized highly until the 1994 crisis. Before the peso devaluation, government officials pointed to the impressive fiscal surpluses generated by the Mexican economy in 1992 and 1993. (See the negative fiscal deficit numbers as percent of GDP in Table 1.) However, what government officials failed to mention was that, in exchange for a lump-sum infusion of cash, privatization leads to a loss for the government of long-term revenues, which are then replaced by smaller, more variable tax revenues from privatized firms (see, for example, Baer and Birch 1991, 1-39; Edwards and Baer 1993; *Latin American Economy and Business* 1994a, 4-5). Moreover, the deficit-reducing effects of privatization may be offset completely by the government's efforts to "sanitize" public enterprises in order to render them more saleable. These efforts often include transferring the company's liabilities to the state, closing portions of parastatal operations, and changing tax and rate structures to minimize the company's role as a provider of government revenues.

In the case of the sale of the CMC, for example, the fiscal impact on the government's net wealth was negative because the price paid for the copper mining company was not sufficient to offset the net present value of the unrecovered loans that the public development bank, or National Financier (Nacional Financiera — NAFINSA), had granted CMC since 1981, when it began experiencing severe financial problems as a result of the downturn in international copper prices. NAFINSA's bad loans to CMC alone caused the bank losses in excess of $36 million. Even in the case of TELMEX, a highly profitable company because of its ability to charge long-distance rates that are much higher than international standards, "the net present value of the fiscal impact is estimated to have been negative if the benefit from [the] reduction in interest rates (to which the sale of stock on the international markets contributed) is not included" (Sánchez and Corona 1993, 28). Additionally, in an effort to sanitize mining concerns, such as Mexicobre and CMC, the Salinas administration phased out the 2 percent to 6 percent royalty tax charged on all mineral production, while also lengthening the rights to exploration from three to six years and the rights to exploitation and development from 25 to 50 years. The government also relinquished mineral rights on almost 2 million acres of national reserves. These mineral-rich lands, primarily in northern Mexico, are now open to private investments. The government retains rights only to a small percentage of the 12.35 million acres it had held since 1932 (*Business Latin America* 1992, 161-162).

The Salinas administration attributed the massive inflow of capital the nation has attracted since 1989 to the favorable investment climate that resulted from the liberalization and deregulation of the economy (Table 3), including privatization. In 1992 alone, Mexico received close to $15 billion in foreign investment, with most coming in the form of indirect or portfolio investments connected to the privatization of public firms and banks (*Mexico Business Monthly* 1993, 5-6; *Latin American Economy and Business* 1994a, 5). As of December 1993, the total accumulated value of foreign investment channeled to Mexico's stock market was $28.1 billion, representing 19 percent of market capitalization (*Latin American Economy and Business* 1994b, 4-5). Although these foreign inflows were instrumental in financing the country's ever-growing current account trade deficits ($21 billion in 1993 and $25 billion in 1994), they also made Mexico overly reliant on foreign capital to keep the economy growing (for further details, see *Latin American Economy and Business* 1992c, 4-5; *Mexico and NAFTA Report* 1993, 4-5; *Latin American Economy and Business Quarterly Update* 1994, 4). The economic debacle unleashed on the Mexican people following the disastrous 1994 devaluation has exposed the short-term dangers associated with an overreliance on highly liquid sources of foreign capital.

PRIVATIZATION AND THE MINIMALIST STATE

From the outset, the Mexican government has been decidedly vague about the nature and scope of its privatization program. During most of the de la Madrid sexenio, the government proceeded cautiously with its "disincorporation program," and it was not until the Salinas administration that government officials even used the term "privatization." When forced to provide an explanation for their policies, the architects of the privatization program usually invoked the idea of allocative and productive efficiency. That is, when private managers are freed from cumbersome government regulations and driven by the profit motive — in a competitive environment — they are invariably more efficient than public managers in producing that mix of goods and services that consumers value the most.

The problem with this version of the efficiency notion is that it ignores the historical fact that corporate bureaucracies can be every bit as inefficient as government bureaucracies, and, more often than not, large corporations, especially in small countries, operate in the absence of significant competition from other producers. The determining factor for productive and allocative efficiency is the kind of market structure in which privatized firms operate, different from ownership per se. In this connection, it is important to point out that in the Mexican case, a significant number of public enterprises "created" during the Stabilizing Development Period (1955-1971) were either the direct result of the state bailing out failed private companies in oligopolistic sectors of the economy or the result of the private sector inviting government participation in the form of financial, administrative, and technical assistance. In other words, because the impending bankruptcy of these monopolistic firms threatened to generate serious repercussions throughout the economic system, the Mexican state had to step in and attempt to substitute its own action for that of the "market," thereby socializing the losses of the capitalists involved (Bazdresch and Levy 1991, 242-43; see Sweezy 1970, 318-319, for the U.S. case).[10]

As this discussion has shown (particularly with regard to the banking subsector, but not limited to it), the privatization movement in Mexico has led to the transfer of relatively profitable public sector firms to the private sector in markets where one or two firms dominate production and sales (Grinspun and Cameron 1993, 32-37). The inherent danger of this is that it may lead to an outcome where private monopolies merely replace public ones. Unless an effective regulatory framework exists, the dominant firm in these markets may engage in monopolistic practices that could eliminate some or all of the efficiency gains promised by privatization enthusiasts.

It is also important to remember in this debate about "efficiency" that many of the goods and services provided by the government and state-owned enterprises are of a public or quasi-public nature. Although the underproduction problem associated with private provision of public goods can be solved by contracting out the production of these goods to private agencies, in accordance with government specifications, and regulations can overcome the underutilization problem, the presence of substantial monitoring costs, cost overruns, and monopolistic pricing could remove the bias of public officials in favor of privatization (Prager 1992).[11] In this connection, the World Bank reports that in the construction of an ambitious 400-mile road in Mexico, the government awarded concessions to private contractors who promised to transfer the road back to the government in the shortest possible time. The short time frame, in turn, motivated private contractors to charge toll rates that were "five to 10 times higher than those in the United States for similar distances" (World Bank 1994, 99). Not surprisingly, the old "free" roads became heavily traveled and congested, while traffic failed to materialize on the new roads. To make matters worse, the World Bank reported that "cost overruns averaged more than 50 percent of projected costs. . . . The Highway of the Sun, from Cuernavaca to Acapulco, for example, cost more than twice the original estimate" (World Bank 1994, 99).

CONCLUSION

Mexican specialist Oscar Humberto Ferrer (1991) has argued that the privatization movement in Mexico is motivated by the need to restore the government-private sector partnership that prevailed during the Stabilizing Development Period (1955-1971). According to Ferrer, the populist and ill-fated policies pursued by the Luis Echeverría Alvarez and Miguel López Portillo administrations broke the political pact that had existed between the state and powerful factions of the private sector. The private sector began to view government pronouncements as credible only after the state — with few foreign credits available and under intense pressure from international organizations such as the International Monetary Fund (IMF) and the World Bank — had implemented a more radical version of disincorporation in late 1987. Ferrer argues that the private sector's compliance with the price guidelines of the Solidarity Pact "attests to the effectiveness of the disincorporation process in changing private sector attitudes" (1991, 55).

The problem with this explanation is that the neoliberal policies sweeping through Mexico go far beyond restoring the government-business partnership that existed during the 1950s and 1960s. These policies constitute a fundamental reversal of the state's traditional role in the Mexican economy and, as such, they undermine, perhaps irreversibly, the state's capacity to guide the economy or intervene on behalf of those economic and social groups that the current neoliberal strategy has marginalized. The privatization movement in Mexico has an ideological dimension whose objective is nothing short of permanently weakening the relative autonomy of the state and, in the process, reducing the power of organized labor and the influence in policy formulation of small and medium-sized businesses, relative to the more powerful, ideological, and dynamic segments of the Mexican capitalist class and their foreign partners (mostly of U.S. origin).

Mexico's privatization and liberalization process has generated widespread and far-reaching economic and political consequences for the country's working poor, small and medium-sized businesses, powerful economic grupos, and the state. First, the double-conditionality of the IMF and the World Bank and the passage of NAFTA have led to the implementation of stabilization measures and market-based structural reforms which have created economic and social burdens that have fallen disproportionately on peasants, the urban working poor, and small and medium-sized businesses. Therefore, the majority of the Mexican people (and ironically, those who were the least responsible for the excesses of the debt-expansion, debt-recycling years) have suffered the most severe economic losses and the most drastic social consequences of the reforms. As the 1994 crisis clearly demonstrates, neoliberal reforms have failed to pave the way for a *sustainable* resumption of economic growth and development based on increasing and broad-based purchasing power. They have also failed to generate and, through their indiscriminate application, have further aggravated the provision of adequate levels of public investment in physical and social infrastructure — key expenditures for the realization of the economic efficiency gains promised by market-oriented reforms. In addition, the ill-advised implementation of these policies has saddled the economy with a huge and growing current account trade deficit, the financing of which further increases the economy's future vulnerability and overreliance on foreign capital, in turn, compromising the nation's sovereignty due to economic events and political decisions undertaken outside Mexico.

Second, the privatization program has led to clear "winners" and "losers," and the winners, economic theory notwithstanding, have not been obliged to compensate the losers. The unprecedented streamlining and deregulation of the Mexican economy has led to a) the total withdrawal of the state from key economic sectors; b) a massive loss of jobs and the trampling of labor rights in the affected industries; c) the promotion of economic concentration rather than competition, particularly in banking, finance, mining, and the airline industry; d) a growing inequality in the distribution of income and wealth in a country that is already one of the most inequitable in the world; and e) the attraction of foreign capital, by means of overly generous terms but mostly into relatively unproductive activities such as financial speculation, thereby undermining real capital accumulation.

Third, privatization has compromised the national patrimony in areas such as energy, mining, banking, and finance, as well as with regard to laws governing the remittance of dividends, profits, royalties, intellectual property rights, and, most important, labor rights. Finally, from the standpoint of political economy, the dismantling and indiscriminate pillage of the state's economic apparatus by powerful domestic and foreign grupos have not only altered the balance of power within the Mexican capitalist class and minimized the state's future role in maintaining overall aggregate demand (and, therefore, the conditions for profitable private investment), but, perhaps more significantly, have also undermined the state's base of loyalty and support (its legitimation function) among the majority of the Mexican people — peasants, the working poor, and owners of small businesses. The dismantling of the state-firm sector means that Mexico now lacks what was, in the past, a traditional and major tool for promoting investment, growth, and economic development.

Notes

1. ECLAC 1994, 61, Table 8.

2. The discrepancy in the figures reported for the first five years can be traced to the government's common — and misleading — practice of including, when listing completed privatizations, entities that had only been authorized to be privatized.

3. Dresser, in this timely and well-researched study, however, observes that PRONASOL, as a program designed to rescue vulnerable sectors of the population from the adverse economic and social effects of the neoliberal policies, leaves much to be desired, despite the government's carefully orchestrated promotion of the program. As a political strategy, it may have helped the Salinas administration diffuse social and political discontent through its administration of highly selective subsidies to regions of the country where the Institutional Revolutionary Party (Partido Revolucionario Institucional — PRI) has faced strong opposition from left-wing forces, such as the Democratic Revolutionary Party (Partido de la Revolución Democrática — PRD), but if it is going to constitute an effective program to end extreme poverty in Mexico, its economic and human resources will have to be increased significantly. In this regard, Dresser points out, "...given the extent of poverty in Mexico, the 1 or 1.5 percent of gross national product (GNP) invested in PRONASOL is insufficient. PRONASOL's 1991 entitlement represents approximately one-tenth of the outlays devoted to interest payments on Mexico's foreign debt. If we were to divide PRONASOL's budget for 1990 by the 17 million people in Mexico who live in extreme poverty, each would receive a daily allotment of 15 cents" (1991, 11).

4. The PEMEX holdings that were scheduled to be sold to the private sector included 30 service stations owned by Compañía Operadora de Estaciones de Servicio, handling about 10 percent of Mexico's domestic sales of gasoline, a 49-percent share in Distribuidora de Gas Natural, a 94-percent holding in Distribuidora de Querétaro, and a 60-percent stake in Tetraetilo de México. (See BIC 1990, 66-67; *Latin American Weekly Report* 1992, 9.)

5. The Salinas administration also allowed private sector firms to bid for service contracts for PEMEX drilling operations, thereby directly challenging the past practice of awarding these and other service contracts to companies owned by the PEMEX union. In addition, many PEMEX-owned businesses in the area of exploration and production, employing approximately 15,000 workers, are slated for privatization. (For further details, see OECD 1992, 93).

6. The divergence in the figures for petroleum is due in part to the pending privatization of several peripheral businesses affiliated with PEMEX's production and exploration divisions. In the petroleum industry, tens of thousands of workers were laid off during 1991 and 1992. The precise number is not known: PEMEX officials claim that 20,000 workers were fired, but labor leaders claim that the figure is as high as 135,000 because the government's figures do not take into account the pending privatization of several of PEMEX's non-priority firms. It is highly probable that ultimately the employment loss will be closer to the higher estimate because the Zedillo administration is under intense pressure to raise needed revenue to meet the pressing economic and social demands generated by the

1994 crisis (*Latin American Economy and Business* 1992d, 4-5; Latin American Newsletters 1992, 4).

7. Elizondo's observations are indirectly confirmed by a recent study released by the Economic Research Institute of the National Autonomous University, which reports that 25 families control 55 percent of the privatized bank assets" (*Mexico Business Monthly* 1994b, 2).

8. See Elizondo 1993, 16-20. For an excellent, comprehensive discussion of how the growing international financial integration of the Mexican economy has affected the degree of economic concentration and, thus, the influence and power of the grupos, see Maxfield 1990, 97-116 and 142-162.

9. "Factoring" refers to the practice by exporting firms of selling the accounts receivable to a third party known as the "factor." The latter is responsible for collecting payments from the buyer. A factor usually buys the accounts receivable at a discount and receives a flat processing fee.

10. A case in point is the role played by NAFINSA (the country's largest industrial development bank), which was instrumental in providing necessary risk capital, financial and technical assistance, and official representation abroad for private investors in the steel, paper, mining, electricity, truck and bus, and sugar industries. This was particularly true during the *Mexicanization* process initiated by the administration of López Mateos (1958-1964) . It should also be pointed out that the actions of the Mexican state are by no means unique: Other developing and developed nations have had to intervene and suspend the actions of "supply and demand" when the social costs were perceived to be too great (for example, the U.S. bailout of Lockheed, Chrysler, and Continental Bank of Illinois at taxpayer expense). For further details, see Ramírez 1986 and Solís 1981.

11. An excellent discussion of the pros and cons of privatization is found in Prager 1992, 301-322.

References

Baer, Werner, and Melissa H. Birch. 1991. *Privatization and the Changing Role of the State in Latin America*. Faculty Working Paper 92-0123 (April). University of Florida, Gainesville, Florida: Bureau of Economic and Business Research.

Banco de México. 1989. *Informe Anual*. Mexico, D.F.

Bazdresch, Carlos, and Santiago Levy. 1991. "Populism and Economic Policy in Mexico, 1970-82." In *The Macroeconomics of Populism in Latin America*, eds. Rudiger Dornbusch and Sebastián Edwards. Chicago: The University of Chicago Press.

Business International Corporation (BIC). 1990. "Mexico: Privatization, Deregulation and Liberalization." In *Privatization in Latin America*. New York: Business International Corporation.

Business Latin America. 1992. "Mexico's New Mining Law Aims To Lure Investors." May 25.

Calderón, Francisco. 1988. "La inversión privada en México, 1970-1987." Centro de Investigación y Docencia Económica (*CIDE): Documentos de Investigación, División de Economía* (September): 1-39.

Calva, José L. 1995. "El nudo macroeconómico de México: La pesada herencia de Ernesto Zedillo." *Problemas del Desarrollo* 26, special edition (January-March): 92.

Cárdenas, Enrique. 1990. "Contemporary Economic Problems in Historical Perspective." In *Mexico's Search for a New Development Strategy*, eds. Dwight S. Brothers and Adele E. Wick. Boulder, Colo.: Westview Press.

Cardoso, Eliana. 1993. "Private Investment in Latin America." *Economic Development and Cultural Change* 41 (July): 833-848.

Carr, Barry. 1986. "The Mexican Left, the Popular Movements, and the Politics of Austerity, 1982-85." In *The Mexican Left, the Popular Movements, and the Politics of Austerity*, eds. Barry Carr and Ricardo A. Montoya. La Jolla, Calif.: Center for U.S.-Mexican Studies, University of California, San Diego.

Casar, María Amparo, and Wilson Peres. 1988. *El estado empresario en México*. Mexico, D.F.: Siglo XXI.

Cornelius, Wayne A. 1986. *The Political Economy of Mexico Under de la Madrid: The Crisis Deepens, 1985-1986*. La Jolla, Calif.: Center for U.S.-Mexican Studies, University of California, San Diego.

Cypher, James A. 1990. *State and Capital in Mexico*. Boulder, Colo.: Westview Press.

Dresser, Denise. 1991. *Neopopulist Solutions to Neoliberal Problems*. La Jolla, Calif.: Center for U.S.-Mexican Studies, University of California, San Diego.

Economic Commission for Latin America and the Caribbean (ECLAC). Various reports, 1991-1994. *Economic Panorama of Latin America*. Santiago, Chile: United Nations.

Economic Commission for Latin America and the Caribbean (ECLAC). 1996. *Statistical Yearbook for Latin America and the Caribbean*. 1995 edition. Santiago, Chile: UN/ ECLAC.

Edwards, Jack K., and Werner Baer. 1993. "The State and the Private Sector in Latin America." *The Quarterly Review of Economics and Finance* 33 (special issue): 9-20.

Elizondo, Carlos. 1993. "The Making of a New Alliance: The Privatization of the Banks in Mexico." *CIDE, Documentos de Trabajo 5*. Mexico, D.F.: Centro de Investigación y Docencia Económica.

Federal Reserve Bank of Dallas. 1995. *The Southwest Economy* 2:7. Dallas: Federal Reserve Bank of Dallas.

Ferrer, Oscar H. 1991. "The Political Economy of Privatization in Mexico." In *Privatization of Public Enterprises in Latin America*, ed. William Glade. San Francisco: ICS Press.

Grinspun, Ricardo, and Maxwell A. Cameron. 1993. *The Political Economy of NAFTA*. New York: St. Martin's Press.

Hanson, Gordon H. 1994. "Antitrust in Post-Privatization Latin America: An Analysis of the Mexican Airlines Industry." *The Quarterly Review of Economics and Finance* 34 (Summer): 190-216.

Inter-American Development Bank (IDB). 1990. *Economic and Social Progress in Latin America 1990, Report*. Washington, D.C.: The Johns Hopkins University Press.

Inter-American Development Bank (IDB). Various reports, 1989-1994. *Economic and Social Progress in Latin America*. Washington, D.C.: The Johns Hopkins University Press.

Instituto Nacional de Estadísticas, Geografía e Informática (INEGI). 1992a. *Central Bureau of Statistics*. Mexico, D.F.: INEGI.

Instituto Nacional de Estadísticas, Geografía e Informática (INEGI). 1992b. *Encuesta nacional de ingresos y gastos de hogares*. Mexico, D.F.: INEGI.

Latin American Economy and Business. 1992a. "The Decisive Year." January.

Latin American Economy and Business. 1992b. "Aspe's Big Gamble." February.

Latin American Economy and Business. 1992c. "Mexico's Vulnerable Stock Market." August.

Latin American Economy and Business. 1992d. "Some Signs of Strain." September.

Latin American Economy and Business. 1992e. "The Glitter Begins to Fade." October.

Latin American Economy and Business. 1994a. "Business Is Split Over Economic Policy." March.

Latin American Economy and Business. 1994b. "From Bad to Worse." May.

Latin American Economy and Business Quarterly Update. 1994. "Mexico," no. 1 (March): 4.

Latin American Newsletters. 1992. "Ira Sindical en Vísperas de NAFTA." *Informe Latinoamericano*. August 13.

Latin American Weekly Report. 1992. August 27.

Lustig, Nora. 1992. *Mexico: The Remaking of an Economy*. Washington, D.C.: The Brookings Institution.

MacEwan, Arthur. 1990. *Debt and Disorder*. New York: Monthly Review Press.

Machado, J., and Wilson Peres. 1986. "Evaluación de la racionalización de la empresa privada." *Empresa pública: Problemas y desarrollo* 1 (1): 36-55.

Martínez, Ifigenia. 1995. "Desarrollo sustentable sectorial y regional. Un proyecto alternativo." *Problemas del Desarrollo* 26 (special edition): 137-169.

Maxfield, Sylvia. 1990. *Governing Capital*. Ithaca, N.Y.: Cornell University Press.

McComb, Robert P., William C. Gruben, and John H. Welch. 1994. "Privatization and Performance in the Mexican Financial Services Industry." *Quarterly Review of Economics and Finance* 34 (special issue): 217-236.

Mexico Business Monthly. 1991a. "Banking and Finance" 1 (9).

Mexico Business Monthly. 1991b. "Commerce, Services" 1 (11).

Mexico Business Monthly. 1992a. "Banking and Finance" 2 (2): 5-6.

Mexico Business Monthly. 1992b. "Overview" 2 (7).

Mexico Business Monthly. 1993. "Banking and Finance" 3 (3).

Mexico Business Monthly. 1994a. "Agribusiness, Fishing" 4 (4): 5-6.

Mexico Business Monthly. 1994b. "Overview" 4 (5): 1-2

Mexico and NAFTA Report. 1993. "Grisby" (September 23).

Miller, Robert. R,. and Mariusz A. Sumlinski. 1994. *Trends in Private Investment in Developing Countries*. Working Paper No. 20, International Finance Corporation. Washington, D.C.: World Bank.

Murguía, Valdemar de. 1986. *Capital Flight and Economic Crisis*. La Jolla, Calif.: Center for U.S.-Mexican Studies, University of California, San Diego.

Noguera, Celso G., and Enrique Q. López. 1987. "Financial Relations and Economic Power in Mexico." In *Government and Private Sector in Contemporary Mexico*. La Jolla, Calif.: Center for U.S.-Mexican Studies, University of California, San Diego.

Organization for Economic Cooperation and Development (OECD). 1992. *OECD Economic Surveys: Mexico*. Paris, France: OECD Publications.

Pazos, Luis. 1993. *El final de Salinas*. Mexico, D.F.: Editorial Diana.

Pazos, Luis. 1995. *Devaluación*. Mexico, D.F.: Editorial Diana.

Prager, Jonas. 1992. "Is Privatization a Panacea for LDCs? Market Failure versus Public Sector Failure." *The Journal of Developing Areas* 26 (3): 301-322.

Ramírez, Miguel D. 1986. *Development Banking in Mexico: The Case of Nacional Financiera, S.A.* New York: Praeger Publishers.

Ramírez, Miguel D. 1994. "Public and Private Investment in Mexico, 1950-1990: An Empirical Analysis." *Southern Economic Journal* 61 (1): 1-17.

Romero, Jaime B. 1991. "El neoliberalismo económico: ¿Un grave retroceso histórico para México?" *Problemas del Desarrollo* 22 (84): 45-62.

Sánchez, Manuel. 1993. "The Privatization Process in Mexico: Five Case Studies." In *Privatization in Latin America*, eds. Manuel Sánchez and Rossana Corona. Washington, D.C.: Inter-American Development Bank.

Sánchez, Manuel, and Rossana Corona, eds. 1993. *Privatization in Latin America*. Washington, D.C.: Inter-American Development Bank.

Solís, Leopoldo. 1981. *La realidad económica mexicana: Retrovisión y perspectivas*. Mexico, D.F.: Siglo XXI.

Sweezy, Paul M. 1970. *The Theory of Capitalist Development*. New York: Monthly Review Press.

Villarreal, René. 1988. *Mitos y realidades de la empresa pública: ¿Racionalización o privatización?* Mexico, D.F.: Editorial Diana.

World Bank. 1994. *World Development Report 1994*. New York: Oxford University Press.

CHAPTER 4

The Argentine Privatization Process and Its Aftermath: Some Preliminary Conclusions

SEBASTIÁN GALIANI AND DIEGO PETRECOLLA

Since the beginning of the 1980s, the world has undergone a major shift in thinking about the appropriate economic role of the state. Privatization of state-owned enterprises (SOEs) has been at the core of this change ever since Britain and France initiated privatization planning. Privatization of government-owned enterprises has taken place across an enormous spectrum of economic sectors and almost the world over, including developing countries such as Argentina. Although the extent, form, and pace of change have varied from country to country,[1] the general trend has been similar: the state gradually has withdrawn from directly producing goods and services.

The privatization debate addresses not only the level of state intervention in the economy, but also whether production should be public or private. Different opinions exist about the relative costs of public and private production. The notion that public ownership is inherently less efficient than private ownership is rooted in the literature on the economics of property rights. Recently, however, the body of literature on industrial organization and contract theory has emphasized both the role of market structure and the institutional environment in which a firm operates as factors influencing efficiency.

In Latin America, widespread agreement exists on the need to integrate the region's economies into world markets. The pursuit of import substitution beyond its successful early stages and the failure to switch to a policy of outward-oriented growth are now recognized as a mistake. The political consensus on the advantages of a mixed economy has been replaced by the goals of reducing state regulation and intervention and promoting the widespread participation of foreign capital.[2]

Although the consensus on a wide set of economic policies is intrinsically limited by differences in normative values, the region's long-term crisis has substantially reduced policymakers' freedom in the design of economic policy. Consequently, the unusual convergence on economic policy reached in the region has been historically biased. In the future, the state's role in the economy will no longer exhibit its post-war characteristics; however, this must not imply a weakening of the state. Instead, the state must be strengthened as it gradually adapts to the role of regulator from that of producer.

SOEs IN ARGENTINA'S ECONOMY: A BRIEF OVERVIEW

In this chapter, we focus on the privatization process of Argentine SOEs. As Jack K. Edwards and Werner Baer (1993) have pointed out, the current privatization process in Latin America has taken a 360-degree turnabout. In the early decades of the twentieth century, the private sector, mainly foreign capital, played a dominant role in Argentina's extractive industries and public utilities. Since then, SOEs have occupied a predominant role in the provision of public services (water supply, communications, electricity, gas, and transportation) and in the exploitation of natural resources (coal, gas, and oil).

As is true with all government-run entities, public enterprises are vulnerable to politics. SOEs have been used as tools to rectify static market failures. Public finance theory views state enterprises as the cure to monopolies and externalities caused by private firms. State enterprises are seen also as tools to modify the structure of payoffs within the economy. In Argentina, as in the rest of Latin America, this modification is achieved through the appropriation of natural resource rents and through subsidies to consumers and certain industrial sectors.[3] Without neglecting the importance of these factors, this chapter emphasizes the decisive influence of macroeconomic considerations in the development, performance, and privatization of Argentina's state enterprises.

Another explanation for the active presence of SOEs in Latin American economies centers on the need to correct the shortcomings of capital markets. This problem can be traced to underdeveloped capital markets and overly risk-averse investors whose myopia prevents them from providing adequate financing for important sectors of the economy. Such an extreme level of risk aversion often is due to the economic and sociopolitical conditions under which investment takes place.

During the first stage of import-substitution industrialization (ISI), in comparison to private industries, public utilities offered not only positive externalities but also strategic complementarities.[4] Consequently, they played a coordinating role in a context where the dynamic market failures mentioned above exacerbated coordination problems. Thus, state enterprises were considered strategic industries for economic development. According to Alexander Gerschenkron (1962), during this period, public investment crowded out private investment. SOEs, however, gradually lost their capacity to influence the path of economic growth and finally became an obstacle to it. The debt crisis of the 1980s contributed significantly to a decline in the dynamism and efficiency of public sector firms,[5] but their deterioration was well under way before that. Beginning in the 1970s, public utility prices fell below the costs of the state firms' factors of production (Gerchunoff and Cánovas 1994). Although significant financially from the point of view of the firms, this drop merely reflected a complex process that resulted in a profound, practically irreversible deterioration of SOE microeconomic efficiency. On the one hand, the decrease was the result of changes in distributive goals. On the other hand, the drop reflected the use of state enterprises as tools of short-run macroeconomic policy. Periodically during the 1980s and 1990s, the government used SOEs to control inflation by allowing the public enterprises' prices to lag behind increases in generalized price levels. As Edwards and Baer (1993) noted, to the extent that state enterprises became less like firms and more like short-run macroeconomic policy tools, the opportunities for economic and political mismanagement increased.

Public utility prices in Argentina have been characterized by 1) a significant gap between the prices charged to residential consumers and those charged to producer firms; 2) a rate level that did not cover SOE costs; 3) an excessively progressive indexation, especially in periods in which residential consumers were favored at the expense of the business sector[6]; and 4) the existence of different specific subsidies, determined by the activity, sector, or region.

The Argentine government and SOE management, suppliers, and unions increasingly urged firms to behave on behalf of their own interests. Although the government could bail enterprises out of financial difficulties, the costs were passed on to society at large. Doing so increased the private sector's costs and reduced the general efficiency of the economy. Thus, as Argentina's economic situation worsened, SOEs were increasingly discredited.

In the early 1980s, the debt crisis and acceleration of inflation substantially worsened the fiscal problem, which had become structural in nature.[7] During that decade, the economy experienced unusually high inflation. The change in contract network, which took place as an endogenous answer to inflation's wealth corrosion, was not enough to moderate the virulent increase in prices, and the economic disturbance produced by high inflation undermined the performance of the public sector, including state enterprises. Wide fluctuations in real wages and abrupt rationalizations caused many good employees to leave public service and demoralized those who stayed. The fiscal crisis finally forced the government to reduce the financing of state enterprises. Public enterprise investment was a prime target for budget cuts. Without investments, the quality of goods and services and the productive capacity of firms quickly deteriorated, eroding the positive effects of other policies undertaken to improve the health of the SOEs. Privatization was a means to bypass financial constraints by turning ownership over to operators better able than the state to provide resources for investment. In cases such as telecommunications, where technological change was unprecedented, this move was essential.

Crises in public finance appear as a systemic phenomenon in economies suffering hyperinflation. Financing public sector deficits lies at the very heart of the problem (Heymann and Leijonhufvud 1995). By the late 1980s, Argentina's public finances had been seriously weakened, and revenues could not easily be augmented. The tax system, lacking a clear design, could not collect broad-based taxes. In place of a systematic budget process, distributive pressures determined public expenditure in an inconsistent manner. Government departments, state enterprises, and other organizations operated under soft-budget constraints,[8] a frequent feature in Argentina (Kornai 1986). Moreover, the market for public bonds did not exist, and the demand for money was reduced to its minimum (Heymann and Navajas 1989).

The overall public sector deficit reached an average of approximately 9 percent of gross domestic product (GDP) during the 1980s. By the end of the decade, the budget deficit problem was extreme, due to the lack of financing. In 1989 and 1990, Argentina suffered rapid inflation, atypical even by the country's own standards (Heymann 1991). In both episodes, the inflation rate moved from a single-digit monthly rate to well above 50 percent within a matter of weeks. This hyperinflation could not be sustained. The state itself was threatened. "When a society has reached this extreme, the alternatives become stark and simple: Stabilize or else" (Heymann and Leijonhufvud 1995). Consequently, the government had to gain control over its fiscal policies. SOE privatization was a key instrument in the stabilization program launched by the administration of Carlos Menem, which took power in mid-1989. However, even if the government argued in favor of reducing its fiscal deficits and its foreign debt by selling state enterprises, the privatization program was regarded as a major element in the structural reform of the economy. Privatization of state enterprises was supposed to deliver significant efficiency gains that would increase social well-being.

This chapter analyzes privatization as a fiscal tool and the interplay between privatization and stabilization in Argentina. Also examined are the issue of efficiency and regulation related to the program's implementation and the main macroeconomic impacts of privatization.

PRIVATIZATION AND EFFICIENCY

Improved efficiency is usually held to be the prime motivation for privatization. Consequently, one would like to answer the following questions for each privatized firm: Is the privatized firm's efficiency better than the performance of its SOE predecessor? If so, is this due to a change of ownership or to a change of the institutional or competitive environment in which the industry is situated? The answer to these questions addresses the larger issue facing both developed and developing nations: Is social welfare better promoted by public or private ownership?

In general, it is argued that the ownership rights arrangement of a firm influences the structure of incentives for management, changing both managerial behavior and the firm's achievements. By privatizing, a government could enhance the efficiency of a poorly performing SOE. Contract theory notes, however, that ownership structure matters only if complete contracts cannot be written (Grossman and Hart 1986).[9] In such a scenario, public and private ownership imply that owners have different goals, consequently, the different levels of performance, as well as different levels of acquisition of information about the firm by outsiders (Laffont and Tirole 1993).

Nonetheless, the simplest economic transactions can be so complex that it is practically impossible to list the entire range of outcomes and contingencies. Privatization and the circumstances under which it is an appropriate instrument to improve efficiency are still relevant issues of the policy agenda.

A firm's behavior is influenced by more than just ownership structure; the competitive structure and regulatory framework in which it operates also affect performance. Moreover, the impact on the company of any one of these three factors is contingent upon the other two (Vickers and Yarrow 1988).

This complex relationship of regulatory framework, competition, and ownership is vitally important because the government frequently retains some rights of control over the firm in the form of regulation, necessary due to the existence of market failures. When firms are privatized and regulated, the results obtained in terms of efficiency and social welfare depend upon the nature of the relationship between the firm and the government (Vickers and Yarrow 1991). Even if one assumes that the management in a privatized firm will reach static internal efficiency — independent of regulatory framework and market structure — this is not sufficient to assert that privatization will generate welfare gains for society. The privatized firm will still have incentives to capture part of the consumer surplus through the pricing structure of the services it sells. In short, the trade-off for the less socially desirable character of private objectives is the possibility that the private sector will pursue its business objectives with greater technical and dynamic efficiency. This resulting trade-off is commonly referred to as "the fundamental trade-off of privatization" by Leroy Jones et al. (1990). The methodology used in many empirical studies that comparatively evaluate the differences in efficiency between private and public firms neglects this trade-off, which leads to a bias in favor of private ownership. This methodology compares profitability, factor productivity, and unit costs instead of estimating the sum of consumer and producer surpluses.[10] "Given some degree of market power, it might be expected that private firms will be more profitable, but this has no direct bearing on the question of economic efficiency" (Vickers and Yarrow 1988).

When evaluating ownership structures in different institutional settings, some settings may be more important than others. Since incentives are not exogenous to the competitive structure and regulatory framework in which a firm operates, theorizing about the relative efficiency of public versus private ownership must prove inconclusive. Moreover, the empirical literature is also indecisive (see, among others, Atkinson and Halvorsen 1986; Boardman and Vining 1989; and Bös 1992).

Rather than assume that a government will play a benevolent role, one must also consider the likelihood that it has its own political goals. These could include, for example, employment for low-skilled workers, locating privatized companies in economically inefficient places, underpricing output, or a specific wage structure. Additionally, it is sometimes argued that SOEs are inefficient because politicians use them as tools to achieve their political objectives (see, inter alia, Boycko et al. 1992). In this analysis, privatization changes the terms of trade in the bargaining between politicians and managers, making it more expensive for politicians to buy the desired "inefficient" outcome. However, the inefficiency of this outcome is exogenously assumed. For example, what argument can be offered against employing low-skilled workers who would otherwise face structural difficulties in getting jobs? What one must evaluate, instead, is whether hiring workers in SOEs is the most efficient way to achieve the goal of higher employment. A government can also pursue these types of goals for electoral reasons. Information asymmetries imply that if the costs imposed on the rest of society are reasonable, politicians may not derive electoral benefits from improvements in SOE economic efficiency. Therefore, the question for the government remains: Why privatize, especially if the government cannot achieve political gains?

If it is assumed that a government maximizes "social welfare," then the ideal objective of an SOE manager is to maximize a linear combination of consumer and producer surplus. The question regarding reasons for privatization can be answered partially as follows: The gain in welfare from privatization can be evaluated as the present value of the change in consumer surplus plus the present value of the change in company profits, valued at the true cost of goods and services after the privatization has taken place. This assumes that the government obtains the maximum price the buyer is willing to pay (Jones et al. 1990). If the gain were positive, the government would want to privatize the firm.

Even if the government takes a political approach and does not maximize social welfare, the government still may have strong incentives to privatize. For example, privatization can take place when distortions, created elsewhere in the economy but related to financial transfers to the firm, are significant[11] and are captured by the government's objective function (welfare maximization). Thus, the objective function of the policymaker accounts for efficiency, financing, and the attainment for specific social goals. The incentives to privatize will become stronger if the privatized firm can accomplish internal efficiency gains at minimal cost to social welfare during periods of economic decline.

THE ARGENTINE PRIVATIZATION PROCESS

Governments that have enjoyed the luxury of planning their privatization programs usually pursue some or all of the following objectives: 1) improvement of efficiency, 2) enhanced competition, 3) wider share ownership, and 4) greater accountability (Button and Weyman-Jones 1994). This was not the case for Argentina, where the privatization program was basically an instrument of the government's stabilization policy.[12]

Privatization as an Instrument for Stabilization

Argentina's economic and institutional crisis at the end of the 1980s forced the administration of Carlos Saúl Menem in 1989 to concentrate on the difficult task of stabilizing the economy.[13] The hyperinflation of 1989 was both an asset and a liability for the new administration, because popular opinion heavily favored stabilization, but failure to achieve it would erode the government's legitimacy. The task required more than just fiscal and monetary measures.[14] It also required a radical change, credible over time, which would lessen current and future fiscal deficits. The market for public bonds reflected the uncertainty over the ongoing fiscal deficit.[15] Private agents' expectations influence public debt values, and those expectations are a function of the fiscal regime in which those agents operate, especially the current net value of the revenue flows that are backing the public debt. To modify those expectations, a necessary condition for stabilization, the administration was forced to introduce profound modifications in tax collection, expenditures, and transfers.

Nevertheless, building an effective tax system is a long-term project. Besides, an effective tax system allows for the possibility of considerable redistribution. Groups that fear an increase in their tax burden can block this type of measure (Heymann et al. 1988). Due to its incentives, the government, seeking to improve the tax system, needed to signal that tax policy would not favor redistribution toward workers and small businesses.[16] At the same time, it would have been very difficult for the government to have recovered the credibility of its fiscal solvency by a mere reduction of current expenditures. This measure would have reduced its financial needs, but it would not have restored the government's access to credit markets. Indeed, government expenditures in hyperinflationary economies are not likely to be large, and, in Argentina in 1989, spending as a portion of GDP was 7 percent lower than at the peak of the decade. The overall public deficit reached 4.8 percent of GDP in 1989. Although this deficit was major, it was well below the average for the decade.

Argentina's massive privatization program was an important instrument of the new administration's stabilization program. Four stages can be distinguished in the process, depending on the specific relationship between stabilization and privatization at any particular moment. During the first stages, the priority was placed conspicuously on raising revenues. Beginning in the third stage, when the expectation of a predictable, low inflation rate had been established, financial goals were relegated to second place. The fourth stage was marked by a return to the idea of placing financial goals first.

Privatization could reinforce the government's credibility if it were interpreted as a component of an invariant, restrictive fiscal policy. By the time the Menem administration took over, the general macroeconomic and microeconomic circumstances provided clear incentives to privatize. Therefore, by massively privatizing state enterprises, the government moved toward solvency, reducing current and future deficits by eliminating high SOE deficits (overall deficits had reached an average of approximately 4 percent of GDP during the 1980s). Through debt-equity swaps, the government reduced its debt service and, consequently, also improved its balance sheet.

To reduce a country's debt by undertaking privatization, a government must capture in the selling price of the companies either the expected internal and dynamic efficiency gains or part of the economic rent that accrues to a firm with market power. In either case, much depends on the regulatory framework. By substantially increasing the real price of the goods produced by the privatized firms and by selling these firms through the debt-equity mechanism, the Argentine government found an instrument of macroeconomic policy. Privatization could be substituted for tax reform or reductions in government spending as the policy initiative required to balance the federal budget. Additionally, the government was responsible for a large external debt. In mid-1988, Argentina declared a moratorium on its foreign debt payments. Stabilization requires a permanent arrangement between a government and its creditors. The former needs to define clearly which commitments it will honor and what relief it will obtain. The latter, however, is not likely to renegotiate debts until it is certain that a serious disinflation program has been implemented (Heymann and Leijonhufvud 1995). The debt-equity swaps produced during privatization in Argentina helped to stabilize the country not only directly but also indirectly, by allowing the country to participate in the Brady Plan debt rescheduling.[17]

Privatization as an Instrument for Raising Revenues

Some economists also argue that revenue-raising is a prime motive for privatization, depending on the circumstances of a particular country and the constraints it faces in the bond market. For example, the British government in the early 1980s voluntarily limited its debt financing to make its anti-inflationary policy more credible (Vickers and Yarrow 1988). Therefore, privatization revenues helped the government to achieve this target. The Argentine government, however, was completely restricted in its access to the credit market. Consequently, privatization also relaxed the government's short-run cash constraint.

When a government seeks revenue targets through privatization, it will most likely restrict competition within the market, thereby causing a deterioration of allocative efficiency. If not, the government will allow the enterprise to appropriate part of the consumer surplus.[18] However, this policy cannot last in the long term.

Nicolás Gadano and Sebastián Galiani (1994) and Sebastián Galiani and Diego Petrecolla (1995) have analyzed the eventual temporal inconsistency of the government's utilization of privatization as a fiscal tool, assuming that the government's main target is to obtain revenues by selling assets. These authors present a model that concentrates exclusively on the trade-off the government faces between the price obtained by selling the enterprise and the cost of operating the SOE. This trade-off is measured in terms of consumer-surplus losses due to the regulatory framework the government establishes. The government, facing substantial fiscal stringency and restricted in its capacity to use alternative tools, transfers a public enterprise to the private sector to obtain revenues. Usually, when privatization takes place, the government establishes, according to its objective function, an optimal regulatory framework for the entire planning horizon. This allows part of the consumer surplus to be appropriated by the enterprise, generating an increased flow of benefits. However, if the government faces an incentive constraint, its first, best policy is not achievable. During the first stage of the Argentine privatization process, in which the authorities assigned priority to price as the main factor in the sale of an SOE, the government probably faced an incentive constraint, and, compelled to stabilize, it sped up and widened the program.

In addition, Argentine firms had to be sold before stabilization occurred, that is, in a context of extreme uncertainty. This was manifested in the shortening of decision horizons. Thus, to be able to sell SOEs, especially those that needed significant levels of new capital, the Argentine government had to guarantee the profitability of those firms undergoing privatization. This explains the government's inability to follow an ideal privatization program "operations manual." Authorities, in order to have valuable assets to transfer to the private sector, had to reduce the economic uncertainty drastically; only then were they able to transfer firms that were highly profitable in the short run. Both motives kept the government from following an ideal sequence, and that failure substantially reduced the benefits of privatization for the whole society. This failure also forced the government to increase the speed and extent of the privatization program, and it reinforced the need to regularize access to capital markets.[19]

Argentina's Rapid and Extensive Privatization

Moreover, the government used the speed and extent of the privatization program to signal a general orientation toward the reduction of state intervention as well as its intention to launch a program of state reform as part of the stabilization plan. The need to send such a signal lost importance as these measures gradually reduced the uncertainty over the future direction of the government's economic policies.

Thus, a remarkable characteristic of the Argentine privatization process was its extent and speed. The program privatized competitive firms as well as monopolies, both natural ones and those in which competition could exist but was legally restricted. It also utilized the mechanism of contracting out the provision of public goods. Overall, the privatization of utilities and natural resources has been of great significance.[20] The Argentine privatization agenda was one of the speediest and most ambitious of the programs carried out by countries that accomplished structural reform goals.[21] Unlike other national privatization experiences and in spite of what had been extensively recommended, Argentina's program focused from the beginning on the transfer of public utilities, often natural monopolies, instead of selling firms in industries where there was potential for competition.

Outcomes: Pros and Cons

Especially during the first stage, the program did not prepare firms to reestablish productive capacity. On the contrary, the performance of SOEs slated for privatization worsened. To restructure these enterprises prior to sale, the government needed time, financing, and credibility — all of which it lacked. Additionally, the grave deterioration of SOEs implied that the government was not the best qualified actor to improve firm performance. To start with, a change in management and management policies was required, as well as the designing of a highly effective incentive system. Without these, an investment project that could improve the profits of the firm could, in fact, reduce them. The government's primary pre-privatization restructuring efforts consisted of a deep rationalization of both labor and management. Prior to privatization, the SOEs had lacked an ethos of productivity. Due to the government's timetable, the principal goal was simply to privatize them. Only the national oil company (Yacimientos Petrolíferos Fiscales — YPF), which was privatized by the end of 1993 after fiscal goals were relegated to second place, was restructured prior to being sold.[22]

During the privatization process, the state did not retain equity in the firm, and the sale of shares on capital markets was marginal. The private consortiums that won the bids received at least 51 percent of the firms' stock, reducing the possibility of a takeover. The absence of capital-market monitoring has been identified as a cost of public ownership. The absence of financial takeovers supports this argument. Since public enterprises are not subject to takeovers, their managers are less concerned about losing their jobs.[23] In contrast, domestic economic groups substantially increased their economic and political power due to the concentration of property resulting from the privatization process.

Especially when privatization changes the distribution of power within a society, the political obstacles to the sale of large SOEs tend to be formidable. In a democratic system, approving the needed legislation can take a long time and usually involves compromises that weaken the government's position. Powerful labor unions and other interest groups often resist privatization. Opposition increases if the firm is sold to foreign investors.

In Argentina, however, privatization was widely supported, reaching a high point of popularity in 1989 with approval ratings of 75 percent. The mid-1989 hyperinflation episode enabled the government to obtain significant support from Congress for a privatization agenda that included extensive state reforms.[24] Groups, including domestic businesses, that were interested in controlling the activities being turned over to the private sector strongly backed the government. International institutions and the international financial community, seeking to swap their shares of the Argentine debt for profitable enterprises, also backed the structural reform program. Surprisingly, the government did not encounter any significant resistance from the unions, and union leaders even participated actively in the process.

This reflects not only the near collapse of SOEs by this point, but also a form of takeover of state enterprises by a powerful coalition of national holding companies, international financial investors, and some foreign operators of public services. The privatization process was greatly affected by the coalition. Before the privatization program took place, the administration was able to pass a law whereby foreign investment was granted equal status with domestic investment. The move was essential to the government's sales strategy, and it led to substantial foreign investment flows associated with privatization. In addition to union leaders' interest in participating directly in certain privatizations, their membership in the political party holding the presidency debilitated them strategically because they could not threaten the government with strikes. Consequently, the government unilaterally controlled whether to compromise over policy reforms (Palermo and Torre 1992).

As emphasized above, the outcome of privatization in terms of "well-being" depends crucially on the design of the regulatory environment. Furthermore, the strategy used to value the assets to be privatized focused on the creation of quasi-rents, where before there had been only financial losses. In order to achieve this goal, the authorities created regulatory environments that allowed the survival of legal monopolies, even in activities in which this would have been controversial, such as long-distance and international telecommunications and commercial air cargo services (Petrecolla et al. 1993). The preservation of a monopolistic environment was a specific characteristic of the Argentine privatization process. Even in cases for which economies of scope favored the restriction of competition, or in the privatization of natural monopolies, the allocative efficiency criteria were blocked. Another conspicuous feature of the privatization process was the delay in the creation of regulatory agencies, staffed by specialized personnel capable of controlling the market power of the new companies and promoting competition (Gerchunoff and Cánovas 1994).

The pricing policy of the firms to be privatized was substantially modified. Preceding a transfer, the authorities adjusted prices to the point that the SOEs became profitable. These adjustments were deepest during the first stage,[25] as the goal at that point was to maximize fiscal revenues through the selling price of the firms. However, despite the profits realized through the adopted pricing policy, the government, facing an incentive constraint, collected revenues substantially lower than under its first best revenues policy.

Thus, during the first stage, and between the approval of the decree authorizing the sale of ENTel, the state telecommunications utility, and the transfer of the company, telephone rates increased almost 720 percent; the exchange rate, 235 percent; and the wholesale price index, 450 percent. When the national airline company, Aerolíneas Argentinas, was privatized, in addition to a general increase in its prices, the enterprise substantially changed relative prices, establishing cross-subsidization of domestic fares to benefit international fares. However, during the third stage of the privatization program, after the electricity privatization, prices decreased across all of the sector's consumption categories. Major consumers, in particular, benefited from this decrease. Following the sale of the national gas company, however, residential consumer rates were raised substantially above the increase in the consumer price index (CPI), while, for industrial consumers, prices increased more than the wholesale price index. For example, the price of natural gas for residential consumption grew 120 percent, twice the increase in the CPI between 1991 and 1994.

Together with the increase in average price levels in privatized firms, changes in the rate structure of many public services have been observed. From one perspective, this policy can be understood as a search for a rate structure guided by efficiency criteria, arising in an environment that assigns greater importance to financial than distributive goals. However, as Fernando Navajas (1992) pointed out, privatization of public enterprises has changed the incentives and composition of the rate structure for different types of consumers. This adds another dimension to the determination of the rate structure. In this sense, the rate structure that penalizes residential consumers and favors industrial consumers seems to reflect a new political equilibrium.

In addition to SOE pricing policy, regulatory considerations exist. Thus, the bidding documents and the contracts for the transfer of ENTel stipulated that the purchasing firms have exclusive permission to provide basic telephone services, but they are also authorized to provide other services such as telex, wireless telephony, and data transmission, under a competitive regime with other suppliers. The coexistence of monopolistic and competitive segments raises the possibility of predation of the competitive services by the enterprises that hold a monopolistic position in certain activities. Technological innovation and the prospect of lifting regulatory barriers to entry are increasingly exposing some portions of the local call-exchanges to competition. However, in Argentina, legal barriers protect the licensed market power position, substantially limiting regulatory action.

In 1991, the government changed the structure of the electricity system when the market was deregulated — a first step in the vertical disintegration of the electric sector. With the new regulation, different enterprises are specializing in each of the three phases of the activity. In the electricity sector, producers compete to sell their product to distributors and large producers. In this context, a decentralized mechanism regulates commercial relations between producers and distributors, while the state regulates transport rates and sales by distributors to consumers (Gerchunoff and Cánovas 1994). Due to the regulatory framework established in the privatization bidding contracts, the electric sector is a "model" case for the Argentine privatization process; however, it is not without its shortcomings. The regulation and functioning of the Argentine electric industry presents many challenges, especially related to consumer confidence, discriminatory practices, environmental regulation, and so forth (Abdala 1994). When the electricity sector was privatized, privatization of YPF and in the steel sector occurred in a regulatory environment that allowed the privatized firms to exert monopolistic power. In these cases, mixing trade opening and privatization did not work (Gerchunoff and Cánovas 1994; Gerchunoff et al. 1994).

The Argentine privatization program had an important direct effect on investment. By setting quantitative and qualitative targets for the improvement of transferred services, the government often demanded substantial investment by the new owners. According to Alberto Petrecolla et al. (1993), investment in gas, telephones, electricity, railroads, subways, highways, ports, and water were predicted initially to jump, to be followed by a sharp decline between 1992 and 2000. Additionally, Petrecolla and his coauthors expected that the productivity of private investment in these sectors would be notably greater than public enterprises exhibited during the 1980s.

Thus, the value of investments in telecommunications, made with the goal of increasing the number of customers and improving the quality of service, is greater than the price paid for the firms. The licensed purchasing firms had more than reached the targets imposed in the bidding contracts by 1995. Electricity generation and gas transportation firms, though smaller in scale, also invested in order to improve the availability of their services, but these investments had not reached the targets established in their contracts (Chudnovsky et al. 1995).

In the mid-1990s, a new order of investment projects arose in Argentina, reinforced by the overvaluation of the domestic currency following stabilization. Investment projects, especially in economic sectors privatized during the first stage of the program, have helped reactivate the economy. However, doubts have appeared about the sustainability of this growth path. Is the Argentine economy able to produce, at prevailing relative prices, the volume of tradable goods necessary to sustain the level of non-tradable production reached? Additionally, this level of production will be more difficult if the productivity gains of the privatized sector do not spill over to the rest of the economy.

Even if it is too early to evaluate the overall impact of privatization on firm efficiency, some preliminary conclusions can be stated. In so doing, one must consider carefully what kinds of evidence are useful in measuring the achievements of privatized industries. Privatized firms have clearly achieved ample overall gains in technical and administrative efficiency. Total factor productivity and the quality of the goods provided have also increased significantly. Notably, at the time of privatization, SOE firms exhibited an extremely low factor productivity level and poor quality in goods and services provided. More time will be needed to evaluate the impact of the combination of weak regulatory agencies and the low target levels of internal efficiency gains required of the privatized firms that still exercise market power. However, it is important to note that allocative efficiency clearly has been seriously damaged by the absence of properly designed regulatory frameworks. This suggests that while privatization may have an impact on industry efficiency, the post-privatization regulatory environment is also critically important.

THE FOUR STAGES OF THE ARGENTINE PRIVATIZATION

As noted, four stages of the privatization process can be distinguished, each characterized by the specific relationship between stabilization and privatization operating at the time.

The First Stage: Canceling Massive Public Debt

The first stage canceled the massive public external debt. To achieve this, the government sold state enterprises (among them, ENTel and Aerolíneas Argentinas) in those sectors with the most substantial rate increases and the least restrictive regulatory frameworks. Privatizations undertaken at this stage demonstrate how the authorities assigned priority to the price at which the government sold the enterprises and to the privatization itself. The end justified the means. In the future, these privatizations are likely to be the main sources of conflict among the government, the regulatory agencies, and the privatized firms. For example, the privatization of ENTel has certain features that can be identified in the model presented in Galiani and Petrecolla (1995). Prior to the privatization, the government implemented a set of policy measures that guaranteed the buyers a high profit. Thus, telephone rates were raised about 90 percent in real terms, resulting in a highly skewed rate structure. The prices for international and long-distance calls were much above international price levels, while rates for local calls were not. The introduction of competition was scheduled for 7 to 10 years after privatization took place, depending on the achievement of certain of the investment targets established by the government at the time of sale. There is a consensus that the price paid by the firms acquiring 60 percent of ENTel can only be justified by conservative estimates of cash flows and a high discount rate. This high discount rate may have been the result of the buying firms' expectations of a change in the regulatory framework, which, in fact, occurred when the regulatory agency allowed competition in the market for international calls before the privatized firm's monopoly had elapsed.

The Second Stage: Easing Short-Term Cash Constraints

In the second stage, revenues from the privatization of oil reserves and ENTel relaxed the government's short-run cash constraint, which had occurred when the government announced the Convertibility Plan, establishing the exchange rate as the nominal anchor of its new stabilization program. The Convertibility Plan limited the operational autonomy of the Central Bank, requiring that its monetary liabilities be less than or equal to its foreign-exchange reserves. This rule effectively limited the Central Bank's ability to create money through the expansion of domestic credit. The government's goal in establishing the Convertibility Plan was to stop inflation, and the Plan made illegal any form of indexation of contracts, including the one for the sale of ENTel, since, under the original terms of the sale, buyers had been guaranteed certain prices and rates of return indexed for inflation. As a result of the renegotiation of the terms of the ENTel sale and the sweeping changes taking place in the Argentine economy as a result of the stabilization plan, the new private owners of ENTel saw the outlook for the firms' profits fall. The government tried to offset this effect by adjusting the rate structure of the firms, but it was blocked in this attempt by the regulatory agency. The experience of ENTel was typical of that of several other companies that had been privatized before the adoption of the Convertibility Plan.

The Third Stage: Emphasis on Allocative Efficiency

In the third stage, after the signing of the Brady Plan and the balancing of the government's budget, financial goals were relegated to second-place, and allocative efficiency was given greater priority than it had received in the previous stages. Regulatory frameworks for the gas and electricity sectors were better designed to promote competition. The government also took measures to promote efficiency, including the gradual offering of shares on the securities markets and careful organization of the bidding to ensure maximum competition. In this stage, privatization seems to be a tool of the structural reform policy oriented toward increasing productivity and efficiency in the economy. This attention to efficiency and productivity was made possible by the success of the stabilization measures adopted and was also required if the measures were to continue to be successful. The privatization of industrial inputs, such as electricity and gas, could not be handled as had previous privatizations, without seriously damaging the sustainability of the Convertibility Plan. This was due to the appreciation of domestic currency during the stabilization process and the resulting financial disincentive to produce and invest in the tradable goods sector.

During the third stage, the government reformed the social security system. The government replaced the pay-as-you-go system with a partially private system based on capitalization of returns. However, the state retains an important redistribution component. The government's main targets in undertaking the reform were to restore the solvency of the retirement system and to set favorable conditions for the development of a domestic long-term capital market in which Argentine residents' savings could be matched with investors' needs. However, the transition to a private system resulted in a larger deficit than under the existing system. This larger-than-expected deficit in the short run was viewed negatively by financial markets that were unable or unwilling to see the long-run benefits that would be derived from the reform.

The Fourth Stage: Placing Financial Goals First

In 1995, the privatization program entered its fourth stage, characterized by the return to placing financial goals first. The Argentine economy faced a recession, after four years of impressive growth, so the government was bound by a short-run cash constraint that compelled it to sell the shares it still owned of enterprises privatized in the third stage. The authorities also announced the privatization of some remaining public enterprises.

As can be appreciated, the relationship between stabilization and privatization is not simple. In particular, it has implied several contractual modifications or at least conflicts regarding the interpretation of some contractual obligations. These resulted from different parties' opportunistic reaction to a sudden and significant change in the state of the economy. To some extent, it is normal to encounter conflicts among firms, regulatory agencies, and the government. After all, governing complex transactions with incomplete contracts is difficult. Policymakers cannot specify in advance all possible modifications or applications of a policy rule since it is impossible to specify all possible contingencies in advance. Transaction costs are higher when contingencies are more difficult to forecast and frame in a clear manner. Consequently, it is expected that the part of a contract that concerns the near future should be more thorough than that concerning the distant future (Williamson 1975). More often, the policymaker is constrained by the unknown factors and must make simple, unconditional commitments. For example, regulators may not be able to specify exact terms of future regulation today because they are unable to establish the characteristics of the goods to be produced in the future or because tomorrow they may learn of new technology that cannot be anticipated today (Laffont and Tirole 1993).

Changes in the regulatory framework should not be surprising, as the "engineering" of regulation is a dynamic process with its own information feedback loop among the regulatory agency, consumers, and the regulated agents (Abdala 1994). Regulation of public services has proved to be a complex challenge. The impossibility of eliminating monopolies has led to tensions between the licensed firms and the regulators (Veljanovski 1991). However, this dynamic regulatory process requires some kind of flexible governance structure. Nabil Al-Naijar (1995) suggests two complementary ways to restore flexibility to the contractual relationship. The first is to introduce ambiguity in the terms of the contracts. The second is to supplement contracts with reputation conventions or the legal system. However, this way of achieving contract flexibility requires, among other things, well-established, efficient, and benevolent regulatory agencies as well as a benevolent government.

Additionally, it is worth emphasizing that the dynamic process of regulation can be path dependent. That is, as in the Argentine case, it can be strongly determined by the way privatization is carried out. For example, a time inconsistency problem can seriously damage the dynamic evolution of the regulatory process. This evolution can also be complicated by a highly unstable macroeconomic environment.

CONCLUSION

The short time elapsed since the enterprises were privatized and the consequent lack of case studies of the privatization process reveal the need to do more research on the subject. The complexity of such an analysis, however, makes this research difficult. Nevertheless, it can be concluded that:

- The performance of state enterprises in Argentina has been determined mainly by macroeconomic considerations. The privatization of SOEs, even in the early stages, was an instrument of the stabilization process.

- Using privatization as a tool of stabilization has had its costs. Poorly managed SOEs were replaced by a variety of powerful, private monopolies with consequent allocative inefficiencies. However, the quality of goods provided by the privatized firms has improved, sometimes substantially. The financial deterioration of the SOEs prior to the implementation of the privatization program and the stream of profits transferred to the private sector have attracted new investments and more investments of larger size. Additionally, privatized firms have increased total factor productivity. However, when considering the evolution of productivity gains and the spillover to the rest of the economy, it is necessary to be more cautious.

- Due to the fiscal goals of the government when conducting privatization, the prospect of conflicts between the regulatory agencies and the firms may increase in the future.

- As privatization proceeds, it is natural for the state to shift from the role of producer to that of regulator, a stage that has not been successfully reached in the Argentine privatization process. This pending issue is central to the new role of the Argentine state. However, due to the characteristics of the privatization process and the complexity of regulation in general, this transformation may not yet be at hand.[26]

Notes

1. For example, the introduction of privatization in the post-communist countries has been an immense break with the centralized command economy and an essential component of the change that implied the fall of the communist regimes. Privatization's principal objective has been the foundation of an economy based on a market mechanism. In the capitalist countries, however, privatization has generally been introduced to reduce the presence of the public sector in the economy.

2. Structural reform is supported not only by the U.S. government and international financial institutions but also, to a great extent, by the Latin American intellectual community. In particular, privatization is regarded as an essential tool to improve efficiency in the allocation of resources. For some countries, however, the privatization of large public utilities such as telecommunications and postal services is not feasible. Additionally, Argentina sold its national telecommunication enterprise (ENTel) to two European state enterprises. In West Germany and the Netherlands, when public utilities were considered inefficient, policies of internal reorganization rather than privatization have been adopted. Similarly, Bolivia has followed a combined strategy entailing the privatization of small- and medium-scale commercial public enterprises and the reform of large public enterprises (see Mallon 1994).

3. For an extensive study of the origin of state enterprises in Latin America, see Werner Baer 1974.

4. In the game theory literature, it is said that strategic complementaries arise if an increase in one player's strategy increases the optimal strategy of the other player's (see Cooper and John 1988).

5. As Werner Baer and Melissa H. Birch (1992) point out, due to the good reputation of many state enterprises in international markets, such enterprises were forced by their governments to borrow more than their optimal level in order to obtain foreign exchange to sustain fixed exchange rates. This fact placed state enterprises in a precarious financial situation and subsequently restricted their access to capital markets.

6. Regarding the progressive incidence of the rate structure in Argentina, Fernando Navajas and Alberto Porto (1990) compared the structure of a quasi-optimal rate, in which efficiency, financing, and distributive equity are considered, with the observed rate structure. They found, for example, that electricity and gas sectors in the mid-1980s used price discrimination unevenly, and the level of progressive incidence was higher than what was predicted by their theoretical model. By 1992, financial and efficiency considerations had led to a greater degree of uniformity in the tariff structure in these sectors.

7. Between 1981 and 1983, the overall public sector deficit experienced a huge increase. By 1983, the deficit reached 15.6 points of GDP. An immense reduction in tax collection also took place, and this was the main factor behind the increase in the public deficit. Also, by that time, due to the nationalization of the external debt, the government increased its financial needs around 4 points of GDP.

8. In few other parts of the public sector did agencies have the ability to overspend to the degree that occurred in SOEs. As a result, attempts to impose financial order were not successful (see Heymann and Navajas 1989).

9. A contract is complete if it is contingent on all variables that are verifiable by a court, even if it is not contingent on some unobservable variables.

10. Consumer surplus is the difference between what a consumer would be willling to pay and the amount actually paid. In economic terms, it refers to the gap between utility and price. Producer surplus is defined as the excess revenue received by producers over production costs. — Ed.

11. It is also assumed that the government is not able to spread out payments to the firms over time, without introducing additional distortions.

12. This does not overlook the fact that fiscal considerations are always present in privatization. Even in a budget-surplus context, the government faces the alternative of protecting allocative efficiency in the privatization (and accepting a lower sales price) or being able to reduce tax reductions or increase expenditures.

13. The administration elected in 1989 was populist. The supposed certainty regarding the measures this administration was going to take played a significant role in the hyperinflation episode of 1989. During the presidential campaign, Menem, following his party's tradition, promised economic growth through government spending with social justice to be achieved via income redistribution in favor of workers.

14. It is worth pointing out that in an unstable economy such as Argentina's, no clear line can be drawn between fiscal and monetary policy due to the fact that governments have very little access to capital markets, while, at the same time, they are not able to abstain from borrowing (see Heymann and Leijonhufvud 1995). It was usual in Argentina to define the budget deficit to include the Central Bank quasi-fiscal "deficit." The Central Bank operated as an "off-budget" channel to transfer resources to various sectors of the economy.

15. The government was completely restricted in its access to the voluntary issue of new debt.

16. The government faced opposition to tax reform until it was mainly based on indirect taxes.

17. Debt-equity swaps are exchanges of bonds or bank loans for ownership rights. The Argentine Brady agreement, named for U.S. Secretary of the Treasury Nicholas Brady, was the first accord in which a debtor country acceded without paying interest already due (US$8.3 billion by the end of 1992). The agreement reached allowed Argentina to reduce both the servicing of the debt and reduction of the debt stock itself.

18. Thus, for example, analyzing the changes in the regulatory policy in Britain during the 1980s, John Vickers (1991) examines the trade-off between the higher price obtained from the sale of a monopoly and the benefits that could be derived from the introduction of competition. Investors recognize that the enterprise will face more competition and regulation as time goes by. Consequently, they discount the price that they are willing to pay for the enterprise.

19. After the Brady agreement, both the private sector and the public sector were able to access the capital markets. It is relevant to mention that debt-equity swaps increase the debtors' incentive to commit capital to investment projects that command a positive net present value. Swaps, by mitigating an investment inefficiency associated with debt over-hang, can be beneficial to both debtor and creditors (see Bowe and Dean 1993).

20. Britain's privatization process was extensive and included utilities. However, its pace differed significantly from Argentina's. "First, industries in competitive markets were privatized. Then, after the government election victory in 1983, a process of privatizing utilities was initiated with British Telecom, followed by British Gas. Further election success in 1987 paved the way for airports, water, and electricity to complete the main utility privatization program. After almost 15 years, all that remain are a number of hard industry cases: postal services, nuclear power, railways, and Scottish water, all of which are currently under consideration for privatization" (Helm 1994). For an extensive analysis of the privatization process in Britain, see John Vickers and George Yarrow 1988.

21. Between 1990 and 1993, among other firms, the Argentine government sold ENTel; the national airline (Aerolíneas Argentinas); four TV channels; petrochemicals; 10,000 km of national roads in the form of concessions; the national railroads (Ferrocarriles Argentinos); oil and gas reserves; Palermo Hippodrome; the Greater Buenos Aires energy generation company (SEGBA); steel companies (Altos Hornos Zapla and SOMISA); oil refineries; state properties; the national gas company (Gas del Estado); the national water company (Obras Sanitarias de la Nación); military industries; the Hidronor energy generation dams; Buenos Aires Subways; and the national oil company (YPF).

22. As in all the other cases, the YPF restructuring was mainly based upon labor reduction. Acording to estimates, between 35,000 and 50,000 workers were fired. However, the management appointed by the government remained in charge. Union leaders' coopera-tion in this privatization was remarkable. Some economists argue that this enterprise could not have been restructured if privatization had not already been scheduled.

23. However, this has little relevance in Argentina since corporate takeovers play a minor role in the economic institutional organization.

24. Congress quickly approved the State Reform Law and the Economic Emergency Law, which authorized the administration to privatize many SOEs and gave it the right to suspend costly industrial subsidies and tax loopholes.

25. "The adjustment of the average level of prices as well as the freedom to design the pricing structure were facilitated by the fact that the first privatizations of public services in Argentina were in the telecommunications and airline sectors, which hardly affect low-income consumers, and have only a moderate impact on the costs of manufacturing firms. Owing to this, it is possible that social tolerance of the adjustment of relative prices was greater than it would have been with other services (in fact, the creation of a toll in order to privatize highway services aroused substantial resistance and necessitated a rapid renegotia-tion of contracts with the private operators)." See Alberto Petrecolla et al. 1993.

26. For a more extensive analysis of the state's continuing regulatory function after privatization, see Martín Rodríguez Pardina, Diego Petrecolla and Guillermo Cruces, 1999, *Regulación y Competencia en los Servicios Públicos Privatizados: Diagnóstico y Propuesta*, Nota No. 3 (Buenos Aires: Fundación Argentina para el Desarrollo con Equidad (FADE).

References

Abdala, Manuel Ángel. 1994. "Transformación y regulación económica en el sector eléctrico argentino." Serie Seminarios, Instituto y Universidad Torcuato Di Tella, Buenos Aires, Argentina.

Al-Naijar, Nabil. 1995. "Incomplete Contracts and the Governance of Complex Contractual Relationships." *The American Economic Review*, Papers and Proceedings (May): 432-436.

Atkinson, Scott, and Robert Halvorsen. 1986. "The Relative Efficiency of Public and Private Firms in a Regulated Environment: The Case of U.S. Electric Utilities." *Journal of Public Economics* 29: 281-294.

Baer, Werner 1974. "The Role of Government Enterprises in Latin America's Industrialization." In *Fiscal Policy for Industrialization and Development in Latin America*, ed. D. Geithman. Gainesville, Florida: University of Florida Press.

Baer, Werner, and Melissa H. Birch. 1992. "Privatization and the Changing Role of the State in Latin America." *Journal of International Law and Politics* 25: 1-25.

Boardman, Anthony, and Aidan Vining. 1989. "Ownership and Performance in Competitive Environments: A Comparison of the Performance of Private, Mixed, and State-Owned Enterprises." *Journal of Law and Economics* 32: 1-33.

Bös, Dieter. 1992. *Privatization: A Theoretical Treatment.* Oxford, England: Clarendon Press.

Bowe, Michael, and James Dean. 1993. "Debt-equity Swaps: Investment Incentive Effects and Secondary Market Prices." *Oxford Economic Papers* 45: 130-145.

Boycko, Maxim, Andrei Sheleifer, and Robert Vishny. 1992. "Property Rights, Soft Budget Constraints, and Privatization." Cambridge, Mass., and Chicago: The State Committee on the Management of State Property. Unpublished manuscript.

Button, Kenneth, and Thomas Weyman-Jones. 1994. "Impacts of Privatization Policy in Europe." *Contemporary Economic Policy* 12: 23-33.

Chudvnosky, Daniel, Andrés López, and Fernando Porta. 1995. "Más allá del flujo de caja. El boom de la inversión extranjera directa en la Argentina." *Desarrollo Económico* 35 (137): 31-62.

Cooper, Russell, and Andrew John. 1988. "Coordinating Coordination Failures in Keynesian Models." *Quarterly Journal of Economics* 103: 441-463.

Edwards, Jack K., and Werner Baer. 1993. "The State and the Private Sector in Latin America: Reflections on the Past, the Present and the Future." *The Quarterly Review of Economics and Finance* 33: 9-19.

Gadano, Nicolás, and Sebastián Galiani. 1994. "Las privatizaciones como instrumento fiscal: Un caso de inconsistencia temporal." *Anales de la Asociación Argentina de Economía Política* 3.

Galiani, Sebastián, and Diego Petrecolla. 1995. "An Ex-Post View of the Privatization Process in Argentina." Paper presented at the International Institute of Public Finance, 51st Congress (Session T26 - The Changing Role of the Government in Latin America), in Lisbon, August 21-24.

Gerchunoff, Pablo, ed. 1992. *Las Privatizaciones en la Argentina: Primera etapa.* Buenos Aires:Instituto Torcuato Di Tella.

Gerchunoff, Pablo, and Guillermo Cánovas. 1994. "Las privatizaciones en la Argentina: Impactos micro y macroecónomicos." *Serie Reformas de Política Pública* 21. Santiago: United Nations, Economic Commission for Latin America and the Caribbean (ECLAC).

Gerchunoff, Pablo, Carlos Bozalla, and Juan Sanguinetti. 1994. "Privatización, apertura y concentración: el caso del sector siderúrgico argentino." *Serie Reformas de Política Pública* 25. Santiago: United Nations, ECLAC.

Gerschenkron, Alexander. 1962. *Economic Development in Historical Perspective.* Cambridge, Mass.: Harvard University Press.

Grossman, Sanford, and Oliver D. Hart. 1986. "The Cost and Benefits of Ownership: A Theory of Lateral and Vertical Integration." *Journal of Political Economy* 94: 691-719.

Helm, Dieter 1994. "British Utility Regulation: Theory, Practice, and Reform." *Oxford Review of Economic Policy* 10: 3.

Heymann, Daniel 1991. "From Sharp Disinflation to Hyperinflation, Twice: The Argentine Experience, 1985-1989." In *Lessons of Economic Stabilization and Its Aftermath*, eds. Michael Bruno, et al. Cambridge, Mass.: The MIT Press.

Heymann, Daniel, and Axel Leijonhufvud. 1995. *High Inflation.* London: Oxford University Press.

Heymann, Daniel, and Fernando Navajas. 1989. "Conflicto distributivo y déficit fiscal: notas sobre la experiencia argentina, 1970-1987." *Desarrollo Económico* 29 (115): 309-329.

Heymann, Daniel, Fernando Navajas, and Ignacio Warnes. 1988. "Distributive Conflict and the Fiscal Deficit: Some Inflationary Games." Working Paper. Buenos Aires: Instituto Torcuato Di Tella.

Jones, Leroy, Pankaj Tandon, and Ingo Vogelsang. 1990. *Selling Public Enterprises: A Cost-Benefit Analysis.* Cambridge, Mass.: The MIT Press.

Kornai, Janos. 1986. "The Soft Budget Constraint." *Kyklos* 39: 3-30.

Laffont, Jean-Jacques, and Jean Tirole. 1993. *A Theory of Incentives in Procurement and Regulation.* Cambridge, Mass.: The MIT Press.

Mallon, Richard. 1994. "State-owned Enterprise Reform through Performance Contracts: The Bolivian Experiment." *World Development* 22 (6): 925-946.

Navajas, Fernando. 1992. "Grupos de presión y estructuras tarifarias." *Estudios*, Fundación Mediterránea, Córdoba, Argentina (July-December): 111-123.

Navajas, Fernando, and Alberto Porto. 1990. "La tarifa en dos partes cuasi-óptima: Eficiencia, equidad y financiamiento." *El Trimestre Económico*, no. 228: 863-887.

Palermo, Vicente, and Juan Carlos Torre. 1992. "A la sombra de la hiperinflación. La política de reformas estructurales en Argentina." Buenos Aires: Instituto Torcuato Di Tella. Unpublished paper.

Petrecolla, Alberto, Alberto Porto, and Pablo Gerchunoff. 1993. "Privatization in Argentina." *The Quarterly Review of Economics and Finance* 33: 67-93.

Rodríguez Pardina, Martín, Diego Petrecolla, and Guillermo Cruces. 1999. *Regulación y Competencia en los Servicios Públicos Privatizados: Diagnóstico y Propuesta*, Nota No. 3. Buenos Aires: Fundación Argentina para el Desarrollo con Equidad (FADE).

Tirole, Jean 1994. "The Internal Organization of Government." *Oxford Economic Papers* 46: 1-29.

Veljanovski, Cento G. 1991. *Regulators and the Market: An Assessment of the Growth of Regulation in the UK*. London: Institute of Economic Affairs.

Vickers, John 1991. "Government Regulatory Policy." *Oxford Review of Economic Policy* 7: 13-30.

Vickers, John, and George Yarrow. 1988. *Privatization: An Economic Analysis*. Cambridge, Mass.: The MIT Press.

Vickers, John, and George Yarrow. 1991. "Economic Perspectives on Privatization." *Journal of Economic Perspectives* 5 (2): 111-132.

Williamson, Oliver. 1975. *Markets and Hierarchies: Analysis and Anti-Trust Implications*. New York: Free Press.

CHAPTER 5

The Impact of Privatization in Peru*

PEDRO-PABLO KUCZYNSKI

N o country in Latin America in the late twentieth century began its program of
economic reform and privatization from a base of such hopelessness as Peru.
The legacy of twelve years of statism during the country's military administration
from October 1968 to July 1980 was compounded during the elected government
of Alan García (1985-1990), which ended in a paroxysm of hyperinflation, deep
economic depression, and narco-terrorism. No doubt because Peru hit an economic
nadir of unheard of proportions, it was possible for a new government to put in place
a program of drastic reforms. These measures were initially very painful to a
population that had already endured great privation and suffering.

THE LEGACY OF MISMANAGEMENT

T he history of Peru from the late 1960s to 1990 is one of almost constant
upheaval. A military government forced its way into power in October 1968;
the coup was inspired more by the frustrated ambitions of General Juan Velasco
Alvarado than by any ideology of revolution, the motive that a number of foreign
commentators subsequently cited. Egged on partly by the admiration of these
outside observers[1] and also by its own nationalistic interpretation of the ideology of
social reform espoused by the Kennedy and Johnson administrations through the
Alliance for Progress, the military embarked on a series of state takeovers. These
began immediately after the coup, with the expropriation of the local subsidiary of
Standard Oil of New Jersey, a target for the intellectual left in Peru for many years.

The takeovers were followed by sweeping land expropriations and strong
government support for communist-led unions, as well as subsidies for a multitude
of public provincial universities that were the springboard for the ideology that
encouraged extremist movements such as Shining Path (Sendero Luminoso).
Initially, as often happens with drastic changes in government, the economy
continued to grow, helped along in this case by the fiscal reforms and external debt
refinancing implemented at the end of the civilian administration of Fernando
Belaúnde Terry (1963-1968) and stimulated by a binge of lending by international
banks to the new nationalistic government. By 1973, however, there were clear
signs of financial strain. It was not until the commodity boom of the second oil
shock, beginning in 1978, that the chronic fiscal deficit started to go down, as the
government levied a massive tax on the country's then-booming exports. Nonethe-

---

* This chapter will appear under the title "Peru" in the author's forthcoming book,
Unfinished Business: Privatization and Reform in Latin America.

less, the inflation that had begun in the mid-1970s was to continue rising increasingly right up to 1990.

The last two years of the military regime (1978-1980) and the first two of the second civilian administration of Fernando Belaúnde (1980-1985) brought a bonanza, despite continuing inflation and the onset of rapidly escalating terrorism, exacerbated by government inaction and the financing of the terrorists by coca growers and traders east of the central and northern Andes. By 1983, the Latin American debt crisis and natural disasters, due to the shift of the "El Niño" ocean current, put an end to Peru's prosperity.

When Alan García, running on a populist platform, was elected by an overwhelming margin in 1985, he was widely seen as a savior. A part of business organized itself as "the twelve apostles," a group that gave the new president the type of fawning admiration reserved for governments that business instinctively fears. The reaction from some circles abroad was equally deferential. An essay in *Foreign Affairs*, "Peru: The Message from García,"[2] published only a few months after his inauguration, was representative of this subjective commentary (Roett 1985). Meanwhile, the new government financed, with the foreign exchange savings from the suspension of debt service begun under Belaúnde, a massive but inevitably short-lived consumption boom with central bank credit. The boom was over very quickly. In order to postpone inflation, an Argentine advisor and a U.S. professor, paid for by the UN, together designed a complex web of controls to hold the exchange rate steady. This system not only decimated exports but also enabled the government to satisfy its voracious appetite for corruption. Sensing collapse, the president, on his second anniversary in power, decreed the nationalization of the commercial banks, as President José López Portillo had done five years earlier in Mexico. Since the García government was rapidly losing authority, the owners of the banks successfully resisted, some by encamping for months inside their bank headquarters.

The final years of the "Message from García" were an orgy of government disorganization, corruption, and escalating terrorism. By the first round of presidential elections in March 1990, government tax revenues had plummeted to about 3 to 4 percent of GNP and inflation was roaring along at an annualized rate of close to 20,000 percent. By then, it was clear to all that drastic change was needed. As early as September 1988, in a representative poll taken by Peru's leading polling organization, 49 percent (versus 35 percent) favored the sale of state enterprises, 80 percent favored incentives for foreign investment, and 61 percent said that inflation was Peru's main problem (Williamson 1990, 93). Eighteen months later, with the country facing even worse economic and security problems, the poorer the economic segment polled, the greater the support for "paying Peru's debts" and "balancing the budget." While support for privatization did not reach the same levels as it did for these more general abstractions, it was clear that a vast majority of Peruvians thought that state companies were corrupt, and 65 percent thought they should be sold (Kuczynski and Ortiz de Zevallos 1990).

Economic crisis motivated these attitudes, but, notably, low-income groups, who had only a limited idea of what market reforms would do to them, supported drastic change. The leading presidential candidate, the well-known author Mario

Vargas Llosa, who had led the fight against García's attempted takeover of the banks, thought that he could appeal to the people's rational interests. He explained what the economic "shock" would entail and what reforms were intended, while the campaign of his opponent, Alberto Fujimori, a professor of mathematics at the agricultural university, emphasized optimism. Vargas Llosa's frankness undermined him; in the end, García threw his party's support to Fujimori. Consequently, Vargas Llosa received a mere one-third plurality in the first round and lost to Fujimori by a wide margin in the runoff election in May 1990.

ORGANIZING PRIVATIZATION

The first task of the government on the economic front was to implement the type of orthodox program advocated by many economists and some businessmen well before the change of government: huge increases in controlled prices (especially utilities) to compensate for past inflation; balancing the budget by drastic cuts in expenditures and big hikes in basic taxes (especially sales taxes, particularly on gasoline); restricting wage increases to the minimum politically acceptable; halting central bank financing for the Treasury; and negotiating support from the International Monetary Fund (IMF). In 1991 came a massive reduction of import barriers, the elimination of state monopolies, simplification of the foreign exchange regime, bureaucratic deregulation, and the beginnings of privatization. Servicing of the external debt, mostly dormant since 1984, began again in 1992, and a Brady deal on the commercial bank debt was finally announced in November 1995.[3]

The initial program went beyond anything that the IMF thought feasible. Some controlled prices, such as gasoline and electricity, went up by a factor of 35! By choking off liquidity and purchasing power and opening the protectionist floodgates to cheap imports, the new government quickly brought runaway inflation to a halt (Table 1). This was not easy to achieve, however: In the months before the election, former Economy Minister Carlos Rodríguez-Pastor and then UN Secretary-General Javier Pérez de Cuéllar decided to introduce President-elect Alberto Fujimori, who had yet to establish an economic team, to the orthodox shock program and to people who might help him carry it out. Fujimori's first economy

Table 1. Economic Indicators

	1990	1991	1992	1993	1994	Prelim. 1995
GDP (percent change)	-5.6	2.6	-1.2	5.8	12.8	6.9
Inflation (percent change, Dec. to Dec.)	7,650	139	57	40	15	11
Real Wages (index 1985=100)	40	46	44	44	51	49
Gen. Govt. Current Revenue (as percent of GDP)	8.8	9.1	11.1	11.0	12.5	12.5

Sources: ECLAC 1996; IDB 1997.

minister, Juan Carlos Hurtado Miller, who implemented the basic shock program, lasted in office only six months, as the inevitable deep recession continued into 1991 and early 1992. The program was refined and extended in the next two years, under Carlos Boloña Behr.

Privatization started slowly with the sale of the state's minority participation in private sector companies and a number of small state-owned assets, such as gas stations (Table 2). Initially, much time was spent, within and outside government, debating whether state companies could be sold for Peruvian government external debt paper, which had traded as low as US$.05 per $1 of nominal obligation in early 1990 — even though, at such a low price, there were very few sellers (chiefly banks). Some in the new government were convinced that allies of Vargas Llosa had bought

Table 2. Proceeds from Privatization
(US$ millions as of March 1996)

	1991	1992	1993	1994	1995	1996*	Total
Value of sales[1]	3	211	147	3,194	903	185	4,611
Income to Treasury	3	211	147	2,527	808	167	3,834
Amount paid in debt paper[2]	-	-	-	95	160	18	270
Investment commitments	-	179	550	1,159	81	170	2,689

1. Includes a $600 million capital investment in the telephone company by Telefónica, which was not income to the Treasury.
2. Calculated at the current market price at the time of the transaction.
*Until March
Source: COPRI 1997.

large quantities of this "giveaway paper" in order to benefit should privatization-for-paper sales be allowed, but this suspicion was patently untrue.

The program ultimately gained strength with the organization of a strong privatization agency, under Energy and Mines Minister Jaime Yoshiyama (a logical location, since the largest companies to be privatized were in the portfolio of that ministry) and with the capture in September 1992 of the Maoist terrorist leader, Abimael Guzmán. Guzmán, a former professor, and his Shining Path movement — a tightly run, fanatical organization that ostensibly advocated a return to pure communism and the destruction of all those who in any way collaborated with capitalism — were responsible for 25,000 killings, mostly of poor peasants and policemen (Gorriti 1990; Palmer 1992). His capture unleashed a small flood of portfolio investment into the tiny Peruvian stock exchange and, in the eyes of foreign companies, greatly improved the country's economic prospects.

The privatization agency (Comisión de Promoción de la Inversión Privada — COPRI) was led by Carlos Montoya,[4] a competent and experienced Stanford Ph.D. in business administration, who was cautious and avoided the limelight. (Fujimori hated grandstanding in his cabinet ministers and close associates, and that had been the principal cause for the departure of Boloña.) The first big coup of the privatization program was the sale in October 1992 of HierroPerú, an iron ore mine, for $120 million to the Chinese steel colossus, Shougang. The second highest bidder, a group led by the steel company of Chile (Compañía de Aceros del Pacífico — CAP) and put together by the author, offered only $24 million, slightly above the minimum price. The enormity of the price paid by Shougang can only be understood in relation to the perilous condition of HierroPerú at the time of sale.

The original iron ore mine had been developed by Marcona, a U.S. consortium specially created in the late 1950s as a low-cost supplier for the Japanese steel industry. The mine has huge reserves (albeit somewhat high in sulphur) near a deepwater port. In a high-volume, low-cost operation, the iron ore is taken by conveyor directly to a processing plant at the port, where it is loaded onto large carriers headed for Asia. After the military took over the mine in 1975, production collapsed, while featherbedding and corruption increased. Except for a brief interlude between 1980 and 1984, when a new independent board and management were put in place, production continued to decline as investment and customers were neglected. By 1990, annual output was barely 2 million tons compared to 10 million tons under the original U.S. management. The long-term future of the privatized mining operation under Shougang remains uncertain; although production has returned to between 5 million and 6 million tons, as promised by Shougang at the time of purchase, the Chinese managers have had trouble keeping the labor force tranquil and increasing productivity in what is essentially a long-distance, captive supplier. More important, low-cost, high-volume suppliers in Brazil, Australia, and India may eventually cause the Chinese to question the wisdom of having their own captive supplier.

COPRI, after the financial success of the sale of HierroPerú, set about planning Peru's major privatizations: two large banks, the electricity generation and distribution system, major mines and smelters, and the state petroleum monopoly (Petróleos del Perú — PetroPerú). Each individual asset to be sold had a special independent privatization board (Comité Especial de Privatización — CEPRI) created to supervise its sale. CEPRIs are small groups, consisting of experts on the particular industry and often people close to the president. The presence of Peruvians of Japanese descent, who make up 0.4 percent of Peru's population, is particularly notable on several important CEPRIs. CEPRIs had significant authority in the privatization process. With the help of specialized consultants, mostly from abroad, much effort went into organizing the assets to be sold, especially electricity, where the two reigning state companies, ElectroLima and ElectroPerú, were split into various, separate distribution and generation units.

In general, the method worked well. Political controversy was largely avoided, and few mistakes were made. On the other hand, progress was much slower than in Argentina, for example, where privatization was largely accomplished within a span of about three years. Generally speaking, the prices obtained by Peru were above average for Latin America, both in relation to most (subjective) measures of country risk and in relation to the generally poor condition of the assets sold. The lesson seems to be that taking time pays off both politically and financially. Peru's experience between 1992 and 1995 does not support the idea, widespread in the literature on Latin American privatization, that state assets were sold off at giveaway prices.

As of mid-1996, the privatization process was about 70 percent complete. The companies that had been sold included two large banks, the telephone company, the bulk of the electricity-distribution system, and most of the state-owned mining companies. However, certain large companies and assets remained under state control because, in some cases, the level of complexity made a company difficult to sell, while, in other cases, the government appears simply to have lost some of the steamroller momentum of earlier years.

Among the remaining companies is Centromin, the former Cerro de Pasco Corporation, which was taken over by the military in 1975. Centromin is a complex company with disparate assets: one of the world's most sophisticated but dilapidated custom smelters, two medium-sized hydroelectric works that supply it, several surrounding mines, a large but uneconomical copper mine, and a railway network. The CEPRI in charge of the Centromin sale attempted to sell off the whole thing in 1994 but found no bidders, partly because of the smelter's immeasurable environmental liabilities and also because of the diversity in its assets. The government was firmly committed to the privatization of this entity, however, and planned to bundle groups of assets in order to improve the prospects for their sale, which was to take place in 1996-1997.[5] Because of its considerable value, the smelter (together with a long-term power-supply contract from the hydroelectric works) should be sold alone; the smaller mines, of lesser value, should be sold individually; while the Cobriza Copper mine is a write-off,[6] the power plants could be sold as a unit (but with the smelter's electricity-supply contract attached — a condition that will no doubt reduce their value).[7]

The case of PetroPerú is somewhat different. There, too, the question of whether to sell the whole or the parts has arisen. Given the overstaffing of the company, the parts are worth significantly more than the whole. Moreover, some major assets, such as the northern Trans-Andean pipeline, are more suitable for a management concession than for an outright sale, which would not generate revenues even close to the replacement value of the pipeline, both long and difficult to construct. However, the key issue in the sale of PetroPerú is political. Because of the lack of exploration since 1984, most of Peru's rapidly dwindling oil production is in the north, near the Ecuadorean border. In an effort to protect jobs that would no doubt be eliminated by privatization, the active and overstaffed union of PetroPerú has taken advantage of Peru's sensitive relationship with Ecuador to revive talk about the "strategic" nature of the oil industry. Despite these inevitable political problems, the government has decided to go ahead with the sale of virtually all the assets of PetroPerú, beginning with the country's two major refineries, which are badly in need of repair and expansion.

Two other large companies remain to be sold: the main Lima water-supply agency (Servicio de Agua Potable y Alcantarillado de Lima — Sedapal) and the 700- megawatt Mantaro Dam in the Central Andes, the largest power plant in Peru, which supplies almost one-quarter of the power in the country's interconnected system.[8] In the case of Sedapal, President Fujimori is said to be influenced by one adviser in particular, who believes that water is a "social" product that ought to be supplied by the state. This attitude seems uncharacteristic of the president, who tends to be highly practical. Lima, in 1996, had a population of almost 7 million, while the water supply system was designed to serve fewer than one-third that number of people. The supply is further diminished by leaks in the aged system.

There is no in-house water supply in the poor areas that ring the city, where 3 million people must rely on scarce public taps or buy water at exorbitant prices. None of these slums — or *pueblos jóvenes* — has sewerage. Less than 10 percent of Lima's sewage is treated: Its discharge into the nearby ocean and into the Rimac River is responsible for cholera epidemics, water-borne diseases, and high infant mortality rates. As in Mexico City, where private management of the water system was successfully started in 1994, Lima faces a severe water shortage in the near future; only the extremely low level of consumption by the bulk of the population is postponing the onset of that crisis. The example of Buenos Aires[9] clearly illustrates that a private concession to a world-class operator can quickly improve the existing water-supply system, gradually extend it, and lower effective costs for the mass of the population.

The sale of the Mantaro Dam is hindered by its size. As was found in Chile, large dams are hard to sell because no one will pay a price approaching replacement or even historic costs. A sale of a percentage with operating control or a concession arrangement may be the most practical solution. While relatively low international oil prices continue, the construction of large dams to produce electricity can rarely be justified: their acquisition, therefore, can only take place at large discounts to their original cost, since most were constructed at a time of much higher energy prices. When the inevitable upheaval of international oil prices arrives, the economics of thermal versus renewable (hydro) power will dramatically change, as happened once before between 1973 and 1982.

In addition to these four major cases, two other significant pending privatizations, the railway system and a network of ports, are still pending. Peru has two limited railway systems, one serving the mining region in the central Andes and the other linking Cuzco and Puno with the southern Pacific coast. A World Bank loan will help finance improvements on the parts of the lines to be sold. Seven major coastal ports and four Amazonian ports will be auctioned off as management concessions.

By the end of 1997, most Peruvian state enterprises had been sold or put under private management. The most significant exception is the water supply; ultimately, the inevitable water shortage, especially for Lima, will probably force some type of privatization.

THE MAJOR PRIVATIZATIONS

The large size of the Peruvian state enterprise sector, built up during the years of the military regime, meant that once the decision to privatize was taken, significant assets had to be sold. From 1970 to 1982, state enterprise in Peru grew more rapidly than anywhere else in Latin America. The public sector got major participation in banking and industry (cement); control of the principal airline; a major part of both the mining industry and petroleum production; and total control of telephones, electric utilities, water supply, and ports, as well as the only steel mill in the country. With the exception of telephones and the steel mill, all the companies were expropriated during the 1970s. While the same tendency was visible in most of Latin America, it was much more pronounced in Peru: From 1970 to 1982, in the

Table 3. Major Privatizations over US$10 million (in millions)

Company/Asset	Min. Price	Sale Price	Investment Commit.	% Sold	Date	Principal Buyer
PetroPerú gas stations	25.0	38.5	-	All	6-8/1992	Several
Public buses (Enatru)	13.0	15.0	-	All	7-8/1992	Workers
HierroPerú (iron ore mine)	22.0	120.0	150.0	100	10/1992	Shougang Corp. (China)
Quellaveco (copper deposit)	9.0	12.0	-	100	12/1992	Anglo American (S. Africa)
AeroPerú (airline)	41.0	54.0	-	72	1/1993	AeroMéxico
Transoceánica (shipping)	21.5	25.2	-	100	11/1993	Glenpoint (Chile)
Cerro Verde (copper mine)	30.0	37.0	485.0	100	11/1993	Cyprus Minerals
CPT/ENTEL (telephones)	535.0	2,002.0	1,000.0	35	2/1994	Telefónica (Spain)
Cementos Yura	30.0	67.0	-	100	2/1994	Gloria (Perú)
Ilo Copper Refinery	67.5	65.0	20.2	100	4/1994	Southern Perú
Cementos Lima	60.7	103.4	-	49	6/1994	Public (stock market)
Edelnor	127.7	176.5	-	60	7/1994	Endesa of Spain
Edelsur	129.4	212.1	-	60	7/1994	Ontario Hydro & others
Interbanc	45.0	51.0	-	90	7/1994	CRP (Peruvian)/Chilean Gp
Tintaya Copper Mine	60 + 55[1]	253.8[1]	85.0	100	10/1994	Magma Copper (U.S.)
Cajamarquilla Zinc Ref.	120 + 40[1]	179.0[1]	20.0	100	11/1994	Cominco/Marubeni
Emsal (salt)	4.0	14.7	-	95	12/1994	Química del Pacífico
EnturPerú (hotels)	33.1	46.8	22.8	100	1994/95	Various
Banco Continental	66 + 60[2]	225.7[2]	-	60	4/1995	Banco Bilbao Vizcaya & Brescia Gp.
Cahua Hydro	21.1	41.8	-	60	4/1995	Peruvian Gp.
Cementos Norte Pacasmayo	15.0	15.0	-	11	6/1995	Public stock market
Edegel (Lima hydro)	273 + 100[1]	489.5[1]	45.0	60	10/1995	Entergy (U.S.) Endesa (Chile) & others
Cementos Sur	11.8	33.3	12.0	100	10/1995	Gloria (Perú)
Etevensa (power plant)	-	-	120	60	1/1996	Endesa of Spain and Peruvian Gp.
SiderPerú	120 + 20[3]	185[3]	30	100	3/1996	GS Technologies (U.S.)

1. Includes nominal debt paper amount shown, which is estimated at market value of about 65 percent. 2. Same as note 1, at 50 percent. 3. US$26 million of paper was submitted with a street value of about US$18 million.

Source: COPRI 1997.

major Latin American countries, state enterprise outlays measured against GDP grew from 9 percent to 19 percent on average, but in Peru, the increase was from 4 percent to 32 percent (Kuczynski 1988, 54).[10]

The task of privatization was thus a very large one for Peru. The process started slowly, not only because of the size of the undertaking, but also because the government had to await an improvement in investment flows and economic growth after the brutal recession following the shock program to stop hyperinflation in 1990. After the first large-scale privatization, that of HierroPerú in October 1992, there followed in quick succession the sale of 72 percent of AeroPerú to a group headed by AeroMexico (itself a subsequently troubled privatized airline); the granting of a concession to a private group made up of Peruvians and individuals from the United States to operate the north coast oil fields formerly owned by Belco Petroleum (which had been nationalized by García in 1985); and the sale of PetroPerú's coastal shipping operation to the Von Appen group of Chile (see Table 3).

After the customary lull for national holidays at the end of July, the next round of privatizations began with the sale of the Cerro Verde copper mine to U.S.-owned Cyprus Mines in October 1993. The Cerro Verde mine was nearly exhausted and required major investments to develop the sulfide ore body below its already exploited oxide ores. Despite the lack of other bidders, Cyprus offered somewhat more than the minimum $30 million bid plus a $485 million investment commitment over five years to build a whole new operation. In the same southern region three months later, Cementos Yura, a medium-sized producer, was sold at more than twice the minimum price to a Peruvian group that borrowed heavily to finance the acquisition. A large copper refinery nearby was sold at the same time, on the second try, to the only logical bidder, the Southern Perú Copper Corporation, controlled by Asarco, a U.S. multinational mining company, which owns the smelter that feeds the refinery.

Privatization got into high gear with the sale in February 1994 of the two telephone companies (one serving Lima and the other the rest of the country). The price for operating control (35 percent plus a capital increase) was $2.002 billion ($1.391 billion for the acquisition plus a capital injection of $611 million into the two merged companies), a truly stunning sum considering the perilous condition and small size of the company, which had only about 600,000 functioning lines. The price paid per line ($3,300, or $10,200 per line, taking into account the 35-percent equity position) was well above the already high prices paid for telephone companies in Venezuela ($2,400 per line) and Mexico ($1,900 per line) and far beyond the prices paid in Argentina and Chile.

The winning bidder, Telefónica of Spain, Spain's largest publicly held company, was seriously interested because Peru had the last sizable telephone company likely to be privatized in South America. Purchasing the Peruvian entity would enable Telefónica to create a large South American phone company. There was the further possibility of creating a large, arc-shaped network (with Chile and Argentina) once Colombia's telephone company was privatized. The other two bidders, Southwestern Bell (which offered $857 million and is one of two foreign partners in Teléfonos de México) and General Telephone and Electronics (GTE) (which bid $803 million and controls the Venezuelan telephone company), did not anticipate these opportunities. Telefónica has three Peruvian minority institutional partners, which it agreed to finance once the surprisingly large bid was announced.

The new company, Telefónica del Perú, immediately reduced its staff by 3,100, out of a workforce of 12,000, and implemented an expansion plan to operate about 1.8 million lines in 1998, something that cost twice the original investment commitment of $1 billion. This expansion was designed to create direct employment that far offset the initial staff reduction. Although the quality of service is obviously still far below industrial-country standards, there has been a remarkable improvement in the waiting time for telephone installation (from seven years to a few weeks) and in the number of public telephones (which tripled to 35,000). Time will tell, but so far the record is one of steady improvement.

The success of the telephone company sale combined with a rapidly growing inflow of portfolio capital into Peruvian debt paper and the Lima stock exchange sparked strong foreign interest in the privatizations that took place after February 1994. These included the Lima area electric-distribution network, which was separated into two companies bought by utilities from Spain, Chile, and Canada; the Tintaya copper mine near Cuzco, for which a U.S. mining company paid somewhat more than the original construction cost[11] — without taking into account intervening inflation; the Cajamarquilla zinc refinery near Lima, sold at near-replacement cost to a Canadian mining company after being mothballed for several years due to a preference from foreign buyers for zinc concentrate for their own refineries, especially in Europe, and two banks — large by Peruvian standards. These two large institutions were Interbanc (the former Banco Internacional, in which Chemical Bank was an investor in the 1960s) and Banco Continental (founded by Chase Manhattan and sold to the Peruvian Brescia group and Spain's Banco de Bilbao-Vizcaya).

During the 1980s, Spanish companies (including Telefónica and the major Spanish banks) had been obsessed with the country risk — or *riesgo país* — of Latin American countries, including Peru. Thus, Spain's renewed interest in its old flagship colony was a notable feature of the Peruvian privatizations. Also notable was the interest of Chilean investors, not only a variety of corporate and portfolio investors but also of pension funds and utilities. The utilities, flush with funds in a limited domestic market, were especially attracted to Peru. They recognized its potential for high growth, given the country's current low level of consumption, and saw an investment climate more congenial than that of Argentina's larger market, where some Chilean utility investments had encountered difficulties. Many Peruvians harbor negative attitudes toward Chile as a result of historical conflicts between the two countries, so it is to the credit of the Fujimori administration that it ignored the ghosts of the past and welcomed the Chilean investors.

The last big utility privatization, in October 1995, was the sale of the generating system for the Lima region, with a capacity of 700 megawatts. A group led by Entergy, a major utility in the southern United States, paid a company value of about $800 million ($475 million for 60 percent of the company), not too far below replacement cost.

Following the reelection of Fujimori as president in July 1995, privatization in Peru slowed somewhat. However, as explained above, this was mostly due to the complexity of the sales and also to the inevitable economic slowdown after the election, which had been preceded by a substantial expansion of government spending — financed partly with privatization revenues — that subsequently led the central bank to tighten credit significantly. Should Peru experience strong export growth and substantial inflows of capital investment into mining and other private sector activities, the slowdown will probably be of short duration.

It is difficult to measure the improvement in productivity of the privatized companies over a short span of years. But in most companies, the improvement — which will ultimately be reflected in profits and, in turn, tax revenue — is large. Tintaya, for example, has almost doubled copper production, even before launching a major investment program to expand the available ore body. In gas stations, typically bought by smaller entrepreneurs, sales rose 50 percent between 1992 and 1994 (admittedly, a period of rapid economic expansion) and profits also rose sharply with the marketing of new, associated products, such as convenience stores (see, for example, *Perú Económico* 1995).

THE IMPACT OF PRIVATIZATION

From the start of privatization in June 1991, with the sale of its minority share in a leasing company, until March 1996, with the sale of its ailing steel mill, the Peruvian government disposed of 71 state-owned assets. The number of individual transactions was much larger, because 78 gas stations, 35 tourism hotels, and a number of fishmeal plants and fishing boats were sold individually. The total value of the sales, without counting concession agreements, was $4.6 billion; of that, $3.8 billion went to the Treasury, with the remainder returning to the companies as initial capital investments, primarily to the telephone company. Peruvian debt paper (at market value) was used to pay for only $270 million of the privatization revenues. Finally, the government extracted investment commitments of $2.7 billion, a figure likely to be exceeded, since the telephone company plans to double its original $1 billion investment commitment between 1994 and 1999 (Apoyo Consultoría 1995).

In order to put these numbers in perspective, total sales proceeds between 1992 and 1995 were, on average, equivalent to about 2.5 percent of annual GNP, somewhat higher than the average for other Latin American countries undergoing privatization. This average conceals large variations from year to year, particularly because the $2 billion privatization of the telephone company and several other large-asset sales in electricity and mining all took place in 1994. The significant fiscal impact of privatization was due to the large size of Peru's state enterprise sector, as well as to the relatively high prices paid at privatization for certain state companies, notably the Peruvian telephone companies, Compañía Peruana de Teléfonos (CPT) and Empresa Nacional de Telecomunicaciones (ENTEL). If the privatizations of PetroPerú and the Mantaro Dam take place,[12] the revenue from those sales will match the average of the previous four years.

Perhaps the most interesting macroeconomic feature of Peruvian privatization is the unleashing of a flow of future investment. This results not so much from the investment commitments made by buyers at the time of privatization as from the new owners' determination — barring some catastrophic event — to expand these enterprises profitably. In a broad-brush, conservative estimate,[13] the minimum investment by the privatized companies between 1996 and 1999 was in the range of $5 billion, about equivalent to 2.5 percent of GNP, the same percentage as the government had collected in the previous four years — not a bad bargain for the Peruvian economy. This volume of investment would never have been achieved had these enterprises stayed in the public sector. This is not simply a matter of the dynamic of public finance, where always scarce resources are needed in long-neglected areas such as education and public health or of the political leanings of the government in power, but simply of ownership. The shareholders of the newly privatized companies see the prospect of growth and returns on their initial acquisition if they are able to expand the enterprises through investment. In the public sector, on the other hand, state-owned companies (SOEs) are the responsibility of everyone (politics) and of no one (no transparent incentives for management), with the result that investment is sometimes governed by what middlemen and functionaries think they can milk out of equipment purchases and the loans to finance them.

New investments in privatized companies will be partly financed through external borrowing, just as the state sector would have done, but the proportion is likely to be somewhat less because of far better operating margins and, in the case of public utilities, less delay in tariff adjustments. Moreover, the borrowing will be on somewhat better terms, given the high credit rating of the foreign parent companies that own the largest privatized Peruvian companies.

On the labor front, privatization so far has not had the effect of greatly reducing the labor force, as occurred in some other countries, notably Argentina. Between 1990 and 1992, the central government itself cut administrative personnel by about 50 percent, but in SOEs, staff reductions prior to privatization were somewhat smaller, ranging from almost none to 25 percent in some mining companies and utilities. The most overstaffed company, PetroPerú, is also the one where privatization is meeting the greatest opposition, precisely out of fear of massive reductions. As an incentive to the labor force remaining in the privatized companies, the privatization law (Legislative Decree 674 of 1991) allows the sale of up to 10 percent of a state company to its workers, either by using their fund for accumulated years of service (in reality an accounting fiction since no state company has created real reserves for that purpose) or through a state subsidy for a sum up to $10,000 payable at an interest rate of 1 percent per month. Only limited use was made of these options, with the largest percentages purchased in the case of the airline (7.2 percent); the Cerro Verde mine (8.4 percent, to be significantly diluted when Cyprus Mines expands the operation); and Interbanc (9.4 percent) (COPRI 1994). The largest SOE privatization, that of the telephone company, was already a long-time quoted company on the Lima stock exchange prior to its sale, principally because potential users were required to buy shares in order to qualify for installation of a telephone line.

Thus, Peru, like many other Latin American countries, did not make a broad-based effort to create "popular participation privatization" of the type that was promoted in Britain (particularly in the case of British Telecom) and in Central Europe and Russia through vouchers, most of which were re-sold. The reason, of course, was the small size of the Peruvian stock market and the lack of institutions that could support its steady growth. The 12 insurance companies operating in Peru in 1994 had a total premium income of only $333 million, compared to $1.8 billion in Chile. The incipient private pension system, begun in 1994, has assets of $600 million, small compared to the Chilean system ($25 billion), and much smaller than most U.S. state-level pension funds (for example, the State of Wisconsin's is $50 billion). If economic growth continues and private pension coverage expands, Peru will achieve indirect popular participation in its largest privatized enterprises, which will, in time, be among the most active companies on the stock exchange as a result of pension-fund investments.

The telephone company was the one case where a major attempt was made to create widespread popular interest in privatization. In mid-1996, the government was selling part of its remaining interest in a flotation totaling about $1.3 billion, of which at least $100 million was made available to small investors in Peru in lots of up to $500 each. Focus groups for potential smallholders, organized by Apoyo, the leading polling organization in Peru, suggested that the government's already optimistic target could be met and possibly exceeded once a shareholder-education effort is completed. Interestingly, the initial reaction of most people questioned was that they thought that participation in the stock market was only for "rich folk."

A final word on a major but hard-to-quantify effect of privatization — the widening net of international investors interested in Peru. Privatization greatly stimulated the interest of portfolio investors, although only two cement companies (a 49-percent share in Cementos Lima and a smaller company in the north) were sold on the stock market. But even so, the large number of foreign corporations bidding in the privatizations and the companies that won (besides Peruvians, the biggest investors were from Spain, the United States, Chile, and Canada) have substantially expanded the competitiveness of the economy. Even in utilities, where competition is more difficult, the existence of companies from diverse backgrounds is not only likely to benefit consumers but also regulators, who will gain from a variety of perspectives and approaches to such things as customer service, integrity, reporting compliance, and so forth.

Italian-Peruvian geographer and historian Antonio Raimondi said over a century ago that Peru was a beggar seated on a heap of gold. Time will tell if the poverty associated with the excessive expansion of state enterprises in the 1970s can be turned into the gold of productive enterprise. Certainly, the privatization effort in the first half of the 1990s was a significant and promising beginning.

Notes

1. See, for example, various pieces in Lowenthal 1975 and Goodwin 1969.

2. The title of the *Foreign Affairs* article played on that of a classic essay, "A Message to García," written by Elbert Hubbard in 1899, about the man he considered the true hero of the Spanish American War — a messenger who braved death by carrying a note behind the lines to the leader of the Cuban insurgents. "It is not book-learning young men need," explained Hubbard in his essay, "nor instruction about this or that, but a stiffening of the vertebrae which will cause them ... to act promptly, concentrate their energies: do the thing — 'carry the message to García!'" —Ed.

3. The Brady Plan, designed in 1989 by then-Secretary of the U.S. Treasury Nicholas Brady, made it possible for Latin American countries to negotiate debt relief with the international banks.

4. Carlos Montoya returned to Peru in 1981 from a post at the World Bank to head Pro-Bayóvar, an entity within the Ministry of Energy and Mines then led by the author.

5. As of late 1999, Centromin was still owned by the government. —Ed.

6. The Cobriza Copper Mine, financed by the World Bank and Interamerican Development Bank in the mid-1970s, was located away from the more promising or bodies discovered years before by Robert P. Koenig, the U.S. geologist who discovered most of the large copper deposits in Peru in the 1930s and 1940s and who became head of Cerro Corporation.

7. The Doe Run Company, a United States-based mining company (the successor to St. Joe Minerals), bought the Cobriza mine for $7.5 million from Centromin Peru in 1998, along with the La Droya smelter. —Ed.

8. Mantaro Dam and Sedapal have not been privatized as of late 1999.

9. See, for example, the presentation by the head of Lyonnaise des Eaux for Argentina at the World Bank/Latin American Economic System (Sistema Económico Latinoamericano — SELA) Conference on Latin America and Caribbean Privatization Conference held in Lima, January 22-23,1996.

10. See Kuczynski 1988 for data. These are not measures of value added, which would probably be roughly half the numbers shown.

11. Tintaya, a high-grade copper mine in a remote southern Andean area, was conceived under the military regime but redesigned and built with possible privatization in view while the author was Minister of Mines and Energy (1980-1982).

12. The biggest refinery of Peru (La Pampilla Refinery) as well as oil Blocks 8 and 8X and the lubricant plant (PETROLUBE) have been privatized. The privatization process for the other units of PetroPerú is still in progress. —Ed.

13. These figures are estimates by the author based on plans announced by companies, investment commitments at the time of privatization, and a 25-percent discount for possible overestimation.

References

Apoyo Consultoría. 1995. *Perspectivas del proceso de privatización en el Perú*. Lima: Editorial Apoyo.

Comisión de Promoción de la Inversión Privada (COPRI). 1994. *Informativo COPRI*. Lima.

Comisión de Promoción de la Inversión Privada (COPRI). 1997. *Informativo COPRI*. Lima.

Comisión Económica para América Latina y el Caribe/UN Economic Commission for Latin America (ECLAC). 1996. *Balance Preliminar de la Economía de América Latina y el Caribe*. Santiago de Chile: ECLAC.

Goodwin, Richard. 1969. "Letter from Peru." *The New Yorker*. May 17.

Gorriti, Gustavo. 1990. *Sendero: Historia de la guerra milenaria en el Perú*, vol. 1. Lima: Editorial Apoyo.

Interamerican Development Bank (IDB).1997. *Annual Report*. Washington, D.C.: Interamerican Development Bank.

Kuczynski, Pedro-Pablo. 1988. *Latin American Debt*. Baltimore: The Johns Hopkins University Press.

Kuczynski, Pedro-Pablo, and Felipe Ortiz de Zevallos. 1990. *Respuestas para los 90's*. Lima: Editorial Apoyo.

Lowenthal, Abraham F. 1975. *The Peruvian Experiment*. Princeton, N.J.: Princeton University Press.

Palmer, David Scott, ed. 1992. *Shining Path of Peru*. New York: St. Martin's Press.

Perú Económico. 1995. February.

Roett, Riordan. 1985. "Peru: The Message from García." *Foreign Affairs* (Winter).

Williamson, John, ed. 1990. *Latin American Adjustment*. Washington, D.C.: Institute for International Economics.

CHAPTER SIX

The Experience of Privatization in the Caribbean

RICHARD L. BERNAL AND WINSOME J. LESLIE

S ince 1983, privatization has taken on increasing importance as a worldwide phenomenon, a trend that has involved a redefinition of the role of the state in the economy. Privatization in this context is one form of divestment and refers to the transfer of ownership of state-owned entities to the private sector.

Beginning in the mid-1970s, there was a worldwide questioning of the efficacy of state-led development strategies, which had failed to achieve the objectives of greater national control over the economy and increased efficiency. Far from contributing to government revenue, many state-owned enterprises (SOEs) had proved to be a drain on government resources. By the early 1980s, therefore, in every region of the world, there was some degree of retreat from a belief in the state as the engine of growth and from a commitment to state intervention in the economy. The notion that the state needed to be directly involved in the production and distribution of goods and services was being replaced with a belief that it should confine itself to the role of facilitator.

The regime of General Augusto Pinochet in Chile commenced the first comprehensive program in Latin America and the Caribbean as part of a wider economic liberalization strategy and an attempt to mobilize foreign investment. After the initial phase of privatization (1974-1978), a second round took place between 1985 and 1989 (Larraín 1995). While Chile's was among the earliest programs to be implemented, the industrialized countries, led by Britain, dominated the process through the mid-1980s in terms of value of assets transferred. In 1981, for example, the partial privatization of British Aerospace raised US$245 million, and, by 1986, the Margaret Thatcher government had launched a sweeping divestment program, which resulted in the privatization of other major enterprises — British Telecommunications, British Airways, Rolls Royce, and British Gas (Chapman 1990). After that, other Organization for Economic Cooperation and Development (OECD) countries — France, Germany, Italy, and Japan — followed suit. The former Eastern Bloc has also pursued privatization, and, as of 1994, this region accounted for 16.5 percent of all privatizations worldwide (*Wall Street Journal* 1995, R4).

In the developing world, privatization initiatives have been a recent phenomenon. In many instances, governments in less developed countries have embraced privatization only as part of the conditionality attached to the structural adjustment programs of the International Monetary Fund (IMF) and the World Bank. Beginning in the mid-1980s, these multilateral institutions began to focus on private sector development and privatization as the path to self-sustained growth. As such, privatization of SOEs became a vital component of a wider program of economic liberalization. In its 1994 *World Economic Outlook*, the IMF maintained that countries that had firmly committed themselves to privatization, such as Chile and Mexico, had experienced higher rates of growth than countries in Sub-Saharan Africa, where progress with respect to divestment was slow (IMF 1994, 50).

According to the International Finance Corporation (IFC), between 1988 and 1993, industrialized countries accounted for 15 percent and developing countries 85 percent of the 2,655 privatization transactions worldwide. These transactions yielded US$271 billion in revenue, and industrialized countries accounted for US$175 billion of that total (IFC 1995b). To date, most of the privatization activity in the developing world has occurred in Latin America and the Caribbean. Between 1988 and 1993, in dollar terms, this region accounted for more than half of all privatization revenues in the Third World (Richard Lawrence 1995, 3A)

This chapter will discuss privatization initiatives in the English-speaking Caribbean. With the exception of Jamaica, the countries in question have been pursuing divestment strategies for only a decade or less. In most cases, reduction in state-owned enterprises (SOEs) has only occurred since 1992. However, tentative conclusions can be drawn about lessons learned from the process, based on this experience. The following analysis will describe the various modalities that Caribbean countries have utilized for private sector involvement in the state sector, and, where possible, it will briefly examine the impact on employment, economic efficiency, and the availability of goods and services.

OBJECTIVES OF PRIVATIZATION IN DEVELOPING COUNTRIES

Frequently, privatization in developing countries is motivated by a desire to do one of the following: 1) improve company performance and efficiency in terms of reliability of delivery, quality, and price; 2) introduce competition in areas long monopolized by government; 3) raise income, as an alternative to raising taxes or incurring further debt; 4) reduce the burden on the government's budget; 5) settle foreign debt; 6) expand or develop the local equity market; 7) encourage industrial development; 8) attract foreign investment; and 9) promote growth and increase equity in income and access to resources (Berg 1988, 185-209).

In addition to privatization, divestment can be undertaken in a number of ways. For example, services traditionally provided by government or the management of SOEs can be contracted out to the private sector. Worker-owned enterprises can also be established, either through employee stock ownership programs or companies formed by government employees to purchase the SOE. Furthermore, an entire SOE or parts of it can be leased to the private sector, or the government can enter into a joint venture with private sector interests or with workers.

INDEPENDENCE AND NATIONALISM: THE ORIGINS OF PRIVATIZATION IN THE ENGLISH-SPEAKING CARIBBEAN

Privatization of state-owned entities in the English-speaking Caribbean must be understood in the context of the nationalism prevailing in the first decade of independence in these countries. Jamaica, Trinidad and Tobago, Guyana, and Barbados became independent between 1962 and 1966; the Eastern Caribbean states, which include Antigua and Barbuda, Dominica, Grenada, Montserrat, St. Kitts and Nevis, St. Lucia, and St. Vincent and the Grenadines became independent in the 1970s. Government involvement in the economy grew during the first few years following independence, largely as an outgrowth of ideology and the political imperative to assert sovereignty and economic independence. In some cases, however, governments felt obliged to take over facilities owned by foreigners who wished to close their operations. In Trinidad and Tobago, for example, the government's acquisition of a controlling interest in British West Indian Airways (BWIA) and its takeover of British Petroleum's holdings on the island were aimed at protecting the income and employment of workers who would have been displaced by these companies' withdrawal. The public sector, therefore, came to play a prominent role in Jamaica, Trinidad and Tobago, and Guyana by the mid-1970s, as the state became directly involved in a wide range of commercial and industrial activities.

Trinidad and Tobago

Public sector ownership rose significantly in Trinidad and Tobago beginning in 1960 with the acquisition of the Telephone Company of Trinidad and Tobago (TELCO) and BWIA. By 1972, the Trinidad government held investments in 35 companies — hotels, telecommunications, petroleum and sugar, banking and finance, as well as manufacturing and industrial development. The Third Five-Year Plan (1969-1973) stated that the public sector would not "hesitate to enter either alone or in partnership with foreign or local private capital into the productive fields of industry, tourism, and agriculture" (Henry 1990, 256). In addition, all public utilities would be owned or substantially controlled by the public sector. The White Paper on Public Sector Participation in Industrial and Commercial Activities pointed to the need for state intervention because of "innate deficiencies in the private sector." In other words, the private sector could not be relied on to be the engine of growth needed to safeguard the country's independence, stimulate economic growth, increase employment, and create an equitable distribution of income (Henry 1990, 256).

The OPEC oil price increase in 1973, resulting in higher levels of domestic crude oil production and a new tax regime for the petroleum sector, significantly augmented government revenues, providing the resources necessary for the further expansion of the state sector. By 1975, the government held 100-percent ownership in major enterprises, such as the Trinidad and Tobago Television Company Ltd., the Trinidad and Tobago Telephone Company, and BWIA. Steps were also taken to increase state participation in natural resource-based industries. Fertilizers of Trinidad and Tobago (FERTRIN) was established as a joint venture with AMOCO.

TRINGEN, an ammonia manufacturing company, was created in a joint venture with W. R. Grace and Company. Between 1973 and 1983, the Trinidad and Tobago government invested TT$7.3 billion (US$1.25 billion) in equity, loans, and advances in the SOE sector (Republic of Trinidad and Tobago 1995, 7-8).

Jamaica

The People's National Party (PNP) government led by Michael Manley, which came to power in Jamaica in 1972, adopted a democratic socialist platform in 1974. The Principles and Objectives of the PNP stated that "in the economic sphere, socialism requires social ownership and/or control of the means of production, distribution, and exchange, which must begin with a dominant public sector which owns and/or controls the commanding heights of economy" (PNP 1979). Accordingly, the government targeted the banking system, public utilities, and the sugar and bauxite companies for public ownership. By 1974, the government had acquired all the outstanding foreign-owned shares in the island's only electric company, Jamaica Public Service Company Ltd. (JPSCo). Three years later, the government purchased the shares of Barclay's Bank, renaming it the National Commercial Bank Ltd. (NCB). Thus, NCB became the first wholly state-owned commercial bank. Sugar plantations were also converted into workers cooperatives, while major changes occurred in the bauxite/alumina industry. In 1974, the government imposed a production tax on Kaiser, Reynolds, Alcoa, and Alcan — the bauxite companies operating in Jamaica — and it announced plans to purchase just over half of their mining operations as well as all the bauxite-producing lands.

By 1979, a total of 185 state enterprises had been established in Jamaica. The state owned all utilities, the largest commercial bank (NCB), 51 percent of bauxite mining operations, 75 percent of sugar output, and 48 percent of hotel capacity. The government also created a state trading corporation responsible for the importation of basic commodities (Bernal 1986, 614-615). Government services, which accounted for less than 7.7 percent of GDP in 1953, rose to 19.22 percent by 1980 (Sampson 1993, 265).

Guyana

Likewise in Guyana, after the ruling People's National Congress (PNC) created a Cooperative Socialist Republic in 1970, nationalization of foreign-owned assets became an important priority for the Forbes Burnham regime, which sought to give the government more control over the economy. By the mid-1970s, the state had taken over key activities earning foreign exchange, such as sugar and bauxite production, public transportation, much of the import trade, and a significant portion of distribution and communications (Thomas 1988, 252). Furthermore, through a group of enterprises under the supervision of the Public Corporations Secretariat, government control extended to pharmaceuticals, timber and log processing, fishing, livestock, printing, and repair workshops. In essence, the state dominated much of the country's economic life.

Grenada

In Grenada, the Maurice Bishop regime, which came to power in 1979, pursued a "mixed economy" approach. However, the People's Revolutionary

Government (PRG) stressed that the state would be the dominant sector and would lead the development process. In late 1979, it established a state-owned bank by acquiring the Canadian Imperial Bank of Commerce, which was about to close its operations on the island. In the tourist sector, the state purchased Holiday Inn and confiscated five other hotels from former Prime Minister Eric Gairy and his supporters. The government also became directly involved in trade through the establishment of a state-owned marketing and import authority. The state became the sole importer of basic consumer items (sugar and rice) and production inputs (such as cement and fertilizer) (Thomas 1988, 241-244).

This high level of government participation throughout the Caribbean in the 1970s was a reaction to what was seen as the negative impact of foreign ownership of sectors and large enterprises. However, it was also a response to the perceived shortcomings of the "industrialization by invitation" development model. This was import-substitution industrialization (ISI) by means of direct foreign investment attracted by generous incentives, such as tax holidays, unrestricted repatriation of profits, and duty-free concessions on imported inputs. Economists believed that this type of foreign investment had resulted in dependent development by reinforcing foreign ownership and a concomitant denationalization of decisionmaking about resource allocation (Manley 1982, 25-37). This was most strongly felt in the mineral-exporting economies — Jamaica, Guyana, and Trinidad — where the mineral sector remained essentially an enclave within the larger economy, more integrated with international markets than the domestic one (Girvan 1976, 30).

THE SHIFT TO PRIVATIZATION

B y the early 1980s, the conviction about the benefits of state ownership and control came to be questioned due to a convergence of several factors. State-owned enterprises had become overstaffed, inefficient, and a drain on public finances. Because of large and persistent fiscal and trade deficits, as well as mounting foreign debt, governments could no longer afford to subsidize unprofitable operations. The weak performance of SOEs also coincided with a worldwide shift toward free-market principles.

In the United States, Ronald Reagan, who expressed a firm belief in private sector-led growth and a free market to allocate resources, had been elected U.S. president in 1980. Reagan's approach was evident in the conditionality attached to U.S. bilateral assistance to the Caribbean, which stressed economic reform, and to assistance from multilateral institutions, such as the World Bank, Inter-American Development Bank (IDB), and the International Monetary Fund. These multilateral institutions required countries to accept privatization and economic liberalization as a condition for receiving loans.

Trends in the Caribbean toward large-scale divestment of government holdings in various sectors of the economy must be evaluated in this context. By the early 1990s, several countries had already undertaken structural adjustment or economic reform programs that included divestment plans. Accordingly, at the 1994 World Bank-sponsored meetings of the Caribbean Group for Cooperation in Economic Development (CGCED) held in Washington, D.C., Trinidad and Tobago, Jamaica,

Guyana, and Grenada were able wholeheartedly to endorse privatization and private sector-led growth as part of their medium-term strategies for economic development.

Guyana

In 1989, the government of Guyana formulated a divestment policy as part of a structural adjustment program. In the previous decades, the high level of public sector control of the economy was associated with declines in both local and foreign investment. SOEs had consistently performed poorly. Twenty of the 28 enterprises under the Public Corporations Secretariat had not been able to pay either taxes or dividends to the central government since the late 1970s. This had contributed to fiscal deficits, which increased from 12 percent to 55 percent of GDP between 1975 and 1989 (Hope 1992, 20).

By the October 1992 elections, 14 public enterprises had been either fully or partially privatized or liquidated. These initial divestitures included Guyana Telecommunications Corporation, Guyana Transport Services Ltd., Guyana Stockfeeds Ltd. (partial), and Demerara Woods Ltd. In 1990, Guyana Telecommunications Corporation was the first to be divested through an asset sale arrangement for US$16.5 million. In 1991, 70 percent of the country's largest bank, Guyana Bank for Industry and Commerce, previously acquired from Barclay's, was sold through a public offering (Esau 1994, 160).

Privatization soon became a controversial issue as many Guyanese expressed serious concerns about the speed with which these early divestments had taken place, the absence of a framework for the process, the lack of transparency of many of the transactions, the failure to achieve optimal prices for state assets, and the fact that the public was unaware of the benefits of divestment. Accordingly, the administration of Cheddi Jagan, which came to power in 1992, halted the divestment process. In the view of the government, "A policy objective of raising money for the fiscal budget is not sufficient to explain privatization to a population which has been conditioned in the past to regard state ownership as beneficial in and of itself. . . . The objective of raising money alone raises the spectre of ad-hocism, recklessness and of desperation, giving rise to doubts as regards the reasonableness of the amounts received from divestment of assets/interest in Public Corporations" (Cooperative Republic of Guyana 1993, 4). Although the government was still committed to privatization in principle, it was felt that the strategy should not be based simply on budgetary concerns but ought to be placed in the broader context of a desire to improve SOE efficiency and productivity through a private sector-led development program.

Revised objectives and guidelines for privatization were outlined in a ministry paper tabled in the Guyana Assembly in June 1993. A Privatization Unit was established to coordinate the process with a cabinet-level Privatization Board, chaired by the Ministry of Finance, that was composed of representatives from labor unions, consumer groups, and the private sector. Phase I began with 10 companies in distribution, transportation, rice milling, paint, fisheries, and foods, the sales of which netted proceeds close to US$30 million. (See Table 1.) Phase II, which involved 16 more profitable companies, began in 1992, but the process initially has encountered some difficulties, partly because of a critical shortage of experts qualified in various aspects of the divestment process.

Since 1995, the process of privatization in Guyana has been proceeding fairly well. (See Table 2.) During the 1995-1996 fiscal year alone, the government divested all its shares in the Guyana Pegasus Hotel and six other enterprises, including Demerara Distillers Ltd. The major assets of the Guyana National Engineering Corporation and 19 percent of the government's shares in Guyana Stores Ltd. were also divested. In 1997, the government also sold its shares in the National Bank of Industry and Commerce, and divested its share of Guyana Stockfeeds for US$900,000. In 1998 and 1999, the government continued with the privatization program, and it is expected that the bauxite companies — LINMINE and BERMINE — will again be brought to the point of sale along with six other companies — Guyana National Printers Ltd. (GNPL), Guyana Pharmaceutical Corporation (GPC), the Versailles Dairy Complex, GNCB Trust, the Wauna Oil Palm Estate, and Guyana Stores Ltd., which will be divested of the remaining government shares. All these entities were brought to the point of sale by the end of 1998 (*Financial Gleaner* 1999). Guyana Airways was privatized early in 1999, and, in October 1999, bids were received for Guyana Pharmaceutical Corporation and Guyana Stores Ltd. There have also been expressions of interest for BERMINE from both ALCAN and ALCOA bauxite companies.

Table 1.
Guyana: Public Corporations Divested, 1989-1992

1. Guyana Timbers Ltd.
2. Guyana Telecommunications Corporation
3. Guyana Nichimo Ltd.
4. Guyana National Trading Corporation Ltd.
5. Guyana Leather Craft Ltd.
6. Livestock Development Company Ltd. (partially)
7. National Paint Company Ltd.
8. Demerara Woods Ltd.
9. Guyana Transport Services Ltd.
10. Quality Foods (Guyana) Ltd.
11. Sijan Place Restaurant
12. Guyana Fisheries Ltd.
13. Guyana Rice Milling & Marketing Authority
14. Guyana Stockfeeds Ltd. (partially)
15. Soap and Detergents Ltd.

Source: Cooperative Republic of Guyana (Ministry of Finance), 1993.

Most significantly, privatization of the Guyana Electricity Corporation (GEC), which should have been completed in 1998, was delayed until Fall of 1999. The Commonwealth Development Corporation (CDC) of the United Kingdom and the Electricity Supply Board International Ltd. (ESBI) were chosen in 1998 as the preferred bidder for a 50-percent equity interest in the GEC. The CDC/ESBI consortium has indicated that they will initially invest about US$23 million in the new company. However, concerns about the political situation, coupled with a devaluation of the Guyanese dollar, has led the CDC/ESBI Consortium to conclude that it will not be able to realize in the near future the 23 percent return on investment stipulated in its agreement with the government. As a result, the consortium has proposed new financial arrangements to invest US$9 million initially and the remainder through a letter of credit over the next four years. Final agreement was reached with CDC/ESBI early in October 1999 when the government accepted these new terms.

Privatization of GEC had previously stalled toward the end of 1997; a Canadian firm, SaskPower Commercial, withdrew its bid for 50 percent of GEC in the wake of the political uncertainty after the opposition contested the election of Janet Jagan as president of Guyana (*Power in Latin America* 1999).

So far, the effects of privatization have been positive. Anticipated large-scale layoffs did not occur, and, in some instances, wages have risen substantially. For example, after privatization of Demerara Woods, the firm raised wages by over 120 percent in 1991 and another 55 percent in 1992. Efficiency has also increased. For example, telephone service has improved noticeably since the privatization of the Guyana Telephone and Telegraph Co. Ltd.

Table 2.
Guyana: Entities Earmarked for Privatization or Restructuring, 1994-1996

1. Guyana Stores Ltd. (GSL)
2. Guyana National Engineering Corporation
3. Guyana Glassworks
4. Shares in Demerara Distillers Ltd.
5. National Edible Oil Company
6. Guyana National Printers Ltd.
7. Guyana Mortgage Finance Bank
8. Guyana Pharmaceutical Corporation
9. Guyana Cooperative Insurance Services
10. Shares in National Bank of Industry and Commerce
11. Guyana National Co-operative Bank (GNCB)*
12. Guyana Co-operative Agricultural and Industrial Development Bank (GAIBANK)
13. Guyana Oil Company Ltd.
14. Guyana Electricity Corporation
15. Linden Mining Company (LINMINE)
16. Guyana Airways Corporation
17. Guyana Sugar Corporation (GUYSUCO)
18. GUYSUCO's Livestock Dairy Project
19. Shares in Seals and Packing Industries Ltd.
20. Versailles Dairy Complex
21. Wauna Oil Palm Estate

* Merged with GAIBANK, restructuring underway.

Source: Embassy of the Republic of Guyana, Washington, D.C., 1998.

However, the government has been criticized for "giving away" some enterprises, by involving speculators who have resold the companies. There have also been questions about the logic of selling profitable enterprises. In addition, the privatization process has not been completely transparent. Observers claim that some of the larger transactions have taken place in private negotiations outside public bidding procedures. These difficulties have made privatization a serious political issue (World Bank 1992, 42-43; World Bank 1994, 28-29). This can clearly be seen in the debate about the divestment of government-owned holdings in the sugar industry. In this regard, there were public concerns that the sale of sugar lands to the private sector would benefit those Guyanese with the financial means to make purchases. As a result, the government of Janet Jagan has stated that sugar companies will not be privatized and sugar lands will not be sold to the private sector. Plans for the partial divestment of GEC to the CDC/ESBI Consortium also encountered initial resistance from the unions and the political opposition. They opposed one of the main conditions of the arrangement, namely, a progressive increase in electricity rates.

Trinidad and Tobago

The Trinidad government continued to acquire equity in various companies until the early 1990s. Indeed, by January 1992, the state's portfolio consisted of shares in 87 enterprises, valued at TT$6.5 billion (US$1.12 billion), in addition to sizeable investments in four public utilities — water, power, transport, and ports. Nevertheless, privatization began in 1987 under the National Alliance for Reconstruction (NAR) government. Forty-nine percent of TELCO was divested for US$80 million, and a new company formed, Telecommunications Services of Trinidad and Tobago (TSTT), via a merger with Cable and Wireless. The government's controlling interest in Trinidad Cement was transferred to private hands through a public offering in 1988, and plans were formulated to divest the remaining 29 percent through a strategic partnership (20 percent) and public offering (9 percent) (Esau 1994, 162). This divestment policy continued under the People's National Movement (PNM) government, which took office in 1991. In that year, the government outlined its approach to ownership of state enterprises, stressing the role of the state as facilitator for economic activity. Accordingly, the state would reduce its holdings in the commercial sector (except in areas of strategic importance, such as oil and gas, and telecommunications or where a crucial social service was being provided). If an operation were important for diversification of the economy and the private sector could not mobilize resources to undertake the investment or if a foreign investor required the participation of the state in a particular project to minimize country risk, state participation in the commercial sector would continue. However, this participation by the state would not be long-term in nature, and divestment to the private sector would take place as soon as it was feasible.

By 1993, the government had identified 30 SOEs for divestment and 12 for liquidation. A Divestment Secretariat was created in the Ministry of Finance to coordinate the process. By mid-1995, several companies had been either fully or partially privatized, including Trinidad and Tobago Urea Company Ltd., Trinidad and Tobago Methanol Company, BWIA, and the Electricity Commission. In the energy sector, the exploration and production activities of Trinidad and Tobago Oil Company (TRINTOC) and the Trinidad and Tobago Petroleum Company (TINTOPEC) were merged to create a new company, Petroleum Company of Trinidad and Tobago Ltd. (PETROTRIN). The nonpetroleum assets of both TRINTOC and TINTOPEC have been divested (Republic of Trinidad and Tobago 1995, 8, 10, 22; Republic of Trinidad and Tobago 1994, 12-13; Republic of Trinidad

Table 3.
Principal Divestments in Trinidad and Tobago as of January 1997

Company	T&T Share-holding	Percentage Divested	Timing	Buyer
T&T Urea Co.	100%	Full	Completed	Arcadian L.P.
Fertilizers of T&T	51%	Full	Completed	Arcadian L.P.
Trinidad & Tobago Priting & Packaging	100%	Full	Nov. 1993	
Caribbean Hotel Dev. Co. Ltd.	99.2%	Partial (Hotel Assets)	June 1994	Bella Forma Resorts
Ethanol Co.	100%	Partial	Completed	Ferrostaal/Helm
BWIA International	100%	Partial	July 1994	Acker & Loeb
PETROTRIN	100%	Partial	1994/95	
T&T Forest Products	100%	Partial	1995	
Trinidad Cement	29.1%	Partial	Aug. 1994	Cementos Mexicanos
Telecommunications Services of T&T		51%	Partial	1995
Electricity Commission	51%	Partial	Completed	Southern Electric/ Amoco Business Dev. Co.
National Flour Mills	100%	Partial	20% 1995 15% 1996 14% 1997	Public issue
Trinidad and Tobago Methanol	100%	Full	69% 1994 & May 1997	Ferrostaal/Helm/ CMC
Shipping Corporation of Trinidad & Tobago	100%	Partial	Jan. 1997	

Source: Trinidad & Tobago Ministry of Finance, 1995.

and Tobago, Status of Divestment Secretariat, 20). Several methods of divestment were utilized, such as competitive bidding, sale of shares on the Trinidad and Tobago stock exchange, sales to former lessees, and the formation of strategic alliances with either local or foreign partners. Under a World Bank-funded US$138 million Water Supply and Sewage Rehabilitation Project, the government evaluated the water sector for possible privatization. As a result, a management contract was awarded to a private company in April 1996 to operate the Water and Sewage Authority. Government holdings in National Flour Mills were sold in two offerings in 1996 and 1997, and the privatization of additional operations are also planned by the end of 1999, including the sale of the Iron and Steel Company of Trinidad and Tobago, the sale of PETROTRIN assets, and the sale of additional shares of the National Flour Mills. (See Table 3).

Trinidad's privatization program had raised TT$3.39 billion (US$542.4 million) as of the summer of 1999. To date, employment losses have been minimal. When Trinidad and Tobago Printing and Packaging and National Fruit Processors were divested, the government settled all outstanding obligations with employees of those companies. Furthermore, the partial divestment of the Trinidad and Tobago Methanol Company will result in increased employment with the construction of an additional methanol plant (Republic of Trinidad and Tobago 1995, 42-44). However, in some instances, divestment has had a negative fiscal impact, as the government has had to assume outstanding liabilities of SOEs to financial institutions or settle obligations to employees. In the case of BWIA, for example, the government agreed to provide funds totaling TT$360 million (US$62.07 million) to cover outstanding loan liabilities, statutory payments, and severance costs, in addition to liquidating loans totaling TT$500 million (US$86.2 million) (Valley 1995).

Grenada

In Grenada, after the overthrow of the Maurice Bishop government in 1983, the new government committed itself to privatization. At that time, the state portfolio of 29 enterprises was reviewed with assistance from USAID. The government decided to utilize various privatization modalities: full divestment for seven companies; the outright sale of several enterprises; conversion of three entities to statutory bodies; liquidation; management contracting; and sale of shares. By 1992, in response to a weak fiscal situation, Grenada began a "self-imposed" three-year structural adjustment program, in which privatization of SOEs was an integral component. In that year, 90 percent of shares of NCB were sold to the Republic Bank of Trinidad and Tobago, and 10 percent to Grenadians and individuals in the Eastern Caribbean. In addition, the government sold most of its shares in Grenada Breweries Ltd. In 1994, 50 percent of the shares in the power company, Grenada Electricity Services Ltd. (GRENLEC), were sold to a U.S. company, WRB Enterprises Inc. (Grenada Ministry of Finance 1994, 3-4), and, in 1995, an additional 40 percent of government shares were sold.

In 1996, the government sold 15 percent of the equity in Grenada Broadcasting Corporation (GBC), and an additional 50 percent in 1997 to the Trinidad firm, Caribbean Communications Network. GBC is now called the Grenada Broadcasting Network. Majority shares in Grenada Telecommunications Ltd. (GRENTEL) have been divested to Cable and Wireless, and the new company is now known as Cable and Wireless Grenada Ltd. Divestment of shares in the Grenada Bank of Commerce Ltd. (GBC), and the Grenada Sugar Factory Ltd. are also underway. Government services, such as road maintenance, garbage collection, security, school maintenance, and computer services, are also to be privatized. Net proceeds from these transactions were estimated at EC$28 million (US$10.4 million) in 1996 and 1997 and EC$7 million (US$2.6 million) in 1998. However, the administration of Keith Mitchell, which came to power in 1995, is proceeding carefully out of concerns about the terms under which the previous government concluded certain privatization agreements. The Mitchell government has held an inquiry into the sale of GRENLEC, originally with a view to reacquiring the company. After negotiations in mid-1998, the government indicated it would honor the terms of the original sale, based on an arrangement to reduce electricity rates to consumers (Government of Grenada 1998, 4, 8).

Barbados

In Barbados, the privatization program is just beginning. In contrast to other islands in the Caribbean, public utility companies in Barbados — electricity, and telephone and telecommunications — have always been privately owned, and the history of public sector ownership has been based on pragmatism rather than on any commitment to a socialist philosophy. For example, the government took over Barbados National Oil Company after Mobil Oil Company, the original investor, decided to sell its shares because of Barbados' relatively low oil reserves. Nevertheless, the government of Prime Minister Owen Arthur, elected in 1994, has committed itself to a divestment program as part of a comprehensive strategy to mobilize local and foreign private investment. State enterprises that are purely commercial in nature will be privatized using various methods, giving priority to the small investor and SOE employees. Initially, plans were formulated to sell the government's interest in the Caribbean Broadcasting Corporation (CBC), but this transaction was placed on hold until the institution's financial situation improved. However, in April 1999, the Caribbean Communications Network, which had acquired majority shareholding in the Grenada Broadcasting Network, made a bid for 60-percent ownership of the television division of CBC. This proposal was made as part of a larger plan to develop a Caribbean Television Network. The government responded that any proposal for private ownership had to fall within the parameters outlined in the 1997 budget speech of Prime Minister Arthur. At that time, he had indicated that no entity in Barbados would be divested to a single owner and that any such transaction had to involve the broad participation of Barbadians. Specifically with respect to the CBC, the Prime Minister had stated that in any divestment of the company, a block of shares would have to be reserved for the staff of CBC, credit unions, trade unions, and individuals. If necessary, the government would retain a minority shareholding with a "strategic" partner. In the case of technology-intensive industries, such as the Barbados National Oil Company, the government will encourage joint ventures to attract needed skills and technology.

Elsewhere, the Arawak Cement Plant has been sold to Trinidad Cement, the Haywards Resort Hotel on the Northwest coast is now privately owned, and the repair services of the Transport Board have been divested. (The Board is now owned cooperatively by the transport workers, operating under a repair contract to the transport company.) There are no plans for further privatization in the transport sector. Indeed, the government has been quick to stress that some SOEs, such as the Transport Board or the Sanitation Services Authority, have a valuable contribution to make to the national interest, and, therefore, they will remain under government ownership (Barbados Labour Party 1994, 16-17, 42; *Daily Nation* 1995, 1).

St. Lucia

St. Lucia has also embarked on a divestment program as part of the economic reform process. St. Lucia has established an Office of Privatization and Private Sector Relations in the Office of the Prime Minister, and the government sees privatization as one of the ways in which it can develop and strengthen the local private sector. In this regard, there are plans to privatize the operations of the St. Lucia Marketing Board over the next three years. In addition, a portion of the government shares in the National Commercial Bank and the St. Lucia Development Bank will be sold to the public. In order to encourage broad local participation in divestment operations, St. Lucians will be offered tax deductions for the purchases of shares in SOEs. The government intends to create a new National Development Fund with divestment proceeds (Government of St. Lucia, 1998, 45).

Dominica

The government of Dominica sold its shares in the Dominica Electricity Company to the Commonwealth Development Corporation for US$21 million in 1996. The private sector is to take on a greater role in the imports of basic commodities, and, as a result, the Dominica Export and Import Agency will no longer have a monopoly on the imports of rice and sugar. The government is also exploring the feasibility of merging the Port and Airport Authorities under private management (Government of the Commonwealth of Dominica, 1998, 45).

Jamaica

Jamaica's privatization initiative began in 1981, following the election of Edward Seaga, who, in campaigning against the Manley regime in 1979 and 1980, committed himself to reducing the government's role in the economy and to privatizing SOEs. Because of a slump in the tourist industry, divestment commenced with the leasing of several state-owned hotels to the private sector. Seaga's government came to power in October 1980, and, although in principle it was firmly committed to privatization, his administration had no long-term privatization policy. Privatization, it was explained at the time, would occur purely on a case-by-case basis, selecting only those enterprises that would be most attractive to private sector buyers (Leeds 1991, 89). In addition, multilateral institutions (IMF, World Bank) and the United States Agency for International Development (USAID) enthusiastically supported the Seaga regime. Beginning with a World Bank Private Sector Development Adjustment Loan (PSDAL) in 1981, disbursements for several loans were linked to the government's progress on its divestment agenda and its efforts to stimulate private sector investment. Through an Export Development and

Investment Promotion project, USAID also became directly involved in the divestment process, providing technical and financial assistance for the government's privatization team.

Other divestments during the Seaga administration included local government services such as sanitation. The operations of public markets were placed in private hands, through service management contracts and short-term leases, and several agricultural properties were also either leased or sold. These early divestment efforts were not undertaken in a coordinated fashion and were not executed in the context of an overall economic strategy. Furthermore, the government downplayed the program, and, as a result, the public was largely unaware of its existence.

By 1985, however, as privatization accelerated, the process began to attract increasing attention. A national policy on privatization was made public only in 1986, with Phase I of the divestment of the National Commercial Bank (NCB). The government sold 51 percent of its equity in NCB in the largest public issue on the Jamaican stock market up to that time. This offering was oversubscribed by 170 percent and attracted 30,000 individual and institutional investors, including 98 percent of the Bank's own employees (Leeds 1991, 86). Phase II took place in 1991, with the government reducing its nonvoting shares by selling six million shares to NCB Trust and Merchant Bank, the trustee for the NCB Employee Share Scheme, thereby increasing employee ownership from 3 percent to 10.5 percent. In Phase III, the remaining government shares (49 percent), originally to be sold by public offering, were disposed of through a private arrangement between the government and a local investment syndicate. According to one source, the government needed the J$526 million (US$13.2 million) in privatization proceeds to meet the budgetary targets in its IMF program.

Ten years after the first divestments, 201 entities and activities had been divested in various categories: markets (80), sanitation (33), farm holdings (50), hotel properties (14), and corporate entities (24) (Stone 1992, 1). Over 50 major companies were handed over to the private sector, including NCB, the Caribbean Cement Company, and the Jamaica Telephone Company. (See Table 4.)

In 1991, the Manley government was re-elected and immediately presented to Parliament a new institutional framework for privatization, which was now being placed in the broader context of liberalization of the economy, as part of the government's goal to transform Jamaica from a state-centered to a more private sector-led, market-driven economy. This strategy was based on three principles: 1) streamlining the public sector through an extensive administrative reform program; 2) removing unnecessary bureaucratic intervention in the market, without compromising the government's role as regulator; and 3) broadening the base of ownership in the local economy (Government of Jamaica 1991, 3). To support privatization efforts, certain macroeconomic reforms were also initiated, including liberalization of the foreign exchange market, deregulation of several areas of the economy, and progressive reduction/elimination of import duties on most goods and raw materials.

The government believed that an aggressive privatization program involving SOEs would result in more efficient enterprises; reduce the drain on public sector resources; secure access to foreign markets, technologies, and capital; and increase

Table 4.
Major Privatizations in Jamaica
1981-1997

Entity/Activity	Method	Proceeds
Versair Flight Ltd. (1981)	Sale of shares	J$1,600,007
Southern Processors Ltd. (1981)	Sale of assets	J$1,573,993
Zero Processing & Storage Ltd. (1986)	Sale of assets	J$3,990,000
National Commercial Bank (1986)	Sale of shares (51%)	J$156,000,000
Caribbean Cement Co. Ltd (1987)	Sale of shares (89.6%)	J$142,651,000
National Hotel Supplies (1987)	Sale of assets	J$6,000,000
Telecommunications of Jamaica (1987)	Sale of shares (19%)	J$285,816,808
Royal Caribbean Hotel (1987)	Sale of assets	J$23,000,000 + US$4,200,000
Serge Island Dairies (1988)	Sale of shares (30%)	J$1,779,000
Telecommunications of Jamaica (1988)	Sale of shares (13.10%)	J$92,752,000
Casa Monte Hotel (1989)	Sale of assets	J$5,000,000
Casa Montego Hotel (1989)	Sale of assets	J$22,400,000
Telecommunications of Jamaica (1989)	Sale of shares (20%)	J$231,764,160
Inn on the Beach (1989)	Sale of assets	J$7,000,000
Wyndham Rose Hall Hotel (1989)	Sale of assets	J$21,900,000 + US$18,000,000
Eden II Hotel (1989)	Sale of assets	J$27,700,000 + US$5,000,000
Jamaica Jamaica Hotel (1989)	Sale of assets	J$45,000,000 + US$8,000,000
Montego Inn (1989)	Sale of assets	J$2,700,000
Hedonism II (1989)	Sale of assets	J$63,200,000 + US$10,750,000
Trelawny Beach (1989)	Sale of assets	J$29,800,00 + US$5,000,000
Jamaica Gypsum & Quarries (1989)	Sale of shares (100%)	J$4,000,000
Wyndham Kingston (1990)	Sale of assets	J$65,000,000
Telecommunications of Jamaica (1990)	Sale of shares (20%)	US$42,760,915
Jamaica Frozen Foods (1991)	Sale of assets	J$8,000,000
Mallards Beach Hotel (1991)	Sale of assets	US$16,000,000
Americana Hotel (1991)	Sale of assets	US$11,000,000
Workers Savings & Loan Bank (1991)	Sale of shares (75.4%)	J$45,000,000

continued...

Table 4. Major Privatizations in Jamaica (contd.) 1981-1997

Entity/Activity	Method	Proceeds
West Indies Glass (1991)	Sale of shares (61.4%)	J$40,000,000
Negril Cabins (1991)	Sale of assets	J$15,000,000
RJR "B" Shares (1991)	Sale of shares (25%)	J$15,700,000
Government Printing Office (1992)	ESOP	
Caribbean Steel Co. (1992)	Sale of shares (51%)	J$15,700,000
Cornwall Dairy (1993)	Sale of land, bldg., machinery	J$9,493,424
Jamaica Soya Products ((1993)	Sale of shares (60%)	J$49,500,000
Skyline Hotel (1993)	Sale of assets	J$100,000,000 approx.
Caribbean Cement Co. (1993)	Sale of shares (9.95%)	J$168,000,000
National Computer Center (1993)	ESOP	
Sugar Estates - Frome, Monymusk, Long Pond, Bernard Lodge (1993)	Sale of factory, equipment, cane lands; lease of cane lands	J$1,360,000,000
Holiday Inn Hotel (1994)	Sale of assets	US$22,000,000
Water Valley (1994)	Sale of land	J$14,000,000
Grains Jamaica Ltd. (1994)	Sale of shares (51%)	J$33,915,000
Eastern Banana Estates (1994)	Sale of shares (50%)	J$287,000,000
Victoria Banana Co. (1994)	Sale of shares	J$43,000,000
Air Jamaica Ltd. (1994)	Sale of shares & assets (70%)	J$270,562,500 + US$18,125,000
Police Garage - partial (1994)	Service contract	
Ashtrom Building Systems Ltd. (1995)	Capital Reorganization	N/A
Trans-Jamaica Airlines (1995)	Sale of shares (80%)	J$20,000,000
Tanners Limited (1995)	Sale of shares (17.5%)	J$494,910
Digital Computer Systems (1996)	Liquidation	J$250,000
NIBBI tractors (1996)	Sale of assets	J$2,478,000
Jamaica Grains & Cereals Ltd. (1996)	Sale of shares (20%)	J$12,000,000
Long Pond Poultry Assets (1997)	Sale of buildings	J$4,500,000

Source: National Investment Bank of Jamaica Ltd., 1997.

Jamaicans' equity participation in their economy. Working with the World Bank in the context of a private sector adjustment loan, the government identified 57 entities, assets, and activities for privatization, representing about 50 percent of the total assets of the public enterprise sector. (See Tables 4 and 5.) These included utilities (power and water); unprofitable major corporations, such as Air Jamaica;

Table 5.
Remaining SOEs to be Fully Privatized in Jamaica
as of 1999

Entities	Form of Privatization
Abbatoirs	Lease of services
Aqualapia Ltd. (Fish Farm)*	Sale of assets
Ariguanabo Company of Jamaica Ltd.	Lease of assets with option to buy
Bath Fountain Hotel and Spa*	Lease of assets
Black River Upper Morass Dev. Co. Ltd.	Sale of assets
Catering (Hospitals)*	Provision of services
Collection Management (Hospitals)	Provision of services
Caymanas Track Ltd.	Sale of shares
Cotton Polyster Plant*	Sale of assets
Geochemical Laboratory	Provision of services
Government Electrical Inspection (non-regulatory)	Provision of services
Hospital Services	Provision of services
Innswood Vinegar Ltd.*	Sale of assets
Jamaica Railway Corporation*	Sale of assets
Kingston Industrial Works Ltd.	Sale of shares
Kingston Port Royal-Portmore Ferry Services	Provision of services
Maintenance of Hospitals & Clinics	Provision of services
Management of Health Equipment	Provision of services
Milk River Bath Hotel & Spa*	Lease of assets
Motor Vehicle Repairs	Contracting Services
Natural Cane Products Ltd.	Sale of assets
Sangster International Airport Terminal*	Concession for both airside and landside operations
Spring Plain/St. Jago*	Sale of Properties
Sugar Estates*	Lease of non-cane lands and residual assets
Tropiculture Ltd.*	Sale of shares
Vehicle Inspection services of the Island Traffic Authority	Contracting services

* Brought to point of sale   Source: National Investment Bank of Jamaica Ltd., May 1999.

sugar factories; the Jamaica Railway Corporation; and the Petroleum Corporation of Jamaica. The government announced that all these transactions would be completed by 1996. Although most privatizations would take place through outright sale, other modalities would be considered, such as long-term leases (particularly for land, government services, and utilities), leasing with an option to buy, concessions, joint ventures, and the contracting-out of services.

With respect to the privatization process, the Ministry Paper tabled in Parliament emphasized that all transactions would be public, fully transparent, and open to local and foreign investors. Both market and book values would apply when establishing the disposal price of SOE assets. Transactions would be at "arms length" and fair with respect to giving equal opportunity to all parties, except in cases with special foreign exchange requirements or where special arrangements were being made for employees. Finally, in cases of possible conflict of interest, the parties involved would not be allowed to participate in the transaction.

In an effort to accelerate private sector development in Jamaica, the government decided the following: 1) all relevant regulatory issues would be dealt with either prior to, or simultaneously with, any privatization; 2) neither direct financing nor loan guarantees would be provided to purchasers; 3) except in public utilities, no new public sector investment, excluding maintenance, would be undertaken prior to privatization; 4) sale of SOEs to other public sector entities would not be considered privatization; 5) unsolicited offers for any enterprise or activity would not be accepted prior to the official advertisement; 6) direct sale or negotiation could not take place without publicly solicited bids, unless the assets involved were so small as to make public bidding economically impractical; 7) when the sale was completed, all aspects of the transaction would be made public; and 8) any minority shares that the government retained would not carry special voting rights.

The formal presentation of this framework marked a second phase in which the government began to take a more centralized and systematic approach to privatization. Three key decisions were made. First, the National Investment Bank of Jamaica (NIBJ), which had been involved in several previous divestment transactions, would coordinate all privatizations, have responsibility for the administrative and operational aspects of the program, and would be accountable to the Office of the Prime Minister. Second, a Privatization Committee, drawn from members of the cabinet, would be established to advise the government on the list of entities or activities to be privatized, the modality proposed for each, and whether to accept or reject offers from private sector investors. Third, for each divestment, an Enterprise Team would be established to conduct the necessary analyses, recommend the appropriate privatization strategy to the cabinet, and coordinate its implementation as approved by government. The team would be led by NIBJ personnel and would be comprised of representatives from relevant government agencies, the SOE, and external consultants.

This latest phase of the privatization program has progressed well. Of the 57 entities targeted for privatization by 1998, over half had either been sold or leased. Since the inception of the program in 1981, divestment by sector has occurred as follows: agriculture, 10 percent; manufacturing, 39 percent; and services, 51 percent (NIBJ, 1994-1995). By 1999, it was reported that 27 additional entities were scheduled to be divested, including the Jamaica Railway Corporation. Bids for the privatization of the Jamaica Public Service Company (JPSCo), the electric utility, were received in 1996, and it was expected that JPSCo would be a private company by the end of that year. By October 1996, the short list of prospective buyers had been reduced to two — Houston Industries Energy Inc. and Southern Electric. However, after several weeks of extensive negotiations, the government rejected these bids because the offer prices were too low, the proposed electricity rates for consumers were too high, and the dividend policy was unacceptable. It now appears that the privatization process for JPSCo will not resume in the near future.

Divestment is proceeding in other areas, however. Government holdings in Jamaica Grain and Cereal Ltd. were sold to Seprod Ltd. in December 1997. As part of the decentralization and reform process in the health sector, private companies now provide catering services, maintenance, equipment management, and security services in all public hospitals. The privatization of Sangsters International Airport in Montego Bay also resumed in June 1998. The prequalification process is now complete, and 12 potential investors have been invited to submit preliminary offers based on a request for proposal (RFP) by mid-January 2000. Four or five applicants will then be invited to submit final offers. If all goes well, the government expects a Final Concession Agreement by May 31, 2000. The Multilateral Investment Fund (MIF), administered by the Inter-American Development Bank, has awarded the government a grant for technical assistance to draft the legal framework for the privatization of the Norman Manley Airport in Kingston. The privatization of the free zones in Jamaica is also being considered as part of the terms of a World Bank loan for export development. In 1998, negotiations were underway with a Swedish firm to assume control of vehicle inspection services. The leasing of sugar lands is also moving forward. Over 300 acres have been leased in Trelawny for a major eco-tourism project. Elsewhere, lands have been leased for freshwater fish production, sea island cotton, and the growing of yams for local consumption. In terms of the Jamaica Railway Corporation, a study commissioned by the NIBJ calls for partial rehabilitation of the line, essentially the Kingston-Spanish Town-Linstead segment, which would be privately operated, after which privatization of the entire operation would take place. In 1999, the government signed a memorandum of understanding for a joint venture with Rail India Technical and Economic Services. Under the agreement, Rail India will own 30 percent of the shares, the government of Jamaica 40 percent, and 30 percent will go to other Jamaican companies. It is expected that passenger and freight service will begin in three phases in May 2000, with service between Kingston and Spanish Town. Also in 1999, the government sold its 43.5 percent shareholding in the Caribbean Cement Company to Trinidad Cement Company for US$29.4 million.

Privatization in Jamaica has had benefits and costs. First, increased employment in agriculture, hotels, and telecommunications have tended to offset job losses in other areas. Second, excluding the privatization of lands, local government operations, and other transactions conducted outside the purview of NIBJ, proceeds from the program since 1981 are approximately US$300 million, which has had a positive impact on the government's fiscal position. Third, customer surveys have revealed noticeable improvements in service, with respect to public sanitation, garbage collection, and hotel service (Stone 1992).

Jamaica is one of the few countries in the region with strong public support for privatization. When the program began in 1981, however, there was little public endorsement of privatization. The change in perspective has been due to a public education program; early divestment successes, such as NCB; attempts to include small investors in the process; increasing transparency; and, finally, a firm commitment to the process by both the government and the opposition.

Nevertheless, there have been difficulties. First, problems in the financial sector since 1996 have complicated the privatization process. In January 1997, the government established a Financial Sector Adjustment Company (FINSAC) to consolidate, recapitalize, and strengthen the institutions in the sector. FINSAC has intervened in the sector through outright acquisition of institutions, injection of capital through the purchase of shares, or by providing liquidity support in the form of FINSAC notes. In the process, FINSAC has assumed control of about 150 entities and holdings owned by these institutions. As a result, the government is in the process of divestment once more to the private sector. So far, several financial institutions have either been merged or sold. Workers Bank, for example, which was privatized in 1999, has been merged with several other institutions to form Union Bank. The government now owns 40 percent of NCB, after the government's majority shares were sold in 1986. Several hotels in the FINSAC portfolio have also been divested, including the Holiday Inn, whose assets had been sold to the private sector in 1994. As of 1999, these divestments have brought in revenues of approximately J$4 billion. However, the cost of the FINSAC intervention overall has been high, amounting to J$8 billion in 1999 alone. Second, other earlier privatizations have continued to require government involvement. With continued difficulties in the sugar industry, the government has had to reassume control of the sugar estates. Furthermore, the government continues to give financial support to Air Jamaica to offset the airline's losses.

Third, a major shortcoming of the program has been that, in many cases, design and implementation of the appropriate regulatory framework have not kept pace with the privatization process. However, since 1993, the government has made some progress in this regard. For certain privatization transactions, such as Telecommunications of Jamaica (TOJ) and the sugar companies, regulatory mechanisms and legislation were included in the agreements. Steps have also been taken to protect and strengthen worker participation in the program. In 1994, an Employee Stock Ownership Plan Act was drafted and passed as part of an employee stock ownership program (ESOP) funded by the Inter-American Development Bank's MIF. The program includes training for employers, employees, and trade union officials. An ESOP Secretariat has also been established at NIBJ.

Other initiatives that have been put in place in the aftermath of economic liberalization also create a propitious environment for subsequent privatizations. Parliament passed a Fair Competition Act in 1993, and a Fair Trading Commission was established to protect consumer rights. An Office of Utility Regulation has been created, again with the assistance of the MIF, to regulate all utilities — energy, telecommunications, water, transport, and ports. Finally, securities legislation is in place, and a Securities Commission is operating to protect investors and ensure transparency in securities trading.

CONCLUSION

The Caribbean now has well over a decade of experience with privatization — a process full of valuable learning experiences for the various economies of the region. The state, for example, rather than being replaced by the private sector in these countries, has generally taken on a new role in the economy. According to Jamaican Prime Minister P.J. Patterson, this new role:

> . . . implies a movement towards catalytic government — one that concentrates on facilitating, on regulating, and on monitoring; one more given to 'steering than to rowing.' But this does not mean, however, that there are not certain situations in which the government must be involved in rowing rather than in steering. There are areas, where because of either the size of the investment or the special facilities that are peculiarly available to the state, some government involvement is both logical and inescapable — e. g., the bauxite industry . . . and airports (Patterson 1993, 6).

Clearly, there is a need for consensus, across the political spectrum and in society at large, for any comprehensive program. The apprehension and potential dislocation that can accompany privatization can be avoided by a carefully orchestrated process of dialogue with all affected parties. The Jamaican experience demonstrates the value of public education and transparency, particularly in the initial stages of privatization, as factors that help ensure success for individual transactions and the program itself.

Moreover, rapid and extensive divestment without a proper framework can lead to disastrous results — as Eastern Europe has illustrated (Nellis 1998, 16-19). For each transaction, proper planning, execution, monitoring, and assessment are necessary. Furthermore, each privatization must be evaluated carefully to determine its relevance to future cases. However, it is important to consider appropriate modalities and the timing for privatization, both for different sectors as well as for enterprises of varying sizes within sectors. The Latin American experience shows that small firms in areas such as manufacturing can often be sold quickly in the early phases of a privatization program, whereas the divestment of public utilities and larger entities with monopoly control is considerably more difficult to achieve (Edwards 1995, 175).

In addition, public perceptions of success are important for subsequent transactions. In Jamaica, for example, in 1987, the share offering of the Caribbean Cement Company was widely viewed as unsuccessful, in spite of the fact that 72 percent of the shares were sold. This divestment was being compared to the NCB share offering in 1986, which had been oversubscribed (Leeds 1991, 120).

It is also important to ensure that there is a proper context for privatization. A competent executing agency with qualified staff is needed, together with the appropriate regulatory framework and the necessary safety nets to protect displaced workers.

ADDITIONAL CONSIDERATIONS

Three further issues need to be considered. First, every effort must be made to encourage the involvement of small investors so that private sector monopolies do not replace those held by the state. Where investment opportunities are spread as widely as possible, particularly to include the participation of employees and small investors, this serves to widen the support for the privatization program, strengthen equity markets, and encourage new forms of savings and investment. Where opportunities for investment cannot be diversified at the time of transfer, the enterprise should be committed to do so in the near future. In Trinidad, for example, the investment agreement with the Acker/Loeb Group for the privatization of BWIA provides for worker ownership of 25.5 percent of the airline, through the creation of an ESOP and the purchase of shares with surplus from the BWIA's existing pension plan (Valley 1995, 8). By contrast, the public strongly criticized the third phase of the NCB share offering, not only because of a perception of a lack of transparency and the apparent financial expediency of the transaction but also because of the lack of broad-based investor/employee involvement.

Second, foreign participation in the investment process must be carefully considered and planned. In Guyana and Grenada, for example, serious concerns were expressed by the public at large about the haste with which early privatizations were undertaken. In the Caribbean, there have often been lively public debates about whether "strategic" industries and activities should be sold to foreign interests or, indeed, whether they should be privatized at all. Governments can mute criticism in this area by ensuring that local investors have the first opportunity to purchase SOEs even if requirements dictate a purchase price in foreign exchange. The Grenadian government, for example, is taking an interesting approach by encouraging regional investors to participate in its privatization program.

Third, in any privatization effort, governments must take steps to protect the interests of the consumer. As such, privatization without a sufficient regulatory framework can lead to a lack of accountability and standards, resulting ultimately in a breakdown in efficiency and performance and re-involvement by the government. This has been the case with the Jamaican urban bus system (Anderson 1990, 234-248). The need for adequate regulation and supervision of newly privatized sectors is particularly important in the financial sector, as the Chilean experience illustrates and, most recently, as the crisis in the Jamaican financial sector as well shows. Governments pay a high price in terms of support when these "checks and balances" are absent (World Bank 1995, 93).

THE GAINS UNDER PRIVATIZATION

Overall, privatization has had some positive effects in the Caribbean. First, generally speaking, employment has experienced net gains from the process. Divestment of agricultural lands in Jamaica resulted in employment increases of 150 percent (Stone 1992, 30). As a result of these and other similar, early gains, the trade unions were supportive of the government's efforts.

Second, efficiency and company performance improved. For example, in the hotel sector in Jamaica, occupancy levels in privatized hotels were above 85 percent, as a result of aggressive marketing strategies, tighter management, and refurbishing (Stone 1992, 19). In Guyana, the privatization of Guyana Telephone and Telegraph Co. Ltd. improved service quality and expanded service. Between 1991 and 1994, the number of subscriber lines increased from 21,000 to 53,600 (Tyndall 1995). In Trinidad, in the first quarter after privatization (February to April 1995), BWIA posted a profit of US$2.04 million, compared to the previous 12 months when the airline had lost US$25.6 million.

Third, privatization has also contributed to the reduction in fiscal deficits, not only because of the initial injection of funds after sale but also due to the elimination of government financing for unprofitable enterprises.

Fourth, the program has attracted foreign exchange from foreign as well as local investors.

It is important to note, however, that privatization is not a panacea. Government priorities must be clear, as there are often important tradeoffs between divestment objectives. Government-owned enterprises cannot be sold indiscriminately based on political expediency, or without due regard to the financial strength of bidders, the quality of management, or the overall economic system being created. In addition, in any new privatization initiative, an effort must be made to learn from the successes and failures of earlier divestments. To ignore these issues is a prescription for failure and only serves to undermine any program. The Caribbean experience shows that under the right conditions, privatization objectives can be met.

This chapter includes the authors' updated material for a previously published version of this paper: Richard L. Bernal and Winsome J. Leslie, *Privatization in the English-Speaking Caribbean: An Assessment*, CSIS Policy Papers on the Americas, Vol. X: Study 7, October 22, 1999 (Washington, D.C.: Center for Strategic and International Studies).

References

Anderson, Patricia. 1990. "Jamaica's Urban Bus System: Deregulation or Public Responsibility." In *Privatization and Deregulation in Global Perspective*, eds. Dennis J. Gayle and Jonathan N. Goodrich. New York: Quorum Books.

Barbados Labour Party. 1994. *Manifesto.*

Berg, Elliot. 1988. "Privatization and Equity." In *Policy Reform and Equity: Extending the Benefits of Development*, ed. Elliot Berg. Washington, D.C.: International Center for Economic Growth.

Bernal, Richard L. 1986. "Restructuring Jamaica's Economic Relations with Socialist Countries, 1974-1980." *Development and Change* 17:4 (October): 607-634.

Chapman, Colin. 1990. *Selling The Family Silver: Has Privatization Worked?* London: Hutchinson Business Books.

Cooperative Republic of Guyana.1993. Ministry of Finance. *Privatization Policy Framework Paper*, June.

Data Resource Systems International Ltd.1995. *Privatization Impact Assessment Study — Jamaica,* May 25.

Edwards, Sebastian. 1995. *Crisis and Reform in Latin America: From Despair to Hope.* Washington, D.C.: World Bank.

Embassy of Guyana. 1998. *Guyana Update* . Washington, D.C. July.

Esau, Joe. 1994. "Privatization: Why the Noise?" *Caribbean Affairs* (September-October).

Financial Gleaner. 1999. "Guyana Government Presses for Provatization" April 9.

Fortune Magazine. 1995. "Privatization: A Tool for Modernization." In "Jamaica: Open for Business the Modern Way." May 1, Supplement.

Girvan, Norman. 1976. *Corporate Imperialism: Conflict and Expropriation.* New York: M. E. Sharpe, Inc.

Government of the Commonwealth of Dominica. 1988. *Medium-Term Economic Strategy Paper*, May.

Government of Grenada, Ministry of Finance. 1994. *Grenada: From Stabilization to Sustainable Growth — The Medium-Term Economic Strategy Paper,* May.

Government of Grenada. 1998. *Medium-Term Economic Strategy Paper, 1998-2000*, May.

Government of Jamaica. 1991. *Ministry Paper No. 34*, June 28.

Government of Saint Lucia. 1998. *Medium-Term Economic Strategy Paper, 1998-2000.* May.

Hanke, Steve H., ed. 1987. *Privatization and Development.* Washington, D.C.: International Center for Economic Growth.

Henry, Ralph. 1990. "Privatization and the State Enterprise Sector in Trinidad and Tobago: Market and Non-Market Issues in a Plural Political Economy." In *Privatization and Deregulation in Global Perspective*, eds. Dennis J. Gayle and Jonathan N. Goodrich. New York: Quorum Books.

Hope, Kempe Ronald Sr. 1992. "Privatization and the Quest for Economic Revival in Guyana." *Caribbean Affairs* 5 (2).

International Finance Corporation (IFC). 1995a. *Annual Report*. Washington, D.C.

International Finance Corporation (IFC). 1995b. *Privatization, Principles and Practice.* Washington, D.C.

International Monetary Fund (IMF). 1994. *Adjustment and Growth in Developing Countries.* Washington, D.C.

Larraín B., Felipe. 1995. "Privatizing the Economies: Lessons from the Chilean Experience." In *Privatization Amidst Poverty*, ed. Jorge A. Lawton. Coral Gables, Fla.: University of Miami.

Lawrence, Richard. 1995. "Privatization Trend is Expected to Continue Expanding Worldwide." *The Journal of Commerce,* September 29.

Lawrence, Vincent. 1995. "Getting on the Fast Track to Efficient Development in Jamaica." Paper presented at Jamaica Investment Conference, Waldorf Astoria, September 21-22. New York.

Leeds, Roger. 1991. "Privatization through Public Offerings: Lessons from Two Jamaican Cases." In *Privatization and Control of State-Owned Enterprises*, eds. Ravi Ramamurti and Raymond Vernon. Washington, D.C.: The World Bank.

Manley, Michael. 1982. *Jamaica: Struggle in the Periphery.* London: Third World Media.

Nellis, John. 1999. "Time to Rethink Privatization in Transition Economies?" *Finance and Development,* June, 16-19.

National Investment Bank of Jamaica Ltd. (NIJB). *Annual Report, 1994-1996.* Kingston.

Patterson, P.J. 1993. "The Emerging Role of the State." Address at the Ministerial Roundtable, Ocho Rios, Jamaica. Kingston, Jamaica: Jamaica Information Service, August 12.

People's National Party (PNP). 1979. *Principles and Objectives of the People's National Party.* Kingston, Jamaica.

Planning Institute of Jamaica.1991. *Economic and Social Survey, 1991, 1992, 1993 and 1994.*

Republic of Trinidad and Tobago. 1994. *Medium-Term Policy Framework 1994-1996.* May.

Republic of Trinidad and Tobago. 1995. Ministry of Finance, Investments Division. *Report on Public Participation in Industrial and Commercial Activities.*

Republic of Trinidad and Tobago. 1997. Ministry of Finance. *Medium-Term Policy Framework, 1998-2000.* December.

Republic of Trinidad and Tobago. 1998. Ministry of Finance — Divestment Secretariat. *Status of Divestment Secretariat, Trinidad and Tobago.* March 31.

Roth, Gabriel. 1987. *The Private Provision of Public Services in Developing Countries.* New York: Oxford University Press.

Sampson, Cezley. 1993 "Structural-Adjustment, Privatization, Trade and Economic Deregulation: The Jamaica Experience." In *Competing Globally: Challenges and Opportunities*, ed. S. Neelamegham. New Delhi: Allied Publishers Ltd.

Sampson, Cezley. 1994. *Privatization in Banking Services (NCB, Ltd.) in a Developing Country.* Mona, Jamaica: Mona Institute of Business.

Stone, Carl. 1992. *Putting Enterprise to Work: A Study of Privatization in Jamaica.* National Investment Bank of Jamaica Ltd. Kingston, Jamaica.

Thomas, Clive Y. 1988. *The Poor and the Powerless: Economic Policy and Change in the Caribbean.* London: Latin America Bureau [Research and Action] Ltd.

Tyndall, Joseph A. 1995. "The Performance and Regulation of Privatized Industries: The Case of the Guyana Telephone and Telegraph Co. Ltd." Seminar on Privatization

Policy Issues, Trinidad and Tobago, July 11-14. CARICOM/Commonwealth Secretariat/CARICAD and UWI/Canada Institutional Strengthening Project.

Valley, Kenneth. 1995. Address by The Honorable Kenneth Valley, Minister of Trade and Industry, on the Occasion of the Signing of the Investment Agreement for the Divestment of BWIA Among the Government of Trinidad and Tobago, BWIA, the Acker/Loeb Group, and Loeb Partners Corporation. Central Bank of Trinidad and Tobago. January 6.

Wall Street Journal. 1995. "What is Privatization Anyway?" October 2.

World Bank. 1992. *Guyana: From Economic Recovery to Sustained Growth.* Report No. 10307-GUY, April 10.

World Bank. 1993. *Jamaica Report,* May 26.

World Bank. 1994. *Guyana: Strategies for Reducing Poverty.* Report No. 12861-GUA, May 6.

World Bank. 1995. *Bureaucrats in Business: The Economics and Politics of Government Ownership.* New York: Oxford University Press.

CHAPTER SEVEN

The Tortuous Road to Privatization in Venezuela

GERVER TORRES

INTRODUCTION

In 1989, after several years of marked macroeconomic disequilibrium, Venezuela introduced broad economic reforms, much like those that other Latin American countries had recently undertaken. The reform package was centered on three fundamental ideas: economic stabilization measures, such as exchange rate unification and price liberation; structural adjustment policies, such as trade opening, tax reform, and reforms of the state apparatus; and compensatory social programs aimed at reducing the effects of the adjustment on low-income sectors of the population. Programs to restructure and privatize state-owned companies were also part of the reform package. (See Table 1.)

Table 1.
Economic Reform Programs

Macroeconomic Stabilization	Structural Adjustment	Social Programs
Exchange Rate Unification	Trade Opening	Direct Subsidies
Liberalization of Financial Markets	Public Sector Restructuring	Implementation of Public Welfare Programs
Price Liberalization	Financial Reform	Unemployment Programs
Elimination of Subsidies and Foreign Debt Renegotiation	Foreign Investment Promotion	Acceleration of Programs Exemptions for Social Investment
		Improvement in Social Services

Source: Author's compilation.

In order to implement these programs, two ministerial commissions were created — one for each project. Within a short time, the "restructuring" commission began to languish, as the limitations and inefficacy of its mission became clear. In contrast, the first privatization operation — the sale of a state-owned bank — was completed in 1990. Thereafter, privatizations picked up speed, reaching the greatest intensity in December 1991, when 40 percent of the stock of the national telephone company was sold to an international consortium. During this period, banks, hotels, sugar refineries, a shipyard, and an international airline were sold; most of the country's ports were decentralized and privatized; and some Venezuelan monopolies were eliminated.

On February 4, 1992, only two months after the privatization of the telephone company, the first of two attempts to overthrow the Venezuelan government that would take place that year occurred (the second happened on November 27). This interrupted the privatization program, which had been moving forward rapidly. Except for the very important opening of the petroleum sector and despite efforts by the administrations that have governed the country since 1992 to continue the process— at least formally, delegating responsibility for its execution to various ministries — the privatization program has not recovered its momentum. The government maintains an ambitious list of companies to be privatized, including sectors such as steel and aluminum that only a few years ago were considered "strategic" and nontransferable to the private sector. Paradoxically, the rhetoric on privatization has intensified to the same degree that its practical realization has been paralyzed. The lack of real and sustained political determination, an adverse macroeconomic context, and the state's limited technical-institutional capacity largely explain the program's stagnation.

An evaluation of the Venezuelan privatization process reveals lessons to be learned and errors to be corrected. However, in assessing the Venezuelan privatization experience, this chapter will be concerned only with those privatizations involving an actual transfer of assets or economic activities from the state sector to the private sector. The chapter does not focus on transfers of other kinds of responsibilities from the government to civil society.

This is, obviously, a reduced concept of privatization. In its true sense, privatization refers to all kinds of transfers of responsibilities, functions, and rights from the public to the private sectors — that is, of the government sector to the non-government sector and from the government to civil society. When neighborhood organizations, for example, decide to assume the functions of policing and enforcing security in residential areas, complimenting or substituting those of the state, a process of privatization is also taking place. When groups of citizens organize and assume functions for the protection of the environment because they think that the government is not performing well or simply because they consider their participation necessary, a privatization process is also taking place. This means that those functions that up to now have been the exclusive responsibility of the government are now assumed totally or partially by the private sector, by civil society. In such instances, there is privatization without involving any commercial transactions or the buying and selling of public assets. Privatization means a reassignment of functions between the state and civil society, in which the society assumes responsibilities that were previously performed exclusively by the state. Privatization is, therefore, a social and political concept as well as an economic one. In Venezuela and all over the world, these kinds of privatizations will continue to take place.

Unfortunately, they are seldom taken into account as much as those that are of a strictly commercial nature. In this paper, however, privatization is treated only in its economic and, more precisely, in its commercial aspects.

THE INITIATION OF THE PRIVATIZATION PROCESS

Initially, Venezuelan privatization formed part of a broader program of economic reforms designed to modernize the economy, making it more open, efficient, and competitive, and granting the market a much larger role in the allocation of resources in the economy than it had previously assumed. This differed dramatically from subsequent privatization efforts made between 1994 and 1996, which occurred in a context decidedly hostile to a market-driven economy, one dominated by numerous controls and government interventions of a micro character in various aspects of the economy.

In order to define privatization policy, the government established objectives, standards, and general lines of action, including the following:

1. Redefinition of the role of the state in the economy,
2. Promotion of efficiency through greater competition,
3. An increase in the supply of goods and services,
4. Development of capital markets,
5. Democratization of wealth, and
6. Improvement of fiscal balances.

Venezuela differed from other countries in its use of privatization as a primary mechanism for rethinking the role of the state in the economy. The aim of transforming the state from a producer and provider of services into an entity that regulates and defines policy was central to the reforms. This contrasted with the more common practice in other countries of defining the promotion of competitiveness and efficiency as the primary or most important objective. Although both goals are related, they are not the same. It is possible to increase economic competitiveness and efficiency — at least theoretically — without redefining the economic role of the state. It may be possible to introduce competition in the economy without the state giving up its role as producer of goods and services. In the final analysis, this is a debate over whether public property is important. If the problem is solely one of economic efficiency, then it could be argued that it can be solved through adequate regulatory frameworks that permit or encourage competition. If, however, the problem refers to what role the state should play in the economy, then the issue of property becomes much more important.

Fears Surrounding Privatization

In regard to privatization, Venezuelans immediately expressed six enormous fears, both real and imagined, that initially raised concerns even among supporters of the initiative. These apprehensions have progressively disappeared to the degree that they have proved to be unfounded.

Price Increases. Around the time of privatization, there is often a rise in the prices of goods and services provided by the companies to be sold. This rise results not from privatization itself but from the need to make the company economically viable. Even without privatizations, if these companies were to be restructured and made to rely on self-financing, the same increases would appear; otherwise, the firms themselves would go bankrupt. If state subsidization were to continue, that would mean higher taxes or an increase in the public deficit; in the end, this would translate into inflation, the worst of all taxes. Traditionally, the prices of public goods and services in Venezuela have lagged well behind production costs. For example, as of 1994, the provision of water in Caracas was billed at less than 20 percent of its cost. In addition, the charge for collecting garbage barely reached 10 percent of its cost. As late as 1996, the price of gasoline was less than 10 cents per gallon.

Frequently, price adjustments accompanying privatizations make it appear to the public that privatization itself is responsible for the rise in prices. However, the private sector cannot grant the subsidies that the state grants to keep prices below costs, and, therefore, increases become necessary sooner or later, following the sale of a state-owned company. The more the prices for goods and services have been subsidized, the larger will be the price increases produced by a privatization.

The marked acceleration in inflation that occurred in Venezuela in the early 1990s, mainly as a consequence of the continued and accentuated fiscal deficit, worsened the problem of consumer price increases. As the prices for public goods and services lagged, the adjustments required to make the privatizing companies more attractive to investors increased. This was the case, for example, in the electricity sector, where the government was reluctant to concede the rate increases necessary to compensate for inflation. However, the implementation of a stabilization program, under an agreement with the International Monetary Fund (IMF), imposed a realignment of the prices for all public goods and services, and thus, with or without privatization, increases occurred.

Unemployment. Often, unemployment accompanies privatization programs. However, three facts explain why this fear did not grow or deepen as a result of Venezuela's privatization experience. First, privatization did not lead to major layoffs of personnel, at least in the short term. This was partly a consequence of both formal and informal agreements made in the sale of the firms, whereby the new owners agreed to maintain the greatest possible workforce stability. The second factor — which in part also explains the first — is that the most important privatizations took place within a context of expansion and growth, making it easier to reabsorb those laid off into the labor force. Third, in some cases, downsizing included attractive terms for employees.

The Venezuelan experience demonstrates that overemployment is not as critical a factor in the privatization of a company as are the rates charged for the product or service or the regulatory framework. Even if the government does not want to undertake a massive labor restructuring before selling a firm, excess employment is relatively easy to negotiate with the new investors, provided it is accomplished sensibly, sensitively, and gradually.

Monopolization. Perhaps the strongest concern was that powerful economic groups would take control of companies that, up to then, had been the property of the state, converting what was considered as belonging to all into the property of one individual — especially an economically powerful individual. The public saw this as a monopolization that would make "the rich richer and the poor poorer." This view had profound ideological roots that could recede only as people learned the true nature of many of Venezuela's "public companies" and gained access to information about the origin and destination of funds these companies managed and the trade unions, professional associations, or politicians that controlled them. For this reason, an educational campaign was critical to the success of the privatization program in the early days of the process.

Many Venezuelans, in fact, feared another aspect of monopolization — where a public monopoly becomes a private monopoly. Generally, privatization in Venezuela has served to increase competition. For example, the telephone company, which had been an absolute public monopoly, became both a system that fostered competition for a wide range of services (the "value-added services") and a temporary monopoly in basic telephone service. In other areas such as ports, banks, sugar refineries, and hotels, the transfer to the private sector also served to increase competition. In some cases, the absence of privatization served to reinforce a monopoly or create a monopoly where one did not previously exist. For example, when Línea Aeropostal Venezolana (AEROPOSTAL) was not privatized, it went bankrupt, leaving practically all of the market to a large private company with which it had competed. Venezuelan public opinion took note of this development.

Denationalization. This form of fear was never particularly strong in Venezuela and decreased after the 1993 economic recession, which made clear the urgent necessity for attracting foreign investment and cast a positive light on the presence of foreign investors in Venezuela. (The exception has been Colombian investors, who, as a result of Venezuela's border disputes with its neighbor, have been less welcomed.) The "golden clause," introduced into the sale contracts of public companies and giving the state veto power over certain strategic decisions, has also diminished denationalization fears, especially among the leaders of political parties. This clause has been used in cases such as that of the national airline.

Weakening of the State. Concern over a possible weakening of the state was present in different debates, especially at the beginning of the privatization program. With the transfer of important public companies to private hands, Venezuelans assumed the state would lose control of the economy. The government, however, argued that privatization would strengthen the state by allowing it to concentrate on those activities that were within its true scope. Certainly, the Venezuelan state weakened considerably in the 1990s, not as a result of privatization but rather as a result of the political, social, and economic crises that the country has lived through. The magnitude of these crises has been so severe and the impact on the state apparatus such that it has become practically irrelevant today to attempt to establish any connection between privatizations and state weakening.

Corruption. The rumors about corruption began to evaporate early on, and the debate over corruption gave way to more important issues, such as what to sell and how to sell. Today, this fear is almost nonexistent, and there is a generalized recognition that the privatizations that took place were accomplished in a transparent manner. In a country where accusations of corruption occupy a preponderant space in the public arena, this is not an issue of minor importance. By privatizing, the space in which corruption may occur diminishes as the state's commercial involvement declines.

Other Serious Obstacles to Privatization

In Venezuela, the obstacles to privatization have varied since the process began in the early 1990s. In addition to the six concerns outlined above, two other sizable forces have stood in the way of the process: those groups motivated by ideology and those motivated by specific interests, especially economic and political. At times, these two groups managed to form strange but powerful alliances that delayed or stopped privatizations, and, by acting directly or through the manipulation of public opinion, they have affected the government's determination to privatize. Nevertheless, as Venezuelan and international experiences have revealed numerous examples of successful privatizations, the ideological opposition has progressively lost ground. The most evident indication of this process is that the economic team that assumed power in 1994 strongly opposed the existing privatization policy but soon became one of its principal champions.

The opposition motivated by special interests, on the other hand, is complex and difficult to defeat. Quite frequently, members of this group declare themselves advocates of privatization as a general policy but oppose specific sales to the degree that their own interests are affected. Who makes up this group, and what motivates them to act? Some are businesspeople whose vocational abilities depend on a public company and who fear the arrival or accentuation of competition if the public firm is privatized. Their strategy tends to be one of making sure that the purchase of the firm includes terms advantageous to them or, if this proves impossible, terms that prevent the particular privatization altogether. Other members of the opposition are businesspeople who maintain commercial relations with public companies to whom they sell or from whom they buy under conditions more advantageous than could be found in the free market. Still others are high-level ministerial officials with authority over the privatizing firms, who believe that their power and influence will decline with the sale of these companies to the private sector. This fear is not unfounded, since a common parameter that a public official uses to measure his or her place in the hierarchy is the number of entities and people formally under his or her command. Privatization thus reduces bureaucratic power, whether real or symbolic. Trade unions, another component of the opposition, have acquired power in public companies to such a degree that, in some cases, they actually control the company. Obviously, privatization directly affects this sector. Other opponents of privatization worth mentioning are groups and political factions that have located spaces within the public companies for exercising clientelistic politics and financing their activities.

All of these interest groups oppose privatization using a variety of arguments. They often contend that the company whose privatization they oppose represents a particular case, a sui generis situation that demands special treatment and an exception to privatization policy. In many cases, these groups are the true owners of the "public companies." That is why it is possible to state unequivocally that many state-owned companies are public only in appearance, since interest groups have already "privatized" them, albeit covertly and in a manner contrary to the interests of the society. Thus, privatization is actually re-privatization, but under-taken as part of public policy, formulated in the interests of society as a whole and not for the benefit of small special-interest groups.

As a result of the articulation of all of these factors, privatization was launched in 1990 with public opinion clearly against it. Polls showed that 70 percent of those surveyed rejected the policy, which was perceived as an effort to sell the country's "crown jewels." However, popular opinion has progressively changed, and a majority of the population has now come to favor privatization. In addition to the public-education campaigns explaining the objectives of privatization policy, a key factor in its acceptance was the intensification of the economic crisis, which predisposed many Venezuelans to drastic changes in their country's economy.

Nevertheless, the climate dominated by state controls and uncertainty over policy directions was unpropitious for privatization and became one of the main obstacles to the process. This climate continues to be a significant impediment. However, as illustrated in the case of CANTV, timing, political astuteness, and leadership can often triumph over a policy environment unreceptive to change only on a temporary basis if the government's ultimate objective is to use regulation of privatized firms as a tool of social policy.

Forces Encouraging Privatization in Venezuela

Legislation. Although Congress was involved at an early stage in the privatization process, it did not necessarily share the vision held by the administration's economic team. Instead, its predominantly hostile posture kept the privatization legislation from being approved until December 1991. In other words, the most important privatizations completed were accomplished without this law. The fact that the process slowed down considerably after the law's approval has led some to think that it was the most important factor in the hobbling of the process. Even when the Telecommunications Law made the process slower, it cannot be said that it was the most important factor in its paralysis. Other factors, such as political determination, the macroeconomic situation, and the weak institutional capacity for speeding up the process had a greater weight and were more decisive in this regard. The 1991 law was the result of a long negotiation between the government and Congress, with Congress attempting to exercise control over privatizations while the executive branch sought the most liberty and autonomy possible. But as the law was being debated, the government took advantage of the time to carry out key transactions, including the privatization of ports, telecommunications, and the national airline. Thus, the most important privatizations were accomplished without the existence of specific legislation on privatization, and, moreover, the process slowed down after the law's approval, leading some to identify it as the program's biggest impediment.

In circumstances in which the government could not count on a congressional majority — as was the case at the beginning of the process — a privatization law could become a true straitjacket, with both congressional and nongovernmental opponents making efforts to delay, impede, or sabotage the execution of transac-tions that are, in and of themselves, quite complicated. For those governments that enjoy broad congressional support, the passing of a privatization law is a very different experience, since this support can help overcome all kinds of legal and administrative obstacles to selling public companies. This can be seen in the case of Argentina.

The Venezuelan Congress continued to be very active in the privatization process. In 1990, it created a privatization commission that conducted ministerial reviews and pronounced opinions on various aspects of the process. As was pointed out, the actions of Congress sometimes made the process more difficult, but a growing tendency in favor of privatization was developing among the representatives, so that occasionally it was the parliamentary commission that called for greater agility on the part of the executive branch in fulfilling the aims of the privatization program.

The executive delegated responsibility for carrying out the privatizations to the Venezuelan Investment Fund (Fondo de Inversiones de Venezuela — FIV). The FIV defined policy, drew up the list of companies to be sold, contracted private firms to produce reports and studies, and, in general, coordinated the whole process. However, for each company the execution of the sale was decentralized to a working committee in which all of the relevant ministries and company personnel participated. This generated some important institutional tensions. For example, the aluminum and iron companies are under the direction of a powerful public entity, the Venezuelan Corporation of Guyana (Corporación Venezolana de Guyana), which has long battled with the FIV for control of privatizations of companies under its authority. In the absence of clear and decisive political determination to move forward with the privatization program, these institutional rivalries proved fatal to the process. Although the FIV minister's cabinet-level rank signals the government's intent to privatize, this ministerial position has not been granted the power to make certain decisions critical to the privatization process, such as, for example, designating or removing the managers of the firms undergoing sale.

Fiscal factors. Venezuela did not escape the fate of those countries that have been forced to undertake privatization programs as a result of pressure from deteriorating fiscal accounts. The years just prior to the implementation of the adjustment program[1] (with its privatization component) were marked by large fiscal deficits that reached 4.4 percent of gross domestic product (GDP) in 1987 and 8.6 percent in 1988. The 1988 fiscal deficit originated solely in the poor performance of public companies. The consolidated deficit of the public companies reached 10 percent that year, but a central government surplus compensated slightly, leaving the final figure at 8.6 percent of GDP.

These public companies encompassed many different sectors and clearly went beyond the public service responsibilities of the state, subtracting strength from the state's sphere of activity where its rule was absolutely indispensable. The Venezuelan public companies — with the exception of petroleum — have represented a significant drain on public finances. In 1990, the Venezuelan state owned approximately 130 commercial firms, of which 60 percent were dedicated to the production of goods typically made by the private sector. Between 1986 and 1990, these companies received direct transfers from the central government equivalent to an annual average of approximately 11 percent of total public spending. (See Table 2.)

Table 2.
Classification of Public Companies by the Kind of Product
or Service Produced, by Percentage, 1995

Semipublic goods (taxable)	27.97%
Semipublic goods (non-taxable)	3.27%
Public goods	8.62%
Private goods	60.14%

Source: Author's estimates.

The fiscal problem caused by public companies was not limited to the deficit that they generated. Public companies also contributed to the national foreign debt. One important part of the operations and investment of the state-owned companies was financed through public indebtedness — especially foreign — which weighs heavily on fiscal accounts. On February 19, 1983, "Black Friday," Venezuelans woke to the reality of an external debt of more than US$30 billion, of which state-owned companies accounted for approximately 70 percent.

The accentuated deterioration of public services, partly as a result of the same fiscal crisis, and the repeated failure to restructure the companies that provided these services opened the path for more radical solutions to the problem of state-owned companies. Eight years of waiting, on average, to get a new telephone line was a stronger argument for privatizing the telephone company than any economic theory.

THE IMPLEMENTATION OF THE PRIVATIZATION PROGRAM

With the exception of the first of the Venezuelan privatization goals previously mentioned — the redefinition of the state's role in the economy — the program's aims were similar to those generally proposed by governments of other countries in their own contexts. When Venezuela initiated its privatization process, countries both within and outside Latin America had already had successful experiences with the sale of public companies. Chile and Mexico stood out as examples and served, on more than one occasion, as references in specific privatization processes. For example, Venezuelan trade unionists were familiar with the Mexican experience through exchanges with officials sent from that country expressly for this purpose.

The Venezuelan economic team that initiated the 1989 reform program shared a vision of the role of the state in the economy that was radically different from the interventionist vision, which had predominated in Venezuela (and Latin America) for many decades. The new vision favored a deep reorganization of the public sector, including privatizing many state-owned companies.

Outlines and Targets of Venezuelan Privatization

The program's targets were periodically stated in the form of a list of firms to be privatized and their anticipated sales revenues. These projected revenues were also included in the national budget. The program targets were achieved — in fact, were superseded — in 1990 and 1991, particularly in terms of the income realized through the sales. However, after that, the government failed to meet its targets for the privatization program, especially in terms of earnings objectives for sales. Since 1992, the targets have remained basically the same and are repeated year after year. The truth is that the targets have grown to the same degree that the percentage of privatizations carried out has fallen. The list of companies for sale has lengthened, as sales planned in previous years fail to be completed. On several occasions, the national government has submitted budget proposals to Congress containing projections for substantial income from privatizations. These estimates have repeatedly failed to materialize. The present situation suggests that the government is conscious of the necessity of going forward with an audacious privatization program but lacks the ability to carry it out.

Notable Features of the Venezuelan Privatization Sales

The sale method employed in the Venezuelan privatization process entailed several notable features aimed at attracting investors while ensuring that the interests of the state would be advanced.

In all cases, the sales were carried out through *public auctions*. Most companies were sold to an investor or strategic partner, who purchased between 40 percent and 100 percent of the company's stock. The stock market was used only infrequently (the sale of the Banco Occidental de Descuento was realized on the stock exchange). However, the government reserved a percentage of stock in certain firms, such as the telephone company, with the express purpose of placing them in the capital markets. All auctions defined a minimum price below which offers would be rejected by the government. The prices paid have varied with respect to that minimum, depending on two factors: the number of competitors bidding and the reigning macroeconomic context. Recent privatizations have been characterized by reduced competition. Some auctions have been declared vacant, or only one interested party has presented an offer. In those where there were multiple bidders, either no premium or only a very small one has been paid over the minimum price.

Strictly Cash Sales have been very unusual in privatization processes in other countries, where credit and debt conversion have been routinely accepted as part of the payment for state assets sold to the private sector. In the Venezuelan case, all privatizations have been carried out on a purely cash basis, and no privatization has been impeded by the establishment of cash as the method of payment.

Often, when a government announces privatization of a company, it begins to receive solicitations and even pressure from potential investors asking for concessions in the sale. When the company to be sold has financial problems, the pressure increases. This is aggravated by the conditions common to developing countries, which suffer economic recessions and other serious problems such as political instability. A frequently requested concession is the granting of special financing mechanisms such as credits and debt conversion schemes. On occasion, it has been claimed that without such mechanisms, the privatization will not be possible. What implications can the granting of special financing have for the sale of a public company?

Credits granted by the state present a problem in that they convert the government into a creditor of the new investors, thus keeping the divested company within the public sector's orbit. Companies sold in this way are at peril of returning to the public sector if the new owners renege on their obligations to the state. Frequently, in Venezuela and other countries, the state has ended up controlling a number of companies because the private investors who received state funds to develop them failed in their efforts or simply defrauded the state.

With respect to the mechanism of debt conversion, when it is spelled out in a privatization program, the mechanism does not produce negative macroeconomic effects — inflationary pressure, among others — that usually accompany the use of this financial mechanism in new investment projects. This is the case because, in a privatization, the state does not issue new funds for the conversion of debt but transfers already existing assets to new investors. In other words, no new money enters the economy. However, the comparison that should be made is not between the conversion of debt into assets (privatization) and the conversion of debt for projects and new investments, but between debt conversion versus cash payment. This comparison makes visible some important disadvantages of the conversion mechanism. The first is complexity. Once the government has decided to accept debt as a means of payment for the sale of public companies, other decisions must be taken: What class of paper is to be accepted? What discount will be applied? These decisions are taken totally at the discretion of the government, and this, in turn, presents one of the problems outlined below, that of transparency. Transparency is acutely important because the public has difficulty in grasping the complexities of the conversion mechanism. Public opinion generally views privatization as an exchange of public assets, buildings, and equipment for "paper" — in other words, debt — which can have a highly negative connotation, especially in countries that are heavily indebted, as is Venezuela. In contrast, everyone understands cash.

If credit and/or debt conversion are considered concessions necessary to attract potential investors, there is no reason why these discounts should not be expressed more clearly and directly in the price ultimately determined by the market at the time of the bidding. It is the market that ought to discount the price to be paid for any amount that can be attributed to country risk, the condition of the company, or any other factor that negatively affects the firm's value. When the price is determined by the market, the "discount" is not a discount; it is simply the price paid by the investor. The only credit that is fully justified within an adequate privatization policy is that granted to the firm's employees so that they can purchase the stocks set aside for them. Using this reasoning, the Venezuelan government has maintained its decision to sell companies for cash and to allow the market to discount the final sales price.

Sales without Restructuring also characterized Venezuelan privatization. Companies have been put on the market "just as they are," with no significant effort at labor or administrative restructuring. The only restructuring that has taken place has been financial, such as was carried out in the telephone company. The decisive policy-making process by which a full schedule of "restructuring" operations gave way to greater emphasis on privatizations in Venezuela was short but intense. Three elements were critical in producing this change: First, opportunity costs associated with the human and financial resources invested in restructuring were particularly high, given the enormous number of problems and demands facing the state. Second, there was a risk of not being able to privatize after having restructured, perhaps because of the disappearance of potential buyers lured away by other, more attractive opportunities. And, third, important signals were missing about the nature and scope of the transformations that otherwise might have reassured the national and international markets.

These factors led the Venezuelan government to move radically in favor of privatization as the best option for dealing with the problem presented by public companies. As for restructuring, the following criteria prevailed: 1) restructuring of companies as a prior step to their privatization only made sense when this would permit or increase competition or when it was the only way a company could be sold; 2) any restructuring to be undertaken would be assumed by those who bought the company rather than by the state; and 3) except when dealing with a simple restructuring, it made little sense to restructure a company to increase its sale price because the associated risks might not be compensated by the potential increase in sale price.

Privatization of the Privatization Process — the Venezuelan approach — took maximum advantage of the experience and knowledge of the private sector in carrying out the sale of state-owned companies. In 1990, a centralized register of private firms was set up in the FIV. Advertisements were placed in the national and international press inviting consulting and service firms, both national and foreign, to list themselves in the register. The Venezuelan privatization process has depended to a large extent on the use of these private firms. On major contracts, consulting firms were selected by public bidding.

Labor Participation has not been as successful as anticipated because of labor's staunch political opposition to privatization in and of itself. A political decision was taken to set aside stock (generally between 10 percent and 20 percent) to be sold at preferential prices to the employees of the privatizing companies.

Transparency. The problem of transparency is acute because the majority of the public does not understand the debt conversion mechanism, which is relatively difficult to grasp. Transparency has been achieved in Venezuela by using a quantitative, measurable criterion — price — to decide who would buy the public companies or the publicly quoted stocks, and all privatizations have been conducted through public auctions, granting *la buena pro* (final approval) to the competitor offering the best price. This mechanism has been extraordinarily effective, and no significant questioning or denunciations of the privatization process have arisen in Venezuela.

THE PRIVATIZATION PROCESS CARRIED OUT

Between 1990 and 1995, a total of 27 firms were sold for approximately $2.4 billion. The highest price paid was for the telephone company, an operation that yielded $1,885 billion, or 78.5 percent of the total privatization income. The majority of the privatizations, including the most important ones, were completed

Table 3.
Companies Privatized, 1990-1995

Sector	Company	Sale Date	Price (US$ millions)
Telecommunications	Telefonía Móvil Celular	5/31/91	97.7
	CANTV	11/14/91	1,880.5
Airline	VIASA	9/9/91	145.0
Naval	ASTINAVE	12/13/91	20.5
Banking	Banco Occidental	10/15/90	9.6
	Banco Italo-Venezolano	3/27/91	61.9
	Banco República	7/2/91	61.9
	Banco Popular	8/31/93	22.2
	Banco de FRC	12/6/94	3.8
	Banco Guyana	12/7/95	6.6
Tourism	Hotel Cumanagoto	2/5/92	3.3
	Hotel Miranda	2/5/92	0.7
	Hotel Jirahara	10/27/92	3.5
	Hotel El Tama	11/27/91	3.5
	Hotel Moruco	12/16/94	0.8
Sugar Refineries	Tocuyo	11/26/91	3.4
	Cumanacoa	5/5/92	2.4
	Río Yaracuy	10/2/92	6.9
	Tacarigua	12/17/92	1.2
	Las Majaguas	2/10/93	8.6
	Ureña	1/27/94	2.9
	Portuguesa	4/20/94	0.1
Dairy	Indulac	6/15/92	14.6
Manufacturing	Cerámicas Cumaná	10/15/92	0.7
	Motonaves CAVN	6/3/94	4.2
	Cementos Catatumbo	9/29/94	2.8
Petroleum	8 area concessions	1/27/96	244.6
Total	**27 Companies**		**2,628.6**

Source: FIV 1996; author's calculations.

in 1991, at the outset of the reform program undertaken by the Carlos Andrés Pérez administration, which had just begun its governing term. The Venezuelan case again proves the theory that profound structural reforms, such as privatizations, have the greatest chance of success at the beginning of an administration, when the new leadership can count on more political support and popular approval. (See Table 3.)

The Oil Industry

The most significant privatization in Venezuela was in the oil industry. For decades, petroleum has represented a substantial portion of fiscal income and of hard-currency inflows, but, even more important, it has been the true motor of the Venezuelan economy. In addition, the presence of oil transcends pure economics through its creation of a special culture or as a means of organizing the state and Venezuelan society. Thus, the manner adopted for the industry's privatization could have more than just an economic impact on the nation.

After operating predominately under the ownership of foreign multinational firms, the petroleum industry was nationalized in 1976 under a legal code that made private sector participation very difficult. Since then, the process of opening the industry to the private sector has been gradually and insistently developing. The process began with outside service contracts (outsourcing), which continue to be in force; later, concessions were given for the exploitation of "marginal" wells (which produce over 100,000 barrels per day). In January 1996, under the program of "petroleum opening," concessions were granted for the exploration and exploitation of geographic areas with oil-producing potential. The state oil company (Petróleos de Venezuela, S.A. — PDVSA) auctioned off 10 areas where extraction was expected to reach approximately 500,000 barrels per day, equivalent to a little less than one-quarter of the country's total oil production. The privatization of the areas took place under a "shared-profits" program through which investors offered the government a percentage of their profits if they found oil. Private investors were chosen, based on the percentage of participation they offered the government. In addition, the state company reserved for itself the right to participate in the new firm that would be constituted if oil were found in economically attractive quantities.

Table 4.
Bids for Exploration and Exploitation Risk Areas, Percentages, 1996

Area	Winning Consortia	Peg Offer
La Ceiba	Mobil, Ven Oel, Nippon	50%
Golfo de Paria Oeste	Conoco	50%
Guanare	Elf Aquitaine, Conoco	50%
Golfo de Paria Este	Enron, Inelectra	29%
El Sombrero	No offer	
Guarapiche	British Petroleum, Amoco, Maxus	50%
San Carlos	Perez Companc	40%
Punta Pescador	Amoco	50%
Catatumbo	No offer	
Delta Centro	Louisiana Land & Exploration, Norcen, Bemton	41%

Source: PVDSA 1996.

The results of the January 1996 bidding were decidedly successful, as much for the solvency of the firms that participated and won areas in concession, as for the percentages of profits offered to the government and the extra premiums paid when bids ended in ties. (See Table 4.)

CANTV: The Venezuelan Telephone Company

In December, 1991, 10 months after the initiation of the privatization process, the FIV held a public bidding in which 49 percent of the stocks of the Venezuelan Telephone Company (Compañía de Teléfonos Venezolana — CANTV) were sold to an international consortium led by the U.S. company GTE at a public bidding. At the same time that the sale was being made, *fideicomiso* (trusteeship) was constituted as a private national bank with another 11 percent of CANTV's stocks that would be available for purchase by the company's employees. With those two operations completed, turning over 51 percent of the telephone firm to private hands, CANTV was no longer a state-owned company.

The plan adopted for the privatization of CANTV was the result of a long process that began initially with a proposal for a simple restructuring of the company without an ownership transfer. The proposal — with no sale of stock and the maintenance of the recently appointed president — had the greatest amount of support within the Pérez government, which began its term in 1989. This majority position within the government included the firm's own management, as tends to occur in most of the privatization experiences, who opposed the sale of the company and other forms of privatization that could dislodge them from control. However, the low quality of the service offered by the company, its dreadful public image, its difficult financial situation, as well as the government's inability to rescue it due to the government's own fiscal limitations, facilitated the task for those who proposed more radical solutions to the problem as it was presented. Consequently, the decision was made to opt for some form of privatization.

The Regulatory Agency

As part of the privatization process, the National Council of Telecommunications (Consejo Nacional de Telecomunicaciones — CONATEL) was formed as a regulatory and supervisory entity of the telecommunications sector. Initially, the autonomy and institutional solidity of this organization were guaranteed by the fact that the council would be created by a law. However, as it was impossible to get such a law passed by Congress, it was created by an executive decree. The project for a new telecommunications law that would replace the one currently in force, dating back to 1940 and modified in 1965, has been stuck in Congress since 1991.

In spite of the meticulous details included in the concession contract, diverse conflicts have arisen between CONATEL and CANTV. The continued technological innovations make it more and more difficult to distinguish boundaries between those services that can be offered competitively and those that remain as monopolies. CANTV was guaranteed the monopoly over basic telephone service for nine years, but imposing this monopoly is ever more difficult. For this reason, some have proposed a re-negotiation between the government and the telephone company, reducing the period of exclusivity in exchange for the immediate and total liberalization of telephone rates. The lesson is clear: in an area like telecommunications, where technological innovations are so numerous and constant, the definition of periods, more or less lengthy, of monopoly rights can become very difficult to guarantee.

At the time of its privatization, CANTV presented the classic problems of many public companies: a technology lag of at least 15 years, unsatisfied demands of 47 percent, a real decline in operating income, overemployment, low investment levels, and a politicized management staff, among others. All of this translated into low productivity and poor service quality. Given the firm's absolute monopoly over the entire telecommunications area and the fact that it regulated and supervised itself, telephone users had no means to demand or to defend their rights as consumers.

Three years after the privatization, many achievements were reported in the telecommunications sector in Venezuela. Investments by the firm during 1992-1994 tripled the amount made by the state during the years 1989-1991. This produced an increase of more than 1 million installed telephone lines (a 50-percent increase in the total number); 732,000 new clients; the installation of more than 23,000 public telephones; and the incorporation into the telephone network of more than 154 rural populations who had never before had service. By 1995, around one of three of the existing telephones in Venezuela had been installed by the privatized company. (See Table 5.)

Table 5.
Improvements in Telephone Service, 1995

Indicators	Before Privatization	After Privatization
Lines installed	1,987,615	2,956,788
Calls completed		
Local	48%	58.8%
National	30%	46.3%
International	19%	52.1%
Calls without any tone lag	50%	98.9%
Public telephones in service	43%	90.0%

Source: CANTV 1995.

The new CANTV has succeeded in overshooting the targets set by the regulatory agency that was created in the course of the privatization. Between 1992 and 1994, CANTV transferred net resources of $117 million to the Venezuelan state. However, CANTV, as a private firm, still confronts many problems. In contrast to what happened in Mexico, where the privatized telephone company became the company of the year in a very short time, the process has been much more complicated in Venezuela.

For example, the real operating income of CANTV grew during the period 1991-1993 at a time when rate increases were less than the rise in the consumer price index and the wholesale price index. This meant that there were gains in efficiency. However, after 1993, the rate increases approved for CANTV by the regulatory authorities were below those agreed upon in the concession contract. This, added to the accumulation of debts to the company by the government, led real operating expenses to begin to fall by the end of 1994. During the years 1992-1995, the delays in rate increase approval caused the company accumulated financial losses on the order of $56 million, while the government's debt to the firm reached $114 million in 1994. All of this led CANTV to reduce its investment plans for 1995 by approximately 40 percent in nominal terms, which implied a very severe reduction, taking into account the inflation rate during this period.

One of the main problems confronted by the privatized company was the failure of the state to comply with the legal agreements (concession contracts) signed as a part of the privatization process and, furthermore, the company's failure to comply with its commercial obligations as a consumer of telephone service. In this case, the state worked against the success of its own privatization policies by the behavior it adopted following the policies' implementation.

The case of CANTV shows that, regardless of the type of ownership of a public service firm, the type of regulation to which the firm is subject can radically affect its operating viability. The Venezuelan government tried various times to use CANTV as a factor in its social policy in order to achieve better income distribution by controlling rates. However, as local and international experience shows, in the end, this results in a losing strategy in which the affected firm is made economically nonviable and those who aspire to benefit from rate controls end up being negatively affected themselves. The CANTV process, therefore, illustrates what can happen when the state does not sufficiently internalize the philosophy of privatization.

THE GREAT FAILURES IN THE VENEZUELAN PRIVATIZATION PROCESS

The Venezuelan privatization process failed in five important areas: the slow pace of privatization, the lack of regulatory frameworks, underutilization of the country's capital markets, the failure to implement employee participation programs, and government failures to live up to its promises

Pace of Privatization

Privatization in Venezuela advanced at a very slow speed, which has reduced the program's credibility. The privatization process essentially halted after February 1992, when the first of that year's two coup attempts occurred. Paralysis set in, despite subsequent administrations' affirmation of the government's desire to continue the process. Even though the government repeatedly announced the same list of companies to be privatized, it has been unable to carry out the sales. The main reasons for the extremely slow pace have been the adverse macroeconomic context and the lack of a clear, defined political will.

Adverse Macroeconomic Context. Venezuela's macroeconomic outlook progressively deteriorated after 1992, first, as a consequence of political instability and, later, as a result of economic policies applied by the government that assumed power in February 1992. At that moment, the economic picture changed radically. The expansion and growth, which had developed between 1990 and 1992, gave way to progressive stagnation and recession between 1993 and 1996. Macroeconomic policies favorable to trade opening and the market economy gave way to tendencies toward accentuated state intervention and control of economic activity. The change in direction reduced the attractiveness of companies slated for privatization, and it continued until May 1996, when an important about-face in economic policy occurred as part of an agreement with the IMF.

Venezuela's experience between 1993 and 1996 shows that, more than the deterioration of the economy, the trend in policy direction can negatively affect privatization. Experiences exist — such as that of Peru in 1992 — in which privatizations took place in the middle of an adverse economic situation but in the framework of policies that pointed toward a market economy, trade opening, and modernization. In other words, it is not so much the gravity of the economic situation as it is policy direction that affects privatizations. The direction of policy in Venezuela until May 1996 was one of the most notable factors contributing to the stagnation of the privatization program.

The application of controls (on prices, interest rates, and exchange rates), such as were operative in Venezuela in 1994 and 1995, increases risk and discourages private investment. For the private investor, it is not clear how to operate success-fully in an environment of price controls, high tariffs on industrial imports, and tough restrictions on profit repatriation. In such a context, privatization is feasible only in sectors such as petroleum and aluminum that operate as enclaves producing primary products directly exported abroad and in which state intervention is minor. For the same reasons, under these conditions, privatization is difficult in the area of infrastructure, where all operations are undertaken within the country and in the local currency.

An illustrative example of how difficult it can be to privatize in a negative macroeconomic context can be found in the Venezuelan electricity sector. For four years, attempts were made to sell a group of electrical generation and distribution companies. Although these companies were relatively well managed and had a promising business outlook as well as potentially interested buyers, the companies could not be transferred to the private sector. The reasons for this included the lack of an adequate regulatory framework, the government's decision to freeze rates for long periods, the public sector's debts to the firms that had yet to be canceled, and so forth. These conditions made privatization difficult, except in isolated buy-sell cases that were motivated by very specific reasons.

Lack of Political Will. Lack of a clear political will to carry out the program also delayed Venezuelan privatization. The political will to privatize can be measured with a five-point test. Venezuela clearly failed on two of the criteria: 1) a cabinet-level official in charge of the privatizations (present); 2) the establish-ment of a cabinet-level committee or intergovernmental executive committee (present); 3) public statements by the highest authority in the country of commit-ment to the program (absent); 4) incorporation into the national budget of the resources estimated to be gained from privatizations (present); and 5) empowerment of the program's director to name and remove officials in the companies to be privatized (absent).

Of these five points, the fifth is critical. It is this power — the power to remove those executives who are not collaborating with the privatization process — that permits the director of privatization to advance with the process. Most of Venezuela's privatization ministers have lacked this power.

Regulatory Frameworks

Venezuela's second failure was the lack of progress on the definition of the regulatory frameworks that, on the one hand, make it possible to know the rules of the game and, on the other hand, stimulate competition. This has been a critical negative factor for the electricity and telecommunications sectors. Although the telecommunications sector had been opened to private capital and the telephone company had been privatized, Congress failed to approve both the Telecommunications Law, submitted in June 1991, and the law designed to give institutional autonomy to CONATEL, the sector's regulatory agency. It appears that in the highest political echelons of the country — in the executive as well as in Congress — there was little awareness of the necessity for and importance of modern regulatory frameworks, especially for those public services being privatized. The statist model, in which the state formulates its own rules at its discretion, according to what it needs, persists as a mode of thinking and acting for most of the country's political leaders.

Capital Markets

Venezuela's third failure is related to its underutilized capital markets. Only one company, Banco Occidental de Descuento, was sold through the stock market. Those operations intended to be realized through the capital markets (such as the sale of the second stock package of CANTV) were notably delayed, as was the case for the whole privatization program in general. The small size of Venezuelan capital markets (total capitalization of the stock markets in Venezuela is not above $4 billion) has fed the argument that the markets have no important role to play in the privatization process. This created a vicious cycle in which economic policy did not stimulate capital markets and capital markets, in turn, could not reinforce economic policy. Policymakers, when placing a large volume of stock, have assigned the Venezuelan capital markets a minimal role or have ignored them altogether because of their small size. This occurred with the telephone company and the opening of the petroleum sector, even though local capital markets could have played a much greater role.

Employee Participation

Venezuela's fourth failure was the inability to implement employee-participation programs as they were initially designed. In general, this was due to difficulties that the privatized companies confronted following their sale. Among other factors, an adverse macroeconomic context, the state's failure to fulfill contractual agreements, and the lack of adequate regulatory frameworks weakened the companies financially and made establishment of the employee-participation programs harder. Obviously, the particular condition of each firm at the time of its privatization played an important role, as did the strategy adopted to achieve employee participation. To give one example, VIASA, the national airline, encountered all three difficulties: 1) a precarious financial situation when it was privatized, which discouraged employees from purchasing the stock set aside for them; 2) difficulties imposed on the company by the state, which continued to be an important partner; and 3) the scheme adopted for employee participation. In a company in VIASA's conditions, the employee-participation program probably should have formed part of the obligations retained by the company, once its financial situation had been cleaned up.

Government Failures

The state itself has also contributed to the stagnation of privatization policy by failing to fulfill some of the agreements the government signed for the purpose of privatizing publicly owned companies. For example, the concession contract for telephone service promised a modification of rates, but the government has prevented timely adjustments on various occasions and has also failed to pay for the state's use of the company's services. Without a doubt, the state's failure to fulfill accords damages the privatized company and sends a dreadful signal to potential privatization investors.

In aggregate, Table 6 shows some of the quantifiable results of privatizations in Venezuela.

Table 6. The Results of Privatization in Venezuela

Total Income	US$2.628 billion
Foreign Investment	US$1.868 billion
New Stockholders	21,375
Reduction in Public Employees	45,000

Source: Author's estimates.

Of the numbers, perhaps the most significant is the amount of foreign investment made in Venezuela through the privatization process. The volume of foreign investment attracted reflects about 40 percent of total foreign investment existing in the country. The other relatively important figure is that of the reduction in the number of state employees. Privatizations yielded a reduction of approximately 3.75 percent of public employees — 1,200,000 persons — in Venezuela in 1992. On the other hand, if only employment generated by state-owned enterprises is taken into account — close to 200,000 persons in 1991 — the drop in employment as a result of privatization rises to 22.5 percent. However, it is in the area of efficiency where the gains from privatization have been greatest. An examination of some of the main privatizations corroborates this conclusion.

The Agenda for the Coming Years: Some Possibilities and Some Dilemmas

The Official Program

Despite scant progress, the Venezuelan government maintains a lengthy list of companies to be privatized. Were these companies actually to be sold, the sale could generate income between $4 billion to $5 billion, which represents approximately 7 percent to 8 percent of 1996 GDP (around $60 billion). This amount is nearly equivalent to one-sixth of Venezuela's foreign external debt, contracted, to a large extent, by the state-owned companies that the government now wants to privatize. However, more important still than the resources that may be generated by privatization, the transfer to the private sector of some of the public companies, such as steel and aluminum, could give a significant impetus to development of some productive sectors in which the country has important comparative advantages.

Table 7. The Privatization Schedule

Sector	Company	Estimated Date
Aluminum	Alcasa	4th Quarter 1996
	Carbonorca	4th Quarter 1996
	Venalum-Bauxilum	4th Quarter 1996
Iron	Fesilven	4th Quarter 1996
	Sidor	1ST Quarter 1997
Telecommunications	49% stock CANTV	2nd- 4th Quarter 1996
Electricity	Enerbar	4th Quarter 1996
	Enelven-Enelco	2nd Quarter 1997
	Sistema Estado Nueva Esparta	4th Quarter 1996
Tourism	Hotel Bella Vista	2nd Quarter 1996
	Hotel Aguas Calientes	2nd Quarter 1996
	Hotel Humboldt—cable lift	4th Quarter 1996
Ports	Port of Central Coast	3rd Quarter 1996
Shipbuilders	DIANCA	3rd Quarter 1996
Financial Sector	Banco de Fomento Regional de los Andes	1st Quarter 1996
	Extebandes	3rd Quarter 1996

Source: FIV 1996.

The Incomprehension of a Policy

Privatizations forecast by the government to take place in 1996 and 1997 have been delayed by problems that illustrate the difficulties preventing privatization policy from being understood. For example:

The Aluminum Sector. In spite of the long time that has passed in the effort to sell the aluminum sector firms and the short time left for meeting the target sale date, basic questions regarding sales strategy, for instance, remain undecided, that is, whether the companies are to be sold as a package to the same buyer or as separate companies. Also to be determined is whether the finance ministry will capitalize the debts that these companies have with the federal government or if they will be ceded to another state entity, such as the Venezuelan Investment Fund. Another decision to be made is whether the state will maintain its guarantee on the debts that the companies have with foreign creditors once privatization is completed. Moreover, no agreement has been reached with the Japanese partners who hold 20 percent of the stock of Venalum and a veto right over important decisions on the firm's future.

Some economists argue that selling the companies as a package will guarantee the privatization of the whole group. Investors would not have the option of buying only the profitable aluminum refineries while avoiding companies that operate in less lucrative parts of the production process. This is the theory of "the steak and the skin and bones," whereby some skin and bones must be added to each piece of steak or the private investors will run off with the steak, leaving the skin and bones to the state. Some important considerations cast doubt on the validity of this theory: 1) a package sale of all the companies reduces the number of potential interested investors and, with it, competition, ultimately lowering the price that can be expected to be paid for the companies; 2) the investors will discount from the sale price the cost of buying companies they do not want, and if they cannot do that, they simply will not buy the package; and 3) if the investors are obliged to buy companies that do not contribute to the efficiency of their global operations, they will later find the means to dispose of firms they do not want, either through sale or bankruptcy. Investor X can reduce Company A to the lowest possible price if forced to buy it as part of a package that includes other firms that he or she finds interesting, while Investor Y may have been interested only in Company A, which he was not allowed to acquire because he was uninterested in or unable to buy the entire package. The steak and skin and bones theory reflects a lack of understanding of how markets and economic agents function and is a fruitless effort to extend the state's control in a totally private-sector-led environment.

CANTV. The most complicated issue facing the government in the sale of its remaining CANTV stock is setting the initial offer price. Political pressure is being brought to set the minimum sale price at the level obtained in 1991, when the international group headed by GTE, mentioned previously in this chapter, bought 49 percent of the stock. However, three factors work against this. First, the portion sold in 1991 included management control of the firm, which implied the payment of a premium. Second, the offerings of telephone company stocks made on the international stock markets has grown considerably since 1991 to the point that some placements have underperformed. Third, Venezuela's economic condition has deteriorated since 1991, and the political risks have increased. The dilemma of the sale of CANTV stock, which confronts the Venezuelan government and political elite, is rooted in their failure to internalize the most substantive aspect of privatization policy: privatization means allowing the market to operate more freely. CANTV's stock will be worth what the market dictates, and this price may be more or less than it was in 1991. To pretend that someone can guarantee a minimum price for the stock at the 1991 level is to fail to understand what markets are all about.

The Electricity Sector. With abundant energy resources, the potential for privatization in the Venezuelan electricity sector is ample. The companies on the state's privatization list have already been evaluated and are well known for the level of investor interest they have generated. Nonetheless, advances in the area of electricity regulation continue to be precarious. The regulation of the sector and the approval of a new electrical service law have not been undertaken. Neither has any regulatory decree been approved that could serve as a transitional mechanism while more solid and permanent legal instruments are agreed upon. Still, also in this context, the government has attempted or hoped to realize some privatizations in the sector. The implicit supposition is that the private sector is an extension of the state, which believes that regulatory frameworks are not required because it will always be the arbiter and a part of economic activity.

Positive Developments

Even more interesting than the companies formally listed to be privatized are the five areas in which some advances have been achieved or appear to be likely in the near future: petroleum, pension funds, reprivatization of banks, regional privatization programs, and the sales of agricultural land.

Petroleum. In the petroleum sector, a gradual process of opening to the private sector began in 1996. Open discussion of the privatization of the industry has been impelled by the enormous debt that the Venezuelan state has with its workers regarding social security payments for which no disposable funds exist. Although the debt has largely been liquidated as a consequence of high inflation suffered in the 1990s, it represents almost $7 billion, or approximately 10 percent of GDP.

A proposal popular among the country's leaders would cancel this debt by swapping it for stock in the petroleum companies, which could constitute a first step in the privatization not just of petroleum activities but of the state company itself. The turnover of stock in the state petroleum companies would require that these companies be taken public as that is the only way to convert the stock into liquid assets. Opening the PDVSA and its affiliated state petroleum companies to private capital as a formula to solve the problem of social security payments would facilitate the sector's privatization. This initiative coincides with another initiative that has also been gaining strength, which would transform the social security system into one of individual capitalization and private pension funds, as has occurred in other countries in the region, such as Chile and Argentina. Were these initiatives to progress, this would significantly speed up the privatization process in Venezuela.

Throughout the world, oil is one of the sectors most open to private foreign investment. Between 1993 and 1995, privatization operations in Venezuela's petroleum sector (sales of stock or property transfers, excluding mergers) accounted for more than $12 billion, and it is estimated that in 1996 that figure will reach approximately $8 billion. The magnitude of the investments, the risk, and the intensification of international competition have led a number of countries to open their petroleum industries to both national and foreign private capital. Eastern Europe, Vietnam, Argentina, Peru, and Canada, to name only a few, are widely promoting the development of the petroleum sector on the basis of private capital.

Opportunities for deals are being lost inside and outside Venezuela under the petroleum sector's current regulatory framework. Given Venezuela's petroleum reserves, if production were to double from the 1995 level, reserves would still last more than the expected life of oil as a source of energy. The industry has begun a process of opening through which the private sector has been ceded the following: 1) marginal wells for its exploitation, 2) new areas to be explored and exploited, and 3) contracted services (outsourcing). However, a debate has slowly begun to surface over a more ambitious privatization process that may include the sale of stock of certain companies to affiliated firms or the holding company itself. Many obstacles to this approach remain to be overcome.

The first obstacle to privatizations including sales of stock is political-ideological. Although this point of view is declining in intensity, some of Venezuela's political elite believe the oil industry ought to be predominantly, if not solely, in the hands of the state and that the sector should not go beyond marginal associations with private capital for specific operations, considered on a case-by-case basis. This vision tends to rest on the mistaken identification of three separate and distinct factors: 1) the size of the country's oil reserves, 2) the business activity directed toward commercially exploiting these reserves, and 3) the state-owned oil company, PDVSA. These three distinct aspects of business elements are confused with each other because they have been intertwined ever since the nationalization of petroleum.

The simple conceptual separation of these three elements can reduce resistance to privatization. Reserves belong and will continue to belong to the state, which will charge a "royalty" for their exploitation. Consequently, the state can keep control of PDVSA and still permit the entrance of independent operators, unaffiliated with PDVSA, to become involved in any area of the oil business. This approach would make it possible to understand that the total or partial privatization of PDVSA — the company itself — would not necessarily lead to the transfer of a public monopoly to a private monopoly or to the loss of ownership of the country's oil reserves. Such a conceptual clarification, which has begun to appear in the country, constitutes the first essential step for defeating the political and ideological resistance to petroleum privatization.

Currently, the participation of private capital in the hydrocarbon industry is determined by Article 5 of the Nationalization Law for the industry. In accordance with this article, the private sector can participate in the oil industry only by establishing service or associative contracts with PDVSA. These contracts and associations are limited to determined areas and require the approval of Congress.

A broader and more intense participation by private capital in the industry, which would permit it to operate without having to associate with PDVSA, requires repeal or substantial modification of the Nationalization Law for petroleum. In the meantime, private sector participation has to be administered, from a legal point of view, on a case-by-case basis. Of great importance, the incorporation of private capital requires the development and strengthening of an autonomous regulatory capacity apart from the state company. A provision that would assist in that strengthening does not exist in Venezuela today. Although regulatory responsibility belongs formally to the Ministry of Energy and Mines, PDVSA, in reality, regulates itself. The ministry lacks the resources and technical capacity to carry out this function. Without first overcoming this weakness, a substantial incorporation of private capital into the oil sector could negatively affect privatization.

To stimulate private participation will also require modifications of the fiscal scheme that applies to the petroleum sector. Under the current code, all activity in the sector is subject to two taxes: a "royalty" equal to 16.6 percent of the price of a barrel of crude oil, and an income tax levied at a rate of 67.7 percent. (Marginal wells, which pay a tax of 34 percent on income, are the only exception.) These two taxes apply to all of the sector's activities without reference to profitability. This fiscal scheme discriminates against those projects that have less relative profitability but that could be, nonetheless, important centers of productive activity.

The Pension System. Venezuelan labor legislation requires all companies to maintain reserves for an amount equivalent to one month's salary for every employee. This benefit is known as "social security for seniority and termination." The adequate amount for the employees is recalculated annually, retroactively, with the last salary payment as the reference point. These funds, which each employee has the right to receive upon retiring from the firm, earn interest according to a rate set by the Venezuelan Central Bank. Although social security contributions are not the only component of the existing social security system in Venezuela, the extreme precariousness of the other elements makes these contributions among the most important, and they could become the base of a modern pension system.

In the public sector, estimates place the amount required for adequate social security reserves at a figure that oscillates between $6 and $7 billion. This forms part of the current structural deficit in Venezuelan public finances. Obviously, the state has had to adopt a long-term financing program to fulfill this debt obligation.

The necessity of transforming the existing social security system offers an opportunity to create private pension funds, improve the situation of workers, and generate positive effects on the domestic savings rate and on national investment. Under the new system, the funds would be administered by private firms, regulated and supervised by the government, and workers would be free to decide in which fund to invest their payments. The funds would compete with each other to capture these resources, offering the workers a range of investment opportunities. Under this system, the workers can have a guarantee that their payments are, in fact, being accumulated and are also being invested in accord with the best opportunities in the market. Moreover, these funds would be converted into an enormous mass of resources that will contribute to the financing of private and public investment.

Reprivatization of Banks. The crisis in the financial system, which erupted after the government took over the second largest bank in the country in January 1994, has left some eight entities in state hands, in addition to other firms owned by the banks the government now controls. The reprivatization of these institutions —

with options such as mergers and liquidations — poses a new task for the Venezuelan state.

The massive reprivatization of the banks is far more demanding in regard to its macroeconomic implications than are sales of industrial or service sector companies. The privatization of a shipbuilding company or a sugar refinery is primarily conditioned by the state of the firm being sold and the outlook for its particular market, for example, its export possibilities. The macroeconomic picture, of secondary importance for industrial and service sector companies, takes precedence as the most important variable in the sale of financial entities.

A geographically close example of a massive privatization of banks is found in Mexico, where in 13 months, between 1991 and 1992, 18 commercial banks were sold for nearly $14 billion. These banks were the product of the process of mergers and closures that followed the 1982 nationalization of around 60 financial institutions. The nationalization took place at the same time that other measures, such as exchange rate and price controls, were introduced. The reprivatization of the Mexican banks occurred in the middle of a program of economic reforms that sought liberalization, opening, integration of new markets, and a redefinition of the role of the state in the economy. In addition, the process unfolded in an economy that had stabilized and in which the exchange rate had been unified and freed, along with prices and interest rates. It had also occurred in the context of strong fiscal and monetary discipline, significant foreign capital flows, and a considerable reduction in inflationary pressure. In other words, the reprivatization of Mexican banks took place amid growing confidence among economic agents, thanks to the economic polices that were being implemented. As a consequence of these factors, all of the banks were sold at prices well above the value assigned by specialized foreign firms contracted to evaluate them.

Regional Privatizations. In 1989, Venezuela initiated a process of decentralization that placed in the hands of regional state governments and municipalities important functions and assets that up until then had been under the control of the central government. Race tracks, ports, airports, mines, education, health services, and other activities have gradually been transferred to local and regional governments. Some of the regional governments, which are chosen in direct elections and may represent parties or positions at odds with the central government, are planning or are already executing privatizations of the activities and properties that have been transferred to them. The government of the state of Sucre has privatized its salt mines and tourism properties and is in the process of privatizing the port of Guiría. The government of the state of Falcón has begun to design, with the assistance of the World Bank, an integrated privatization program that includes different sectors.

Privatization on a regional scale can demonstrate some of the obstacles that slow privatizations at the national level. For example, the attempts by some regional governments to advance the privatization of electricity firms (as was the case with El Occidente in Falcón) or of water distribution (as in Monagas) pressured national authorities and Congress to create or modify the regulatory frameworks. The initiation of privatization processes, such as the granting of concessions to private companies for the maintenance of roads at the state level, can also create important demonstration effects. The granting of concessions to private companies for the maintenance of roads in some regional entities of the country has begun to produce these effects.

Sales of Land in the Agricultural Sector. A substantial percentage of Venezuela's agricultural production takes place on lands where legal title is precarious or uncertain. This has a doubly negative impact by limiting investment in infrastructure and other long-term investment activities, and, as the land cannot be used as a security guarantee, by making it difficult for farmers to obtain bank financing.

In 1960, all of the unused land in the country was transferred to the National Agrarian Institute (Instituto Agrario Nacional — IAN), along with extensive land that had previously been expropriated. As a result, of the 30 million hectares of land suitable for cultivation in Venezuela, IAN today owns approximately 15 million hectares. In addition, almost all irrigation drainage projects have been constructed on IAN-controlled land.

As an extraordinarily underutilized form of capital, these lands could be privatized to meet two goals. The first would be to regularize the ownership and property holdings of hundreds of thousands of families that have worked these lands for years. Purchase price and financing could be designed to take into account the economic situation of those acquiring the land. The privatization program's second goal could be to incorporate investors with the capacity to develop and exploit existing infrastructure, at the same time that they legally promise to respect the rights of small producers already established in the area. The state could retain significant amounts of land or could make the sale of it subject to certain conditions or objectives. However, it makes little sense to allow more than half of Venezuela's best land to be unproductive or only partially developed due to uncertain ownership.

In the agricultural sector, there are other government-controlled assets, such as coffee plants or cacao storage facilities, which can be privatized immediately to inject new resources and vitality into the country's agrarian economy.

THE LESSONS FROM VENEZUELA'S PRIVATIZATION PROCESS

The Venezuelan privatization process offers interesting lessons, some of which match the experience of other countries, while others are relatively new:

1. The Venezuelan experience proves conclusively that successful privatization demands a context of macroeconomic policies compatible with the market economy. Controls and excessive interference by the government in macroeconomic issues discourage private investment.

2. Privatization is perceived by economic agents — external and internal — as one of the most important signs of a government's determination to reform the economy. The absence of privatization contributes to a lack of confidence and uncertainty.

3. Privatization has its best chance at the beginning of an administration's tenure in office, when political capital is at its highest.

4. Those companies for which new executives are appointed with the specific mandate to carry out the privatization have the greatest probability of being successfully transferred to the private sector.

5. Cash as a method of payment is not an impediment to the sale of public companies, as has often been argued.

6. The problem of unemployment — which is the greatest fear generated by privatization programs — diminishes considerably if the privatization takes place in a context of economic growth, and if certain arrangements, such as generous severance payments, retraining, outplacement, gradual workforce reductions, and so on, are negotiated with the private investors.

IMPLEMENTING PRIVATIZATION: 20 MAJOR ISSUES FOR POLICYMAKERS

The Venezuelan privatization experience illustrates lessons that policymakers in other countries would do well to consider as they implement privatization measures. When a government decides to sell a company or a group of companies, many relevant and practical issues must be addressed. The way in which the following issues are approached affects the results of the privatization process, making the difference between success and failure.

1. Restructuring before Privatization. Governments usually face the dilemma of whether to restructure companies before privatizing them. Some policymakers argue that restructuring will facilitate the sale of the company or increase its value. Others fear that restructuring may lead to a loss of windows of opportunity or momentum. They would also argue that restructuring demands additional managerial and financial resources that the public sector lacks. However, what guidelines should governments apply to this issue? Are there areas where governments have comparative advantages for restructuring a company? Is restructuring worth doing?

2. How Much to Sell. When it comes to divesting a company, governments must decide what percentage of shares to sell: 100 percent? 50 percent? 40 percent? The reasons for and the implications of selecting any of these percentages must be evaluated carefully. A government may decide to sell just 40 percent of a company because it is facing political resistance to privatizing it completely. Or it may decide to sell the same percentage as part of a financial strategy to raise the value of the shares before selling the rest of the company. Nevertheless, to remain as a shareholder of a privatized company can have high costs for the state, including investments of more money. So, what are the implications, constraints, and best strategies when it comes to deciding how much to sell?

3. Loans and Credits. In most cases, potential buyers want the most credit as cheaply as possible from the government, even if a loan is not really needed. In some cases, it will be argued that if a government does not extend generous credit, it may be impossible to sell the company. How is it possible to know if this is so? How beneficial is it for governments to facilitate the selling of enterprises by giving credit? What does international experience tell us about the pros and cons of different methods of payment? What are the political and economic implications of each one?

4. Public Offering or Private Tender. Most governments consider the promotion of capital markets as a main objective of privatization. However, public enterprises frequently are not listed on the stock market and are not in an acceptable financial condition to raise money easily in equity markets. Capital markets in developing countries are generally weak, which sometimes leads governments to adopt private tenders as a more effective way to divest assets. However, that may leave a major objective of the privatization program unfulfilled. Therefore, how can a government strike a balance between the need to bring strategic investors in rapidly and to develop its domestic capital markets?

5. Defining a Minimum Price. If a government wholeheartedly commits to privatization, it implies accepting a market-determined sale price for companies being divested. However, for many reasons, governments have to establish a minimum or base price as a reference point for the negotiation or bidding process. To arrive at that price, the government conducts a variety of valuations of the company, which often produce an array of results from which it must choose. The final criterion for setting a price is often political. With this in mind, what elements should be considered when determining the minimum or base price?

6. The Criteria for Choosing the Buyer. Most economists agree that the criteria for choosing the final buyer of a public company in competitive bidding should be as transparent as possible. This requires quantifiable criteria, the simplest of which is price. However, should price be the ultimate criteria for selecting a buyer? Are there ways to ensure that, while holding to price as the ultimate element for selecting the winning bidder, other qualitative criteria are also established?

7. Lumping Together Good and Bad Companies. There are all kinds of entities in the realm of the public sectors: healthy, well-managed companies and deficit-ridden, badly run companies. Some governments tried to privatize poorly performing companies by attaching them to ones that were more attractive. The argument is that if the government does not sell in "packages," it will be left with all the losers. If the private sector is obliged to buy bad companies, however, it will find a way to get rid of them eventually, making the privatization process less transparent. Therefore, is it a good policy to oblige the private sector to buy companies that it finds unattractive? When governments have packaged companies, how has that strategy succeeded?

8. Selling to a Foreign Public Company. Some governments have sold their enterprises to other foreign public companies. Can such a transfer be considered a privatization? Beyond this theoretical question, what are the practical implications of such a sale? How does it affect a private company's autonomy from politically motivated actions? What have been the experiences of other countries that have attempted this type of sale? And should governments preclude foreign state-owned companies from participating in privatization programs?

9. Labor Participation. Most privatizing governments have adopted labor-participation programs. Nevertheless, the modalities can vary widely from one country to another and even within the same country. It is recognized that a well-designed labor-participation program may 1) give viability to the privatization program, 2) contribute to create a culture of shareholders, and 3) add value to the company being sold. On the other hand, many labor-participation programs have not worked out as initially planned because 1) workers were not able or did not want to buy shares; 2) they found they could not sell their shares when they wanted to because the markets lack sufficient liquidity; and 3) in general, they have not been realizing the returns they expected as shareholders. What are the critical elements for a successful labor-participation program?

10. The Opportunity to Sell. In some cases, public officials or other relevant parties argue against selling a company because the conditions make it necessary to sell at below the best possible price. This usually occurs in a precarious macroeconomic environment and when private sector agents show a lack of confidence. The question can be posed in the following terms: Is privatization a policy to be implemented only when the macroeconomic environment is healthy or is it a means to improve the macroeconomic environment?

11. Selling Companies in a Particular Sequence. Different rationales have been offered for different sales sequencing. Some argue that it is better to gain experience by selling small companies first, before moving to the medium-sized and larger firms. Others would sell profit-making companies to ensure that the first privatizations are successful, making the entire process easier and more successful. But is it possible for governments to decide the sequencing of the process? Is it really relevant? What are the forces determining the sequencing of privatization programs?

12. Role of the Private Firms in the Privatization Process. All governments are aware of the importance of private firms in privatization programs. Most recognize the need for investment banks and accounting and legal firms, among others, to carry out privatization programs successfully. However, it is not always clear to what extent and under what conditions such participation should take place. How much work should be done by the government internally, and how much should be contracted out? Is it preferable to contract a large, leading private firm that would subcontract services in each privatization or to hire private firms individually for specific tasks? What should characterize the structure of incentives given to private firms contracted by the government to carry out the privatization program?

13. Proceeds from Privatization. To win public support for the privatization program, it is extremely important to explain what the government intends to do with the privatization revenue. There is a general consensus that proceeds should not be used to finance current expenditures but should be used to retire debt or finance other forms of capital expenditure. Nevertheless, governments undertaking large privatization programs are trapped in large fiscal deficits that generate inflationary pressures and other macroeconomic imbalances. In those cases, it might be argued that, even when used to finance current expenditure, the proceeds from privatization contribute significantly to economic recovery by helping to achieve rapid fiscal consolidation and macroeconomic stabilization. What is an appropriate balance when allocating privatization proceeds?

14. Privatization Laws. Some privatization programs occurred in a legal framework that included a general law on privatization. In other cases, governments have acted by issuing decrees or creating less complex legal instruments. Depending on the circumstances, a general law may give strong legal and political support to privatization, or it may make things more complicated and difficult. What criteria can officials use to determine whether a general law on privatization would be useful?

15. Regulatory Frameworks. Governments are always advised to establish a clearly defined regulatory framework prior to undertaking a privatization. In technical terms, there is an ideal order to follow in defining this framework, but governments face opportunities and limitations that sometimes make that impossible. Given that only a very small window of opportunity may exist, if a government does not privatize under the right conditions and at the right time, it might not be able to privatize at all. Therefore, depending upon the specific sector or industry, a key question to be answered is: Which elements of the regulatory framework must be defined before privatization, and which may be defined progressively during and after privatization?

16. Centralizing the Process. How centralized should the process of privatization be? This is an issue that has been frequently debated. Some economists call for a highly centralized process, arguing, on the one hand, that uniformity of principles and general guidelines is extremely important, and, on the other hand, that centralization is the best way to assure this. Other analysts, however, while recognizing the need for common principles and general guidelines, favor a decentralized execution of the program in order to expedite the process. How much centralization is optimal?

17. Transparency. "Transparency" is probably the word most often used by governments when they talk about privatization. All want transparent privatizations. So far, the term has been reduced to mean little more than "competitive bidding." Is this all that transparency means? Is competitive bidding always transparent? What about the way in which the information about the company is released? Are the bidders prequalified? Is the selling contract negotiated? What are the most critical elements to ensure transparency in a privatization program?

18. Political Will. It is commonly said that political will is the most important prerequisite to privatize. But what does it mean to say that a particular government has the political will to privatize? Does it mean that there is a public statement announcing such a policy or that there is an official list of public enterprises to be sold? Does political will mean elected officials shunning clientelistic practices for the larger national good? Does political will have to exist at the beginning of the privatization process, or is it possible to build it as the program proceeds?

19. Public Awareness Campaigns. Although most governments recognize the importance of a public awareness campaign for the success of a privatization program, very few have undertaken comprehensive initiatives. Is it possible that public awareness does not really matter as much as it is often claimed, or is the lack of initiatives a general pitfall in many privatization programs?

20. Apparent versus Genuine Objectives of the Privatization Policy. When it comes to defining the objectives of privatization policy, most governments maintain that the primary objectives of the policy are to enhance the general efficiency of the economy and to promote competition. Nevertheless, when a judgment must be made on how the process has been carried out, it may become obvious that fiscal reasons were the true motivations for privatization. Efficiency and fiscal balance can be contradictory at times. A government might be tempted to give monopoly rights to an investor as a way to get more money for the company being sold. This would be good for the treasury and bad for the economy. How can this temptation be avoided? What definitions could be included in the privatization policy with regard to the enhancement of efficiency and the promotion of competition?

Venezuela's tortuous road to privatization vividly illustrates the problems, prospects, obstacles, and opportunities inherent in the process. Examining both the achievements and setbacks in implementation, one cannot escape the immutable reality that privatization cannot succeed without the convergence of political and economic leadership and elevation of the national interest above parochial demands.

Note

1. The three-year International Monetary Fund (IMF) adjustment program was an orthodox program of liberal economic reforms, imposed shortly after the inception of the Carlos Andrés Pérez administration in February 1989. The program led to a new debt-repayment arrangement with commercial bank creditors and also increased fuel and transport prices.—Ed.

References

Adam, Christopher S., William P. Cavendish, and Percy S. Mistry. 1992. *Adjusting Privatization: Case Studies from Developing Countries*. London: J. Currey. Published in association with Queen Elizabeth House, University of Oxford.

Banco Central de Venezuela. 1996. *Annual Report, 1992-1995*. Caracas, Venezuela.

Barnes, Guillermo. 1992. *Lessons From Bank Privatization In Mexico*. Washington, D.C.: Country Economics Department, The World Bank.

Beesley, M.E. 1992. *Privatization, Regulation and Deregulation*. New York: Routledge.

Boeker, Paul H. 1993. *Latin America's Turnaround: Privatization, Foreign Investment, and Growth*. San Francisco: International Center for Economic Growth and Institute of the Americas: ICS Press.

Bogetic, Zeljko, and Michael Conte. 1992. *Privatizing Eastern European Economies: A Critical Review and Proposal*. Washington, D.C.: Europe and Central Asia Region, World Bank.

Bouin, Olivier. 1992. "Privatization in Developing Countries: Reflections on a Panacea." Policy Brief (International). Washington, D.C.: Development Center of the Organisation for Economic Co-operation and Development (OECD).

Bouin, Olivier, and Charles Albert Michalet. 1991. *Rebalancing the Public and Private Sectors: Developing Country Experience*. Paris: Development Center of the Organisation for Economic Co-operation and Development (OECD); Washington, D.C.: OECD Publications and Information Center.

Bradburd, Ralph. 1992. *Privatization of Natural Monopoly Public Enterprises: The Regulation Issue*. Washington, D.C.: Country Economics Department, World Bank.

Claudon, Michael, and Tamar L. Gutner. 1992. *Comrades Go Private: Strategies for Eastern European Privatization*. New York: New York University Press.

Compañía Venezolana de Teléfonos (CANTV).1995. *Reporte de Actividades, 1992-1995*. Caracas, Venezuela.

Dallago, Bruno, Gianmaria Ajani, and Bruno Grancelli. 1992. *Privatization and Entrepreneurship in Post-Socialist Countries: Economy, Law, and Society*. New York: St. Martin's Press.

Denizer, Cevdet, and Alan H. Gelb. 1992. *Mongolia: Privatization and System Transformation in an Isolated Economy*. Washington, D.C.: Country Economics Department, World Bank.

Earle, John, Roman Frydman, and Andrzej Rapaczynski. 1993. *Privatization in the Transition to a Market Economy: Studies of Preconditions and Policies in Eastern Europe*. New York: St. Martin's Press.

Economides, Nicholas, and Susan Rose-Ackerman. 1992. *Differentiated Public Goods: Privatization and Optimality*. New York: Leonard N. Stern School of Business.

Elling, Martin E. 1992. "Privatization in Germany: A Model For Legal and Functional Analysis." Vanderbilt University Law School, Nashville, Tenn.: *Vanderbilt Journal of Transnational Law* 25 (Nov):581-642.

Fondo de Inversiones de Venezuela (FIV).1996. *Informe Anual de Actividades, 1991-1995.* Caracas, Venezuela: Fondo de Inversiones de Venezuela.

Fondo de Inversiones de Venezuela (FIV). 1996. *Venezuela, Un País de Recursos y Oportunidades.* Caracas, Venezuela: Fondo de Inversiones de Venezuela.

Foster, Christopher D. 1992. *Privatization, Public Ownership, and the Regulation of Natural Monopoly.* Oxford, England.: Blackwell.

Glirorov, Vladimir. 1992. *Justice and Privatization: Communist Economies and Economic Transformation.* London.

Guislain, Pierre. 1992. *Divestiture of State Enterprises: An Overview of the Legal Framework.* Washington, D.C.: World Bank.

Haskel, Jonathan, and Stefan Szymanski. 1992. "Bargaining Theory of Privatization." *Annals of Public and Cooperative Economics.* Belgium: International Centre of Research and Information on the Public and Cooperative Economy (CIRIEC).

Heald, David. 1992. "How Much Privatization Should There Be in Developing Countries?" *Annals of Public and Cooperative Economics.* Belgium:International Centre of Research and Information on the Public and Cooperative Economy (CIRIEC).

Heilman, John G., and Gerald W. Johnson. 1992. *Politics ad Economics of Privatization: The Case of Wastewater Treatment.* Tuscaloosa, Ala.: University of Alabama Press.

Hilke, John C. 1992. *Competition in Government-Financed Services.* New York: Quorum Books.

International Centre of Research and Information on Public and Cooperative Economy (CIRIEC). 1991. *Public Versus Private Enterprises: In Search of the Real Issues.* Liège, Belgium: University of Liège, Department of Economics.

Kocsis, Gyorgyi. 1992. "Uncertain State of Privatization." *New Hungarian Quarterly* 33(Winter):113-120.

Lewis, Russell. 1992. *Recent Controversies in Political Economy.* London, New York: Routledge.

Ministerio de Transporte y Comunicaciones. 1991. *Plan Nacional de Telecomunicaciones.* Caracas, Venezuela.

Modzelewski, Witold. 1992. "Alternative Options of State-Owned Enterprise Privatization." Working papers. Poland: Instytut Finansow.

Mohnot, Sohan Raj. 1991. *Privatization: Options and Challenges in the Context of Comparative Advantage of Public and Private Enterprise Models.* New Delhi, India: Center for Industrial & Economic Research (CIER).

Mullineux, Andrew. 1992. "Banks, Privatization and Restructuring in Poland." Working Paper. University of Birmingham, Alabama: International Finance Group.

Newbery, David M.G. 1992. "Role of Public Enterprises in the National Economy." Working Paper. Cambridge University: Department of Applied Economics (DAE).

Newbery, David M.G. 1992. "Capacity-Constrained Supply Function Equilibria: Competition and Entry in the Electricity Spot Market and Compensation and Regulation in the English Electricity Industry." Working Paper. Cambridge University: Department of Applied Economics (DAE).

Novgorod, Nizhny. 1992. *A Background Brief: Mass Small-scale Privatization.* Washington, D.C.: International Finance Corporation.

Nuskey, Sharon. 1992. *Privatization.* New York: Conference Board.

Privatization. 1992. London: Euromoney Publications Ltd.

Organisation for Economic Co-Operation and Development (OECD). Secretariat. Committee on Competition Law and Policy. 1992. *Regulatory Reform, Privatization, and*

Competition Policy. Paris: Organisation for Economic Co-operation and Development; Washington, D.C.: OECD Publications and Information Center.

Ott, Attiat F., and Keith Hartley. 1991. *Privatization and Economic Efficiency: A Comparative Analysis of Developed and Developing Countries.* Brookfield, Vt.: E. Elgar Publications.

Petróleos de Venezuela (PDVSA). 1996. *Informe Anual, 1994-1995.* Caracas, Venezuela.

Poznanski, Kazimierz Z. 1992. "Privatization of the Polish Economy: Problems of Transition." *Soviet Studies,* 641-664.

Project Liberty. 1991. "The Social and Political Consequences of Decentralization and Privatization." Meeting report, presented at the Workshop on the Social and Political Consequences of Decentralization and Privatization, Gdansk, Poland, 10-12 April, 1991. Cambridge, Mass.: Project Liberty, John F. Kennedy School of Government, Harvard University Press.

Ramamurti, Ravi. 1992. "Why Are Developing Countries Privatizing?" *Journal of International Business Studies* 23(2):225-249.

Rodríguez Cabrero, Gregorio. 1991. *Estado, privatización, y bienestar: Un debate de la Europa actual.* Barcelona: ICARIA.

Santamaría, Marco. 1991. *Privatizing Social Security: The Chilean Case.* New York: Federal Reserve Bank of New York.

Savitt, Ronald. 1992. *Privatization and the Consumer. New Hungarian Quarterly* 33(Winter):121-124.

Schmidt, Klaus M. 1991. *The Costs and Benefits of Privatization.* Bonn: Rheinische Friedrich-Wilhelms-Universitat.

Siebert, Horst. 1992. *Privatization: Symposium in Honor of Herbert Giersch.* Tübingen, Germany: J.C.B. Mohr (Paul Siebeck).

Stella, Peter. 1992. *Tax Farming: A Radical Solution for Developing Country Tax Problems?* Washington, D.C.: International Monetary Fund, Fiscal Affairs Department.

The Privatization Manual. 1993. London: Euromoney Publications Ltd.

Torres, Gerver. 1992. *¿Quiénes ganan? ¿ Quiénes pierden? La privatización en Venezuela.* Caracas, Venezuela: Editorial del Banco Consolidado.

Vial, Joaquín, and Eliana A. Cardoso. 1992. *¿Adónde va América Latina?: Balance de las reformas económicas.* Santiago: Corporación de Investigaciones Económicas para Latinoamérica (CIEPLAN).

Viravan, Amnuay. 1992. *Privatization: Financial Choices and Opportunities.* San Francisco: ICS Press.

Voszka, Eva. 1992a. "Not Even the Contrary Is True: The Transfigurations of Centralization and Decentralization." *Acta Economica: Periodical of the Hungarian Academy of Sciences* 44(1-2): 77-94.

Voszka, Eva. 1992b. "Changes and Dilemmas of Privatization in Hungary." *Annals of Public and Co-Operative Economy.* (Belgium: CIRIEC) 2:317-323.

Welfens, Paul J. 1992. Foreign Investment in the East European Transition. *Management International Review.* (Wiesbaden, Germany) 32 (3):199-218.

Whitfield, Dexter. 1992. *The Welfare State: Privatization, Deregulation, Commercialization of Public Services: Alternative Strategies for the 1990s.* Concord, Mass.: Pluto Press.

World Bank. 1992. *Case Studies from Chile, Malaysia, Mexico, and the U.K.* Conference on the Welfare Consequences of Selling Public Enterprises, Washington, D.C., June 11-12. Washington, D.C.: Country Economics Department, World Bank.

CHAPTER 8

Privatization in Brazil:
Toward an Evaluation

JUAREZ DE SOUZA

B razilian industrialization over the last 50 years has been based on significant
state intervention, which increased steadily after World War II until the
economic crisis of the early 1980s. Government investments in the productive
sectors included steel, mining, railroads, electric power, petroleum, chemicals,
petrochemicals, telecommunications, and other public services. In addition, a
complex system of financial mechanisms and institutions was developed. These
included the creation of the National Bank of Economic Development (Banco
Nacional de Desenvolvimento Econômico — BNDE) in the early 1950s to provide
long-term financing for the development of productive capacity; the creation of the
Central Bank and the reform of the national financial system in 1964; the enlarge-
ment of the Banco do Brasil's activities; the creation of other federal financial
institutions for regional development objectives; and the institution of indexation
to cope with high levels of inflation.

The government's role in promoting development was both necessary and
productive. In some cases, the private sector (both domestic and foreign) was not
interested in investing in the country's development projects (due to lack of capital
in relation to the magnitude of required investments, differential risk assessments,
and other factors). In other cases, for political reasons, the state assumed a strategic
role in the provision of infrastructure. In this process, the state created external
economies for the private sector, and economic "take-off" was facilitated. Most of
the state's productive investments in the Brazilian economy can be seen as a
nonreversible platform (or guarantee) for private investors, both domestic and
foreign. The vast majority of the country's manufacturing industry resulted from
this state strategy, which was based on direct and indirect government intervention
through effective demand, credits, subsidies, managed prices of inputs and outputs,
and favorable commercial policies.

From the 1930s until the mid-1980s, state intervention in the Brazilian
economy had a positive effect. The state contributed to the installation of basic
industrial sectors, spurred rapid economic growth, and expanded opportunities for
private sector investment and employment. As long as the state could finance large-
scale investment with public enterprise revenues, fiscal surpluses, foreign and
domestic loans, and through inflationary means, the overall performance of the
economy after World War II was remarkable. Until the 1980s, Brazil sustained an
annual average rate of economic growth of around 7 percent, which meant that gross

domestic product (GDP) was doubling each decade. This performance partially explains why structural problems in Brazilian society, such as unbalanced urban-rural growth, increased poverty, low levels of education, income concentration, and state inefficiency in several areas, were neglected for so long.

At the beginning of the 1980s, two basic questions were raised in Brazil, reflecting the appearance of neoliberal thinking around the world: First, could the state continue to lead the country's economic growth as it had been doing? Second, could the state afford additional, and much needed, productive investments and, at the same time, address the "social debt," taking into account the economic realities prevailing internationally?

Considering the financial bottlenecks experienced by the federal government in the early 1980s, expressed not only in fiscal difficulties but also in reduced sources of potential financing, the answer to these questions was undoubtedly negative. In spite of certain profitable state firms, such as Petrobrás; the iron-ore producing Companhia Vale do Rio Doce (CVRD); Usinas Siderúrgicas de Minas Gerais (Usiminas); and Banco do Brasil, new investment in the state productive sectors was traditionally financed in part from budgetary sources. After the onset of the foreign debt crisis, Brazil was forced to generate a trade surplus to repay its foreign debt. Since the Brazilian foreign debt was, in fact, public debt, its servicing became a fiscal problem as well.[1]

In fact, part of the country's foreign debt service was transformed into domestic public debt. As a consequence, the government's current spending on the rollover of the public debt, together with the increasingly inflationary macroeconomic environment, did not allow officials to maintain their traditional management of the economy. Despite the recessionary measures implemented under International Monetary Fund (IMF) rules, neither the public debt nor the inflationary problems were solved. On the contrary, the overall performance of the Brazilian economy deteriorated as it underwent a structural transformation. The previous pattern of economic development vanished.

Brazil survived the economic and external ideological earthquakes of the 1980s. In the domestic political arena, there was a transition from a military regime to democracy in 1985. The new government, known as the New Republic, undertook measures ranging from the elimination of the "Conta-Movimento" (the Brazilian treasury's unrestricted demand deposits at the Banco do Brasil, institutionalized by the military regime) to nonorthodox stabilization programs, such as the Plano Cruzado (February 1986), the Plano Bresser (1987), and the Plano Verão (1989). Attempts to control inflation and service the foreign debt created a financial burden for Brazil's government, weakening the public sector as a whole and debilitating state firms in particular. The development model based on long-established state investment in heavy industry had come to an end, primarily due to the exhaustion of the state's capacity to save and leverage funds from both domestic and external sources.

It was in this macroeconomic context that the privatization rhetoric evolved in Brazil. In 1981, the military government created the Special Privatization Commission, and, in 1988, the democratic regime of José Sarney (1985-1990) introduced the National Privatization Program (Programa Nacional de Destatização

— PND), but privatization between 1981 and 1989 resulted in the sale of only 38, primarily small, firms. The approximate revenues amounted to an insignificant US$700 million.

Privatization's slow start in Brazil has been attributed to the lack of sufficient political support for the program. Privatization was not a topic of discussion in civil society, and, perhaps because of the political transition taking place during this period, government administrations failed to provide strong support or leadership. Some authors argue that the sale of firms in the 1980s was possible only because it was well known that most of the firms had involuntarily become state property as a result of their failure to thrive in the private sector (Paiva 1994). Thus, the government's sale of firms between 1981 and 1989 can be viewed as "reprivatization." Although this period has its historical and economic significance, the present chapter focuses instead on the PND launched in April 1990.

THE NATIONAL PRIVATIZATION PROGRAM (PND)

Characteristics and Objectives

The neoliberal wave hit the Brazilian economy in the early 1980s, primarily as a result of high U.S. interest rates. The impact of restrictive monetary policy in the United States, together with expansionary fiscal measures undertaken by the Reagan administration (1981-1989), was strong enough to lead Brazil into economic crisis. The ideological shift, however, did not reach Brazil until the end of the decade. In 1989, for the first time in 29 years, Brazilians directly elected a civilian president. The campaign platform of the winner, Fernando Collor de Melo (1990-1992), was based on neoliberal thinking and included proposals for a drastic reform of the state's economic role, the opening of the economy to foreign capital, and the curbing of quasi-hyperinflation. The PND was born in this environment.

As soon as the Collor administration took office in March 1990, it adopted a series of strong measures,[2] including the creation of the PND. The following month, after debate and discussion in Congress, the PND was transformed into Federal Law N° 8031. The program's basic objectives were to 1) reorient the strategic position of the state in the economy by transferring to the private sector those activities that were inappropriately exploited by the public sector, 2) contribute to the reduction of the public debt and to the improvement of the state's profile, in order to better balance the public sector finances, 3) allow new investments in enterprises and activities to be transferred to the private sector, 4) contribute to the modernization of the country's industrial infrastructure, expanding its competitiveness and reinforcing entrepreneurial capacity in the economy, and 5) contribute to the strengthening of capital markets through the increased supply of stocks and bonds and the democratization of capital property in the firms slated for sale in the PND.

Under the Collor administration, privatization was defined as the alienation by the federal government of all rights that directly or indirectly (through other government-controlled firms) allow it "preponderance in administrative deliberations" and the power to elect the majority of the firm's managers. Privatization also included the alienation of the federal government's direct and indirect minority participation in the capital of other firms.

Initially, the PND included 1) enterprises directly or indirectly controlled by the government, 2) those created by laws, and 3) private firms absorbed in the past by the government for any reason. Beginning in January 1995, official financial institutions (including some state government financial institutions) and public services under concession also were included. The PND could not, and did not, include public and mixed enterprises that, as constitutionally mandated, were controlled exclusively by the state, for instance, enterprises in sectors such as petroleum, telecommunications, or nuclear energy and its derivatives. The Banco do Brasil, official regional financial institutions, and the State Reinsurance Agency also were excluded. Congress, however, subsequently decided in 1995 that those state monopolies would no longer be covered by constitutional mandate, and it also abolished restrictions on foreign investment in the mining sector.

Besides the obvious sale of the state's shares in firms slated for privatization (preferably by dispersion of capital among stockholders, workers, suppliers, and consumers), the PND also permitted capital opening (even without subscription rights), transformation, incorporation, sale or leasing of assets and equipment, and even the dissolution or partial deactivation of enterprises in order to sell their assets. Finally, in February 1995, Congress approved a law granting public service concessions, which made available a new set of investment opportunities for the private sector.

The implementation of the PND was based on the creation of an Executive National Privatization Committee (Comissão Diretora do Programa Nacional de Desestatização — CDPND) composed of individuals chosen by the president of Brazil and by the manager of the National Privatization Fund.[3] In 1995, the new government of Fernando Henrique Cardoso transformed the CDPND into the more powerful Privatization Council (Conselho Nacional de Privatização — CNP), composed of the ministers of Domestic Affairs (Casa Civil), Planning, Finance, Federal Administration and State Reform, and the minister to whom the privatizing firm reported. Although the CDPND had had the authority to approve the forms of payment and the new Council could only recommend them to the president, the Council had the power to "determine the destination of the resources derived from the privatization," preferably to pay debts of and to the state.

Since the beginning of the program, the National Bank of Economic and Social Development (Banco Nacional de Desenvolvimento Econômico e Social—BNDES) — formerly known as BNDE — played the role of "secretariat" for the PND and was responsible for lending administrative and technical support to the officials involved; helping the officials hire consulting firms for the valuation of the companies undergoing sale; determining minimum prices, conditions, and forms of sales; carrying out specific studies prior to privatization; publishing public notices (*editais*) specifying the conditions under which the sale would occur; and preparing information required by the Council for its decisionmaking. The management cost for the program was fixed at 0.2 percent of the net value obtained from the sales. BNDES was one of the oldest government industrial development agencies in Brazil, and, having a highly trained technical staff, the banking institution was well prepared for its mission.

Prior to a sale, public notices published in the official record (Diario Oficial da União) and in the country's major newspapers stated the conditions for privatization and outlined the basic financial and economic situation of the firm. Companies were sold through auctions on the stock exchange, with pre-established quotas for employees and investors. It should be noted that the law limited the sale of stock to foreigners to 40 percent of the voting capital. In order to avoid criticism and make the privatization process more transparent, the vice president who assumed office in January 1993 after Collor's impeachment — Itamar Franco (1992-1995) — prohibited the participation of employee pension funds belonging to the state enterprises and of administrative agencies directly involved in the sale process. Since this measure was promptly recognized as capable of damaging the PND because it would reduce the number of potential qualified Brazilian buyers, his decision was quickly rescinded (Decree 786/93). The restriction on foreigners was removed in June 1993, when the government revised the PND.

Basic Changes in the PND

From the beginning of the PND until the Medida Provisória No. 327 in June 1993, three possible forms of payment were accepted: credits that private financial institutions had with the firms subject to privatization; internal public debt papers issued by the privatizing firms, which were due and subject to co-obligation by the Federal Treasury; and deposits and other assets held in the Central Bank as a result of Collor's 1990 stabilization plan. Thus, the PND's design represented a classic case of the exchange of public debt for public assets, which permitted the private banking system to get rid of bad debt. Under this plan, the Federal Treasury not only would free itself from the burden of loan guarantees but also could access funds that had been blocked in the Central Bank.

Following the reforms in June 1993, the president of Brazil had the power to define the acceptable forms of payment. By that point, the government had recognized that the use of government bonds in privatization did not necessarily mean the automatic retirement of public debt, since the seller frequently was not the central government but enterprises under its control (such as Petroquisa S.A., Petrofértil S.A., Banco do Brasil S.A., etc.). Under such circumstances, "there was only an exchange of the comptroller's shares for government debt paper, which created a serious problem for the balance sheets of these firms, since they were exchanging profitable stock for 'rotten paper' which had almost zero liquidity" (see Paiva 1994; National Congress Commission's Report 1994).[4] In order to solve this problem, the Planning Ministry allowed the exchange of those debt instruments for other government bonds with longer expiration periods.

General Performance of the PND[5]

By June 1995, the PND included 73 firms, 40 of which were directly controlled by the federal government. The remaining 33 were firms in which the government held a minority share through its ownership of Petroquisa and Petrofértil, subsidiaries of Petrobrás S.A. Of the 73 firms, 34 enterprises were sold, of which

21 were directly controlled by the state and 13 were minority shares of the Petrobrás subsidiaries. According to BNDES, nine more state-owned firms (SOEs) were also privatized — including the largest of the electric power companies (Furnas, Eletronorte, Eletrosul, Chesf, and Electrobrás) and the railroad (RFFSA), which have only recently been included, and one official regional bank (Meridional). Eighteen minority shares in Petroquisa and Petrofértil were also sold.[6] Finally, five firms were excluded from the PND, and seven have had their privatization interrupted, either by judicial order or because liquidation was recommended.

Privatization began at the end of 1991, with the sale of Usiminas and Cosinor in October and November of that year, and the program intensified in 1992 and 1993 with the sale of firms in the petrochemical and the fertilizer sectors. (The most important privatized firms, both in terms of relative sale value and sectoral relevance or ranking, are presented in Tables 1 and 2.) Privatization of the steel, petrochemical, and fertilizer sectors was virtually complete by the end of 1993, except for the sale of the above mentioned CVRD and Petrobrás, whose monopoly power has been constitutionally mandated. These two firms are special cases that will be examined at the end of this chapter.

The results of the privatization program, as measured by sale revenues in relation to the total number of companies sold, were unremarkable. Total sales between 1991 and 1993 amounted to $8.6 billion, plus $3.27 billion of the firms' own transferred debts (see Table 1). Although this represented 69.4 percent of the $17 billion estimated for the sale of the industrial enterprises during the first phase of the PND from 1981 to 1989, this amount is insignificant considering that "state involvement in the construction of the country's steel industry was extensive: the total invested by the government in the firms that had been privatized by June 1993 (Usiminas, Companhia Siderúrgica Nacional [CSN], Acesita, and Companhia Siderúrgica Tubarão [CST]) — was $10.751 billion" (Tourinho and Vianna 1994). The government also held an additional $3.6 billion corresponding to the net assets

Table 1.
PND's Sectoral Relevance

Sector	Sales Revenues	
	US$ millions	Percent
Total	11,873.4	100.0
Siderurgy	8,187.6	69.0
Chemical and Petrochemicals	2,178.6	18.3
Fertilizer	493.5	4.2
Others	618.2	4.2
Embraer	455.6	
Celma	95.6	
Mafersa	49.3	
Minority Participations	395.5	3.3

Sources: BNDES 1995a and b.

Table 2.
Relative Shares of Privatization by Firm
(Percentages)

Enterprises	Firm's Sale Value/ Total PND Sale	Firm's Sale Value/ Total Sectoral Sales
Usiminas	22.7	34.9
CSN	17.4	26.9
Copesul	10.0	45.8
Açominas	7.0	10.8
Cosipa*	6.8	10.5
Acesita	5.4	8.4
CST	4.1	6.4
PQU	3.4	15.3
Petroflex	2.7	12.4
Ultrafértil	2.4	49.2
Fosfértil	2.1	43.5
Goiasfértil	0.2	3.1
Arafértil	0.1	2.6
Embraer*	2.2	55.0
Celma	1.1	26.0
Mafersa	0.6	14.0
Other Minority Participations	4.6	-

Sources: BNDES 1995a and b, Tables V and VII.
*Sales process not concluded.

of Companhia Siderúrgica Paulista (Cosipa), Açominas, and Cosinor, in which the government held, respectively, 100 percent, 99.9 percent, and 99.8 percent of the total capital. Thus, the $8.6 billion received from privatization represented only 59.7 percent of the amount the government had invested in the steel sector alone.[7]

According to the BNDES's report on the results of the PND, the state had invested $27 billion in the firms privatized from 1991 through 1993 (BNDES 1995b). If one adds to this the government investment in Embraer, an aircraft company, and Petroquímica União, S.A. (PQU), which were sold in 1994, the State's total investment reached $28 billion. Thus, the ratio of the sale value of the firms to total investment was only 0.24. The government's return from the PND was less than one-fourth of what it had invested in the firms. This indicates how far off the setting of the minimum sale price (based primarily on discounted cash flows) was from the current investment value of the companies undergoing sale.[8]

Even worse, the average ratio of sale value to minimum established price was 1.15, indicating little competition among buyers at the auctions. The best auction performances were delivered by a few firms: Cosipa (1.44); Açominas (1.81);

Piratini (2.44); Mafersa (2.58); PPH (1.36); Acesita (1.26); Copesul (1.26); and Fosfértil (1.26). As of mid-1995, revenue for all sales concluded under the PND had reached $1.6 billion. Of that figure, only 18.6 percent had been paid in cash, while 81.4 percent had been paid with "rotten money" (*moedas podres*), that is, with public debt paper that had little value in market terms and near-zero liquidity when redeemed at par value (Table 3). These data suggest that from 1991 through 1993, the PND created windfall gains for the private sector, which acquired capital and productive capacity in key industrial sectors of the economy at a minimal price and, above all, paid for these purchases with nearly worthless debt paper redeemed at par value. The forms of payment used in the privatization process will be discussed below in light of PND's impact on the public debt.

Table 3.
Forms of Payment Used in the PND
(Percentages)

Siderbras Debts	Privatization Certificates	State's Securitized Debt	Foreign Debt	Fiat Money	Means
15.8	15.0	32.5	0.8	18.6	18.1

Source: BNDES 1995a, Table V.

Table 4.
PND — Buyers' Distribution

Domestic Financial System	Private Pension Funds	National non-Financial Firms	Foreign Capital	Individual Investors
28.8	15.8	42.0	5.5	7.8

Sources: BNDES 1995a and b.

THE MICROECONOMIC IMPACT OF THE PND

One of the most important microeconomic results of the PND derives from the policy decision on how to accomplish privatization. Certain results were guaranteed when it was decided that individual firms, rather than holding companies, would be sold, and that such sales would be carried out using market concepts such as auctions, discounted cash flows, net assets, and business risk. In Brazil, since the government seems to have overlooked the effects that the centralization and concentration of capital and production would have in the privatized sector, it is worthwhile to examine the results of the government's methods in carrying out privatization.

An interesting feature of the PND was the distribution of sale mechanisms and buyers. In the PND's first phase, 85.6 percent of the privatized firms were sold through auctions on the stock exchange, 3.4 percent were sold to the firms' own

Table 5.
Share of Voting Capital After PND
by Group of New Owners

Steel Sector	% of voting capital
Usiminas	
Pension Funds (Previ, Valia, etc.)	22.7
Nippon-Usiminas	13.8
Companhia Vale Rio Doce (CVRD)	15.0
Bancos Bozano, Simonsen; Econômico; and others	28.2
Distribuid. Aço	4.4
Employees	9.6
CSN	
Previ-CSN and others	12.5
Docenave	9.4
Grupo Vicunha	9.2
Bamerindus,Bradesco, and other banks	29.3
Employees	11.9
Açominas	
Cia Min.Part.Industrial	26.8
Mendes Jr.	7.6
Aços Villares	6.8
Commercial Banks: SRL	13.4
Commercial Banks: BCN	9.9
Employees	20.0
Cosipa	
Brastubo	34.4
Anquilla	23.0
Employees	20.0
Acesita	
Pension Funds (Previ, Petros, and others)	29.1
Commercial Banks: Safra	8.8
Real	5.6
Bancesa	4.2
Employees	12.4
Cosinor	
Gerdau Group	99.8
Piratini	
Gerdau Group	89.8

Petrochemical Sector	% of voting capital
PQU	
Unipar	30.0
Petroquisa	17.5
Consorcio Polinvest	13.0
Polibrasil	6.8
Employees (Reserve)	9.8
Copesul	
Consorcio PPE	28.8
Employees	10.0
Individual Investors	10.0
Commercial Banks	11.4
Pension Funds (22)	7.1
Foreigners (26)	4.8

Fertilizer Sector	% of voting capital
Ultrafértil	
Fosfértil	90.0
Employees	10.0
Fosfértil	
Consorcio Fertifós	68.5
Companhia Vale Rio Doce (CVRD)	11.5
Employees	10.0
Banco Bamerindus	6.0

Aeronautics Sector	% of voting capital
Embraer	
Banco Bozano, Simonsen Ltd.	16.1
Employees	10.0
Sistel	9.8
B. Brasil Previ	9.8
Other Pension Funds (18)	9.9
Foreigners	4.0

Source: BNDES 1995a.

employees, and the remaining 11 percent were sold to the public at a fixed price and subject to quotas per investor (BNDES 1995a). Most buyers were concentrated among nonfinancial national firms (42 percent); followed by institutions belonging to the national financial system (28.8 percent); and the private pension funds that belong to the employees of state-owned firms (15.8 percent), such as Banco do Brasil and Petrobrás (Table 4). Thus, these three groups of buyers accounted for 86.6 percent of all sales revenue, while individual investors bought 7.8 percent and foreign capital purchased 5.5 percent. In this sense, one can say that privatization has not denationalized the economy, although it seems to have exacerbated the tendency toward centralization and concentration of industrial capital, despite the participation of workers' and employees' pension funds. In all cases, firms or groups of entrepreneurs ended up holding the majority of the voting capital in the privatized firms. The changing structure of the voting capital in these firms, as shown by the percentages belonging to the new owners' groups, speaks for itself (Table 5).[9]

Tourinho and Vianna (1994) argue that during the implementation of the PND, there was an ongoing preoccupation that privatization might result in a highly concentrated industrial structure — both in terms of market power and capital control. According to the authors, as a consequence of the strategy of selling individual firms instead of the state holding companies, together with the diversification of stockholders, "the competition among firms in the major privatized sectors (steel, petrochemicals, and fertilizer) will occur with the pursuit of profit maximization for the stockholders" (1994, 84). As to the control of capital, Tourinho and Vianna analyzed the index of concentration for these three sectors using an indirect measure. They divided the firms' current sales among their major stockholders and constructed the sectoral concentration index based on the share of the sector's sales attributed to those owners. The percentages of the sectoral sales thus controlled by the four and eight owners of the largest firms (measured by revenue) in two of these sectors, both prior to and after privatization, are reproduced in Table 6.

These indices show that the capital concentration falls for the four-firm concentration ratio, but it rises for the eight-firm concentration ratio. Can one conclude that by "comparing the several capital concentration indices before and after privatization, one verifies that there was no capital concentration increase" (Tourinho and Vianna 1994) for the fertilizer and steel industries? Since these

Table 6.
Capital Property — Concentration Index

Situation	Fertilizers			Flat Steel Products		
	Number of Firms	Cr4	Cr8	Number of Firms	Cr4	Cr8
Prior PND	51	34.5	19.0	6	91.6	8.4
After PND	51	33.0	20.6	6	22.5	9.4

Source: Tourinho and Vianna 1994, 85.

indices do not capture the dynamics involved, it is useful to consider the case of the fertilizer sector in detail.

Tourinho and Vianna argue that "Fosfértil was acquired by a consortium formed by a large number of firms from the sector, by integrated producers of semi-finished steel — in a process of verticalization of the productive chain — and by financial institutions. Later the privatized Fosfértil bought Goiasfértil and, more recently, Ultrafértil. The state's minority participation of Petrofértil in the Indag group was also sold" (1994). Fosfértil, indeed, was acquired by Fortifós, a consortium composed of a subset of the firms in the sector, and by two banks, Bamerindus and América do Sul. Fortifós bought 68.5 percent, Bamerindus acquired 6 percent, and América do Sul bought 1.6 percent of the firm's ordinary voting capital. This corresponds to 76.1 percent of the firm's capital and, therefore, constitutes decision-making control. Because Fosfértil had acquired Goiasfértil and Ultrafértil (90 percent of their voting capital), the Fortifós group dominates the fertilizer market. Tourinho and Vianna fail to mention that Petrofértil's minority participation in Indag, a petroleum company based in São Paulo, was acquired by IAP S.A. A member of Fortifós, this São Paulo fertilizer firm holds 65 percent of Indag's voting capital and is, therefore, sole owner of Indag. In summary, there can be little doubt that Fortifós is in a position to exert significant control in the fertilizer business in Brazil.

Tourinho and Vianna believe that "the elevated number of firms in this activity guarantees permanent competition among them" and that, in the sector, competition "is also favored by the recent reductions in import tariffs, which allowed nearly 40.2 percent of all phosphate raw material currently consumed in the country to be imported, compared to 1989, when imports represented just 8.9 percent of domestic demand" (1994). In the fertilizer sector, competition from imports is significant, given recent trade liberalization in Brazil.[10] However, the statement referring to "the large number of firms" should be better qualified. According to the National Congress Commission's Report (1994, 62-102), there are approximately 300 small and mid-sized firms in the sector (intermediate processors and distributors of fertilizer) in the country. However, it is a market in which about 20 firms are producers, and the majority of the firms that acquired formerly state-owned companies through the PND also own large intermediate processing plants.

Although Tourinho and Vianna did not define the kind of competition they had in mind, by all traditional measures, the new industrial structure brought about by the PND has not differed from the tendency of capitalism toward concentration of ownership. Monopolies and oligopolies maximize results, primarily strategic ones, and, in an open economy, they also compete. Thus, the competition and competitiveness one might expect will not differ from that found in other oligopolist sectors of the economy.

The fertilizer industry was in state hands not by chance but because of a lack of private interest in this basic sector in the late 1960s. In the following decade, the government took it over for strategic reasons, including integration with the petrochemical sector (in response to technical considerations, such as the use of leftover gas from petroleum refineries) and for the development of the agricultural sector (for example, food production, grains for export, and energy substitutes, particularly alcohol). As the National Congress Commission's Report (1994) points out, "The participation of state firms in the fertilizer sector is still subordinate to the predominating logic of the petroleum industry and its derivatives at a world level. . . . This strategy is also justified from a technical point of view, since the fertilizer, petrochemical, and fine chemical sectors constitute a natural extension of the original business. Also, out of the 17 largest world enterprises in the fertilizers sector, including Petrofértil, 12 are state firms, 4 are private, and one of them is mixed capital; all of them are linked to the largest petroleum firms."[11] Thus, according to the National Congress Commission's Report, the privatization of the fertilizer sector is part of a strategy to break the chemical arm of Petrobrás, since the petroleum area has, to date, a constitutional barrier to the entry of the private capital.[12]

An analysis of capital control and market power in the petrochemical and steel industries after privatization would be similar to that outlined above for the fertilizer sector. The difference is a matter of degree, not substance, except for the role of the pension funds and the CVRD's participation in the steel industry auctions. In the steel privatization, the most important buyers included 1) major national private banks and other financial institutions, especially Bamerindus; Bozano, Simonsen; Econômico; Safra; Real; Bradesco; and Unibanco; 2) pension funds belonging to the employees of SOEs (B. Brasil-Previ, Petros-Petrobrás, CSN, CVRD, and others), which acquired 29.1 percent of Acesita, 22.7 percent of Usiminas, and 12.5 percent of CSN; 3) CVRD, which bought 15 percent of Usiminas and 15 percent of CST; 4) Gerdau, a private national group, part of the Brazilian steel industry for a long time, this firm bought Cosinor, Cosipa, and Piratini; and 5) firms already operating in the sector, such as Nippon-Usiminas (which acquired 13.8 percent of Usiminas); Kawasaki Steel (which bought 13 percent of CST); Brastubo and Anquilla (which acquired 57.4 percent of Cosipa); and Companhia Mineira Participaçoes Industriais e Comerciais, Mendes Junior, and Aços Villares (which together bought 41.2 percent of Açominas).

This distribution of ownership means that vertical and horizontal integration in the production sphere and the extension of links to financial capital are taking place. It means also that the firms' synergy in the sector may well result in future economic benefits, such as higher technological levels, productivity gains, reductions in production costs, and so forth.

A complete microeconomic evaluation of the PND would, theoretically, cover all three sectors where privatization is complete. However, the petrochemical and fertilizer sectors have been in private hands for only a short period, and their operations involve a large variety of raw materials and products that are interconnected in a complex industrial chain. Under these conditions, the microeconomic effects require more time to mature and, consequently, to produce the data necessary for an analysis of the impact of privatization. Moreover, given these conditions and their importance for the entire PND, the steel sector looks most appropriate for a more advanced (yet still preliminary) microeconomic evaluation. (Summary statistics for the Brazilian steel industry are found in Table 7.)

Brazilian iron and steel production runs from crude steel to flat and long products; semi-finished products (slabs, ingots, blooms, and billets); pig iron; and

Table 7.
Economic Indicators for the Steel Sector

Specification	1990	1991	1992	1993	1994
Active Own Workforce (Thousands)	112.8	103.2	94.3	87.7	83.2
Sub-contracted Workers (Thousands)	19.7	19.1	16.1	14.5	15.0
Total Active Workforce (Thousands)	132.6	122.3	110.4	102.3	89.3
Payroll (US$ million)	2,368	1,604	1,609	1,842	1,868
Net Sales (US$ million)	10,627	9,117	9,772	10,856	11,629
Investments (US$ million)	494	339	341	625	690
Crude Steel Production (1000 ton)	20,567	22,617	23,934	25,207	25,747

Source: IBS 1995.

sponge iron. Crude steel production was 20.6 billion tons in 1990 and reached 25.7 billion tons in 1994. Rolled products (flat and long) varied from 14.7 to 17.3 million tons in the same period. This overall performance reflects production increases of 25 percent and 17 percent, respectively, and it shows the growth trend of Brazil's share in the world production of crude steel. Thus, having moved from a position of 18th in 1970 to 10th in 1980, Brazil began the 1990s as the seventh leading world producer of steel, before falling to ninth in the first half of the 1990s. Despite this slight relative decrease, the country has gained market share in terms of both Latin America and the world. Market shares totaled 53.5 and 2.7 percent in 1990 and 56.2 and 3.6 percent in 1994 (see IBS 1995).

Crude steel production is concentrated in integrated steel firms, responsible for almost 90 percent of production. The rest is distributed among several private firms. State-owned firms Acesita, Açominas, Cosipa, CSN, CST, and Usiminas accounted for 78.8 percent of production in 1990; but, following privatization, their share increased to 81.8 percent in 1994.

The production of rolled products — common and specialty steel (flat and long products) — also had been dominated by SOEs such as CSN, Cosipa, Usiminas, Acesita, and Piratini, which accounted for two-thirds of this production in 1990. By 1994, they controlled 68.3 percent of the output, reflecting an increase of 2.5 percent after privatization. Production of common steel long products was, and still is, distributed among several private firms, except for the participation of the formerly state-owned CSN. This firm has grown its share from 0.88 percent in 1990 to 1.56 percent after privatization.

In an open economy, there is an invisible line between micro- and macroeconomic impacts. Brazilian imports of steel products are restricted to certain flat and long products, amounting to 196 million tons in 1990 and reaching 205 million tons in 1994, an increase of 4.1 percent. More importantly, however, both domestic and external demand are rising. Brazil's consumption of iron and steel products grew from 9 billion tons in 1990 to 12 billion tons in 1994, while the external commercial balance in steel grew from $2.5 billion in 1990 to an annual average of $3.3 billion from 1991 through 1994.

The steel sector has improved its external performance and responded to domestic demand, although Brazil still has one of the lowest levels of per-capita steel consumption in the world (98 kg/inhabitant versus Japan's 647 and the United States' 400 kg). The country has maintained its structural competitiveness, which derives from long-term public investments in the sector, relatively cheap labor and raw-material costs, and from technological developments. In the Brazilian steel industry, as a result of 20 years of public investment in fixed and human capital, the personnel are highly qualified and their technical capacity is up to date.[13]

In the first half of the 1990s, the performance of the steel sector (Table 8) was excellent, both in terms of productivity gains (68.9 percent) and in profit margins (27.5 percent). Since the wage bill rose just 6.5 percent in dollar terms, productivity gains were mostly transferred to profits and, consequently, were used to finance investments. Steel production is capital- and technology-intensive and demonstrates the serious problem of labor absorption. Despite a real production increase, productivity gains, and market expansion, the number of jobs in the steel industry decreased 25 percent in this period, undeniably a direct effect of technological improvements.

Table 8.
Economic Performance of the Steel Sector

Years/ Variables	Wage Bill/Workers	Production/ Workers	Investments/ Sales	Investments/ Workers
1990	17.85	155.10	4.65	3.72
1994	19.00	261.90	5.93	7.01
% Change	6.50	68.90	27.50	88.00

Note: Calculations based on the data given by IBS 1995.

The privatized firms' performance follows this pattern, as enterprises reduced employment levels — although at a lower rate of 19.3 percent — despite real increases in all the other relevant variables (sales, profits, and productivity). While average prices in the sector have decreased 12.6 percent in the first half of the 1990s, the formerly state-owned firms have kept their prices constant. Thus, the relative increment of their profit margins (128 percent) came from market expansion (13.5 percent) and, above all, from labor-productivity gains. That is, the joint effect of labor reductions (almost 20 percent), together with an increase in physical labor productivity of 40 percent and the firms' market power (as indicated by their market share), explains the profit-margin performance, since average prices were kept constant and real wages increased only 6.5 percent.[14]

In short, privatization in the Brazilian steel industry resulted in a rise in production concentration, since former SOEs have increased their share of production in crude, common, and specialty steels. By reducing employment by 20 percent of its pre-PND level and increasing labor productivity by 40 percent, these firms increased their profit margin to a level four times higher than that found in the steel sector as a whole. Unquestionably, steel production is a profitable business for those who acquired the firms through the PND.

THE MACROECONOMIC IMPACT OF THE PND: 1990-1995

During the first half of the 1990s, Brazil experienced two stabilization programs: the Collor Plan of March 1990 and the Real Plan of July 1994.[15] In both cases, prior to the adoption of the stabilization programs, Brazil was facing quasi-hyperinflation, with monthly inflation rates that varied from 50 to 84 percent between the end of 1989 and March 1990 and from 30 to almost 50 percent in the first half of 1994. Brazil's privatization program was undertaken in this inflationary environment, and the contribution of the PND to economic stabilization will be analyzed below.

The PND's Impact on Inflation, Production, and External Balances

To analyze the PND's contribution to economic stabilization, it is necessary to compare the evolution of prices in the privatized industrial sectors to industrial inflation and to overall inflation in the period (Table 9). For an analysis of the PND's impact on inflation, price changes after the second semester of 1992 should be considered.

A comparison of overall price movements (general and wholesale) with those in the privatized sectors reveals that the PND has not provoked special price changes in private enterprises. Inflation rates in privatized industries have been, by and large, lower than the economy's overall rate of inflation. This sectoral behavior was also present under the Real Plan (Table 9). Except for the steel sector in 1992, sectoral

Table 9.
Annual Inflation Rates (%)

Years	General Prices	Wholesale Prices	Iron, Steel, and Derivatives	Plastic Materials	Fertilizers
1990	2,739.7	2, 734.7	2,186.8	2,561.8	2,822.0
1991	414.7	404.7	383.6	406.1	442.3
1992	991.4	976.9	1.190.9	1.232.0	907.2
1993	2,103.8	2,064.6	2,050.8	1,899.7	1,602.9
1994	2,406.9	2,278.9	2,187.9	1,861.1	2,173.0
July 1994 to March 1995	44.4	41.0	27.4	31.8	31.5

Note: Inflation rates were calculated from Fundação Getúlio Vargas's price index (2, 4, 32, 56, and 57). For the chemical and petrochemical sector, the "Plastic Materials Index" was taken as a proxy for the whole sector.

Source: *Revista Conjuntura Econômica*, March 93, March 94 and May 95.

prices have had annual inflation rates lower than those verified for the whole economy. In this sense, the PND's impact on stabilization has been positive, taking into account that oligopolies mark up prices based on production costs, among other factors, and that the economy was completely indexed in this period — from foreign exchange to wages, and including virtually all financial assets.

The PND's impact on production levels is also an important macroeconomic consideration. The industrial capacity utilization index for the 1992-1994 period averaged 74.8, indicating that this industrial sector was operating with a level of idle capacity around 25 percent. Since a strong industrial recession affecting the privatized sectors occurred from 1990 through 1992, the period between 1993 and 1994 provides important data on the impact of privatization on production. Given the average rate of growth of industrial production (7.5 percent), one can conclude that, of the privatized sectors, only metallurgy had outperformed that growth rate, since the sector's production averaged 9.25 percent, while chemicals and plastics (which include fertilizers and products derived from petrochemicals) stood at 5.7 and 5.8 percent, respectively. The steel sector, therefore, led industrial growth in recent years, and it can be argued that its privatization contributed to this performance.

Since the PND affected state-owned industrial firms belonging to sectors that traditionally have had much to do with Brazil's foreign trade, it is reasonable to examine the evolution of the country's import spending in these privatized sectors. If the rate of change of foreign purchases in these sectors had been greater than the rate of change of the country's industrial production as a whole and since the PND was accompanied by a general reduction in external tariffs, the disparity between the two rates would suggest that the privatized sector was losing ground to producers from abroad and that the new owners had not been internationally competitive. In December 1990, the average tariff level was 31.2 percent, but, by July 1993, the tariff had fallen to 14.2 percent. Between March and September 1994, with the implementation of the common external tariff established in the Southern Common Market (MERCOSUL) agreements,[16] the average tariff dropped to 11.3 percent — close to levels in industrialized countries. (See Banco Central do Brasil 1994).

From 1990 through 1993, current spending on imports of steel, inorganic and organic chemical products, and fertilizers had a positive average rate of growth of 2.6 percent, 6.3 percent, 27.8 percent, and 42 percent, respectively. Comparing those rates with the 7.5 percent average for industrial growth, it is clear that the performance of the organic chemical and fertilizer sectors has been poor, and domestic producers in these sectors are losing ground to producers from abroad. They have not been competitive, and they are paying the price of trade liberalization, just as was predicted by those who argued for privatization.

A similar analysis of the export side of Brazil's balance of payments could be conducted, comparing export growth rates with rates of industrial production. However, given the country's dependence on fertilizer and petrochemical imports, the steel industry is more relevant when the impact on exports is considered. Brazil plays a major role in global steel markets. With privatization, many traditional direct and indirect government subsidies were eliminated, and a more realistic foreign exchange policy was adopted. Domestic steel products have remained internation-

Table 10. Public Sector Fiscal Results
(Averages — Percent of GDP)

Period	Primary	Operational	Debt Burden	Inflation	PIB
1983-1987	2.1	4.1	6.1	210	4.1
1988-1993	2.2	1.7	3.8	1.237	0.4
1991-1994	2.9	0.1	3.0	1.479	2.4

Sources: See Paiva 1993 for the 1983-1987 and 1988-1993 averages. See Banco Central do Brasil 1995 for the averages for period 1991-1994. GDP rates were obtained from the Instituto Brasileiro de Geografia e Estatística (IBGE).

Table 11.
Operational Deficit and Net Borrowings
(As Percent of GDP — Annual Averages)

Period	External	Domestic	Monetary Base	Operational
1983-1987	0.12	1.66	2.54	4.08
1988-1993	1.12	0.53	3.32	1.67
1991-1994	2.2	0.6	2.8	0.0

Note: The operational deficit of the government is obtained from the primary deficit (actual fiscal revenues and expenditures) plus the real spending on public debt interest. Thus, either from the budget or from the borrowing needs, "below or above the line," the government's performance can be analyzed. For the purposes of this study, both concepts are useful.

Source: Banco Central do Brasil 1995.

ally competitive, however, and the sector has kept its positive role in the country's balance of payments. Thus, while at the beginning of this decade steel was already responsible for more than one-fifth of Brazil's foreign trade surplus, following privatization, it accounted for more than one-fourth, reaching 27.9 percent in September 1994 (IBS 1995). Given that Brazil had commercial deficits from November 1994 to May 1995, the steel sector's performance was significant.

Impact on Public Finance

Brazil accumulated an enormous social debt by the end of the 1980s, and, given the income and regional inequality, this debt stood to jeopardize the economic, social, and political system of one of the world's largest economies. Thus, one of the major objectives of PND was to reduce the public debt and improve its profile so that interest rates would fall, stimulating private investment in the country's productive capacity and eliminating the speculation in public bonds that had dominated Brazilian financial markets. It was thought that, with a more manageable debt, the government would be able to resume its fundamental role in society: providing education and health services, basic sanitation, support for science and technology, environmental protection, and public security. In doing so, the government would adopt sound fiscal and monetary policies that would return the country to its development path.

For more than a decade, governments in Brazil imposed a substantial fiscal burden on the population by means of deficit-reduction policies (Tables 10 and 11). These policies were implemented together with price- and wage-freeze programs, the freezing of financial assets, conventional restrictive economic policies such as monetary and credit squeezes, and cuts in SOEs' investments. Nevertheless, despite a decline in foreign interest rates in 1991 and 1992, the overall result was *stagflation* — periods of very high inflation combined with recession.

Thus, in 1990, despite Collor Plan I, the country experienced the worst recession in its post-war history. The fundamental Brazilian macroeconomic problem seems to result from the exhaustion of public financing and, as a consequence, the redefinition of a growth model in which the state would no longer play a leading role. After the change in the supply of foreign financing at the end of 1982, internal financial markets were not capable of financing the Brazilian government's borrowing requirements without putting pressure on domestic interest rates, the monetary base, and, consequently, the rate of inflation. In summary, the data show that the public debt burden was so high that — even with the federal government's decade-long "primary surpluses" (1983-1994); the freezing of financial assets (including demand deposits); the confiscation of financial assets and savings; and the adoption of intermittent price and wage freezes — the "fiscal problem" did not change substantially.[17] As a consequence, the monetary base has been the most important source of public financing but at a cost of extremely high rates of inflation.

The net public debt in Brazil averaged 37 percent of GDP in the first half of the 1990s (for the composition of this debt, see Tables 12 and 13). When new external financing ceased, the government raised domestic interest rates in order to substitute domestic public debt and attract foreign capital. This short-run policy required an increase in domestic interest rates, primarily in 1992, which, in turn, raised the government's debt service and squeezed its profile even more.

Even if the PND had raised more revenues, the financial burden of the already existing public debt has left the PND incapable of structurally changing public sector borrowing requirements. From 1990 through 1993, estimated GDP for Brazil ranged from $406.1 to $473 billion, while the debt service burden averaged approximately 3 percent of GDP. Thus, the $17 billion in estimated sales revenues from the PND would not cover even two years of public sector financial requirements. Actual revenues, however, reached just $8.6 billion (excluding $3.3 billion of transferred debt). Moreover, part of the sales revenue did not go to the Federal Treasury, since the state owned only part of the industrial capital sold. Moreover, only 18.6 percent of the revenue was in cash; the rest was "rotten money." In the end, the revenue from the PND did not cover even one year of the government's current debt servicing requirements.

In terms of the stock of public debt, the picture was worse. The net debt for the federal government and the state firms from 1991 through 1994 averaged $115 billion (Table 12). Both the estimated $17 billion and the $8.6 billion obtained from

Table 12.
Net Public Sector Debt (in US$ billions)

Years	1991	1992	1993	1994	1995*
Total Debt	144.2	150.5	150.2	180.9	181.7
Internal Debt	52.8	74.8	84.8	127.3	127.8
External Dept	91.4	75.8	65.4	53.6	53.9
Federal Government and Banco Central	48.3	49.2	43.9	77.2	76.5
State Enterprises	68.6	63.9	64.1	43.1	43.4
State and Local Governments	27.3	37.4	42.2	60.5	61.8

*Balances in January 1995.
Source: Banco Central do Brasil 1995, 108-109.

Table 13. Net Public Sector Debt
(percent of GDP)

Years	1991	1992	1993	1994	1995*
Total Debt	43.5	42.8	38.6	31.0	30.4
Federal Government and Central Bank	14.6	14.0	11.3	13.2	12.8
State and Local Government	8.2	10.6	10.8	10.4	10.4
State Firms	20.7	18.2	16.5	7.4	7.3

*Balances in January 1995.
Source: Banco Central do Brasil 1995, 108-109.

the PND revenues fall far short of this figure and could not ease either the financial burden or the borrowing requirements of the public sector in Brazil.[18]

Finally, during the Cardoso administration, the PND has expanded to include the electric power sector, the giant CVRD, and public services, such as the federal railroad and telecommunications. It is useful to consider the likely impact of their sale on the fiscal situation. As mentioned earlier, the total value of "rotten money" securities to be used in the PND was based on $8.5 billion of domestic debt paper and $37.6 billion of foreign debt instruments. By 1995, $6.9 billion of those "domestic privatization currencies" and only $68 million of the "external privatization currency" were used in the sales. Thus, the domestic balance is too low for the requirements of the future PND, and external bonds are, by the Brazilian Senate's determination, subject to a 25 percent discount of their par value. Therefore, new currencies will have to be utilized and the so-called social currencies may well be the candidates.

CONCLUSION

B y the mid-1990s, the privatization of state firms in Brazil, begun in 1991, had largely concluded for three basic industrial sectors of the economy, namely, steel, petrochemicals, and fertilizers. Of the 34 firms sold to the private sector, the state directly controlled 21. Thirteen were indirectly controlled, through minority stock participation by Petroquisa and Petrofértil, subsidiaries of Petrobrás, the state-owned petroleum monopoly.

The revenues from the PND were unremarkable: $8.6 billion paid in one or another of the forms of payment allowable under the program plus $3.27 billion corresponding to the firms' own transferred debt. This represents only a little more than two-thirds of the total revenues expected from the program and is far less than the $28 billion the state had invested in those enterprises. The minimum price criteria — primarily based on discounted cash flows, net assets, and other tangible market signals — may have significantly undervalued the firms, given the substantial uncertainty regarding the composition of future cash flows, evolution of prices, market expansion hypotheses, the discount rate, and the estimation of the firms' non-tangible values. On average, the ratio of fixed minimum prices to sales value was 1.15, indicating the absence of competition among buyers participating in the auctions. In addition, only 18.6 percent of the purchase payment was made in cash, with most of the remainder paid in "rotten money."

Regarding the microeconomic impact of the PND, it should be noted that auctions accounted for 85.6 percent of the sales, the firms' own employees purchased 3.4 percent, and the public bought the remainder at a fixed price and subject to quotas set for certain classes of investors. On the other hand, most buyers were nonfinancial national firms (42 percent), including domestic industrial groups, followed by national financial institutions (28.8 percent) and pension funds. These three groups accounted for 86.6 percent of all sales, while individual investors and foreigners accounted for 7.8 percent and 5.5 percent, respectively.

In spite of this "democratization of capital," privatization in Brazil did not escape the tendency to move toward the centralization and concentration of capital and production. In the fertilizer sector, for example, a single, private consortium acquired industry control, by holding a controlling share of Fosfértil, which, in turn, controlled Ultrafértil and Goiasfértil. The existence of some 300 small and middle-sized firms (intermediate processors and distributors of fertilizer) in Brazil did not change the new market structure significantly, since approximately 20 firms were producers, and the majority of the acquiring firms also owned large processing units.

The new control of capital and market power derived from the PND was similar, whether one examines the fertilizer sector or the petrochemical and steel sectors, except that, in the last case, the most important buyers were national private commercial banks, industrial groups whose firms already operated in the sector, and the pension funds of state-owned firms. In short, vertical and horizontal integration in production took place, with links extending to the financial capital arena. The synergy among the privatized firms may well result in future economic benefits, such as higher levels of technology, productivity gains, reduction in production costs, lower prices, and higher wages.

In this sense, it seems the PND reflects the evolution of capitalism and its globalization as well. For a developing society realizing that atomistic competition no longer exists, the design of a model to deal with issues of market power, by democratically creating regulatory institutions and defensive mechanisms, may be the most important challenge that lies ahead.

Throughout the 1980s and the first half the 1990s, Brazil experienced extremely high rates of inflation followed by several stabilization programs, beginning with José Sarney's short-lived, anti-inflationary Plano Cruzado in 1986. Thus, the implementation of the PND took place in an economic environment characterized by a sequence of quasi-hyperinflationary episodes followed by recession and stabilization programs. Comparing the calculated inflation rates for the privatized sectors with the country's industrial inflation and the general price level, one finds that price increases in the privatized sectors were, by and large, lower than the economy's inflation rates (except for the steel industry in 1992), and this behavior persisted even under the Real Plan. In this sense, the PND's impact on stabilization was positive.

Given the brief time that has elapsed since the initiation of the PND and the fact that industrial production recovered its 1989 level only in May 1994, it is too early to examine the program's impact on gross domestic investment. However, by comparing the average rate of industrial production in 1993 and 1994 with the rates for the privatized sectors, one sees that the PND accomplished its output objectives, with the steel sector leading industrial growth rates.

An examination of the country's post-privatization spending on imports of steel, inorganic and organic chemical products, and fertilizers with respect to domestic industrial growth revealed that both the petrochemical and fertilizer sectors lost ground to producers from abroad. They were not competitive and paid the price of trade liberalization. Since the country is dependent on fertilizer and petrochemical imports, the examination of net exports focuses on the steel sector.

Brazil plays a large role in the global market for iron and steel products. The country is competitive in this industry, and the sector has increased its contribution to the country's total exports, despite the implementation of a more realistic foreign exchange rate policy and the removal of many traditional direct and indirect subsidies. Although the sector was responsible for one-fifth of Brazil's trade surplus at the beginning of the 1990s, by 1994, when it reached 27.9 percent, it was responsible for more than one-fourth.

A major PND objective was the reduction of public debt and an alteration of its composition. By selling unprofitable assets and getting rid of costly debt, it was anticipated that the government would be able to take care of public services while leaving the leadership of economic growth in the hands of the private sector. In this regard, the PND's results (revenues of $8.6 billion plus $3.3 billion of transferred debt) were disappointing, whatever public finance indicator is chosen. The net debt for the federal government and the state firms from 1990 through 1994 averaged $115 billion; if local government is included, the net debt reached $181.7 billion in January 1995. Despite the structural changes in Brazil's fiscal policy since 1982 (when the IMF's macroeconomic policies went into effect) and the freezing of financial assets under the Collor Plan in March 1990, the average rate of public debt service for domestic and external debts was around 3 percent of GDP. Thus, the PND's estimated $17 billion sales revenues for this phase of the program would not have covered even two years of the public sector's financial burden. The real outcome was worse, especially when one considers that of the $8.6 billion, only 18.6 percent was paid in cash.

If the PND is to have a significant impact on the reduction of public debt, perhaps the Brazilian government should consider setting a minimum amount of fiat currency (that is, cash) to be used in the auctions, emphasize the exchange of long-term treasury bonds for short-term ones, and, above all, improve the criteria for fixing minimum prices. By doing so, the PND may help solve one of the most difficult problems facing the Brazilian economy: to reduce and restructure the public debt and rescue the state's capacity to invest.

Notes

1. Beneath the foreign exchange problem underlying the servicing of the foreign debt was a clearly understood and acknowledged fiscal problem. Moreover, most of the trade surplus was generated by the private sector. Consequently, the Brazilian Senate carefully established its 1990 resolution on import capacity and economic growth parameters for the debt renegotiation.

2. The *medida provisória* (provisory measure), for example, was instituted to allow the executive branch of government temporarily to implement urgent programs, projects, and policies. Congress then decides, within 30 days, whether the measures will be transformed into law. See Article 62 of the Brazilian Federal Constitution for full details.

3. This fund is nonmonetary and composed of stocks belonging to the firms included in the PND.

4. "Rotten paper," or *moedas podres*, also called "rotten money," was public debt paper having little value in market terms and near-zero liquidity when redeemed at par value.

5. Unless otherwise noted, statistics in this section come from BNDES 1995a and 1995b.

6. The sale of Petroquisa shares has been suspended by the president of Brazil. See BNDES 1995a and 1995b.

7. For a criticism of the PND's results as a whole, see the National Congress Commission's Report for 1994; for an apology, see Tourinho and Vianna 1994.

8. See BNDES 1995b, 22. The values are based on the state's capital invested, plus "previous adjustments" less distributed profits. For Embraer and PQU, the author considered only the state's share in their net assets (*ativo total* and *patrimônio líquido*), respectively.

9. State monopolies and oligopolies have been transferred to the private sector without the establishment of any safeguards such as the golden share used in the British case.

10. Brazil is poor in potassium. Although domestic production in this field did not exist until 1985, it corresponded to 8 percent of the estimated national consumption at the beginning of the 1990s and has slightly increased over the 10 years following 1985. On the other hand, the internal production capacity in phosphates reached 85 percent in 1990 and, in 1991, production capacity in nitrogenous fertilizers reached 75 percent of estimated domestic consumption.

11. According to an executive from the Ipiranga Group, the most important result of the PND in this sector was the regionalization of the domestic market, due to the end of freight subsidy. Prices in these markets are set by the coastal markets, and the tariff reduction has induced an alignment of domestic prices to those observed in United States. See *Jornal do Brasil* 1994.

12. In mid-1995, Congress agreed to the "flexibilization" of the Petrobras's monopoly by approving a constitutional amendment that authorizes the government to hire private firms to operate Brazil's petroleum business.

13. In addition to promoting education in the fields of mining and metallurgy, the Brazilian government had also granted special fiscal incentives since 1976 to those enterprises implementing development and capacity-expansion projects. Eligible companies were exempt from 95 percent of IPI for domestic sales (established by Law 7554/86 and in effect through 1996). For 1995, this fiscal incentive was estimated at $257 million and another $140 million was expected for 1996.

14. It has been assumed that real wages in firms previously owned by the state also followed the tendency verified in the overall steel sector.

15. Named for the *real,* Brazil's new currency at the time, the plan was an all-encompassing stabilization program intended to reduce prices and inflation. — Ed.

16. A free-trade zone established by Brazil, Argentina, Paraguay, and Uruguay in 1991, during the Collor administration, to provide for its members' free movement of goods, improve services and factors of production; and establish common external tariffs and trade policies, among other things.

17. See Paiva 1993, 18. Paiva's conclusion discusses a period after the IMF's policies were instituted in Brazil, and, although recently the fiscal situation has been quite different, the "fiscal problem" persists.

18. The government's rhetoric on the PND is entirely unrealistic. Even the usually clever Fernando Henrique Cardoso speaks of privatization as if it were a magical solution, reminding us of Reagan's "voodoo economics" of the early 1980s.

References

Amaral, Adriano B. 1995. "Estudos sobre a Dívida Interna e Externa." Mimeo.

Banco Central do Brasil. 1994. *Boletím.* 30 (12) (December): 31.

Banco Central do Brasil. 1995. *Boletím.* April: 31.

Banco Nacional de Desenvolvimento Econômico e Social (BNDES). 1994. *Avaliação dos Resultados da Privatização do Sector Siderúrgico Brasileiro.* Gandara & Kaufman Consultores Asociados.

Banco Nacional de Desenvolvimento Econômico e Social (BNDES). 1995a. *Programa Nacional de Desestatização — Sistema de Informações.* March 1995.

Banco Nacional de Desenvolvimento Econômico e Social (BNDES). 1995b. *Programa Nacional de Desestatização — Sistema de Informaçoes.* May 15.

Comissão Diretora do Programa Nacional de Desestatização (CDPND). 1994. *Relatorio de Atividades e Resultados, 1993.*

Instituto Brasileiro de Siderurgia (IBS). 1995. *A Siderurgia em Números, 1995 - Estatísticas da Siderurgia,* several issues.

Jornal do Brasil. 1994. April 15.

National Congress Commission's Report (Comissão Parlamentar Mista de Inquérito). 1994. *Relatorio Final,* May.

Paiva, Silvia Maria C. 1994. "A Privatização no Brasil: Breve Avaliação e Perspectivas." *Análise Conjuntural* (2nd trimester): 104-117.

Paiva, Stella Maria G. 1993. "Deficit Público e Financiamento." Mimeo.

Revista Conjuntura Econômica. March 1993.

Revista Conjuntura Econômica. March 1994.

Revista Conjuntura Econômica. May 1995.

Tourinho, Octavio A. F., and Ricardo L. L. Vianna. 1994. "Avaliação e Agenda do Programa Nacional de Desestatização." *Perspectivas da Economia Brasileira* 1: 65-92.

CHAPTER NINE

Privatization in Colombia: Competition and Labor Adjustment in the Electric Power and Telecommunications Industries

MAURICIO CÁRDENAS

Beginning in the mid-1980s, a wave of privatization spread throughout most of Latin America. More than five decades of state intervention in the region's economies had produced substantial public budget deficits, inefficient industrial firms and public utilities, uneven social welfare levels, and unsatisfied consumer needs. However, it was the debt crisis of the 1980s that ultimately precipitated a radical change of the economic model. This change resulted in a renewed role for foreign investment, which has partially replaced state interests in many industries. For domestic investors, the change of economic model has entailed both challenges and opportunities to enhance their own competitiveness. The impact on workers and consumers, in contrast, has been mixed.

Although Colombia's pattern of development spared the country some of the more acute effects of state intervention, privatization became a key policy within the framework of the economic internationalization that started in the late 1980s. Indeed, it is no wonder that transportation infrastructure (seaports and railways) became the first target of privatization efforts, since the inefficiencies of state-owned enterprises (SOEs) in these areas had caused major bottlenecks and excessive costs for import and export activities.

The next step in the privatization process was the telecommunications and public utilities infrastructure (mainly, the electric power industry). Financial and technological limitations in the traditional state-owned companies opened the way for various forms of privatization: subcontracting, concessions, and joint ventures. By the late 1980s, historical restrictions on the presence of foreign investment had been lifted, making it attractive for overseas investors and/or operators to engage in the revamping of existing firms and the establishment of new ones.

The privatization process next targeted the country's highway infrastructure and the social security system. Colombia learned from the mistakes of the Mexican experience and granted toll-road operation concessions in exchange for modern design and construction projects. Due to the large sums involved, foreign engineering firms entered into joint ventures with domestic firms. By adapting the model of the fully privatized Chilean social security system, Colombia established a mixed pension and health services sector, with various private organizations (some utilizing foreign expertise and investment) competing against a revamped state provider.

Privatization policies have also been applied in the oil, banking, and manufacturing industries. Major oil discoveries compelled the Colombian government to reduce the role of the state-owned company in this industry to ensure sufficient funds for exploitation, which were usually provided directly by foreign operators. In addition, deregulation and reprivatization of the financial services industry attracted some foreign capital and encouraged competition. (In the mid-1980s, more than half of the nation's banks had been nationalized due to corruption and insolvency.) The government's industrial development agency also sold its shares in most of the manufacturing joint ventures it had shared with private capital since the 1960s and 1970s, most notably in the automotive, paper, and shipbuilding industries.

Although Colombia's privatization policies have increased foreign investment, the speed and extent to which this has occurred are relatively less than in other major countries in Latin America. This sluggishness is due to the historically smaller role of the state in the Colombian economy, the strengthening of the few large domestic economic groups through diversification, the legal and political barriers faced by some of the more significant privatization projects, and the negative image of the country among potential foreign investors because of drug- and guerrilla-related violence.

The diversity of industries undergoing privatization and the renewed interest of foreign and domestic investors indicate positive prospects for the new economic model. However, expected improvements in the public budget, efficiency levels of industrial and public utility operations, social welfare, and consumer satisfaction have not yet been measured precisely and over the long term. As of 1995, results were reasonably good with regard to the public budget, acceptable with respect to efficiency levels of privatized concerns, and regressive in the areas of social welfare and consumer satisfaction. While business and the well-to-do have benefited from significant quality improvements, higher service rates and consumer prices have further deteriorated the average person's standard of living.

The advance of privatization in Colombia has been conditioned by legislative changes, most made after the 1991 constitutional reforms. Although revenue from privatization reached only US$700 million between 1989 and 1991, it rose to almost $1.6 billion between 1992 and 1994 (75 percent of the 1994 figure corresponds to the sale of cellular-phone operation licenses). In contrast to other Latin American countries, Colombia has passed no general legislation on privatization; rather, Congress has issued specific laws at each stage in the process. Only in December 1995 was a relatively comprehensive legal framework developed, enabling the government to overcome the obstacles it had faced periodically in the courts. These obstacles were usually related to employee stock ownership in privatized companies and the ability of the government to restructure public agencies. The new funding requirements for social expenditures, mandated by the Ernesto Samper administration (1994-1998), also affected privatization. Because of the lack of a comprehensive legal framework, the pace of privatization slowed dramatically during 1995, thus restricting expected social investment. The main focus of this chapter will be the privatization experiences of two of the industries, electric power and telecommunications, in which specific laws have most significantly transformed the traditional rules of the game.

IMPETUS FOR PRIVATIZATION

With the exception of public utilities and the operation of seaports and railways, the private sector has participated all along in virtually every economic activity in Colombia. As a result, the state's share of the gross national product (GNP) has remained under 25 percent, and the fiscal deficit has usually been held to manageable proportions. Even before the current trend toward privatization, the fiscal deficit was approximately 2 percent of GNP.

Internal political developments, namely, a wave of civic strikes and the subsequent decentralization laws passed in the mid-1980s, called into question the operation of public utilities, especially with regard to poor reliability and high cost for residential customers. Decentralization laws opened the door for experimentation with alternative arrangements at the municipal and regional levels. From that point forward, the operation of public utilities — starting with aqueducts — included privatization components such as subcontracting, employee and former-employee co-ownership, operation by consumer associations, and so forth. These new organizational arrangements usually entailed significant labor adjustments and contributed to solving the reliability problems that had led to their creation. Additionally, in the case of electric power supply and telecommunications, the new organizations also contributed to enhancing the competitiveness of industrial and commercial customers.[1]

During the César Gaviria administration (1990-1994), a general criticism of the management of SOEs was articulated in a far-reaching series of legal efforts promoting privatization. Moving beyond its previous concerns with the social unrest derived from inefficient operation of public utilities, the government sought to reduce the comparatively high cost of services provided by the state-owned power generation companies, which had reduced the competitiveness of domestic industry. In addition, international lending institutions pressured the power companies to improve efficiency; however, major, ongoing expansion projects prevented them from being privatized. Indeed, private investors were initially reluctant to invest in the companies due to their precarious financial situation and high labor costs. The regulatory framework initiated in 1992, however, increased the private sector's participation in both investment in new power plants and the operation of overhauled state-owned plants.

Around this same time, the national telecommunications company was restructured to make it more competitive in an increasingly deregulated market. Attempts to sell this firm to private investors — following the example of Colombia's neighbors in the Southern Cone — stopped in 1992 because of a labor strike and the ensuing political reaction. The government ultimately decided to redefine the company's role under a new regulatory framework promoting joint ventures with private operators.

The constitutional changes promoted by the Gaviria administration in 1991 made all these privatization and deregulation measures possible. Specific legislation that resulted from these changes allowed the privatization of state-owned public utilities, as well as the formation of new companies owned by private investors.[2] In typical Colombian fashion, the new legal framework maintained subsidization mechanisms. This time, however, the subsidies came directly from the national budget via transfers to low-income consumers, rather than from industrial and higher-income consumers via cross-subsidization (Peñalosa 1993, 29-36).

By 1995, most investment by domestic or foreign entrepreneurs in public utilities had taken place in the electricity power and telecommunications industries. Whereas deregulation had advanced rapidly in the electric power industry since 1992, tighter controls for private participation remained in the telecommunications industry. This was reflected in a higher level of competition among electricity suppliers than existed among long-distance telephone service providers; in fact, competition was present only in cellular and international long-distance services. Plans for deregulating domestic long-distance service were deferred to 1997. Nevertheless, a de facto privatization of local carriers had already started in 1992 by means of joint ventures led by foreign telephone companies.

Because the state's stake in most industries other than public utilities was small, and political and labor opposition to drastic reforms was strong, little effort was made in Colombia to develop a comprehensive set of privatization policies. The public sector in Colombia was transformed in the early 1990s. Even before the 1991 Constitution came into force, laws authorizing mass layoffs and liquidation of state agencies had been passed. Under the new Constitution, "restructuring-of-the-state" decrees led to further layoffs and to the liquidation or merger of a number of government agencies. Privatization was secondary at that point, especially after the Gaviria administration's failure to sell the national telecommunications company in 1992. However, privatizations during this time were managed on a case-by-case basis, not as part of a comprehensive set of policies. Most occurred in the banking industry, in which the government had intervened (without nationalizing it) in the 1980s because of a financial crisis, and also in the manufacturing sector, where a government credit agency had promoted joint ventures with private counterparts for as long as the infant-industry argument could hold. However, as legislation developed, based on the 1991 constitutional reforms, and the government searched for short-term funding for its social programs, privatization acquired greater importance in the country and began to appear in public utilities, where the state has always played a traditional role. In this chapter, the main focus will be the privatization experiences of the electric power and the telecommunications industries, due to their significant impacts on the economy and the diverse paths they have taken. These cases provide an example for other privatization processes in the country, particularly with respect to the management of labor adjustment and incentives for increased competition.

PRIVATIZATION IN THE ELECTRIC POWER INDUSTRY

The regulatory framework under which power companies operated was revised only one year after the 1991 Constitution established the possibility of private competition in the public utilities sector. According to the new framework, even if SOEs were not privatized, they still had to become cost effective and thoroughly transform their relationships with both suppliers and customers (Arias 1993, 15-26). The power rationing that the country faced in 1992 catalyzed the elaboration of a privatization plan.

Between 1980 and 1990, the power generation capacity in Colombia doubled, from 4,177 megawatts (MW) to 8,356 MW. Simultaneously, the electric power industry's foreign debt increased from $860 million to $5.2 billion. Throughout the decade, investment in the industry represented 24 percent of total public investment. As a result, by 1990, 96 percent of all municipalities and 41 percent of rural areas had access to the national grid (Ochoa 1991). At the same time, by 1990, annual subsidies approached $250 million, and energy losses had risen to 21.6 percent from 17.3 percent in 1975. Accounts receivable were also unacceptably large. Higher interest rates and currency devaluation combined to create a situation in which the electric power companies' current cash resources were sufficient to meet only 44 percent of their foreign debt service (Ochoa 1991).

During that time, industrial customers accounted for more than 27 percent of all electricity consumption in Colombia. Almost 80 percent of the total consumption took place in the steel, chemical, food processing, cement, textile, oil refining, and paper industries. On average, these industries purchased 70 percent of their electricity from local and regional power companies; the remainder was self-generated. The big electricity-consuming industries constituted virtually all of the self-generation capacity in the country, with four industries alone (oil, paper, chemicals, and cement) supplying more than 93 percent of all electricity purchased by power companies from third parties (Ángel 1991).

By 1990, electricity expenses paid by Colombian industry represented an average of 1.5 percent of all value added. In the case of the seven industries listed above — along with the wood, glass, rubber, plastic, and ceramic goods industries — the percentage ranged from two to more than seven times the average. Some have argued, then, that electricity costs are a determining factor of international competitiveness for certain industries (Ángel 1991).

According to a 1988 comparison of electricity rates for industrial customers conducted by Boston Consulting Group, in Colombia the average price for a kilowatt-hour was about the same as in the United States, 60 percent higher than in Mexico, 25 percent higher than in Venezuela, and 30 to 50 percent lower than in most European countries. Unfortunately, reliability and technological problems affected the continuity of production and further increased actual costs of electricity utilization in all industrial zones, but especially along the Caribbean coast and in Boyaca province (Ángel 1991).

Until the early 1990s, Colombian industrial customers paid higher rates (as much as 50 percent higher in Bogotá) than did institutional customers, such as government agencies, or individuals. The rationale was the need to subsidize residential electricity customers. Indeed, by 1993, subsidies worth over $1.2 billion had reduced the rates for the average residential consumer to only 49 percent of the true cost (Restrepo 1993, 87-95).

Substantial regional variations with regard to the rates for industrial customers also existed. For instance, the largest power company on the Caribbean coast charged a rate 50 percent higher than that charged by a company in the interior, for the alleged reason that fuel oil-based electricity plants were more costly to operate than coal- and hydro-based plants.

In response, the Gaviria administration redefined the electric power industry policy in 1991 to reduce subsidies to residential customers, set rates for industrial customers that were congruent with true generation and distribution costs, and eliminate unjustified regional rate differences. Accordingly, the National Department of Planning (Departamento Nacional de Planeación — DNP) announced that the average rate would increase over three years from only 75 percent to 90 percent of the true cost. The DNP also announced that rate increases would be proportionately lower in cases where a comparatively higher rate already existed, as with Bogotá's industrial customers (Restrepo 1993).

The Gaviria administration pointed to a crisis of the entire electric power industry, which needed to be solved through major restructuring. Inefficiency, energy losses, unpaid accounts receivable, unreliable service or no service at all, and arbitrarily defined rates were among the critical problems — not to mention the size of the power companies' foreign debt, which represented one-third of all public foreign debt.

A turning point in collective bargaining took place against this backdrop in 1991. The industry-wide labor union managed to bring together workers from 16 regional power companies, along with those from Bogotá's power company, to present a common front in a nine-month negotiation with top government officials. Anticipating the impact on labor of restructuring the industry as a whole, the union succeeded in keeping long-held benefits for its older affiliates, while accepting a transitional framework for newer workers.

An unforeseen event soon highlighted the prolonged nature of restructuring in the electric power industry and accelerated its privatization. Spurred by limited hydroelectric power generation (the source of close to 80 percent of Colombia's electricity) that resulted from drastic changes in weather patterns, delays in new project construction, and poor maintenance, a significant countrywide rationing of electricity began in March 1992 and lasted one year.[3] Following this experience, government planners concluded that unless a privatization strategy was implemented, the funds (more than $4 billion in direct investment) needed to meet a growing demand for electricity between 1993 and 2000 would not be available. While the privatization strategy was being defined, the government agency in charge of providing funding to the power companies established monitoring programs patterned after those followed by multilateral financial institutions. In addition, the National Energy Commission (Comisión Nacional de Energía — CNE) was created to promote private participation in the industry and competition among the SOEs (Restrepo 1993, 13).

A group of Cartagena's most important entrepreneurs launched the first private venture in contemporary Colombia to generate electricity for their own consumption and to sell the surplus (cogeneration) to the regional grid. Most of these entrepreneurs ran heavy industries and had been seriously affected by the unreliability of the regional state-owned power company. Turning to a U.S. subcontractor, who set up the generation plant in record time and became its operator, the entrepreneurial group from Cartagena became self-sufficient in energy production. Under a long-term agreement guaranteeing the purchase of all surplus electricity, which the U.S. operator had negotiated with the SOEs, the group started selling surplus electricity to the regional grid at a rate 25 percent lower than the rate at which they had been purchasing electricity from the state-owned utility. Interestingly, the new thermal plant employed 50 people, with only 10 in administrative positions. The small size of the new plant's workforce contrasted dramatically with the large workforce in the region's state-owned thermal plants, providing a strong argument for restructuring the electric power industry as a whole (Sáenz 1995).

Favorable legislation developed shortly afterward, leading to the appearance of other forms of privatization in the electric power industry, including subcontracting with foreign firms for technological modernization or operation and with former workers' cooperatives for maintenance services in restructured, state-owned thermal plants.[4] According to Marcel Silva, legal advisor to the national electricity workers' union, subcontracting arrangements prevailed as the privatization mechanism of choice in the industry. Silva clearly identified their impact: Referring to a 50 MW plant operated in the Tolima province by a U.S. firm, he argued that other plants with a similar generation capacity — which were still managed by the state — had six to eight times the workforce but lacked the profitability of the former. In addition, according to Silva, the average salary of a skilled technician might be three or four times higher in the subcontracted operation, discouraging union affiliation (Silva 1995).

For more than a decade, the most successful state-owned public utility company, located in Medellín, had provided a model based on a mixture of sound management practices and subcontracting with private vendors (Chamucero 1995).[5] Between 1992 and 1995, 12 privately managed or owned generation plants were established in the country, most of them resulting from the overhaul of preexisting plants (Silva 1995). With the exception of two hydroelectric operations in the Huila and Valle provinces, all of these plants were thermal (Silva 1995).

In Barranquilla, Colombia's fourth largest city, a mixed enterprise involving some foreign investment was created to promote the expansion of the state-owned power company. It was expected that under new management and with the implementation of new technology only 100 out of the original 240 employees would keep their jobs. The restructured plant would have a generation capacity of 750 MW and would constitute a technological leap forward. However, the bidding process was highly controversial due to apparent biases in the selection of the equipment supplier. The media also criticized the terms granted to the foreign operation in the licensing contract, given the much higher financial costs involved (as opposed to softer loan options to which the state-owned company might have resorted), the subsidization of fuel provided by the state-owned oil company, and the promise to transfer government funds to the private operator when authorized rates did not provide the stipulated level of profit (Sanclemente 1994, 4-5).

In Colombia's southwestern provinces (where Cali, the second largest city, is located), a privatized regional power company emerged when the environmental authority was divided into two different organizations. The national electricity workers' union (Sindicato de Trabajadores Eléctricos de Colombia — Sintraelecol), demonstrating its ability to adapt to changing labor-market and ownership conditions, established a new local in the privatized company (Forero 1995).[6] Despite the liquidation of a few minor state-owned regional power companies, the merger of various company-based unions into the national organization allowed the membership to double between 1987 and 1995. The number of affiliates working for 30 different power companies increased from 7,500 to 15,000 employees (Forero 1995).

The new law on public utilities made it mandatory to privatize, at least partially, all local and regional SOEs in the electric power industry before the end of 1995, by compelling them to issue stock that might appeal to investors. According to the government privatization plans, it was expected that the private sector would provide more than 60 percent of the investment required for the expansion of Colombia's power supply during the rest of the century (Sanclemente 1994).

However, the legal framework continues to support the state's participation in the sector since distributors must pay a fee for the use of the state-owned transmission grid, even though they can now purchase energy from the generator offering the most competitive rates and quality of service, regardless of its geographical location or type of ownership. This legal framework permits subsidies to low-income consumers, to be administered directly by the restructured (or mixed) electric power companies from funds transferred to them from the national budget (Silva 1995).

According to the 1991 Constitution, the ownership transition in the electric power industry contemplated preferential access to stock for currently employed workers, facilitated by soft loans from the energy industry's state financial agency (Financiera Energética Nacional — FEN). During 1995, the Sintraelecol union debated whether to encourage their members to purchase the stock. The union leadership was concerned about the true value of the shares (given the high indebtedness of the state-owned power companies and the emergence of private competitors) and the fate of workers who had already been laid off as restructuring advanced in anticipation of privatization (Silva 1995). Specialists are most concerned about whether the joint-venture arrangement negotiated for the expansion of the Barranquilla power company will become a model for future privatizations, given that it provides the private operator with a number of advantages at the expense of its state-agency partners (Sanclemente 1994).

In general, privatization in the electric power industry advanced at a fast pace. The Colombian government's concern with reliability, rates, capacity expansion, and technological innovations has opened the door for a growing number of foreign operators to participate in joint ventures. Because the independent National Energy Commission (Comisión Nacional de Energía — CNE) controls rates and regulations fostering competition, residential and industrial customers have benefited from the new environment. It is still too early to estimate the true size of subsidies and their fiscal cost. However, it is clear that both the privately owned or operated power plants and the restructured state-owned plants are managed more efficiently and with a smaller workforce than in the past. Although most of the workers have managed to regroup in a single national union — one of the few in the country that does negotiate a common contract on behalf of members across the industry — the traditional politicians' clienteles have lost much of the ground they had held in the electric power industry since the 1960s.

THE TELECOMMUNICATIONS INDUSTRY

In 1992, when the Gaviria administration announced the privatization of the national telecommunications company, Telecom, it cited three main arguments for doing so: high rates for international long-distance service (which subsidized domestic long-distance service); high labor and pension benefits costs (augmented by a growing population of retired personnel); and insufficient financial resources to engage in needed technological innovations (Ramírez 1995). As had happened in the electric power industry, cross-subsidization of telecommunications services had allowed low-income consumers, smaller cities, and rural regions to enjoy low rates. However, in contrast to the electric power industry, revenues from the state-owned long-distance provider were used to subsidize all other telephone rates. In addition, these revenues contributed to a significant surplus, which the government used to offset deficits in other sectors.[7]

Under the privatization framework, some subsidies for the low-income population and rural regions were retained; however, according to union sources, it was unlikely that the transfers from the national budget announced by the government would ever take place (Salazar 1995).[8] In the meantime, rates for domestic telecommunications services increased moderately. In contrast, rates for international services were lowered, in response to the entrance of competition into a market previously managed as a source of revenue for the national government.

According to top officials at Telecom, labor adjustments were required to allow for the investments needed to prepare for a deregulated and more competitive environment (Rincón 1995). In 1995, a voluntary early retirement program reduced the workforce by 30 percent. During the previous three years, extensive subcontracting and joint ventures had kept wages from increasing, despite growing revenues. Telecom's unions had opposed these policies; however, after an apparently successful strike against privatization in April 1992, workers became divided over how to continue their opposition to privatization. In the meantime, Telecom's competitors and joint venture partners had thrived in an environment wary of any future labor-led shutdowns of telecommunications services. In this social context, the government's privatization measures were advanced without any consultation with organized labor.

Privatization of the telecommunications industry in Colombia had been based on the establishment of joint ventures and granting of operating licenses, presumably to promote competition and technological innovation.[9] In the case of the licenses granted for cellular phone operations, however, another objective was pursued through privatization: generating transferable funds to support investment in the government's social programs.[10]

Unlike their counterparts in other Latin American countries, private long-distance operators in Colombia have not been required to invest in new infrastructure; rather, they are granted the right to use existing state-owned infrastructure. Demonstrating the government's willingness to keep Telecom technologically modern, the company has invested in an inland extension of the submarine fiber-optic cable connecting the United States and Colombia.

Domestic long-distance service was slated for deregulation in 1997. There is the possibility that the major local-service operators, all of them owned by the respective municipalities, will develop joint ventures with Telecom or other private operators in order to compete in the new environment. In the cellular industry, joint ventures already integrate state-owned local phone companies and private foreign firms.

Privatization in the telecommunications industry has advanced at a slower pace than in the electric power industry. Initial opposition by militant labor unions and lack of political support in Congress hindered both restructuring and privatization measures undertaken by the Gaviria administration. Telecom was a net cash generator for the government and provided acceptable long-distance service, which made its sale to private investors unpopular. However, the reaction of the unions, which shut down the country's telecommunications systems for almost two weeks in 1992, demonstrated to businesses, private citizens, and the state itself the vulnerability of reliance on a monopoly such as Telecom. Accordingly, a de facto privatization soon took place with the emergence of technological alternatives provided by nonregulated telecommunications sources and an increasing number of joint ventures operated by foreign companies. Since then, Telecom's share of international long-distance service has declined, and it is expected that major competitors will emerge following the deregulation of the domestic long-distance market. In the meantime, significant labor adjustment has taken place in Telecom without an articulated response from the once-strong unions.

CONCLUSION

Although privatization has become a household word in Colombia, its meaning is somewhat different from that in other Latin American countries. To begin with, there has not been much to privatize. The private sector in Colombia has always been present in almost all industries of the economy, including the most dynamic ones. An exception, at least since the 1940s, has been public utilities, where SOEs held virtual monopolies. In the public sector, power supply and telecommunications companies have traditionally accounted for the largest share of investment and assets. While the electric power companies have run deficits for many years due to subsidized rates, costly foreign debt, and high operating expenses, the national telecommunications company has been a net cash generator for the government.

Despite their different financial standings, both industries have undergone some degree of restructuring and privatization, beginning with the Gaviria administration and continuing under the Samper administration. The process has advanced faster in the electric power industry than in the telecommunications industry, but joint ventures have predominated over complete privatization in both cases. Foreign operators have become partners or contractors of SOEs. Competition has been stimulated by newly created independent commissions, which have developed a more market-oriented policy environment.

Because of anti-inflationary policies, the continuation of some preexisting cross-subsidization schemes, and the creation of new subsidization schemes, rates for service have not changed significantly for the average residential customer. Competition in both industries has primarily benefited industrial and commercial customers through increased service reliability and lower rates. Labor unions have reacted differently in the two industries. In the electric power industry, layoffs and contract clause reversals have stimulated the regrouping of most workers into a single national organization. In the telecommunications industry, in contrast, divisions among competing unions have intensified, and membership has dropped dramatically. Finally, politicians in Congress have become increasingly supportive of privatization and have issued laws providing the framework for government decrees. Most state-owned power and telecommunications companies are surviving but in a downsized form and often as a joint venture with private interests.

Notes

1. The author co-organized a conference on alternative approaches to managing public utilities in Latin America held at the Universidad de los Andes in Bogotá (March-April 1995), which was sponsored by the Organization of American States. Managers from privatized, community-operated, or transformed state-owned public utilities presented their cases. One of the main lessons from the conference is developed in this chapter: labor redundancy and political interference have been associated with the inefficient operation of public utilities, while labor adjustment and a focus on customers have usually accompanied restructuring or privatization processes.

2. Some private participation already existed in public utilities. The telecommunications industry was nationalized in the 1940s, whereas private companies — mainly foreign-owned — had been active in the electricity industry until the early 1960s, though their presence declined significantly after the late 1940s.

3. Poor maintenance, in turn, was caused by restrictive government monetary policies aimed at reducing public spending to control inflation, as well as by difficulties in the execution of the maintenance program during the nine-month labor negotiations in 1991 and 1992.

4. See Silva 1995.

5. Roberto Chamucero is a member of the executive committee of Colombia's largest public employee's federation (Federación Nacional de Trabajadores al Servicio del Estado — Fenaltrase). According to Chamucero, whereas Medellín's public utility employed 7,000 people on a permanent basis, maintenance and technical operations were performed by 13,000 workers hired by subcontractors on an as-needed basis.

6. José Forero is a member of the executive committee of Sintraelecol, the national electricity workers' union. Many members who joined the new local had been experiencing deteriorating work conditions. As their previous employer (a regional state agency) was liquidated, the workers were compelled to accept a decrease in their basic pay and benefits from the new private employer in order to keep their jobs.

7. The only "cash cows" for the Colombian government were Telecom and Ecopetrol, the oil company. In addition, because of macroeconomic monetary policies, the government increasingly restricted the amount of reinvestment taking place in both companies. Thus, throughout the 1990s, almost 40 percent of Telecom's financial surplus was transferred by the national government to deficit-ridden sectors for reasons of monetary policy (Ramírez 1995).

8. Carlos Salazar is a member of the telecommunications workers' union's (Asociación de Trabajadores de Telecomunicaciones —ATT) executive committee. ATT, originally the technicians' association at Telecom, has turned into an industry-wide union with bargaining capacity in various state-owned local phone companies.

9. Joint ventures have increased rapidly in recent years and will continue to grow. According to high-level officials at Telecom, the company became the owner of approxi-

mately 350,000 lines through its direct investment in local carriers (which has taken place since the early 1980s, mainly in mid-size cities). Private operators began to appear in joint ventures in 1992 and became the temporary owners of 500,000 lines (temporary in the sense that, after 10 years, the ownership of the lines will return to Telecom). It is estimated that the number of private operators in joint ventures will double between 1995 and 1999, virtually privatizing Telecom's operation of local carriers (Ramírez 1995).

10. Approximately $250 million paid for operating licenses for cellular phones was transferred to the national government's social programs in 1994. Despite a legal controversy over the rights of municipalities to those funds, the national government later resorted to similar arguments over the need to transfer funds to social investment programs to justify further privatizations.

References

Ángel, Carlos Arturo. 1991. "Opciones para la participación privada en el sector eléctrico colombiano." Position paper submitted by the National Industrialists Association to the Conference on Privatization, Cartagena, Colombia, August.

Arias, Enrique, ed. 1993. *Alternativas de privatización para el sector público colombiano.* Bogotá: Universidad Externado de Colombia.

Arias, Enrique. 1993. "Privatización en América Latina." In *Alternativas de privatización para el sector público colombiano,* ed. Enrique Arias. Bogotá: Universidad Externado de Colombia.

Chamucero, Roberto. 1995. Interview by author. Bogotá, May.

Forero, José. 1995. Interview by María Victoria Whittingham, graduate research assistant, Universidad de los Andes, Bogotá, June.

Ochoa, Francisco. 1991. "Perspectivas de privatización en el sector eléctrico colombiano." Position paper submitted by the National Energy Commission to the Conference on Privatization. Cartagena, Colombia, August.

Peñalosa, Enrique. 1993. "Eficiencia, distribución del ingreso y privatización." In *Alternativas de privatización para el sector público colombiano,* ed. Enrique Arias. Bogotá: Universidad Externado de Colombia.

Ramírez, Gustavo. 1995. Interview by Iván Ariza, Jorge Rendón, and Santiago Salazar, graduate research assistants. Bogotá: Universidad de los Andes, June.

Restrepo, Juan Camilo. 1993. "Estado y sector privado participan conjuntamente en la prestación de servicios públicos." In *Alternativas de privatización para el sector público colombiano,* ed. Enrique Arias. Bogotá: Universidad Externado de Colombia.

Rincón, Alejandro. 1995. Interview by Iván Ariza, Jorge Rendón, and Santiago Salazar, graduate research assistants. Bogotá: Universidad de los Andes, June.

Sáenz, Alicia. 1995. Interview by author. Bogotá, March.

Salazar, Carlos. 1995. Interview by María Victoria Whittingham, graduate research assistant. Bogotá: Universidad de los Andes.

Sanclemente, Carlos. 1994. "La realidad de las privatizaciones eléctricas." *Nueva Frontera.* 965: 4-5.

Silva, Marcel. 1995. Interview by author. Bogotá, May.

CHAPTER 10

Conclusion: Comparative Analysis of the Privatization Experience

MELISSA H. BIRCH AND JERRY HAAR

It is far too early to know with any degree of certainty what contribution the privatization of public enterprises in Latin America will make to the region's future economic growth and development. Latin American privatization began in Chile in 1974, and the process there is virtually complete; in Brazil, it began in earnest in 1991, where its future direction is uncertain. The shape, pace, and direction of privatization vary throughout the region. However, even though a definite conclusion as to privatization's "success" or "failure" cannot be made at present, it is important for both research and policy purposes to understand how privatization has evolved in the countries of Latin America. Policymakers and business professionals need to be able to assess the necessity for and direction of mid-course adjustments in order to achieve privatization's goals and intended benefits.

To understand the initial effects of privatization and to document the process of structural change and economic reform, we asked scholars in eight Latin American countries to examine privatization experiences and to assess both the macroeconomic and microeconomic impacts of each program. Specifically, we asked them to examine how privatization has affected macroeconomic stabilization and the fiscal balance; quality and quantity of services; employment, wages, and productivity; and the promotion of free trade. The findings of these studies are summarized here, along with the lessons that the editors believe may be drawn from this experience.

IMPACT OF PRIVATIZATION ON MACROECONOMIC STABILITY AND FISCAL BALANCE

Privatization in Latin America is generally associated with the quest for macro-economic stabilization and fiscal balance by governments in the region in the wake of the debt crisis. Yet, privatization's effects vary substantially among countries across the region and even within single countries over time. In the short run, the structure, scope, and terms of payment of the privatization program itself seem to have significant impact on the macroeconomic outcome. In the long run, which perhaps is more important, privatization has lent credibility to economic reform policies and has sent a positive signal to foreign and domestic private investors.

Argentina

The Argentine experience illustrates many issues central to privatization in Latin America. Public enterprises in Argentina exemplified the many roles these companies were expected to play in developing countries. State-owned enterprises (SOEs) were established in the post-war period to promote employment creation, regional integration and development, income redistribution, and economic stabilization. Prices of goods and services produced by public enterprises were used, for example, to redistribute income across income groups and between industrial and residential consumers. The government's policy of allowing price increases for public enterprise outputs to lag in times of high inflation was designed to dampen inflationary expectations. By the end of the 1980s, the practice of using public enterprise as a tool of macroeconomic management in Argentina had severely damaged the financial health of the firms, leaving them with significant investment and, hence, technological shortfalls.

In the midst of the economic and political crisis of 1989, the administration of Carlos Saúl Menem turned to privatization of public enterprises as a means to make credible an enormous change of government policy and to alleviate the immediate fiscal emergency.[1] Thus, Argentina's privatization program began in haste, with the sale of two large firms in monopoly markets. The debt-equity swaps permitted in the financing of the sales subsidized the (mostly foreign) buyers, and the incomplete regulatory framework for the future operation of these firms made possible the continuation of significant monopoly power. Sebastián Galiani and Diego Petrecolla, in Chapter 4 of this volume, argue that the high rate of return this arrangement guaranteed was necessary to mitigate the great uncertainty surrounding economic decisionmaking in the country. Although these sales yielded little cash, they made a significant contribution to macroeconomic stabilization by eliminating some of Argentina's foreign debt burden.

The second phase of privatization began after the passage of the Convertibility Law,[2] when it was clear that the anchor of the new macroeconomic stabilization program would be the foreign exchange rate. In this phase, the sale of Argentine oil reserves and shares of stock in telecommunications served to relax the government's short-run cash constraints, and it also signaled to international markets a continued commitment to economic reform. By the third wave of privatization, Argentina had a Brady Plan[3] in place and a balanced fiscal position. Financial objectives lost priority as questions of allocative efficiency became preeminent. Gas and electricity firms were sold in a process that yielded less revenue for the government but was more competitive and efficient and included a regulatory system that was better defined and oriented toward competition as well. Unfortunately, as the 1995 recession set in, the government's attention turned again to financial considerations, and the next wave of privatization was dominated by revenue-raising goals.[4]

The Argentine privatization process was perhaps most successful in terms of its ability to reduce foreign debt and contribute to fiscal and macroeconomic stabilization and was particularly effective in attracting the return of flight capital and permitting Argentina's reinsertion into international capital markets. However, as of 1998, Argentina's foreign debt was almost double what it was during the debt crisis and the massive capital outflows that occurred in the wake of the Mexican devaluation in 1994 — suggesting that the situation continues to be quite fragile.

Brazil

The pace of privatization in Brazil has been slower and its scope less extensive than in certain other Latin American countries, though the government's financial need is among the greatest in the region. Between 1991 and 1993, Brazilian privatizations raised the unremarkable amount of less than US$12 billion, far below the $28 billion the government had invested in the enterprises it sold. Privatization in Brazil took place in the context of very high rates of inflation and two stabilization programs, the Collor Plan (March 1990) and the Real Plan (July 1994). Two main objectives of privatization were to reduce the public debt and to alleviate the burden of debt service. However, despite the revenues raised and the internal debt that was retired, Brazil's debt overhang continues to represent a significant challenge to policymakers. In Chapter 8, Juarez de Souza notes that revenues from the program have failed to cover annual debt-service requirements, much less reduce the debt stock significantly. The $17 billion raised from 1990 through 1995 was insufficient to cover two years of the public sector's financial requirements; in fact, revenues could not even cover one year of debt-servicing obligations. Given its deep discount on secondary markets, the widespread use of "rotten" money[5] complicates the analysis of fiscal impact. Only 18.6 percent of the revenues raised were paid in cash.

Privatization is only a small part of the dramatic stabilization programs Brazil has undertaken. Price increases in the privatized industries, however, have been generally lower than the overall rate of inflation in the economy, thus having a positive, if relatively small, impact on the economy. This price behavior is significant in view of the oligopolistic nature of the sectors and the almost fully indexed nature of the economy. The price pattern is perhaps explained by the above-average levels of idle capacity in the affected industries, with idleness in the 1992-1994 period averaging 25 percent.[6]

The Caribbean

The fiscal impact of privatization in the English-speaking Caribbean has been mixed. Asset sales or leases created financial inflows and, in some cases, also reduced budget outflows, following the elimination of subsidies to unprofitable firms. However, in the case of other countries in the region, privatization increased the financial burden, as the government absorbed the outstanding debt or the unpaid obligations to employees of firms being privatized. For example, the government of Trinidad and Tobago paid $62.7 million to cover loan losses and severances, plus $86.2 million for liquidating loan losses.[7] Nevertheless, in most cases, privatization in the English-speaking Caribbean has been effective in attracting foreign exchange and, thus, easing pressure on the balance of payments. The National Investment Bank of Jamaica, for example, has raised $275.5 million from privatizations since 1981; this excludes lands and local government operations.

Having reviewed a decade's privatizations, Richard L. Bernal and Winsome J. Leslie, in Chapter 6, are able to identify features common to successful privatization programs: timing, a competent executing agency, an appropriate regulatory framework, and necessary safety nets for displaced workers. They report that privatization in the Caribbean has resulted not in the private sector replacing the state, but rather in the state acquiring a new role, one that Jamaican Prime Minister P.J. Patterson has likened to "steering" rather than "rowing." Therefore, privatization's final macroeconomic impact may still remain to be determined. In any event, the privatization trend continued through the last decade and included Guyana Airlines, Guyana Electricity, Barbados' Arawak Cement Plant, and Sangers International Airport in Montego Bay, Jamaica.

Chile

Unlike the experience in so many Latin American countries, where privatization was driven by an immediate fiscal or stabilization necessity, the Chilean process issued from an ideological commitment to the free market.[8] As Rolf J. Lüders points out in Chapter 2, instead of supporting a stabilization program, privatization revenues in Chile subsidized social spending in the 1970s and, in the 1980s, supported infrastructure expansion related to the country's new export-promotion strategy. The privatization program's impact on the fiscal side, though greater than that of Great Britain in terms of magnitudes relative to budget and gross national product (GNP), was far less significant than its impact on the competitiveness of the economic environment and the creation of rapid and sustained economic growth. The public sector did receive $2.5 billion up to the end of 1989, and the revenue effect varied from 0.1 percent to 10.6 percent of gross domestic product (GDP). The role of the regulatory environment, both as applied to the private and non-privatized sectors, was crucially important in achieving this result.

Colombia

Privatization's impact on macroeconomic stability and fiscal balance in Colombia has been less dramatic than in other nations in the hemisphere. First, the country emerged relatively unscathed from the Latin American debt crisis of the 1980s, a beneficiary of sound fiscal and monetary management. Second, the state has never played an exceptionally large role in the national economy, accounting for less than 25 percent of GDP. However, the diversity of the privatization activities, involving the country's telecommunications, electricity, and ports sectors, and the keen interest manifested by foreign investors certainly produced positive effects on the public budget.

Additionally, constitutional changes promoted by former president César Gaviria in 1991 facilitated the privatization process and adoption of deregulation measures. The new legal framework continued the use of subsidization measures, the subsidies coming from the national budget via transfers to low-income consumers, rather than from industrial and higher-income consumers. This feat yielded a modest negative impact on the federal budget while meeting the social needs of the lower strata of society and maintaining the political support of the private sector and wealthier groups.

Colombia's unprecedented economic recession in the late 1990s dealt a severe blow to public finances between 1997 and 1999. As the privatization process slowed under former President Ernesto Samper, the declining demand for electric power and other services caused foreign investors to delay their involvement. However, before the recession took its toll, Bogotá's heavily indebted electric company was sold for $2 billion to Chilean and Spanish investors, and the Caribbean coast regional electricity system (Corelca) was sold to U.S. and Venezuelan investors for $1 billion. In addition, current President Andrés Pastrana has infused new momentum into the privatization process, and, despite the nation's current economic and political difficulties, the privatization drive is expected to continue.

Mexico

The Mexican privatization program spans three administrations, but its single-minded focus on fiscal issues varies only in terms of the magnitude and urgency of the revenues sought by the program. The lack of widespread political support for the concept is clear. As Miguel D. Ramírez points out in Chapter 3 of this book, prior to Carlos Salinas de Gortari's *sexenio*,[9] the sale of state-owned enterprises was referred to as a "disincorporation program," rather than "privatization." In the beginning, the program closed more firms than it sold, reducing subsidy outlays by the federal government but contributing only slightly to revenue generation. As the economic crisis of the 1980s persisted, Mexico's need for funds increased, and attention turned to the sale of larger, sometimes profitable public enterprises.

Revenues from the sale of state-owned enterprises in the late 1980s were greater than expected and are credited with helping Mexico attain the significant budget surpluses that were so widely touted in the international press and so effective in attracting foreign investment in the early 1990s. From 1989 to 1992, proceeds from privatizations accounted for 6.5 percent of GDP; from 1982 to 1987, the state divested approximately one-third of its holdings in mining and manufacturing, and its contribution to national output declined by 27 percent. Funds from the privatization sales financed the National Program of Solidarity (Programa Nacional de Solidaridad — PRONASOL) — social programs for the poorest segments of Mexican society. Privatization also reduced the quantity of Mexico's outstanding internal debt; however, certain sales resulted in net losses for the government. For example, the selling price of the Cananea copper mine was less than the net present value of the loans made to the company by NAFINSA, the national development bank.

Privatization, especially when accompanied by the other market-oriented reforms of the Salinas administration, generally contributed to improving the fiscal balance of the Mexican government, and it also served to enhance the credibility of the government's commitment to a new economic policy orientation. This, in turn, resulted in significant capital inflows that helped bring an end to the economic crisis of the 1980s, although they failed to create sustained economic growth.[10]

Peru

Privatization in Peru, conducted as part of a larger program to redefine and reduce the role of the state in the economy, was probably more important for the signal it sent to the international business community than for its impact on the fiscal or macroeconomic condition of the country. From 1990 through 1994, revenues averaged approximately 2.5 percent of GNP—higher than the average for privatizing countries in the region. Perhaps more important, in Chapter 5, Pedro-Pablo Kuczynski estimates that Peruvian privatizations triggered foreign investment inflows equal to another 2.5 percent of GNP. From 1996 through 1999, owners of privatized firms were expected to expand their investments, producing a significant macroeconomic impact, which could amount to as much as $5.5 billion, or 2.5 percent of GDP.[11]

Venezuela

As in Peru, the direct impact of privatization on fiscal conditions in Venezuela was small, averaging less than 1 percent of GNP from 1990 through 1995. During those years, only 26 firms were privatized, producing $2.4 billion in revenues, with the privatization of the phone company, CANTV, accounting for 78.5 percent of that amount. Privatization's role in attracting foreign investment to Venezuela, however, has been more significant. From 1990 through 1995, foreign investment from privatization approached $2 billion during that same period, or approximately 40 percent of all foreign investment in the country. Since 1991, when privatization revenues represented 4.1 percent of GDP, privatization's share has been insignificant. However, if the government were to reinvigorate the program, it could generate potential earnings of $4 billion to $5 billion, or 7 percent to 8 percent of GDP, an amount equal to one-sixth of the nation's public sector foreign debt.

To date, 44 companies have been privatized in telecommunications, agriculture, banking, electricity, tourism, iron, and steel. Nearly $5 billion in revenues have been generated from the sale of state-owned enterprises, and more than 40,000 employees hold shares in privatized companies.

While the former government of Rafael Caldera initially opposed privatization, it made an about-turn and, indeed, continued the process.[12] Current President Hugo Chávez, although a strong critic of privatization, seems less opposed to the concept, despite the fact that to date he has not taken any action in this arena. His administration has indicated, however, that it plans to privatize additional sectors such as aluminum, but the process is being hampered by macroeconomic conditions and the lack of privatization experience among the top echelons of government.

IMPACT OF PRIVATIZATION ON QUANTITY AND QUALITY OF PRODUCTION AND THE PROMOTION OF FREE TRADE

The impact of privatization on the competitive environment and the quantity and quality of goods and services produced is directly related to the nature of the companies sold, the design of the privatization program, and the scope of other economic reforms in the economy. When an industry can be considered a natural monopoly, the details of the regulatory setting are crucial to determining the outcome of the privatization program. In other cases, limited domestic competition can be enhanced by exposure to foreign competition accomplished by trade liberalization policies or by breaking a large firm into several smaller ones. The experience in Latin America shows that all of these methods have been used, to varying extents and with varying success, to achieve allocative efficiency and free trade. For example, the twin forces of privatization and liberalization have boosted Brazilian steel exports so that they now account for 28 percent of Brazil's foreign trade surplus. Also, were Venezuela to privatize its petrochemical sector fully, export earnings would be huge, significantly affecting the current account balance and macroeconomic health of the nation.

Argentina

Given the large number of natural monopolies privatized in the Argentine program and the haste with which the program began, it is not surprising that competitive outcomes have been few. Armed with a regulatory framework that permitted high profits (telephone tariffs were raised 90 percent *before* privatization) but required significant new investment, the newly privatized firms in Argentina quickly set out to exploit their contracts. As a result, while Argentine consumers experienced generally higher prices, they were usually given better quality service. To illustrate, between 1991 and 1995, installed telephone lines increased from 1.9 million to 2.9 million.

As economic theory would suggest, in inadequately regulated monopolistic industries, supply was restricted, and some consumers were priced out of the market.[13] From a political standpoint, this suggests that there will be pressure to renegotiate the terms of the regulatory arrangement. Some renegotiation has already taken place, and Galiani and Petrecolla suggest in Chapter 4 that more can be expected, especially if macroeconomic instability returns. Thus, the final impact of Argentina's privatization program may be a more competitive economy that provides more and better quality goods and services.

The nature of capital flows generated by privatization is an interesting feature of the Argentine process. Privatization in Argentina has attracted a substantial intraregional investment, especially from Chile. Moreover, certain newly privatized firms, such as the national oil company (Yacimientos Petrolíferos Fiscales — YPF), have actively sought international acquisitions to fill gaps in their competitive position and to improve management capability.

Brazil

The Brazilian privatization authorities decided early on to sell individual firms rather than industry holding companies, thus setting the scene for at least some degree of competition in each market. Because fertilizer, petrochemicals, and steel are contestable if not competitive markets, issues of regulation are somewhat less significant in the Brazilian case. However, the concentration of share ownership in a few banks, pensions funds, and other large national firms may offset ostensibly competitive pressures. This seems to be particularly true in the fertilizer industry, where several firms operate but ownership is highly concentrated in the Fortifós group. International fertilizer imports resulting from a significant decline in tariffs constitute the meaningful competition in this industry.

The steel industry also exhibits a notable concentration of ownership, and its distribution after privatization suggests that vertical and horizontal integration are taking place. Some improvements in technology, productivity, and costs may also be expected. Steel production increased approximately 25 percent after privatization, and, although Brazilian steel was exported even before privatization, net exports of steel have increased by nearly 50 percent, suggesting that its quality meets international standards.

The liberalization policies of the Collor and Cardoso administrations and the country's increasing integration in the Southern Cone have substantially eliminated the tariff protection offered to the industrial sectors where privatization occurred. Despite increased international competition, the restrictive credit conditions, and the decline in global demand in 1998-1999 for leading manufactured exports such as steel, Brazil is poised to strengthen both its intraregional and extraregional trade performance in 2000 and beyond.

The Caribbean

Bernal and Leslie estimate in Chapter 6 that sales and service improved in many privatized firms. In hotels, for example, renovations and more aggressive advertising resulted in more tourists, better accommodations, and increased efficiency of operations. Customer surveys report that telephone service and public sanitation, including garbage collection, also improved. In Guyana, for example, telephone subscriber lines grew from 21,000 in 1991 to 53,000 in 1994.

Chile

Chile's privatization program was critical to establishing its free market and free trade environment. The reduction of tariffs on imports, from as much as 700 percent in the early 1970s to a uniform 11 percent in the 1980s, exposed the economy to significant foreign competition. A clear regulatory framework, based on marginal analysis, and the deregulation of much of the economy (with the notable exception of capital markets) established a similar level of competition for nontradable sectors. Lüders, in Chapter 2, emphasizes the importance of understanding the Chilean privatization program in the context of widespread economic reforms and the role of this context in determining the outcomes of privatization with respect to both efficiency and equity. He stresses repeatedly that both the privatized firms and those remaining under government ownership (yet administered as if they were private) aimed to boost efficiency and equity.

Data on the quality of goods and services produced by firms before privatization are not available, but statistics do exist that attest to the customer orientation of these firms. Moreover, increased exports of products produced by formerly state-owned firms suggest that quality meets international standards. To illustrate, the Chilean telephone company increased the number of phone lines by 174 percent, and ENERSIS boosted investment in electricity distribution by 254 percent. Laboratorio Chile witnessed a surge in new products produced each year, going from 20 before privatization to 40 afterward, and new investments, which were negative during the

1980s, grew significantly following privatization, representing 7.5 percent of sales and 43 percent of profits from 1992 through 1994. Exports grew from $200,000 in 1985 to more than $6.5 million in 1994, indicating improved product quality.

Mexico

The impact of Mexican privatization on the quantity and quality of service is particularly difficult to judge. Prior to privatization, basic services in Mexico had not deteriorated to the extent that they had, for example, in Argentina. Although some increase in the quality of economic services has been noted, in certain cases, improvements in quality have been less than expected (airlines) or slower to appear (telecommunications).

The degree of change in quantity of output and services is also unclear. The government has withdrawn entirely from certain sectors such as mining, automobiles, and auto parts, and it is estimated that its share of total production is down by about 30 percent since privatization began. As a result, total economic activity in certain areas has declined significantly. Yet, output in the mining and automobile sectors increased, following a rise in international copper prices and significant rationalization of production in the automobile industry.

The process of privatization in Mexico and the nature of the regulatory framework have tended to yield industrial concentration, which, in the worst cases, has merely substituted a public monopoly for a private one. When considered in light of the general opening of the Mexican economy to international competition that took place during the 1980s, some of the effects of privatization on competition are mitigated but only in the tradable sectors. In toll roads, for example, privatization has resulted in more miles of road but at prices that made them inaccessible to most drivers and resulted in overuse and rapid deterioration of the "free" roads still owned by the government.

Peru

Although it is early to assess the competitive impact of privatization in Peru, it can be reported that, in general, mining output has risen at privatized facilities, sales and profitability of gas stations have increased, and telephone service has improved. Many monopolies and near-monopolies persist, but Kuczynski argues persuasively in Chapter 5 that privatization has successfully stimulated new foreign investment in many Peruvian industries, resulting in an overall increase in goods, services, and competition.[14]

Colombia

In Colombia, as Mauricio Cárdenas explains in Chapter 9, privatized and state entities that have subcontracted the provision of services to private vendors have experienced improvements in quality and quantity of services. As a result of market opening and trade liberalization, Colombia's export competitiveness also has been enhanced. The electric power and telecommunications sectors are cases in point. The quantity, quality, and pricing in these sectors have benefited from constitutional changes aimed at promoting privatization.

Strikes by organized labor and electric power rationing due to climatic factors, along with poor administration of the existing systems, created popular sentiment for private sector solutions. Even where government companies maintained control, subcontracting, joint ventures, and contracting out to private vendors resulted in improved services and lower rates. For instance, a consortium of companies in Cartagena developed power generation for their own use and sold surplus power (co-generation) to the regional grid at a rate 25-percent lower than what they had been paying. Thus, privatization and deregulation in power and telecommunications resulted in lower rates and improved service for industrial, commercial, and residential consumers, which, in turn, enhanced the competitiveness of both domestic and export-oriented industries.

Venezuela

Gerver Torres reports in Chapter 7 notable increases in efficiency and the quality and quantity of service in both the telephone and airline companies following privatization in Venezuela. Telephone lines grew from 1.9 million in 1991 to 2.9 million in 1995; of all public phones, those in service grew from 43 percent to 90 percent; and, of attempted calls, the percentage of successfully completed local, national, and international calls jumped from 48 percent, 30 percent, and 19 percent to 59 percent, 46 percent, and 52 percent, respectively.

Although the privatization of the telephone company converted a government-owned monopoly into a privately owned monopoly, competition in a wide range of peripheral, value-added services has flourished. Other sectors, such as hotels, sugar refineries, banking, and ports, reported increases in competition as well. Foreign ownership in these areas generally has been welcomed, but there is some resistance to more extensive foreign ownership in the petroleum sector. The failure of the government to define clearly the regulatory environment that will govern industries characterized by the absence of multiple competitors has limited the state's ability to privatize the electric power industry and may limit the competitiveness of many other industries in the future.

IMPACT OF PRIVATIZATION ON EMPLOYMENT, WAGES, AND PRODUCTIVITY

Privatization in Latin America seems to have been accompanied universally by reductions in employment and increases in productivity, although governments sometimes carried out employment reductions prior to selling firms. The results with regard to wages and living standards, however, are more mixed. Given the extremely depressed state of most Latin American economies prior to privatization and the breadth of concurrent economic reforms, it is difficult to come to any conclusion regarding the specific effects of privatization on income distribution and living standards. Income distribution has worsened in most countries examined here, and, in certain countries, privatization appears to have contributed to industry concentration. Sorting out how these features relate, if at all, will require additional time and data. Results in this area may have to be judged on a firm by firm basis.[15]

Argentina

In Argentina, total factor productivity increased dramatically in the newly privatized firms, reflecting both the extremely deteriorated state of the firms when they were sold and changes in management and personnel made after the sale. In most privatized firms, the sales contract and/or the exigencies of the market required the new management to make significant investments in the company. Massive layoffs accompanied most privatizations, and significant price increases for goods and services occurred both immediately prior to the sale and under the new ownership. The business press has reported widely on the decline of employment at the Argentine oil company, YPF, which dropped from more than 50,000 to about 5,000 employees, and Galiani and Petrecolla note in Chapter 4 that prices at ENTel, the telecommunications company, rose approximately 270 percent in real terms between the announcement of the sale and the transfer of ownership.

Brazil

Privatization in Brazil has been associated with significant employment reductions, although the more circumscribed scope of the program has limited the magnitudes considerably. Productivity in the Brazilian steel industry increased nearly 70 percent in the post-privatization period, and profit margins rose approximately 27 percent. Employment in the steel industry fell by about 25 percent, but the wage bill rose 6.5 percent. While average prices in the sector decreased by 12 percent, newly privatized firms kept their prices constant, reflecting either their market power or improved product quality. These figures suggest that the increasing profitability of the privatized companies could generate significant sums for reinvestment and continued technological improvement in production.

The Caribbean

Employment losses associated with privatization in the Caribbean have been less than expected, and some wage increases have been reported. In Trinidad and Tobago, layoffs were minimal, and in Guyana, wages in one privatized firm rose by 120 percent. In certain cases, job losses from one privatization have been offset by employment expansion in other privatized companies. A number of firms reported increases in efficiency. In the case of Jamaica, increases in employment in agriculture (by 150 percent), tourism, and telecommunications have offset job losses in other areas. Additionally, in Trinidad and Tobago and Jamaica, the strengthening of worker participation through Employee Stock Ownership Programs (ESOPs) has had a positive impact on industrial relations in those countries.

Chile

Lüders contends in Chapter 2 that privatization has not resulted in employment losses in Chile. He notes, "Privatization, as distinguished from measures in general to increase 'X' efficiency, probably has a positive employment effect." During the 1976-1979 business expansion, newly privatized firms increased employment by 21.2 percent, while the rest of the private sector did so at 1.5 percent. A sample of 10 large core state enterprises *all* increased employment by an average of 10 percent before *and* after privatization. ENTEL, for example, boosted employment by 200 percent between 1985 and 1991. Once the optimum employment level has been reached, Lüders believes that employment will expand with output, which in many privatized firms varies significantly with the business cycle. Thus, employment losses are associated with reaching the efficient level of employment and with the level of output, not with the nature of the ownership of the assets.

Although Lüders points out that data on income distribution are conflicting, a main objective of Chilean privatization was diffusion of share ownership. This, combined with tightly regulated natural monopolies and financial markets and deregulated competitive markets, has resulted in a decline in the degree of industrial concentration and an increase in the level of activity and efficiency of capital markets. Cristián Larroulet (1994) reports that the 10 largest shareholders of the two largest commercial banks owned 66 percent of the shares prior to 1982; after intervention and privatization, they owned only 5.5 percent of the net worth of the same banks. Ironically, privatization in Chile might be termed "socialist" if one considers only the nature of corporate governance in Chile's major private firms. Lüders reports that at the end of 1988, "workers directly controlled over 50 percent of the members of the Board of Directors in IANSA (the sugar beet company) and over 40 percent of CAP (the steel mill); SOQUIMICH (the nitrate monopoly); and Laboratorio Chile (a pharmaceutical company). If directors appointed by the pension fund administration firms are included, all these enterprises are now controlled by workers or their representatives."

Mexico

In Chapter 3, Ramírez has documented the impact of the Mexican privatization program on employment and income. Although labor productivity has increased dramatically in many privatized firms, privatization has resulted in the direct loss of 200,000 to 250,000 jobs, to which must be added indirect employment losses associated with the closure of private sector businesses when the public enterprises in smaller cities were liquidated. More important, perhaps, is the significant change privatization has effected in the balance of power in Mexico among organized labor, big business, and the government. Taken together with the other reforms of the Salinas period and the passage of North American Free Trade Agreement (NAFTA), privatization has increased the concentration of economic power among the large *grupos*, while driving down real wages and working conditions and undermining the process of collective bargaining. It is not surprising, then, that income distribution has become much more skewed. The share of income going to the top decile of the population rose from 33 percent in 1984 to 38 percent in 1989, so that, by the end of that decade, the richest 10 percent of the population enjoyed incomes approximately 24 times higher than the level of the poorest 10 percent of the population. Moreover, the share of national income going to labor declined from 42 percent in 1982 to 31 percent in 1994.

Peru

Job losses in Peru have been fewer than feared, with the majority of layoffs occurring in mining and public utilities. The central government cut administrative personnel by 50 percent; however, staff reductions in state firms ranged from none to 25 percent. Some attempts have been made to reserve up to 10 percent of privatized companies' shares for their workers. A stockholder education campaign was launched to increase interest and participation in share ownership among small savers in future rounds of privatization.

Colombia

As the Colombian state has never had a major share in the economy other than in public utilities, employment impacts at the macro level have not been significant. Nevertheless, labor cost reduction was clearly an issue in the restructuring of both the electricity and telecommunications sectors. Traditionally, Colombian unions have been activist; their strength, both actual and potential, presumably influenced the design of a "soft-landing" approach to labor adjustment, which was embodied in the management and implementation of Colombian privatization. In the electricity sector, a strong union front succeeded in maintaining benefits for older affiliates, while anticipating a transitory regime for new workers. Employee stock ownership and the consolidation of a myriad of unions into one national entity were also positive factors in that sector. In telecommunications, deregulation and privatization created an environment that promoted competition, and, thus, labor-led shutdowns lost their influence. The labor adjustment program of Telecom, the national telecommunications company, necessary to secure the investments needed to compete in the new environment, included a 30-percent reduction in the workforce. Subcontracting and joint ventures enabled Telecom to cap the payroll while business grew; this was accomplished through voluntary early retirement.

The recent economic recession has severely impacted the labor market, with the unemployment rate rising from 8 percent in the early 1990s to nearly 20 percent at the turn of the century. The former monopoly in long-distance service, Telecom, downsized from 10,000 workers in the mid-1990s to only 6,000 at the end of 1999. Personnel reductions in the privatized electric power industry were even more drastic.

Venezuela

As a result of both formal and informal negotiations between the government and private buyers, massive layoffs of personnel were avoided wherever possible, and attractive severance packages were offered where necessary. Small reductions in employment associated with privatization were politically tolerable in the early phase of privatization because the generally buoyant performance of the economy permitted laid-off workers to find work in other companies quickly. Approximately 45,000 public employees were dismissed.

LESSONS FROM EXPERIENCE

The lessons from the Latin American privatization experience indicate that the *regulation, monitoring,* and *management* of the post-privatization process — not to mention the need for coherent, well-designed, competitive, and transparent privatization initiatives at the outset — are vital factors that determine whether the intended results of privatization will be achieved in the long run.[16] It has become clear that privatization is a process that evolves over time, permitting mid-course correction, as in Chile and Brazil, and responding to the changing needs of the state, as in Argentina and Mexico.

The direct impact of the sale of state-owned firms on government budgets has been smaller than some might have anticipated, but privatization's symbolic role in establishing the credibility of changes in government policy has been perhaps more significant in the achievement of macroeconomic stability.[17] State-owned enterprises may have been "loss-leaders," but their sale was a successful ploy in luring flight capital, and eventually foreign capital, back to Latin America after the debt crisis. It is worth noting, however, that although balance-of-payments constraints have eased substantially in the region, all the countries considered here, except Chile, still have large fiscal deficits and are consistently unable to meet fiscal targets. Moreover, in countries such as Argentina, by 1997, the external debt was almost twice the "debt-crisis" level of the 1980s.

Another lesson that can be drawn from the experience reviewed here is the importance of market structure and suitable regulation. Privatization does not create competition or provide the outcomes that result when a competitive market operates. As Bernard Tenenbaum notes, "Private investments require new-style regulation that is limited, transparent, and 'lets managers manage'" (1995, 29). Those privatizations that cause rent-seeking behavior that results in price-gouging and that deregulate instead of regulate in their attempt to stimulate true competition (telecommunications is the most glaring example of failure in this regard) clearly jeopardize a meaningful and lasting transformation of the state sector (Manzetti 1997). The high proportion of natural monopolies among governments' holdings makes this point particularly important. The highly concentrated nature of domestic industries — even those in potentially competitive markets — in most of these countries reinforces the concern. The case of Chile, the pioneer in privatization and widely heralded for the apparent success of its program, warrants more study, not for its privatization program but for its regulatory prowess, especially in capital markets.

The Argentine case illustrates the trade-off between a high sale price and allocative efficiency inherent in the privatization process. As instruments of public policy, not only in their operation but also in their sale, public enterprises have the potential to raise revenue for the fiscal side in the short run or contribute to allocative as well as productive efficiency in the economy in the long run. The higher sale price of a monopoly was a significant temptation for the financially strapped Argentine government. The dangling uncertainty about future regulation, however, opens the question of renationalization. At what point do foreign investors cite changing regulations as virtual expropriation and exit the market?

In all but a few cases of individual firms in the Americas, privatization seems to have resulted in increased operating efficiency. Costs, particularly employment, have been reduced, and productivity has increased. Profits have risen in most cases, and significant new investment seems to be taking place in the newly privatized firms. The immediate impact on wages and living standards, however, seems to be negative, except perhaps in the Chilean case. Although causation is by no means established and this short-run result might be consistent with theory, it poses a problem in the political sphere. Privatization took place at the end of the "lost decade" of the 1980s, which was characterized by the increasing impoverishment of a substantial portion of the region's population. The market-oriented reforms of the 1990s were sold to the public as measures that would turn that situation around. The outcomes have fallen short of expectations. In several countries, unemployment has reached all-time highs, simultaneous with a substantial curtailment in social spending.[18] Thus, privatization faces a challenge — in terms of achieving productive efficiency — as the continuation of foreign investment and the sustainability of the political commitment to reform in fragile democracies are called into question.

In brief, then, a cross-national assessment of privatization in the Americas yields several important conclusions:

- Even beyond its immediate financial and economic impacts, privatization sends an important signal to investors, both foreign and domestic, that the government is serious about implementing economic reforms, unleashing private initiatives, and assuring that the state plays an increasingly smaller role in the economy.

- Privatization's chances of success are enhanced if a government makes it a key initiative at the beginning of its administration and if it is coupled with a larger and broader program of economic reform and market liberalization. A public communications program aimed at explaining the purposes and intended benefits of privatization is a prudent and pragmatic way to advance the political acceptance of privatization.

- The economic and political impacts of workforce reduction will be far less negative in an environment where the economy is growing, private businesses are expanding, and privatization is carried out in selected sectors and implemented incrementally.

- The full, intended benefits of privatization can occur only in economies that are market-oriented, liberalizing, non-monopolistic (including private monopolies), and truly competitive, where the entire process of privatization is transparent and monitored fairly and efficiently.

- Privatization by itself may create or exacerbate problems of income inequality. To assure the desired efficiency outcomes, privatization must be accompanied by adequate regulatory and tax reforms. Outside of Chile, employee stock ownership plans have had little effect in mitigating the concentrating effects of privatization on income, wealth, and asset ownership.

As the privatization process enters subsequent phases in Latin America and the Caribbean (and as it is applied more extensively in other areas, such as Eastern Europe), it is vitally important to evaluate its impact continually within the context of the dual changes — political and economic — that are occurring simultaneously in the region. Although neoliberal reforms and democratization remain the chosen paths for the vast majority of the hemisphere's nations, economic liberalization may negatively influence the political and social processes that are taking place in these developing economies. Such economic liberalization, in turn, may result in setbacks for the institutionalization of democracy and free-market policies.

This volume's review of the experience of Latin American and English-speaking Caribbean nations yields helpful lessons about the design, implementation, and expected results of privatization programs. Such information may be useful to countries just beginning privatization programs and to countries considering adjustments as their programs enter a new phase. Much can be learned from studying the finer details of individual programs, but many questions also arise. The process of privatization is not complete in the Americas, and it may take a number of years before an equilibrium is reestablished in the ongoing search for the appropriate relationship between the public and private sectors in the economies of the region.

Notes

1. An alternative policy strategy would have been the implementation of significant tax and budgeting reforms, but this would have required a much longer time horizon in terms of planning, implementation, and expected results.

2. As Sebastián Galiani and Diego Petracolla explain in Chapter 4 of this volume, the Convertibility Plan was part of an effort by the Argentine government to stabilize the national economy by establishing a fixed exchange rate based on the U.S. dollar. "The plan limited the operational autonomy of the Central Bank, requiring that its monetary liabilities be less than or equal to its foreign-exchange reserves. This rule effectively limited the Central Bank's ability to create money through the expansion of domestic credit." — Ed.

3. See Chapter 4, note 17.

4. Since 1995, the most important privatizations in Argentina have been the National Post and the International Airport. Additionally, several public enterprises and banks have been sold. In other developments, the government has sold several share lots of the firms it had privatized before 1995.

5. See Chapter 8, note 4, for a definition of this term.

6. The privatization process continues in Brazil, albeit not at its earlier pace. Beyond railroads, telecommunications, and financial services, other public services such as highways and water systems will be privatized. However, in spite of the revenues produced from the sale of state-owned companies, the public debt reached more than R$510 billion (or more than half of GNP), and net federal public debt has increased from R$96.8 billion (10.8 percent of GNP) in October 1998 to R$216.8 billion (22.3 percent) in October 1999.

7. In the case of Jamaica, the Financial Sector Adjustment Company has incurred high costs in consolidating, recapitalizing, and strengthening institutions in the financial sector; additionally, the government itself continues to provide support to some earlier privatizations, including Air Jamaica.

8. Chile's macroeconomic needs were managed with the traditional tools of monetary and fiscal policy, although the institutions wielding these tools underwent significant reforms.

9. The Spanish word for the six-year term of office.

10. In the late 1990s, Mexico's fiscal health was challenged by the enormous costs associated with the bailout of the privatized banking system, which, by late 1998, had reached a staggering sum close to US$65 billion — equal to nearly 18 percent of GDP. An externally commissioned investigation, the Mackey Report, found undercapitalization of privatized banks, risky lending behavior, and extensive criminal activity in the operations of seven banks. The cost of servicing the bailout debt in 2000 could total $13.7 billion.

11. Privatization, however, does not always provide a solution to the economics of the marketplace. Aeroperú, the national airlines, ceased operations early in 1999, besieged by competition from a low-cost operator, major U.S. airlines, and LanChile on the international

routes; the domestic recession of 1998-1999; and a very large debt of over $170 million. Its Mexican owners, followed by Delta Airlines, had injected almost $100 million into it, with little to show for their efforts. The government of Peru, committed to fiscal responsibility based upon a belief in market solutions, refused to bail out the airline.

12. The Caldera government sold its remaining shares in the telephone company (49 percent), privatized the Orinoco iron and steel company (Siderurgia del Orinoco — SIDOR); sold concessions to several tourist sites; and took first steps toward privatizing the electricity sector by putting the state of Nueva Esparta's electricity company in private hands.

13. The privatization of the Buenos Aires water and waste treatment company would seem to be an exception. French investors kept the monopoly rights but were required to meet certain investment levels. Water prices have gone down, and service appears to have improved.

14. Nevertheless, Peru's privatization efforts slowed in the second Fujimori administration, when the president became preoccupied with securing a third term. Despite a few significant privatizations, such as the La Oroya smelting complex and two former Centromin zinc mines (San Cristóbal and the original Cerro de Pasco mine), the nationalistic attitude of the Ministry of Energy and Mines in the late 1990s produced large negative consequences. As a case in point, in 1998, the government rejected the Royal Dutch Shell-Mobil plan to develop the Camisea gas deposit — a large discovery made 15 years earlier.

15. Although, theoretically, it should be possible to make estimates based on aggregate data, the apparent absence of lump-sum payoff schemes and a political system strong enough to make them stick makes this approach suspect in a practical sense. See Jones, Tandon, and Vogelsang (1990) for one attempt at a theoretical appraisal.

16. For a comprehensive, state-of-the-art treatment of regulatory issues and the postprivatization environment in Latin America, see Luigi Manzetti, ed., 2000, *Regulatory Policy in Latin America: Post-Privatization Realities* (Coral Gables, Fla.: North-South Center Press at the University of Miami).

17. This finding is consistent with other studies, such as Ramamurti (1996).

18. Craig Torres (*Wall Street Journal*, October 29, 1996, A16) reported that serious crime has increased in several Latin American cities, especially Mexico City and Buenos Aires, and he attributes this to the poor economic conditions in both countries and, in Mexico, to the absence of a serious reform of the judiciary.

References

Jones, Leroy P., Pankaj Tandon, and Ingo Vogelsang. 1990. *Selling Public Enterprises: A Cost-benefit Methodology.* Cambridge, Mass.: MIT Press.

Larroulet, Cristián. 1994. "Efectos de un programa de privatizaciones: El caso de Chile (1985-1989)." *Estudios Públicos* (Santiago) 54 (Autumn).

Manzetti, Luigi. 1997. *Privatization and Regulation: Lessons from Argentina and Chile.* North-South Center Agenda Paper Number 24. Coral Gables, Fla: North-South Center at the University of Miami.

Manzetti, Luigi, ed. 2000. *Regulatory Policy in Latin America: Post-Privatization Realities.* Coral Gables, Fla.: North-South Center Press at the University of Miami.

Ramamurti, Ravi. 1996. *Privatizing Monopolies: Lessons from the Telecommunications and Transport Sectors in Latin America.* Baltimore: The Johns Hopkins University Press.

Tenenbaum, Bernard. 1995. "The Real World of Power Regulation." *World Bank Viewpoint,* Note No. 50 (June): 1-4.

Torres, Craig. 1996. "Mexico City Crime Alarms Multinationals." *Wall Street Journal,* October 29: A16.

Contributors

Richard L. Bernal
Ambassador of Jamaica to the United
States and Permanent Representative
to the Organization of American States
Washington, D.C.

Melissa H. Birch
Associate Professor and Director of
the Center of International Business
University of Kansas
Lawrence, Kansas

Mauricio Cárdenas
Associate Professor, School of
Business Administration
Universidad de los Andes
Bogotá, Colombia;
Visiting Professor, Department of
Business and Management
Instituto Tecnológico y de Estudios
Superiores de Monterrey (ITESM)
Mexico City, Mexico

Juarez de Souza
Associate Professor of Economics
Economic Advisor to the Brazilian
Senate
Brasília, Brazil

Sebastián Galiani
Senior Researcher and Professor
Instituto Torcuato di Tella
Buenos Aires, Argentina

Jerry Haar
Senior Research Associate and
Director of the Inter-American
Business and Labor Program
The Dante B. Fascell North-South Center
University of Miami
Coral Gables, Florida

Pedro-Pablo Kuczynski
CEO
Latin America Enterprise Fund
Managers, L.L.C.
Miami, Florida

Winsome J. Leslie
Economic Attaché
Embassy of Jamaica
Washington, D.C.

Rolf J. Lüders
Professor of Economics
Instituto de Economía PUC
Santiago, Chile

Diego Petrecolla
Senior Researcher
Instituto Torcuato di Tella
Buenos Aires, Argentina

Miguel D. Ramírez
Professor of Economics
Trinity College
Hartford, Connecticut

Gerver Torres
Senior Privatization Specialist
Private Sector Development
Department
The World Bank
Washington, D.C.

Index

A

Acciones y Valores de México. *See Accival*
Accival (Acciones y Valores de México) 64
Acesita 182, 184, 188-189
Acker/Loeb Group 136
Açominas 183, 188-189
Administradoras de Fondos de Pensiones. *See AFPs*
administrative reform 128
Aerolíneas Argentinas 5, 87, 89
AeroMexico 57, 61-62, 107
AEROPOSTAL (Línea Aeropostal Venezolana) 145
AFPs (Administradoras de Fondos de Pensiones) 33
Agrarian Reform Corporation. *See CORA*
Agricultural Promotion Program. *See PROCAMPO*
airlines 8-10, 59-61, 105, 110, 136-137, 147, 225
  company 87
  Guyana 220
  industry 62, 69
  international 5, 142
  Mexicana 57-58, 61
  national 9, 145
Alessandri, Jorge 16
Alfonsín, Raúl 5
Allende, Salvador 14-16, 18, 24, 40
Alliance for Progress 99
Almacenes Nacionales de Depósito 58
Altos Hornos de México, S.A. 58, 61

aluminum sector 10, 162
Alvarado, Juan Velasco 99
Alvarez, Luis Echeverría 68
Amazonian ports 105. *See also ports*
América do Sul Bank 187
American debt crisis 220. *See also debt*
AMOCO 117
anti-inflationary policies 213. *See also inflation*
Antigua 117
Arawak Cement Plant 126, 220
Argentina 1-2, 4-5, 42-43, 77-92, 103, 107-108, 110, 148, 163-164, 218, 223, 225, 227, 230
  crisis of 1989 218
Arthur, Owen 126
Asarco (American Smelting and Refining Company) 107
Asia 103
Asian Tigers 14
Australia 103
automobiles 225. *See also transportation*

B

Bamerindus 187-188
BANAMEX (National Bank of Mexico — Banco Nacional de México) 64
Banco Atlántico 64
Banco Continental 108
Banco de Bilbao-Vizcaya 108
Banco de Chile 30
Banco de Santiago 30

Banco de Comercio. *See*
  BANCOMER
Banco do Brasil 178
Banco Nacional de México. *See*
  BANAMEX
Banco Nacional do Desenvolvimento
  Econômico e Social. *See BNDES*
Banco Occidental de Descuento 150,
  159
Banco Promex 64
BANCOMER (Commerce Bank —
  Banco de Comercio) 64
banks, banking 7, 9-10, 56, 58-60, 64-
  66, 69, 101-103, 105, 108, 117,
  142, 145, 166, 180, 187, 196, 204,
  222-223, 226, 228
  assets 65
  Barclay's 118
  commercial 14, 25, 39, 40-41, 64, 100,
    166, 196, 228
    debt 101
    nationalization of 100
  community 66
  domestic 22
  industry 206
    competition and efficiency in 65
  international 99
  investment 170
  nationalized 58-59, 64
  private 188
  privatization of 53
  privatized 64
  regional (Meridional) 182
  reprivatization of 163, 165-166
  sector 9
  subsector 67
  system 64-65, 118, 181
Barbados 117, 126
Barbados National Oil Company 126
Barbuda 117
Barclay's. *See banks*
Barranquilla 209, 210
bauxite 7, 118, 121, 135
  alumina industry 118
Belaúnde Terry, Fernando 99-100
Belco Petroleum 107

BERMINE 121
BIOMASTER 43
Bishop, Maurice 118, 125
Black Friday 149
BNDES (National Bank for Economic
  and Social Development — Banco
  Nacional do Desenvolvimento
  Econômico e Social) 6, 180, 182,
  183
Bolivia 1
Brady Deal 101
Brady Plan 83, 90, 218
Brazil 1, 5-6, 103, 177-198, 217, 219,
  223-224, 227, 230
Brazilian Senate 195
Brescia group 108
Britain 10, 36, 77, 111, 220
British Aerospace 115
British Airways 115
British Gas 115
British Petroleum 117
British Telecommunications (British
  Telecom) 111, 115
British West Indian Airways. *See*
  BWIA
budget deficits 1, 203
Burnham, Forbes 118
BWIA (British West Indian Airways)
  117, 123, 125, 136-137

C

Cable and Wireless Grenada Ltd. 126
Cajamarquilla 108
Caldera, Rafael 222
Cali 210
Canada 108, 111, 119, 164
Canadian Imperial Bank of Commerce
  119. *See also banks*
Cananea copper mine 58
Cananea Mining Company. *See CMC*
CANTV 147, 155-157, 159, 162-
  163, 222

CAP (steel company of Chile —
Compañía de Aceros del Pacífico)
103, 228
mill 31, 35, 41
capital
flight 9, 57
flows 19, 22, 40, 166, 223
foreign 22, 67, 69, 77-78, 166, 179,
186, 194, 204, 230
markets 8, 10, 22, 40, 78, 84-85, 143,
150, 157, 159, 169, 179
impact of privatization on 40
capitalism
institutional 31
labor 30
popular 9, 30, 40
traditional 31
Cardoso, Fernando Henrique 6, 180,
195, 224
Caribbean 1, 4, 7, 11, 115-137, 207,
208, 219-221, 224, 227, 231-232
Caribbean Broadcasting
Corporation. *See CBC*
Caribbean Cement Company 128,
133, 135
Caribbean Communications Network
126
Caribbean Group for Cooperation in
Economic Development. *See
CGCED*
Caribbean Television Network 126
Cartagena 209, 226
CBC (Caribbean Broadcasting
Corporation) 126
CDC (Commonwealth Development
Corporation) 121-123, 127
Celulosa Arauco 42
cement 9, 105, 111, 119, 123, 128,
130, 133, 135, 207
plants 7
Arawak 126, 220
Cementos Yura 107
Central Andes 104-105
Centromin 104
CEPRI (Comité Especial de

Privatización) 103-104
Cerro Verde (copper mine) 107, 110
CGCED (Caribbean Group for
Cooperation in Economic Develop-
ment) 119
Chase Manhattan Bank 57
Chávez, Hugo 222
Chemical Bank 108
chemical plants 7
Chesf electric power company 182
Chicago Boys 15-16
Chile 1, 5, 7-10, 13-43, 53, 103, 105,
107, 108, 111, 115-116, 149, 163,
220, 224, 227
Chinese 103
Christian Democrats 14, 31
civilian governments 4. *See also
governments*
CMC (Cananea Mining Company —
Compañía Minera de Cananea) 58,
61, 66.
CNE (National Energy Commission
— Comisión Nacional de Energía)
208, 210
co-generation 226
Cobriza copper mine 104
CODELCO (National Copper Corpo-
ration — Corporación Nacional de
Cobre) 20-21, 31, 35-36
Colbún-Machicura 20
collective bargaining 23, 62, 208,
228
Collor de Mello, Fernando 6, 179,
181, 191, 194, 198, 219, 224
Collor Plan 191, 194, 198
Colombia 1, 8, 107, 203-213,
220, 225, 229
1991 Constitution 204, 206-207, 210
Colombian Congress 8
Comisión de Promoción de la
Inversión Privada. *See COPRI*
Comisión Nacional de Energía. *See
CNE*

Comité Especial de Privatización. *See CEPRI*

Commerce Bank. *See BANCOMER*

Commonwealth Development Corporation. *See CDC*

communications
  local and long-distance 25
  satellite 56

Companhia Siderúrgica Paulista. *See Cosipa*

Companhia Siderúrgica Tubarão. *See CST*

Companhia Vale do Rio Doce. *See CVRD*

Compañía de Aceros del Pacífico. *See CAP*

Compañía de Teléfonos de Chile. *See CTC*

Compañía Minera de Cananea. *See CMC*

Compañía Peruana de Teléfonos. *See CPT*

company performance 116, 137

comparative advantage 17, 161, 168

competition 8, 10, 65, 67, 69
  international 2
  lack of 3
  market 2

CONAF (National Forest Corporation — Corporación Nacional Forestal) 32

CONASUPO (food distribution and marketing firm) 58

CONATEL (National Council of Telecommunications — Consejo Nacional de Telecomunicaciones) 155, 159

concessions 5, 9-10, 21, 24, 68, 105, 132, 150, 151, 154, 166, 180, 203
  duty-free 119
  extensive use of 7

Confederación de Trabajadores Mexicanos. *See CTM*

Consejo Nacional de Telecomunicaciones. *See CONATEL*

Constitución, S.A. 42

consumer
  groups 120
  interests of 136
  satisfaction 44, 204

contract theory 77, 80

contracted services (outsourcing) 164

contracting-out 132
  extensive use of 7

Convertibility Law 218

Convertibility Plan 5, 89, 90

Copesul 184

copper. *See also mining*
  company 14
  mines
    Cerro Verde 107, 110
    Cobriza Copper 104
    Cyprus 107, 110
    iron 9
    Mexicobre 58, 66
    Tintaya 108
  refinery 107

COPRI (Comisión de Promoción de la Inversión Privada) 102-103, 110

CORA (Agrarian Reform Corporation — Corporación de la Reforma Agraria) 32

Corelca 221

CORFO (Corporation for Production Development — Corporación de Fomento de la Producción) 13, 24, 30, 41

Corporación de Fomento de la Producción. *See CORFO*

Corporación de la Reforma Agraria. *See CORA*

Corporación Nacional de Cobre. *See CODELCO*

Corporación Nacional Forestal. *See CONAF*

Corporación Venezolana de Guyana. *See Venezuelan Corporation of Guyana*

Corporation for Production Development. *See CORFO*

corruption 6-7, 100, 103, 145-146, 204
Cosinor 182
Cosipa (Companhia Siderúrgica Paulista) 183, 188-189
CPT (Compañía Peruana de Teléfonos) 109
credit control 22, 40
crisis of 1989, Brazil 218
CSN (Usiminas, Companhia Siderúrgica Nacional) 182, 188-189
CST (Companhia Siderúrgica Tubarão) 182, 188-189
CTC (Compañía de Teléfonos de Chile) 30-31, 41
CTM (Mexican Workers Union — Confederación de Trabajadores Mexicanos) 61
customs duties 13, 19
Cuzco 105, 108
CVRD (Companhia Vale do Rio Doce) 6, 178, 182, 188, 195
Cyprus Mines 107, 110

D

de Castro, Sergio 16
de la Madrid, Miguel 51, 55, 57-58, 64, 67
debt
  conversion 150-152
  crisis 1, 2, 51, 78-79, 100, 178, 203, 217-218, 220, 230
    American 100
  -equity 8, 25, 83
    swaps 19, 41
  external 59, 83, 89-99, 101-102, 149, 161, 198, 230
  foreign 5, 19, 25, 51, 80, 83, 116, 119, 149, 178, 195, 207, 208, 212, 218, 222
  public 6, 82, 89, 178-179, 181, 184, 193-194, 197-198
    domestic 6, 178, 194
    external 1
    internal 181

declining investment 57
Demerara Woods Ltd. 120
denationalization 119, 145
Departamento Nacional de Planeación. *See DNP*
deregulation 36, 51, 66, 69, 101, 128, 204, 206, 212, 220, 224, 226, 229
  competition 69
  labor rights 69
  loss of jobs 69
development strategies, state-led 115
Diesel Nacional 60
Dina Camiones (trucks) 60
disincorporation 9, 55, 57, 60, 68
  program 67, 221
distribution of income 62, 63, 69. *See also income distribution*
  equitable 117
divestiture of public enterprises 3
divestment 115-116, 119-121, 123, 125-128, 132-137
Divestment Secretariat 123
DNP (National Department of Planning — Departamento Nacional de Planeación) 208
domestic
  debt 6, 195
  investment 53, 86
Dominica 117, 127
Dominica Electricity Company 127
Dominica Export and Import Agency 127
dual changes — political and economic 231

E

Eastern Caribbean 117, 125
ECLAC (United Nations Economic Commission for Latin America and the Caribbean) 4
economic
  and political, dual changes 231
  development model
    inward-looking 13

economic, *continued*
   growth 1, 14, 19, 36, 39, 51, 53-54, 69,
      78, 107, 111, 117, 168, 177-178, 197
      and investment 1
      stabilization 9-10, 51, 141, 191
      and reform 9
Ecuador 104
Ecuadorean border 104
education 7-8, 13, 17, 21, 23, 34-35,
   37, 41, 110-111, 147, 166, 178, 193
   public 32, 35, 134-135
   stockholder campaign 229
efficiency 5, 13, 18, 23, 36, 37-39, 54,
   65, 67-69, 77, 78-84, 86-88, 90,
   115-116, 120, 122, 136-137, 143,
   157, 160, 162, 171-172, 178, 204-
   205, 208, 218, 223-224, 226-228,
   230-231
   allocative 5
   economic 4
   firm 3
   gains 2
   greater 10
   increase 3
   of the firm 3
   reliability of delivery, quality, and price
      116
El Nacional newspaper 59
El Niño 100
El Occidente electricity firm 166
electric
   company 6, 118, 166, 182
   -distribution network 108
   power 25, 30, 56, 177, 182, 195, 203,
      205-213, 221, 225-226, 229
   utilities 42, 105
electricity 5, 7, 9, 14, 20, 23, 30, 35,
   41, 78, 88, 90, 101, 103-105, 109,
   123, 126, 133, 159, 166, 206-210,
   218, 220, 222, 224, 229
   companies
      state-owned 5
   -distribution system 104
   privatization 87
   residential electricity customers 208
   sector 87-88, 90, 144, 158, 163, 229
   system 87, 221
Electricity Commission 123

Electricity Supply Board International
   Ltd. *See ESBI*
Electrobrás 182
ElectroLima 103
ElectroPerú 103
Eletronorte 182
Eletrosul 182
Employee Stock Ownership Plan Act
   134
Employee Stock Ownership
   Programs. *See ESOP*
employees
   co-ownership 205
   of firms 219
   -participation programs 159
   stock ownership 204
      plans 7
employment 3, 13, 23, 37, 39, 44, 55,
   56, 61, 81, 108, 117, 125, 133, 136,
   144, 160, 177, 190, 217, 218, 226-
   230
   creation 2
   losses
      job 61, 133, 227-228
      indirect 228
   levels 24
   over- 144, 156
   privatization, effects on 61
Empresa Nacional de
   Electricidad. *See ENDESA*
Empresa Nacional de Petróleo. *See*
   ENAP
Empresa Nacional de
   Telecomunicaciones. *See ENTEL*
ENAP (National Petroleum Company
   — Empresa Nacional de Petróleo)
   20
ENDESA (National Electric Company
   — Empresa Nacional de
   Electricidad) 30, 35
energy 69, 134, 164, 210
   industry 210
   losses 207-208
   nuclear 56, 180
   prices 105
   production 209

resources 163
sector 124
substitutes 187
ENERSIS 41, 224
English-speaking Caribbean 116-117,
219, 232
ENTEL 30, 42, 87, 89-90, 228
ENTel 5, 227
ENTEL (Empresa Nacional de
Telecomunicaciones) 109
Entergy 108
equity market 116, 136, 169
ESBI (Electricity Supply Board
International Ltd.) 121-123
ESOP (employee stock ownership
program) 116, 134 227
Espírito Santo 6
Europe 108
Central 111
Eastern 58, 135, 164, 231
European Union 19
exchange rate 21, 51-53, 87, 89, 100,
141, 158, 166, 197, 218
export 8, 19, 21-23, 25, 42-44, 51-52,
99-100, 119, 133, 166, 187, 192,
197, 203, 223-226
growth 109, 192
promotion strategy 220
Export Development and Investment
Promotion 127
Exportadores Asociados 59
expropriations 15, 18, 99
external
borrowing 110
debt 59, 83, 89, 101-102, 149, 161,
198, 230
refinancing 99

F

Fair Competition Act in 1993   134
Fair Trading Commission 134
Falcón 166
Federal Law N° 8031 179

fertilizer 6, 58, 61, 117, 119, 182,
186-188, 192, 196-197, 223-224
imports 224
Fertilizers of Trinidad and
Tobago. *See FERTRIN*
FERTIMEX 58
FERTRIN (Fertilizers of Trinidad and
Tobago) 117
fideicomisos 57
finance 69
public 2, 78-79, 110, 119, 148, 165,
193, 197, 221
Financial Sector Adjustment
Company. *See FINSAC*
FINSAC (Financial Sector Adjustment
Company) 134
fiscal
balance 3, 10, 143, 172, 217, 220-221
deficits 82, 120, 148, 170, 230
reduction in 80, 137
impact of privatization 37, 109, 219
policies 80, 83, 197
reforms 99
fishing 118
boats 109
fishmeal plants 9, 109
FIV (Venezuelan Investment Fund —
Fondo de Inversiones de Venezuela)
148, 152, 155
Fondo de Inversiones de
Venezuela. *See FIV*
foreign
capital 22, 67, 69, 77-78, 166, 179,
186, 194, 204, 230
companies 59, 102, 212
corporations 111
debt 5, 19, 25, 51, 80, 83, 116, 119,
149, 178, 195, 207-208, 218, 222
burden 218
exchange market 128
investment 3, 10, 23, 25, 41, 52, 66, 86,
100, 115-116, 119-120, 145, 160,
163, 180, 203-204, 209, 221-222,
225, 231
investors 7, 9, 23, 25, 59, 86, 132, 145,
204

foreign, *continued*
    ownership 9, 56, 119, 226
Fortifós 223
Fosfértil 184, 187, 196
free
    trade 19, 32, 223-224
        promotion of 217, 222
    zones 133
Fujimori, Alberto 9, 101-102, 104,
    108-109
Furnas electric power company 182

G

Gairy, Eric 119
García, Alan 99-101, 107
gas 5, 9, 59, 78, 87-88, 90, 101-102,
    109, 115, 123, 144, 187, 218, 225
    state-owned 5
GATT (General Agreement on Tariffs
    and Trade) 51
Gaviria, César 205-206, 208, 211-
    213, 220
GBC (Grenada Bank of Commerce
    Ltd.) 126
GBC (Grenada Broadcasting Corpora-
    tion) 125
GEC (Guyana Electricity Corporation)
    121-123
General Agreement on Tariffs and
    Trade. *See GATT*
General Telephone and
    Electronics. *See GTE*
GNCB Trust 121
GNP (gross national product) 8, 100,
    109-110, 205, 220, 222
GNPL (Guyana National Printers Ltd.)
    121
Goiasfértil 187, 196
government
    corruption 6
    policy
        changes 218, 230
    spending 54, 83, 109
    tax revenues 100

GPC (Guyana Pharmaceutical
    Corporation) 121
Great Britain 9-10, 36
Grenada 117-118, 120, 125, 136
Grenada Bank of Commerce Ltd. *See*
    GBC
Grenada Broadcasting Corporation.
    See GBC
Grenada Broadcasting Network
    (formerly GBC) 125-126
Grenada Electricity Services Ltd. *See*
    GRENLEC
Grenada Sugar Factory 126
Grenada Telecommunications
    Ltd. *See GRENTEL*
Grenadines 117
GRENLEC (Grenada Electricity
    Services Ltd.) 125-126
GRENTEL (Grenada Telecommunica-
    tions Ltd.) 126
gross national product. *See GNP*
Grupo Bursátil Mexicano 64
Grupo Falcón 62
Grupo Industrial Maseca 65
Grupo Minero de México 61
grupos 8, 64, 69, 228
GTE (General Telephone and Elec-
    tronics) 107, 155, 162
Guiría 166
Guyana 117-122, 136-137, 148, 224,
    227
Guyana Airlines 220
Guyana Airways 121
Guyana Bank for Industry and
    Commerce 120
Guyana Electricity Corporation. *See*
    GEC
Guyana National Engineering Corpo-
    ration 121
Guyana National Printers Ltd. *See*
    GNPL
Guyana Pegasus Hotel 121

Guyana Pharmaceutical
    Corporation. *See GPC*
Guyana Stockfeeds Ltd. 120, 121
Guyana Stores Ltd. 121
Guyana Telecommunications Corpora-
    tion 120
Guyana Telephone and Telegraph Co.
    Ltd. 137
Guyana Transport Services Ltd. 120

H

Haywards Resort Hotel 126
health 7-8, 13, 17, 23, 37, 41, 79
    facilities 34
    insurance 23, 33, 34
    organizations 23
    public 32, 110
    reforms 34
    sector 133
    services 21, 23, 33, 166, 193, 204
HierroPerú 102-103, 107
highway 88
    infrastructure 8, 203
Holiday Inn 119, 134
hotels 7, 9-10, 109, 117, 119, 127,
    133-134, 137, 142, 145, 224, 226
housing 13, 17, 23, 32, 34
    market 23
    programs 34
    public 37
    subsidies 23, 34
    tourism 109
Houston Industries Energy Inc. 133
hydroelectric operations 209
hyperinflation 57, 79, 80, 82-83, 86,
    99, 107
    quasi- 179, 191
        episodes 197

I

IAN (National Agrarian Institute —
    Instituto Agrario Nacional) 167
IANSA (the sugar beet company) 35,
    43-44, 228
IDB (Inter-American Development
    Bank) 119, 133-134

IFC (International Finance Corpora-
    tion) 116
IMF (International Monetary Fund) 2,
    68, 69, 101, 115-116, 119, 128, 144,
    158, 178, 198
import substitution 77
import-substitution industrialization. *See
    ISI*
imports 8, 52, 101, 127, 187, 189,
    192, 197
    fertilizer 224
    industrial 158
    tariffs on 224
income distribution 15, 24, 62, 157,
    226, 228. *See also distribution*
Independent-Conservatives 14
India 103
industrial
    customers 207, 208, 211
    development 116-117, 180, 204
inflation 5, 21, 78, 89, 100-101, 144,
    194, 219
    acceleration 79, 144
    annual 192
    attempts to control 178
    rates 1, 14-15, 21, 23, 52, 57, 79, 157,
        191, 194, 197
        high 79, 163, 194, 218
        low 83
        reducing 5
    industrial 191, 197
    inpact on 191
    levels of 177
    program 51
    rapid 79
    wealth corrosion 79
infrastructure expansion 220
Instituciones de Salud
    Previsional. *See ISAPRE*
institutional
    capitalism 31
    customers 207
Instituto Agrario Nacional. *See IAN*
insurance companies 111
Interbanc 108
interest rates 13-14, 18, 22, 25, 30, 40, 52,
    64-66, 158, 166, 179, 193-194, 207

International Finance
  Corporation. *See IFC*
International Monetary Fund. *See*
  IMF
intraregional investment 223
investments 21, 24, 31, 33, 37, 39,
  42-44, 52, 64, 66, 79, 88, 92, 107,
  110-111, 117, 123, 151, 156, 164,
  168, 177-179, 194, 211, 222, 224,
  227, 229
  and economic growth 1
  capital 109
  declining 57
  direct 52
  domestic 53, 86, 197
  equity 57
  finance 190
  foreign 3, 10, 23, 25, 41, 52, 66, 86,
    100, 115-116, 119-120, 145, 160,
    163, 180, 203-204, 209, 221-222,
    225, 231
  government 177
  indirect 14
  overall 53
  private 230
  public 190
  tesobono 53
  utility 108
investors
  foreign 7, 9, 23, 25, 59, 86, 132, 145,
    204
  international 111
  small 9, 111, 134, 136
Iron and Steel Company of Trinidad
  and Tobago 125
ISAPRE (Instituciones de Salud
  Previsional) 34
ISI (import-substitution industrialization) 78, 119
Itamar, Franco 6, 181

J

Jagan, Cheddi 120
Jagan, Janet 122-123
Jamaica 116-119, 127-128, 130, 132-
  137, 220, 227
Jamaica Grain and Cereal Ltd. 133

Jamaica Public Service Company. *See*
  JPSCo
Jamaica Railway Corporation 132-133
Jamaica Telephone Company 128
Japanese steel industry 103
Johnson, Lyndon B. 99
joint ventures 8, 21, 126, 132, 203,
  204, 206, 210, 211-213, 226, 229
  extensive use of 7
JPSCo (Jamaica Public Service
  Company) 118, 133

K

Kennedy, John F. 99

L

labor
  capitalism 30
  force 33, 103, 110, 144
  leaders 16
  participation 152, 169
  standards 61
Laboratorio Chile 35, 43, 224, 228
Latin American Depositary Receipts 9
layoffs 122, 144, 206, 213, 227-229
leases 219
  extensive use of 7
  short-term 128
  long-term 132
legal framework 133, 170, 204, 206,
  210, 220
Legislative Decree 674 of 1991 110
liberalization 22
  of the economy 128
Lima 104-105, 107-108, 110-111
Lima water supply agency. *See*
  Sedapal
Línea Aeropostal Venezolana. *See*
  AEROPOSTAL
LINMINE 121
livestock 118
"lost decade" 1, 231

M

macro level 229

macroeconomic
  instability 1
  policy 78-79, 83
  stability 3
  stabilization 5, 170, 217, 218
Mafersa 184
management contracting 125
Manley, Michael 118
market structure 5, 40, 67, 77, 81,
  196, 230
Marxist 14
Medellín 209
Menem, Carlos Saúl 5, 80, 82-83, 218
Mercado Común del Sur. *See*
  MERCOSUR
MERCOSUL (Southern Common
  Market) 192
MERCOSUR (Southern Cone
  Common Market — Mercado
  Común del Sur) 19
Meridional. *See banks*
METRO (Santiago Subway — Metro
  de Santiago) 20
Metro de Santiago. *See METRO*
MexCobre 61
Mexican devaluation in 1994   219
Mexican Workers Union. *See CTM*
Mexicana Airlines 57-58, 61
Mexico 1, 5, 9-10, 51-70, 100, 107,
  116, 149, 156, 166, 207, 221, 225,
  228
Mexico City 57, 105
Mexicobre copper mine 58, 66
Mexico's Grupo Xabre 57
MIF (Multilateral Investment Fund)
  133-134
military
  administrations 99
  government 4, 7, 19, 25, 32-33, 35, 99,
    178
  regime 17-18, 35-36, 38, 100, 105, 178
mineral-exporting economies 119
mining 36, 56, 58, 60, 69, 109, 177,
  221, 225, 228
  Canadian 108

Cerro Verde (copper) 107, 110.
Cobriza Copper 104
companies 59-61, 66, 107, 110
concerns 66
Cyprus (copper) 107, 110
firms 40
industry 105
interests 61
iron 9
Mexicobre (copper) 58
operations 103, 118
ouput 225
region 105
sector 180
state-owned 6, 104
Tintaya (copper) 108
United States 108
Mitchell, Keith 126
Mobil Oil Company 126
Monagas 166
monitoring 68, 85, 135, 208, 229
monopolies 2-3, 17, 23-24, 38-39, 78,
  85-86, 91, 155, 187, 212, 222, 225
  legal 17, 36, 86
  natural 3, 17, 23-24, 38-39, 86, 223,
    228, 230
    regulation of 25
  power 5
  private 67, 92, 231
    sector 136
  state 101, 180
  statutory 3, 10
  utiltity 23
monopolistic 67-68, 86,-88, 223, 231
monopolization 144, 145
Montserrat 117
motor vehicles 60
multilateral assistance 7
Multilateral Investment Fund. *See MIF*

N

Nacional Financiera. *See NAFINSA*
Nacional Hotelera 57
NAFINSA (National Financier —
  Nacional Financiera) 66, 221
NAFTA (North American Free Trade
  Agreement) 19, 51-52, 59, 62, 67,
  69, 228

NAR (National Alliance for Reconstruction) 123
National Agrarian Institute. *See IAN*
National Alliance for Reconstruction. *See NAR*
National Bank for Economic and Social Development. *See BNDES*
National Bank of Industry and Commerce 121
National Bank of Mexico. *See BANAMEX*
National Commercial Bank Ltd. *See NCB*
National Copper Corporation. *See CODELCO*
National Council of Telecommunications. *See CONATEL*
National Department of Planning. *See DNP*
National Development Fund 127
National Development Plan (Plan Nacional de Desarrollo) 56
National Electric Company. *See ENDESA*
national electricity workers' union. *See Sintraelecol*
National Energy Commission. *See CNE*
National Financier. *See NAFINSA*
National Flour Mills 125
National Food Program. *See PRONAL*
National Forest Corporation. *See CONAF*
National Investment Bank of Jamaica 219. *See NIBJ*
national oil company. *See YPF*
National Petroleum Company. *See ENAP*
National Privatization Program. *See PND*
National Program for Integrated Rural Development. *See PRONADRI*
National Solidarity Program. *See PRONASOL*

NCB (National Commercial Bank Ltd.) 118, 125, 127-128, 134-136
neoliberal 6, 53-54, 178-179
  economic
    policies 1
    reforms 10
  policies 59, 68
  reforms 1, 51, 58, 63, 69
  restructuring 51
  strategy 51, 62
  thinking 179
new technology 3, 91, 209. *See also technology*
NIBJ (National Investment Bank of Jamaica) 132-134
Norman Manley Airport 133
North American Free Trade Agreement. *See NAFTA*

O

Ocean Garden 59
OECD (Organization for Economic Cooperation and Development) 115
Office of Utility Regulation 134
oil 5, 9, 56, 78, 123, 163-164, 204, 207
  -based electricity 208
  business 164
  company 59, 85, 124, 126, 210
  crude 165
  fields 9, 59, 107
  industry 104, 154, 164
  OPEC 117
  prices 57
    international 105
  -producing potential 154
  production 104, 117, 154
  refining 207
  reserves 89, 126, 164, 218
  sector 165
  shock, second 99
oligopolistic 67, 219
Organization for Economic Cooperation and Development. *See OECD*
outsourcing 154, 164

P

Pacto de Solidaridad Económica. *See Solidarity Pact*
Pastrana, Andrés 221
Patterson, P.J. 135, 220
PDVSA (state oil company — Petróleos de Venezuela, S.A.) 154, 163-165
PEMEX (Petróleos Mexicanos) 58-60
pension 13, 17-18, 21-23, 30, 32-33, 35, 111, 136, 165, 223, 228
  funds 6-8, 19, 31, 33, 40, 108, 111, 163, 165, 181, 186, 188, 196
  investments 111
  system
    private 23
    reform 40
People's National Congress. *See PNC*
People's National Movement. *See PNM*
People's National Party. *See PNP*
People's Revolutionary Government. *See PRG*
Pérez, Carlos Andrés 154-155
performance improvements 3
Peru 9-10, 41, 43, 99-111, 158, 164, 222, 225, 228
  coastal shipping 9
petrochemical 6, 56, 58-61, 177, 182, 186-188, 192, 196-197, 223
Petrofértil S.A. 181-182, 187-188, 196
Petróleos de Venezuela, S.A. *See PDVSA*
Petróleos del Perú. *See PetroPerú*
Petróleos Mexicanos. *See PEMEX*
petroleum 14, 20, 36
  industry 6, 10, 154, 188
  production 105
  sector 10, 117, 142, 159, 163-165
Petroleum Company of Trinidad and Tobago Ltd. *See PETROTRIN*
PetroPerú (state petroleum company — Petróleos del Perú) 103-104, 107, 109-110

Petroquisa S.A. 181
PETROTRIN (Petroleum Company of Trinidad and Tobago Ltd.) 124-125
pharmaceuticals 118
Pinochet, Augusto 7, 15, 17, 115
Piratini 184, 188-189
Plan Nacional de Desarrollo. *See National Development Plan*
PNC (People's National Congress) 118
PND (National Privatization Program — Programa Nacional de Desestatização) 6, 179-184, 186-188, 191-198
PNM (People's National Movement) 123
PNP (People's National Party) 118
Pontifical Catholic University of Chile. *See PUC*
Pontificia Universidad Católica de Chile. *See PUC*
popular capitalism 9, 30, 40
Port and Airport Authorities 127
portfolio
  capital 108
  investment 52, 66, 102
  investors 108, 111
Portillo, José López 100
Portillo, Miguel López 68
ports 24, 88, 105, 123-134, 142, 145, 147, 166, 220, 226
  Amazonian 105
  network of 105
power sectors 8
PPH 184
PRG (People's Revolutionary Government) 118
pricing policy 86, 87
printing 118, 125
private sector 1, 3, 8, 10, 14, 16-19, 21-25, 29, 32, 35-36, 38-42, 55-57, 67-68, 78-79, 81, 84, 86, 92, 102, 109, 115-117, 119-120, 123, 127-128, 130, 132, 134-136, 142, 144-

private sector, *continued*
  146, 148, 150, 152, 154, 158, 161,
  163-165, 168-170, 179-180, 184,
  196-197, 205, 210, 212, 220, 226-
  228, 232
privatization 5
  board 120
  diversity of activities 220
  electricity 87
  employment
    effects of 39
    wages, and productivity 3
  fiscal impact of 37, 109, 219
  free trade 3
  gas and electricity 5
  impact on production 60
  industries 3
  macroeconomic stability 3
  on capital markets, impact of 40
  process 13, 15, 18-19, 21, 33, 35, 37,
    40, 53, 56, 59-63, 77-78, 82, 84-86,
    88-89, 91 92, 103, 123, 132, 134,
    142, 143, 147, 150, 152, 155, 157,
    159 160, 163-164, 166-169, 170-171,
    181, 184, 203, 206, 218, 220-221,
    229-231
  products and services 42
  program 1, 3, 5-10, 13, 37, 53, 55-56,
    60, 67, 69, 80, 82, 88, 90, 92, 102,
    121, 125-126, 128, 132, 135-136,
    142, 144, 145, 148-151, 158, 159,
    163, 166-171, 178-179, 182, 191,
    217-230, 232
  quantity and quality of production 222
  regulation, monitoring, and manage-
    ment 229
  unit 120
PROCAMPO (Agricultural Promotion
  Program — Programa Nacional del
  Campo) 55
production costs 144, 188, 192, 197
productivity 3, 32, 44, 81, 85, 88, 90,
  92, 103, 109, 120, 156, 190-191,
  217, 224, 226-230
  gains 62, 88, 92, 188, 190, 197
Programa Nacional de
  Alimentación. *See PRONAL*
Programa Nacional de Desarrollo
  Rural Integrado. *See PRONADRI*

Programa Nacional de Desestatização.
  See PND
Programa Nacional de Solidaridad.
  See PRONASOL
Programa Nacional del Campo. *See
  PROCAMPO*
PRONADRI (National Program for
  Integrated Rural Development —
  Programa Nacional de Desarrollo
  Rural Integrado) 55
PRONAL (National Food Program —
  Programa Nacional de
  Alimentación) 55
PRONASOL (National Solidarity
  Program — Programa Nacional de
  Solidaridad) 55, 59, 221
Provida and Santa María 30
PSDAL (World Bank Private Sector
  Development Adjustment Loan)
  127
public
  auctions 150, 152
  debt 6, 82, 89, 178-179, 181, 184, 193-
    194, 197-198
    domestic 6, 178, 194
    external 1
    internal 181
  education 32, 35, 134-135
  finance 2, 78-79, 110, 119, 148, 165,
    193, 197, 221
  utilities 5-9, 17-19, 78, 85, 110, 117-
    118, 123, 132, 135, 203, 205-207,
    210, 212, 228-229
Public Corporations Secretariat 118,
  120
PUC (Pontifical Catholic University
  of Chile — Pontificia Universidad
  Católica de Chile) 15-16
pueblos jóvenes 105
Puno 105

R

Rail India Technical and Economic
  Services 133
railroad 21, 56, 58, 88, 177, 182

railroad, *continued*
(RFFSA) 182
federal 195
Mexican 9
railway system 105
Reagan, Ronald 119, 179
Real Plan 6, 191, 197, 219
real wages 23, 62, 79, 190, 228
recession 5, 8, 18-19, 21, 24-25, 37,
51, 90, 102, 107, 145, 150, 158,
178, 192, 194, 197, 218, 221, 229
regulation 17, 22, 23, 33, 35, 39, 77,
80, 87-88, 91-92, 136, 147, 157,
163, 223, 229, 230
regulatory 3, 22, 87, 91, 134, 163,
165, 223, 230
agencies 86, 88-92, 155-156, 159
authorities 157
environment 86, 88-89, 220, 226
framework 30, 67, 80-81, 83-84, 88-91,
134-136, 143-144, 157-159, 163-
164, 166, 171, 205-207, 218, 220,
223-225
institutions 197
issues 5, 132
laws 23
measures 32
reforms 231
system 218
Renovación Nacional 31
repair workshops 118
Republic Bank of Trinidad and
Tobago 125
request for proposal. *See RFP*
revenues 1, 3, 22, 24-25, 36-39, 60,
66, 79, 83-84, 86-87, 89, 100, 104,
109, 116-117, 134, 149, 177, 179,
182, 194-198, 211, 219-222
RFP (request for proposal) 133
Rimac River 105
Rolls Royce 115
rotten money 6, 184, 194-196
Russia 111

S

Salinas de Gortari, Carlos 51, 58, 64,
221
Samper, Ernesto 204, 213, 221
Sangsters International Airport 133
sanitation 7, 128, 133, 193, 224
Sanitation Services Authority 127
Santiago Stock Exchange 25, 31, 41
Santiago Subway. *See METRO*
Sarney, José 6, 178, 197
SaskPower Commercial 122
satellite communication 56
Seaga, Edward 127-128
securities market 90
Sedapal (Lima water-supply agency
— Servicio de Agua Potable y
Alcantarillado de Lima) 104
Sendero Luminoso. *See Shining Path*
Seprod Ltd. 133
Servicio de Agua Potable y
Alcantarillado de Lima. *See*
Sedapal
sexenio 9, 51, 53, 55, 58, 67, 221
share ownership 40-41, 82, 223, 228-
229
Shining Path (Sendero Luminoso) 99,
102
shipyard 10, 142
Shougang 102, 103
Sindicato de Trabajadores Eléctricos
de Colombia. *See Sintraelecol*
Sintraelecol (national electricity
workers' union) 210
social
market economy 15-16
programs 55, 59, 206, 212, 221
compensatory 141
security 8, 33, 165
-financed health services 23
payments 163
reserves 165
system 90, 165, 203
tax 34
taxes 32

social, *continued*
  services 8, 13, 19, 23-24, 32
  spending 220, 231
  welfare 55, 80-82, 203-204
socialist 31, 126, 228
  platform 118
  states 58
SOEs (state-owned enterprises) 5-6,
  9-10, 13-15, 17, 19, 20-21, 24-25,
  30-44, 77-79, 81, 84-86, 91, 110,
  115-116, 119-120, 123, 125-128,
  132, 136, 182, 188-190, 194, 203,
  205, 207-210, 212-213
  gas and electricity companies 5
  mining 6, 104. *See also mining*
  performance of state-owned enterprises
    8
  privatization 80, 110
Solidarity Pact (Pacto de Solidaridad
  Económica) 57, 68
SOQUIMICH (the Chilean nitrate
  company) 35, 41, 228
Southern Cone Common Market. *See
  MERCOSUR*
Southern Perú Copper Corporation
  107
Southwestern Bell 107
Spain 107, 108, 111
Special Commission for De-Statization 5
Special Privatization Commission 178
Special Secretariat for the Control of
  State Enterprises 5
St. Kitts and Nevis 117
St. Lucia 117, 127
St. Lucia Development Bank 127
St. Vincent 117
stabilization 69, 80, 82-85, 88-91,
  170, 181, 192, 197
  program 57, 80, 83, 89, 144, 178, 191,
    197, 218, 219-220
Standard Oil of New Jersey 99. *See
  also oil*
state enterprises 5, 56, 60, 78-80, 83,
  86, 89, 91, 105, 111, 118, 123, 126,
  181, 227
  sale of 100

state oil company. *See PDVSA*
state ownership 7, 36, 119, 120
state petroleum monopoly. *See
  PetroPerú*
state-owned enterprises. *See SOEs*
steel 5-10, 14, 57-58, 60-61, 88, 102-
  103, 105, 109, 142, 161, 177, 182-
  183, 186-197, 207
  industry 224, 227
    employment in 227
    Japanese 103
  mill 31, 35, 41, 228
steel company of Chile. *See CAP*
stock
  exchange 5, 8, 25, 31, 40-41, 64, 102,
    108, 110-111, 125, 150, 181, 184
  market 9, 57, 64, 111, 150, 159, 162,
    169
    Jamaican 128
    Mexican 66
    Peruvian 111
  ownership 7, 13, 31, 35, 134, 204, 231
    employee 116
stockholder education campaign 229
strikes 86, 226
  civil 205
structural
  adjustment 2, 10, 115, 119-120, 125,
    141
  problems 178
subcontracting 8, 203, 205, 209, 211,
  226, 229
subsidies 1, 21, 23, 32, 38, 78-79, 99,
  144, 177, 192, 197, 206-211
subways 88
sugar 7, 43-44, 61, 117-118, 127
  companies 123, 134
  estates 134
  factories 132
  industry 123, 134
  lands 133
  mills 58, 60
  output 118
  plantations 118
  production 118
  refineries 10, 43, 142, 145, 166, 226

T

tariffs on imports 224
tax
  policy 82
  system 79, 82
technology 42, 62, 126, 156, 190,
  194, 197, 224
TELCO (Telephone Company of
  Trinidad and Tobago) 117, 123
Telecom 211-212, 229
telecommunications 2, 5, 7-9, 23, 30,
  39, 42, 58, 79, 86-88, 115, 117,
  120, 123, 126, 133-134, 147, 155-
  156, 159, 177, 180, 195, 203, 205-
  206, 211-213, 218, 220, 222, 225-
  230
Telecommunications of Jamaica. See
  TOJ
Telecommunications Services of
  Trinidad and Tobago. See TSTT
Telefónica de España 9
Telefónica del Perú 108
Telefónica of Spain 107
Teléfonos de México 107
telephone company 5, 9-10, 30-31,
  41, 58-60, 103, 107-111, 117, 123,
  128, 137, 142, 145, 149, 150-152,
  155-156, 159, 162, 206, 224-226
Telephone Company of Trinidad and
  Tobago. See TELCO
TELMEX 9, 58, 66
Temex (Petrochemical company —
  Tereftálatos de México) 58
terrorism 99, 100
Thatcher, Margaret 115
Third Five-Year Plan (1969-1973)
  117
timber and log processing 118
Tintaya copper mine 108
TINTOPEC (Trinidad and Tobago
  Petroleum Company) 124
TOJ (Telecommunications of Jamaica)
  134

toll roads 5, 9
Trans-Andean pipeline 104
transparency 6-8, 151-152, 171
Transport Board 127
transportation 8, 15, 56, 78, 120
  firms 88
  infrastructure 203
  public 118
  sector 8
  services 7
TRINGEN 118
Trinidad and Tobago 117-119, 123,
  125, 227
  government of 219
Trinidad and Tobago Methanol
  Company 123, 125
Trinidad and Tobago Oil
  Company. See TRINTOC
Trinidad and Tobago Petroleum
  Company. See TINTOPEC
Trinidad and Tobago Printing and
  Packaging 125
Trinidad and Tobago Television
  Company Ltd. 117
Trinidad and Tobago Urea Company
  Ltd. 123
Trinidad Cement Company 133
TRINTOC (Trinidad and Tobago Oil
  Company) 124
TSTT (Telecommunications Services
  of Trinidad and Tobago) 123
Tupac Amarú Revolutionary Move-
  ment. See MRTA

U

Ultrafértil 187, 196
unemployment 23, 144, 168, 229, 231
unions 23, 61, 79, 86, 123, 212-213,
  229
  Colombian 229
  communist-led 99
  company-based 210
  credit 126
  labor 86, 120, 212-213
  Telecom 211
  trade 136, 145-146

United Nations Economic Commission for Latin America and the Caribbean. *See ECLAC*
United States 9, 42, 52, 68, 107-108, 111, 119, 127, 179, 190, 207, 212
United States Agency for International Development. *See USAID*
USAID (United States Agency for International Development) 15, 125, 127-128
Usiminas 182, 188-189
Usiminas, Companhia Siderúrgica Nacional. *See CSN*
Usinas Siderúrgicas de Minas Gerais (Usiminas) 178

V

value-added services 145, 226
Vargas Llosa, Mario 100-102
Venezuela 10, 107, 141-172, 207, 222, 226, 229
Venezuelan Central Bank 165
Venezuelan Congress 148
Venezuelan Investment Fund. *See FIV*
Versailles Dairy Complex 121
VIASA (Venezuela national airline) 160
Von Appen group 107

W

W. R. Grace and Company 118
wages 3, 13-14, 23, 58, 122, 192, 197, 211, 217, 226-230
  and price restraints 57
  bill 190, 227
  real 62, 79, 190, 228
water 20, 23, 30, 32, 78, 88, 103-105, 123-125, 130, 134, 144, 166
Water and Sewage Authority 125
Wauna Oil Palm Estate 121
welfare 81, 82. *See also social welfare*

workers 5, 8, 10, 30-31, 34-35, 40, 57, 61-62, 110, 116, 165, 170, 180, 203, 208-209, 211, 213
  cooperatives 118
  displaced 135
  employed 210
  employment of 117
  in production process 62
  low-skilled 81
  on strike 23
  on the defensive 62
  pensions fund 186
  redistribution toward 82
  retired 34
  severance payment rights 23
  social security payments 163
  transport 127
  union 209, 210
  unionized 61
  unskilled 62
Workers Bank 134
World Bank 1, 2, 68-69, 105, 115, 119, 125, 127, 130, 133, 166
World Bank Private Sector Development Adjustment Loan. *See PSDAL*

Y

Yacimientos Petrolíferos Fiscales. *See YPF*
YPF (Argentine national oil company — Yacimientos Petrolíferos Fiscales) 85, 88, 223, 227

Z

Zedillo Ponce de León, Ernesto 51